ENGLISHNESS AND EMP

Englishness and Empire 1939–1965

WENDY WEBSTER

OXFORD
UNIVERSITY PRESS

OXFORD
UNIVERSITY PRESS

Great Clarendon Street, Oxford OX2 6DP

Oxford University Press is a department of the University of Oxford
It furthers the University's objective of excellence in research, scholarship,
and education by publishing worldwide in

Oxford New York

Auckland Cape Town Dar es Salaam Hong Kong Karachi Kuala Lumpur
Madrid Melbourne Mexico City Nairobi New Delhi Shanghai Taipei
Toronto

With offices in

Argentina Austria Brazil Chile Czech Republic France Greece
Guatemala Hungary Italy Japan South Korea Poland Portugal
Singapore Switzerland Thailand Turkey Ukraine Vietnam

Oxford is a registered trade mark of Oxford University Press
in the UK and in certain other countries

Published in the United States
by Oxford University Press Inc., New York

British Library Cataloguing in Publication Data
Data available

Library of Congress Cataloging in Publication Data
Data available

ISBN 978–0–19–925860–4 (Hbk.) 978–0–19–922664–1 (Pbk.)

1 3 5 7 9 10 8 6 4 2

Typeset by Laserwords Private Limited, Chennai, India

Printed in Great Britain
on acid-free paper by
Biddles Ltd,
King's Lynn, Norfolk

For Anna

Acknowledgements

This study owes a great debt to the Arts and Humanities Research Board. Their Research Leave award in 2001–2 enabled me to undertake much of the work on which the book is based. My involvement with this research dates back to 2000, and some of the material in the book was originally published elsewhere. Material in Chapters 5 and 6 appeared in an essay ' "There'll Always Be an England": Representations of Colonial Wars and Immigration, 1948–1968', *Journal of British Studies*, 40 (October 2001), 557–84. Material in Chapter 3 appeared in an essay 'Reconstructing Boundaries: Gender, War and Empire in British Cinema, 1945–50', *Historical Journal of Film, Radio and Television*, 23 (March 2003), 43–57. Material in Chapters 3 and 5 appeared in an essay 'Domesticating the Frontier: Gender, Empire and Adventure Landscapes in British Cinema, 1945–59', *Gender and History*, 15 (April 2003), 85–107.

In writing this book, I have incurred two further large debts. The book began when I read Bill Schwarz's memorable comment on the conventional historiography of decolonization—that it presented a 'stunning lack of curiosity' about its impact on the metropolis. I am heavily indebted not only to Bill's work on the end of empire, but also to the support and encouragement he has given throughout the writing of the book, and his invaluable comments. My second great debt is to Mike Paris, who generously shared his vast knowledge of film, loaned me countless videos, and read several chapters in draft. Without his encouragement I would never have embarked on this project.

I have benefited from a number of Conferences—at the Universities of Calgary, Central Lancashire, Glamorgan, London, Leipzig, Manchester, Melbourne, Rouen, and Toronto. I would like to thank the British Academy for funding my attendances at Calgary and Melbourne, and all those who organized these Conferences, especially Harriet Jones for all the annual events at the Institute of Contemporary British History. People from whose ideas and comments I particularly benefited include Alison Blunt, Barbara Bush, Kathy Castle, Shani d'Cruze, Peter Hansen, Clare Midgley, Katy Pickles, John Ramsden, Myra Rutherbridge, and Stuart Ward. I am especially grateful to Stuart Ward, who, despite the demands of a new job in Copenhagen, read chapters in draft.

The Department of Historical and Critical Studies at the University of Central Lancashire was a very good place to be while researching and writing the book. Its ethos of generosity and co-operation owed a great deal to Joe Pope, Head of Department until his retirement in 2003. I am indebted to Joe's encouragement of all research activity, including my own. Like Joe, my colleagues in history made their combination of generosity, wisdom, and wit seem effortless.

Finally, I have to thank my family for their forbearance during my many mental absences from contemporary life—often quite prolonged. Rick watched many films on empire and the Second World War without complaining. Anna, glazing over whenever the word 'empire' was mentioned, helped me to keep things in some perspective. This book is for her.

Contents

1
Introduction

Did loss of imperial power and the end of empire have any significant impact on British culture and identity after 1945? Within a burgeoning literature on national identity and Britishness in the past twenty years, there has been surprisingly little attention to this question. In 1996, Bill Schwarz suggested that the conventional historiography of decolonization had presented a 'stunning lack of curiosity' about its impact on the metropolis.[1] A range of work exploring the role of empire in shaping ideas about what it meant to be English or British focused mainly on the period from the eighteenth to the early twentieth centuries.[2] Angela Woollacott, reviewing the impact of such work, confidently and succinctly claims: 'It is now well established that colonialism has been an interconstitutive process that shaped British society and culture.'[3]

Until recently the post-1945 period remained immune from such approaches, but in the new millennium, a debate about the domestic consequences of the end of empire began to emerge. In 2001, Stuart Ward challenged the common answer to the question of the impact of loss of

[1] Bill Schwarz, '"The Only White Man In There": The Re-Racialisation of England, 1956–1968', *Race and Class*, 38 (1996), 65.

[2] Linda Colley, 'Britishness and Otherness: An Argument', *Journal of British Studies*, 31 (1992), 309–29; Linda Colley, *Britons: Forging the Nation 1707–1837* (New Haven: Yale University Press, 1992); Catherine Hall, *White Male and Middle Class: Explorations in Feminism and History* (Cambridge: Polity, 1992); Clare Midgley, *Women Against Slavery: The British Campaigns, 1780–1870* (London: Routledge, 1992); Antoinette Burton, *Burdens of History: British Feminists, Indian Women, and Imperial Culture, 1865–1915* (London: Chapel Hill, 1994); Laura Tabili, *'We Ask for British Justice': Workers and Racial Difference in Late Imperial Britain* (Ithaca: Cornell University Press, 1994); Anne McClintock, *Imperial Leather: Race, Gender and Sexuality in the Colonial Contest* (London: Routledge, 1995); Mrinalini Sinha, *Colonial Masculinity: The 'Manly Englishman' and the 'Effeminate Bengali' in the Late Nineteenth Century* (Manchester: Manchester University Press, 1995); Simon Gikandi, *Maps of Englishness: Writing Identity in the Culture of Colonialism* (New York: Columbia University Press, 1996); Bill Schwarz (ed.), *The Expansion of England: Race, Ethnicity and Cultural History* (London: Routledge, 1996); Antoinette Burton, *At the Heart of Empire: Indians and the Colonial Encounter in Late Victorian Britain* (Berkeley: University of California Press, 1998); Clare Midgley (ed.), *Gender and Imperialism* (Manchester: Manchester University Press, 1998); Ian Baucom, *Out of Place: Englishness, Empire and the Locations of Identity* (Princeton: Princeton University Press, 1999); Angela Woollacott, *To Try Her Fortune in London: Australian Women, Colonialism and Modernity* (Oxford: Oxford University Press, 2001); Linda Colley, *Captives: Britain, Empire and the World, 1600–1850* (London: Jonathan Cape, 2002); Catherine Hall, *Civilising Subjects: Metropole and Colony in the English Imagination, 1830–1867* (Cambridge: Polity, 2002).

[3] Woollacott, *To Try Her Fortune*, 9.

imperial power on British culture and identity—that there was none, or at
least not very much. He named this view the 'minimal impact thesis'.[4] Ward
argued that historians' broad agreement on a thesis which emphasized that
'the mass of people, as they had all along, cared very little', and that 'as far as
the majority of the population was concerned it (the empire) was given away
in a fit of collective indifference'—suggested the grip of historiographical
orthodoxy.[5] Reflecting on the current state of such debate in 2003, Stephen
Howe suggested that 'The received wisdom that decolonisation had aston-
ishingly little impact on Britain itself, that public opinion remained largely
indifferent to it, and that its cultural resonances were scattered, minor, and
largely ephemeral is being questioned rather than overturned'.[6]

Much imperial history has mined official documentation to explore the
activities of policy making elites in imperial politics, economics, and
administration, focusing on an exploration of what has been called the
'official mind'.[7] Work on the domestic dimension of imperial decline has
often taken a similar approach.[8] Those who question the assumption that
the end of empire had little impact in Britain have generally focused on
cultural history. John MacKenzie pioneered a wide range of work which
showed how deeply imperialism was embedded in British popular culture
into the mid-twentieth century, and beyond.[9] Stuart Ward's edited collec-
tion sets out 'to examine popular understandings of imperial decline as

---

[4] Stuart Ward, *British Culture and the End of Empire* (Manchester: Manchester University Press,
2001), 4.

[5] Bernard Porter and David Cannadine, quoted in Ward, *British Culture*, 3.

[6] Stephen Howe, 'Internal Decolonization? British Politics since Thatcher as Post-Colonial
Trauma', *Twentieth Century British History*, 14 (2003), 289.

[7] This phrase was first used in Ronald Robinson and John Gallagher with Alice Denny, *Africa
and the Victorians: The Official Mind of Imperialism* (London: Macmillan, 1961).

[8] David Goldsworthy, *Colonial Issues in British Politics, 1945–1961* (Oxford: Clarendon Press,
1971); R. F. Holland, *European Decolonization 1918–1981: An Introductory Survey* (Basingstoke:
Macmillan, 1985); John Darwin, *Britain and Decolonization: The Retreat from Empire in the Post-
War World* (Basingstoke: Macmillan, 1988); John Darwin, *The End of the British Empire: The
Historical Debate* (Basingstoke: Macmillan, 1991); P. J. Cain and A. G. Hopkins, *Crisis and
Deconstruction, 1914–1990* (London: Longman, 1993); Stephen Howe, *Anti-Colonialism in British
Politics: The Left and the End of Empire 1939–1964* (Oxford: Oxford University Press, 1993); Philip
Murphy, *Party Politics and Decolonization: The Conservative Party and British Colonial Policy in
Tropical Africa, 1951–1964* (Oxford: Clarendon Press, 1995); Nicholas Owen, 'Decolonisation and
Postwar Consensus', in Harriet Jones and Michael Kandiah (eds.), *The Myth of Consensus: New
Views on British History* (Basingstoke: Macmillan, 1996), 157–81; John Darwin, 'Decolonization
and the End of Empire', in Robin Winks (ed.), *The Oxford History of the British Empire*, Vol. V:
Historiography (Oxford: Oxford University Press, 1999), 541–57.

[9] John MacKenzie, 'Heroic Myths of Empire', in John MacKenzie (ed.), *Popular Imperialism and
the Military* (Manchester: Manchester University Press, 1992), 109–37; John MacKenzie, *Propaganda and Empire: The Manipulation of British Public Opinion 1880–1960* (Manchester: Manchester University Press, 1984); John MacKenzie (ed.), *Imperialism and Popular Culture* (Manchester:
Manchester University Press, 1986); John MacKenzie, 'The Popular Culture of Empire in Britain',
in Judith Brown and Wm Roger Louis (eds.), *The Oxford History of the British Empire*, Vol. IV: *The
Twentieth Century* (Oxford: Oxford University Press, 1999), 212–31: John MacKenzie, 'The
Persistence of Empire', in Ward, *British Culture*, 21–36.

articulated through a wide variety of cultural channels and institutions'.[10]
Bill Schwarz's work addresses the cultural and symbolic manifestations of
decolonization, and suggests that 'It may be that it is in the domain of
mental life ('culture'), particularly, that we can establish connections between the end of the Empire and transformations in the domestic scene'.[11]
Both Schwarz and Howe, thinking about the kinds of history that such an
enquiry involves, converge on the idea that questioning the minimal impact
thesis might involve discovering post-colonial Britain in 'unexpected
places'.

Englishness and Empire builds on this work in cultural history, exploring
national self-representation in a period when Britain was on the cusp of
transition from imperial power to post-imperial nation. How were narratives of nation reworked in a period when colonial rule was widely contested
by anti-colonial nationalisms and the process of decolonization gathered
pace? What was the impact on narratives of Britishness and Englishness of a
diminution of British territories and a contraction of its frontiers? How
were the legacies of empire portrayed? Were habits of mind associated with
colonialism dismantled as rapidly or as extensively as British colonial rule,
or did they outlast the end of empire?

Through a focus on popular narratives of nation told in mainstream
British media, this book is concerned with the diverse and complex ways in
which loss of imperial power was registered. It identifies a range of stories
told about Britain and England after 1945 that registered such loss. It also
considers reworkings of diverse stories about empire through which the
imperial dimensions of British identity leaked into other narratives of
nation.[12] Some empire stories had emphasized power and conquest, the
manliness and militarism embodied in the soldier hero, the adventure
landscape. Others had invoked the idea of a 'civilizing mission', and the
high-minded hero, self-sacrificing and dedicated to the fulfilment of this
mission. Most had claimed Britishness as a global identity, and the power,
influence, and authority associated with a world role. One version of such
global identity showed what Stuart Ward has called a 'racial community of

---

[10] Ward, *British Culture*, 12.

[11] Bill Schwarz, 'Claudia Jones and the *West Indian Gazette*: Reflections on the Emergence of
Post-Colonial Britain', *Twentieth Century British History*, 14 (2003), 265. See also Schwarz, 'The
Only White Man In There'; Bill Schwarz, 'Black Metropolis, White England', in Mica Nava and
Alan O'Shea (eds.), *Modern Times: Reflections on a Century of English Modernity* (London: Routle-
dge, 1996), 182–207; Bill Schwarz, 'Reveries of Race: The Closing of the Imperial Moment', in
Becky Conekin, Frank Mort, and Chris Waters (eds.), *Moments of Modernity: Reconstructing Britain
1945–1964* (London: Rivers Oram, 1999), 189–207.

[12] Many of these stories corresponded to the diverse meanings of empire that P. J. Marshall
groups under two broad headings—the 'authoritarian empire' as a source of power and military
greatness for Britain, and the 'libertarian empire' that embodied liberal values. See P. J. Marshall,
'Imperial Britain', *Journal of Imperial and Commonwealth History*, 23 (1995), 379–94.

Britons' in empire—white Australians, Canadians, New Zealanders, bound to Britain by close ties of kinship and culture.[13] Another version developed racial imagery that demonstrated British power, authority, and superiority, where 'others' in empire were primitive, childlike, savage, irrational, and sometimes effeminate against British civilization and modernity. As empire ended, these stories were transposed onto other narratives, especially narratives of the Second World War. They spilled over into narratives of British–American relations. They were variously modernized, disavowed, lampooned, or reclaimed as heritage in volatile, shifting, and contradictory narratives of nation.

Ignorance about empire in Britain—particularly the ignorance demonstrated in a Social Survey of Public Opinion in Britain on Colonial Affairs in 1948—has been used by a number of historians to buttress the minimal impact thesis. This survey found that only 49 per cent of those questioned could name one colony, only 25 per cent knew the difference between a colony and a Dominion, while 3 per cent named America as a British colony. In the year after Indian and Burman independence, only 46 per cent of respondents named India, Pakistan, or Burma when asked to think of 'any British colonies which, in the past year, have been given more responsibility for governing themselves'.[14]

This was an ignorance continually encountered by those arriving in Britain from colonies and former colonies. In a wartime broadcast on BBC radio by Learie Constantine, the Trinidadian cricketer, repeated in 1946, he spoke of meeting a 'blank wall of ignorance' in Nelson in Lancashire where he lived: 'Many questions were asked and many showing truly astonishing ignorance of conditions and people in the Colonies. The working man in England has no idea of what's happening in the Colonies. We knew far more about you when we came than you do about us.'[15] Constantine's discovery that he knew far more about Britain than Britain knew about 'conditions and people in the Colonies' was shared by many migrants to Britain from empire and Commonwealth, before and after the Second World War. But many were shocked to discover that the England they saw at first hand on arrival bore little resemblance to the England they had learnt about in school.[16]

This evidence of extensive ignorance about empire and Commonwealth could be understood as a manifestation of an imperial mentality, and the

[13] Stuart Ward, 'The End of Empire and the Fate of Britishness', paper to the British World II Conference, University of Calgary, July 2003.

[14] G. K. Evans, *Public Opinion on Colonial Affairs*, June 1948 (London: HMSO, 1948).

[15] Learie Constantine, *Tonight's Talk*, BBC radio broadcast, 3 Sept. 1943, repeated 14 October 1946.

[16] Wendy Webster, *Imagining Home: Gender, 'Race' and National Identity 1945–64* (London: UCL Press, 1998), 41–4.

power relations that shaped the direction in which knowledge flowed. It was a mentality about which Harold Macmillan was somewhat apologetic in a BBC radio broadcast on 'The Colonial Effort' during the Second World War. As Parliamentary Under-Secretary for the Colonies, Macmillan urged his audience to welcome colonial troops, technicians, and lumbermen in Britain, and suggested that when they encountered 'a man in uniform in the street with a dark skin and a smiling face' they should stop and chat. In such an encounter, he suggested, 'you will find that he will know a great deal about England'. He added: 'He will certainly, I am afraid, know a great deal more about us than we know about him.'[17]

Evidence about ignorance of empire might suggest that questions about the impact of decolonization in Britain can only be properly investigated through studies of 'the official mind'—manifested, for example, in memoranda and reports by the Colonial Office. Such studies focus on people who were engaged with the issues, and well informed about them. But the media archive is a rich source for exploring questions of national and imperial identity. It suggests that the dismantling of empire was not safely sealed off in debates at the Colonial Office, and the impact of loss of imperial power by no means confined to matters on which people were well informed, whatever those might be, nor to matters that were specific to empire and knowledge of what Learie Constantine called 'the conditions and people in the Colonies'. A study of the mainstream media archive can move beyond questions about the extent of people's ignorance to explore how far, and in what contexts and 'unexpected places', imperial identity and loss of imperial power resonated in popular narratives of nation.

Benedict Anderson's study of the origin and spread of nationalism, first published in 1983, remains highly influential for work on questions of national self-representation, national identity, and nationalism.[18] Defining a nation as an 'imagined political community', he emphasizes the significance of systems of cultural representation—systems of language, education, and mass communication—to the processes through which people come to imagine that they have a shared identity as members of a national community. Print capitalism and printed media, he argues, served as the material foundation for the emergence and dissemination of a sense of shared nationality.

Anderson's study does not extend to the development of cinema, radio, and television in the twentieth century, which—together with the development of a popular press in the late nineteenth century—dramatically increased the audiences who could be involved in a sense of shared nationality. The development of motion pictures in the twentieth century meant

[17] Harold Macmillan, 'The Colonial Effort', BBC radio broadcast, 28 July 1942.
[18] Benedict Anderson, *Imagined Communities: Reflections on the Origin and Spread of Nationalism* (London: Verso 1983).

that visual images became increasingly significant and reached a wider audience. Visual imagery was crucial to the dissemination of what Anne McClintock has argued is a key factor in the power of nationalism since the late nineteenth century: the organization of mass national commodity spectacle. The ritual objects of spectacle that McClintock lists—including flags, uniforms, maps, anthems, and military displays—featured prominently in empire films of the 1930s, in Second World War films of the 1950s, and in the television broadcasts of the Coronation of Queen Elizabeth II in 1953 and Winston Churchill's funeral in 1965.[19] Through developments in visual technology, these spectacles reached a vast audience.

Visual imagery is a key source for *Englishness and Empire*. Although it examines a range of representations of nation and empire in printed media and radio, the contours of the study generally follow the narratives told through prolific filmic and television imagery: the Second World War, the Coronation and Everest, colonial wars of the 1950s, Churchill's funeral. The impact of developments in visual technology was demonstrated in 1953, when the nation went on public display for the Coronation. An estimated 20 million viewers in Britain—almost half the population—watched the live broadcast on television—the first of its kind. The BBC estimated that the overseas audience who heard or viewed at least part of the Coronation broadcasts 'probably exceeded 150 millions, and may have approached the regions of 200 millions'.[20]

In Salisbury in Southern Rhodesia, queues to see a film of the Coronation—*A Queen is Crowned*—began at dawn, and people were still queuing at five in the evening.[21] In Britain, it was the most popular film at box offices in 1953. Despite the increasing competition from television, cinema in Britain retained a mass, if declining, audience in the 1950s—an average each week of 26.3 million in 1951, 22.7 million in 1955, and 17.6 million in 1957.[22] Even as late as 1959, as John Ramsden has observed, this average weekly audience—by now down to 14.5 million—was more than the numbers of homes with televisions, and roughly equivalent to the total circulation of all daily national newspapers.[23] The film archive is particularly important to this study. Cinema remained a key site for the production and consumption of mass-mediated meanings of national identity in the

[19] McClintock, *Imperial Leather*, 374–5.
[20] External Broadcasting Audience Research, Report on Reaction to Coronation Broadcasts Overseas, August 1953, BBC Written Archives Centre (hereafter, BBC WAC), E3/20 Audience Research Overseas, Coronation, Reaction, Overseas 1953.
[21] *Daily Telegraph*, 11 June 1953.
[22] See Paul Swann, *The Hollywood Feature Film in Postwar Britain* (London: Croom Helm, 1987), 6.
[23] John Ramsden, 'Refocusing "The People's War": British War Films of the 1950s', *Journal of Contemporary History*, 33 (1998), 36.

1950s. Geoff Eley, reflecting on the value of film as historical source, suggests that it can provide 'a screen for contemporary anxieties and dilemmas', expose key shifts in social and cultural history, and offer access to popular memory.[24]

In focusing on popular culture, *Englishness and Empire* traces three narratives that were prominent in the media in the period from the declaration of war against Germany in September 1939 to the funeral of Winston Churchill in 1965. Chapters 2–3 look at a narrative of what I have called here a 'people's empire' which mobilized ideas of welfare, development, and egalitarianism. Developed in wartime propaganda and in the immediate aftermath of war, this narrative faded rapidly after the mid-1950s.

The term 'people's empire' had no currency either within this period or subsequently, although the term 'British Commonwealth' carried similar meanings, increasingly displaced the language of empire, and, after 1948, often became simply 'Commonwealth'. I have used 'people's empire' because of its usefulness in suggesting correspondence between ideas of Englishness and empire during wartime and in its aftermath. The Second World War was characteristically portrayed in wartime as a 'people's war'— a term which did have currency, and which served to democratize national identity, emphasizing the common people and unity across differences of class and gender. A corresponding 'people's empire' showed a wartime empire that pulled together across differences of race and ethnicity. 'Partnership' was the slogan first coined in 1942 to encapsulate the relationship between Britain and empire. In the immediate aftermath of war, it was revised to an egalitarian ideal of 'equal partners'. A 'people's peace' that emphasized welfare at home, especially through the post-war development of the welfare state, corresponded closely to the rhetoric of a 'people's empire' that emphasized ideas of welfare and development.

The narrative of a 'people's empire' proved short-lived. It had little currency in Britain after the mid-1950s, but it did enjoy one moment of considerable development. Chapter 4 looks at Coronation year in 1953 as a moment that marked a post-war high-point in this narrative. The timing of news that men had reached the summit of Everest, which appeared in the press on Coronation morning, provided this narrative with new heroes. There was considerable success in associating the 'people's empire' with modernity, youth, and optimism, as well as moral seriousness, a wide consensus in the media about its importance, and an increasing tendency to call it 'Commonwealth'. Although 'empire' and 'Commonwealth' were often used interchangeably, the 'people's empire' promoted in Coronation

---

[24] Geoff Eley, 'Finding the People's War: Film, British Collective Memory, and World War II', *American Historical Review*, 106 (June 2001), 818–38.

year emphasized the ideal of a multiracial community of equal nations that would maintain Britishness as a global identity through transforming and modernizing its imperial dimension.

The 'people's empire' collided with a completely different narrative developed in the period that invoked a quiet, private, and domesticated identity, and showed empire as a threat to Englishness. Chapters 5 and 6 consider the siege narratives that were characteristic of colonial wars and immigration. Both showed England as a domestic sanctuary threatened by violation—in empire and at home. Reworking old ideas of 'little England', they constructed Englishness against empire and particularly against immigrants. The opposition between Englishness and immigrants represented the nation through reference to the small-scale and familiar—hearths, homes, families, streets, neighbourhoods. Englishness was increasingly invoked as an intimate, private, exclusive identity that was white. In much of this imagery it is hard to imagine that Britain had ever occupied a position as a colonial power or continued to embrace a global identity through the transition from empire to Commonwealth. The English spend much of their time indoors, and their major preoccupation is keeping themselves to themselves.

A third popular narrative told a story of national greatness that focused on the Second World War. Once the war was over, the 'people's war' was subject to very considerable revision. Chapters 3 and 7 explore the Second World War narratives of the 1950s and the celebration of national greatness at the funeral of Winston Churchill in 1965, and argue that these bore strong traces of imperial identity. The idea of heroic British masculinity, transposed from an imperial to a Second World War setting, offered a far more exclusive image of nation than the 'people's war'. Second World War narratives took an opposite trajectory from stories of a 'people's empire' and provided more popular and enduring stories of nation. They took up themes of much pre-war imperial adventure, focusing on a homosocial world in which men demonstrated courage, endurance, and humour away from home, and overcame all obstacles and adversaries. The 1950s Second World War film became a vehicle for the celebration of a high-minded hero—self-sacrificing, authoritative, and decisive in action—drawing on the imperial masculinity associated with the traditional values of a middle- or upper-class, public-school educated gentleman.[25]

By 1965, Second World War as well as imperial heroes were the target of considerable levity—lampooned and satirized across a range of media, including film, radio, and television. But Churchill's funeral, as a

---

[25] For imperial masculinity, see Jeffrey Richards, 'Boy's Own Empire: Feature Films and Imperialism in the 1930s', in MacKenzie (ed.), *Imperialism and Popular Culture*, 140–64; John MacKenzie, 'The Imperial Pioneer and Hunter and the British Masculine Stereotype in Late

culminating moment in the process by which a romance of manliness was transposed onto the Second World War, demonstrated the continuing investment in the Second World War as a symbol of national greatness told as a heroic and masculine story of national destiny. Chapter 7, focusing on Churchill's funeral, explores its significance as a marker not only of the eclipse of a 'people's war', but also of the final demise of narratives of a 'people's empire'. Its story of valour and victory, honouring a great leader as the personification of national greatness, excluded almost any reference to the Commonwealth. Alongside the major theme of the Second World War, it was not Commonwealth, but empire and Britain's imperial past that were invoked. The empire, once consigned to history, was unyoked from the Commonwealth, and reclaimed as part of British heritage.

In exploring these popular narratives, *Englishness and Empire* focuses on their interplay of ideas of racial and gender difference. Alison Light's work has demonstrated the extent to which a domesticated version of Englishness, emphasizing hearth, home, and herbaceous border, was developed between the wars. This version of Englishness not only highlighted the female sphere of domesticity, but also the quiet, pipe-smoking Englishman, tending his garden.[26] It was extended during the Second World War, she argues, in a celebration of a 'common people' characterized by quiet courage, and 'a sporting little country batting away against the Great Dictators'.[27] Light views these developments as a move away from 'formerly heroic and officially masculine public rhetorics of national destiny and from a dynamic and missionary view of the Victorian and Edwardian middle classes in "Great Britain" to an Englishness at once less imperial and more inward-looking, more domestic and more private—and in terms of pre-war standards, more "feminine".'[28]

Popular imagery of empire between the wars nevertheless remained overwhelmingly masculine. Some popular fiction and books written for girls and women had female heroines, but the bulk of empire stories in children's literature and comics, popular fiction and films of the empire genre focused on active and expansive masculine heroism and were

Victorian and Edwardian Times', in J. A. Mangan and James Walvin (eds.), *Manliness and Morality: Middle-Class Masculinity in Britain and America 1800–1940* (Manchester: Manchester University Press, 1987), 176–98; Graham Dawson, *Soldier Heroes: British Adventure, Empire and the Imagining of Masculinities* (London: Routledge, 1994); Susan Kingsley Kent, *Gender and Power in Britain, 1640–1990* (London: Routledge, 1999); Kelly Boyd, *Manliness and the Boys' Story Paper in Britain: A Cultural History, 1855–1940* (Basingstoke: Palgrave, 2003).

[26] Alison Light, *Forever England: Femininity, Literature and Conservatism Between the Wars* (London: Routledge, 1991), especially 1–19.

[27] Ibid. 8.

[28] Ibid.

addressed to an audience of men and boys.[29] Martin Francis, noting the continued celebration of traditional adventure culture between the wars in fiction and film, suggests that 'there were definite limits to the "domestication" of the male in the aftermath of the Great War'.[30] During the Second World War the quieter home-loving hero—what Sonya Rose has called 'the temperate hero', a figure in strong contrast to the goose-stepping, jack-booted Nazi—was represented particularly on the British home front, but also found his counterpart in representations of white Australians, Canadians, and New Zealanders.[31] But Winston Churchill called the nation to heroic deeds associated with imperial identity, and much imagery of the imperial war effort continued to show martial masculinity, attributing to Indian and African troops the qualities that martial race theory ascribed to particular ethnic groups—courage, loyalty, discipline (when well led), and physical prowess.

Narratives of a 'people's empire' which aligned Englishness with empire, as well as siege narratives that showed empire as a threat to Englishness, were increasingly feminized in the 1950s, often foregrounding white women. In empire, white women could represent a range of attributes—intrepidity, courage, moral strength, benevolent concern for the welfare of the colonized—but in the context of colonial wars they also became symbolic of national weakness and vulnerability. In the metropolis, the white woman guarding the boundaries of her home against invasion became a common image of a nation under siege by immigrants. White women also guarded sexual boundaries against 'miscegenation'. If black migration to Britain brought a fear of the collapse of boundaries between colonizers and colonized, black and white, it was particularly through a breaching of this internal frontier that such a collapse was imagined.

Once the war was over, empire and Second World War imagery took opposite trajectories, and the Second World War narrative began to occupy much of the territory that the empire narrative vacated. Flags, anthems, military displays, and uniforms faded from view in the 'people's empire' and proliferated in imagery of the Second World War which, in the 1950s, offered a heroic and masculine narrative of national destiny. In so far as the war was not shown as an exclusively British enterprise, often with a

---

[29] Richards, 'Boy's Own Empire'; Kathryn Castle, *Britannia's Children: Reading Colonialism Through Children's Books and Magazines* (Manchester: Manchester University Press, 1996); Richard Phillips, *Mapping Men and Empire: A Geography of Adventure* (London: Routledge, 1997); Michael Paris, *Warrior Nation: Images of War in British Popular Culture 1850–2000* (London: Reaktion, 2000); Boyd, *Manliness and the Boys' Story Paper.*

[30] Martin Francis, 'The Domestication of the Male? Recent Research on Nineteenth- and Twentieth-Century British Masculinity', *The Historical Journal,* 45 (2003), 643.

[31] Sonya Rose, *Which People's War? National Identity and Citizenship in Wartime Britain 1939-1945* (Oxford: Oxford University Press, 2003), Ch. 5.

particular emphasis on English masculinity, the only imperial figures incorporated were white Australians, Canadians, and New Zealanders. Very occasionally Caribbeans, Indians, and Africans are visible in these narratives, but, like white women, and especially women engaged on active war service, they provide a backcloth to the main story, and largely disappear from view.[32] By the 1960s, as an imperial past was reclaimed as part of national heritage unyoked from the Commonwealth, it was increasingly remasculinized and, like the Second World War, incorporated into the celebration of a manly nation.

The incorporation of white Australians, Canadians, and New Zealanders into 1950s narratives of the Second World War suggests the importance of a racial version of the 'people's empire' that contrasted with the ideal of a multi-racial community of equal nations. The term 'Commonwealth' continued to be widely used to signal white settler communities in Australia, Canada, New Zealand, and sometimes South Africa—a 'racial community of Britons'. In their turn, many people of these communities identified as British in the early 1950s.[33] These different racial versions of the 'people's empire' run through most discussions of Britain's imperial and Commonwealth identity and are encapsulated in the debate in *The Times* following the anonymous attack (by Enoch Powell) published in the newspaper in 1964 in which he named the Commonwealth a 'gigantic farce'. An editorial defended the Commonwealth as 'the greatest effort at a multi-racial society of nations the world has seen'. A letter-writer, also defending the Commonwealth, criticized the bid to join the Common Market for its 'shameful treatment of Canada, Australia and New Zealand', but argued that '*They* are the countries that really mattered. The rest, I agree, could well be dispensed with.'[34] By 1964 'the rest'—former British colonies that joined the Commonwealth on independence—comprised India, Pakistan, Ceylon, Ghana, Malaya, Nigeria, Cyprus, Sierra Leone, Tanganyika, Jamaica, Trinidad and Tobago, Uganda, Zanzibar, Kenya, Malawi, Malta, and Zambia.

The media archive, while a rich source for exploring questions about how far imperial identity and loss of imperial power resonated in popular narratives of nation, has little to say about how audiences responded. The BBC undertook audience research, and I have made some use of this here, along with Mass Observation reports, newspaper reviews of films and television programmes, letters to newspapers, and some autobiographical evidence.

[32] For very brief glimpses of black and Asian servicemen see, for example, *Appointment in London* (Philip Leacock, 1952); *The Bridge Over the River Kwai* (David Lean, 1957).

[33] James Belich, *Paradise Reforged: A History of the New Zealanders from the 1880s to the Year 2000* (London: Allen Lane, 2001), 320.

[34] *The Times*, 4 Apr. 1964.

These sources are often problematic. A female British clerk, aged 22, contributing anonymously to a survey of British cinemas and their audiences published in 1948, recorded her response to what she calls 'historical pictures' made just before the Second World War. 'These films', she wrote, citing amongst others *Lives of a Bengal Lancer*, 'gave me an exultant pride in my own country, and her achievements.'[35] Her response is interesting as a young adult female's reaction to imperial adventure. In printed media this was addressed predominantly to boys and men, but empire films were popular at box-offices in Britain in the 1930s and were viewed by women, as members of cinema audiences. Her response is also interesting because the imperial adventure that she cites was a Hollywood celebration of the British empire. British films of the 1930s empire genre were perhaps, for her, less immediately memorable. Or perhaps she saw none. But how representative is her response?

These difficulties are compounded by the size of the audiences for popular narratives—diverse, among other factors, by gender, class, sexuality, age, race, ethnicity, and geographical location. Prem Chowdhry's pioneering study has shown that the reactions of many Indians to the empire film of the 1930s and 1940s were very different from the British female clerk's 'exultant pride in my own country'. When *The Drum*—a British-made imperial adventure—was released in Bombay in 1938, it caused wide-scale protests which took the police more than a week to bring under control. In tracing the popular and official protests against the empire film's projections of India—including Hollywood as well as British films of empire—Chowdhry shows how they shaped the politics and cultural policies both of colonizers and of Indian nationalism, prompting the banning of screenings in India and the shelving of production plans.[36] Post-war films set in India also pose questions about audience diversity. What does it mean that *Black Narcissus* (1947), discussed here as the first empire film to focus on a community of white women, became a cult movie for white lesbians?

Englishness and Empire focuses on questions of national self-representation in mainstream media, and not on diverse audience responses in different local social and cultural contexts. But it is also concerned with the media's engagement and address to diverse audiences—another question for which the media archive is a rich source. The mainstream media were deeply entangled in questions of nation—not only projecting imagery of nation and empire, but also claiming for themselves a key role in national

[35] Quoted in J. P. Mayer, *British Cinemas and Their Audiences* (London: Dennis Dobson, 1948), 84.

[36] Prem Chowdhry, *Colonial India and the Making of Empire Cinema: Image, Ideology and Identity* (Manchester: Manchester University Press, 2000).

life and identity. These were claims through which they often cast nation and empire in their own image, showing modern systems of communication bringing people together across barriers of space and time, and providing the means for participation in a sense of shared nationality.

The period saw three particular moments when the media cast themselves in the role that Benedict Anderson attributes to them—speaking for the nation, projecting themselves as the means by which people were enabled to imagine their shared identity as members of a national community. In wartime, at the Coronation, and at Churchill's funeral they projected their role in forging national unity—bringing millions of people together to hear Churchill's wartime speeches, to focus on the crowning of a Queen in 1953, and on a naval gun carriage bearing Churchill's coffin in 1965. Most media at these moments converged on images of unity—the sing-song on the wartime home front and the marching troops 'away', world-wide rejoicing at the Coronation with particular attention to rejoicing in the Commonwealth and empire, tributes to Churchill. At such moments the nation becomes a media audience, scattered across millions of homes, simultaneously 'listening in' to wartime radio, or watching public ceremonial on television. The idea of a united media audience and a united nation converge. Divisions and conflicts in nation and empire as well as diverse audience responses are obscured. There is only consensus.

But who was invited to participate in this sense of shared nationality? Who was excluded? Who spoke for the nation? How did the media address their diverse audiences? In looking at these questions, this study traces the different versions of nation constructed in different contexts and through address to different audiences.

Within the period, there was considerable effort to address black and Asian audiences in the wartime empire—through, for example, the Empire Service of the BBC, founded in 1932, and the work of the Colonial Film Unit, set up in 1939, which made films addressed to a black African audience.[37] Recruitment to the war effort was a key goal of propagandists—whether this was the need to recruit women to war industries in Britain, Indians to the armed forces, or, before December 1941, America to the allied cause. This meant that imagery of nation and empire as well as the audiences addressed became increasingly inclusive. But the address to Asians and Africans in empire was contained within the assumption of their inferiority. Indian audiences were seen as ignorant, childlike, and

---

[37] For the BBC Empire Service, see Gerard Mansell, *Let Truth Be Told: Fifty Years of BBC External Broadcasting* (London: Weidenfeld and Nicolson, 1982). For the wartime Colonial Film Unit, see Rosaleen Smyth, 'The British Colonial Film Unit and Sub-Saharan Africa, 1939–1945', *Historical Journal of Film, Radio and Television*, 8 (1988), 285–98.

deficient in understanding.[38] African audiences were assumed to be visually illiterate.[39] The idea of audience thus replicated the construction of colonizers and colonized in much imagery of empire: modern and civilized against backward and primitive. The BBC showed some consciousness of the racial diversity of its wartime audience at home, and radio broadcasts incorporated some black and Asian voices. Learie Constantine made a number of broadcasts to British audiences on radio. Una Marson, who arrived in Britain from Jamaica in 1932, offered a black woman's voice, but she broadcast mainly on the Empire Service to people in the Caribbean, and rarely to audiences in Britain.[40]

Constantine and Marson had few successors in the 1950s and 1960s. In the context of colonial wars and immigration, ideas of nation and the audience that the media addressed defined both as a white community. This is particularly evident in characteristic questions posed by the media about colonial wars—'Are we being weak'—and about black and Asian immigration: 'What about this colour problem of ours?' and 'Would you let your daughter marry a Negro?' The 'ours' and 'you' of such questions offered a version of nation, as well as of the audience addressed, which not only excluded immigrants but was defined against them.

Loss of imperial power was also marked by a dwindling attention to a traffic in imagery between metropolis and empire/Commonwealth. Such traffic had a long history, serving to enlarge and dignify British identity. A range of spectacles were staged in empire in the nineteenth century which conveyed British authority and power and endowed these with mystique. At durbars in India and palavers in Africa, colonized did obeisance to colonizers in scenes of considerable splendour.[41] When royalty visited, the colonized were expected to produce themselves as a form of spectacle for their entertainment, particularly in displays of dancing. Imagery of these spectacles was widely disseminated in the metropolis. James Ryan's work shows the importance of photography to the production of imperial spectacle in Britain and its empire in the nineteenth and early twentieth centuries in a traffic in images between 'home' and 'away'.[42] Imperial epics made between the wars—like *Sanders of the River* (1935), set in Africa—incorporated images

---

[38] Chowdhry, *Colonial India*, 17–28.

[39] See James Burns, 'Watching Africans Watch Films: Theories of Spectatorship in British Colonial Africa', *Historical Journal of Film, Radio and Television*, 20 (2000), 197–211.

[40] For Una Marson, see Delia Jarrett-Macauley, *The Life of Una Marson, 1905–65* (Manchester: Manchester University Press, 1998).

[41] For a discussion of palavers see Barbara Bush, *Imperialism, Race and Resistance: Africa and Britain 1919–1945* (London: Routledge, 1999), 93–6, 298–9. Bush notes that in northern Nigeria, durbars, based on the spectacular Indian durbars—which included the Delhi durbar of 1877 at which Queen Victoria was proclaimed empress of India—were introduced.

[42] James Ryan, *Picturing Empire: Photography and the Visualisation of the British Empire* (London: Reaktion, 1997).

of both palavers and displays of dancing. Empire also provided the spectacle of military displays, adventure landscapes associated with exploration and discovery, and anthropological images that demonstrated British modernity and civilization against the colonized as primitive and backward. British media productions of imperial identity could then be projected back to empire, displaying the large and dignified identity to which empire audiences belonged.

A traffic in imagery between metropolis and empire/Commonwealth reached a post-war high point in Coronation year when stories showed the movement of people, loyal addresses, and gifts from empire and Commonwealth to London, but also a reverse movement through Elizabeth II's extensive tour of Commonwealth and empire. After the Coronation, imperial spectacle continued to be produced away as well as at home, but could no longer be relied upon to magnify British identities. It remained strongly associated with royalty in images of Queen Elizabeth II's tours of empire and Commonwealth in the 1950s and 1960s, when the elaborate displays laid on for her entertainment were broadcast to audiences at home on television news. But another characteristic imperial spectacle of the period was one which marked the end of British colonial rule: the ceremony of lowering the flag.[43]

Media traffic in imagery between metropolis and empire was dominated by British productions, focusing on a unity centred on the metropolis, from a metropolitan perspective. But in another traffic—between America and Britain/empire—Britain's position was far less secure. In the 1930s, 80 per cent of films consumed in Britain and much of empire—including India—were American, and the lion's share of box-office receipts to producers went to Hollywood.[44] Britain's subordinate position in the film industry was one of the main complaints of those who were concerned about the Americanization of British culture between the wars. The *Sunday Chronicle* in 1924 went so far as to suggest: 'It is not a question of our public becoming Americanised. That has already happened . . . Our own people actually view the world through American spectacles.'[45]

Such subordination was evident in American influences on British projections of nation and empire—in wartime through concerns about American anti-imperialism, and in the post-war period through American

[43] For a discussion of independence day ceremonies see Nicholas Owen, ' "More Than a Transfer of Power": Independence Day Ceremonies in India, 15 August 1947', *Contemporary Record*, 6 (1992), 415–51.

[44] Hollywood's share of the Indian market fell very rapidly in the decade after the early 1930s—from 80% to 45% of all releases. See H. Mark Glancy, *When Hollywood Loved Britain: The Hollywood 'British' Film 1939–45* (Manchester: Manchester University Press, 1999), 17.

[45] Quoted in Andrew Higson, *Waving the Flag: Constructing a National Cinema in Britain* (Oxford: Clarendon Press, 1995), 19.

finance for British–American film productions and concerns to get British productions into American markets. American influence on imagery and genre also produced an increasing merger of the empire genre in film with the Hollywood western. By the mid-1950s, as westerns were imported by the new commercial television companies, one of the most common visual images of adventure consumed in Britain portrayed the American frontier. As imperial adventure merged with the western or was displaced by it, the traffic with America meant that adventure narratives consumed in Britain continued to magnify white identities but—despite the prolific Second World War genre in film—these were as likely to be American as British.

In a period when first empire and then Commonwealth came to be seen as increasingly outmoded, there was considerable investment in finding a post-imperial identity that signified modernity. What was Britain's relationship to America? Did a 'special relationship' with America serve to enlarge and dignify British identity? What was the significance of America to the making of post-imperial Britain? These are large questions and this book offers only tentative answers.

The period 1939–65 produced a bewildering array of highly contradictory answers to these questions. A widespread adoption of American popular culture in Britain, especially in youth culture, suggested very considerable enthusiasm for American modernity. But conflicting stories about British–American relations were shaped by varied histories and legacies. Britain's former global empire and increasing loss of a world role interacted with other legacies to produce versions of America that were characterized less by enthusiasm for a modernized identity than by pervasive anxiety about national decline. The wide adoption of American popular culture in Britain intensified anxieties about American power. Those who deplored Americanization and the erosion of a distinctive British culture identified American culture as hyper-modern—modernity gone awry. In this story of British–American relations, Britishness was threatened by America.

Another story claimed a continuing world role and power, authority, and influence for Britain through a 'special relationship' with America. The idea of a 'special relationship' produced a heroic, public rhetoric of national destiny in which America and Britain jointly provided the world with moral leadership, representing freedom and democracy. This story had echoes of imperial identity, for those who acclaimed this 'special relationship' often represented British–American relations, like relations between white settler communities and metropolis, as relations based around ties of common heritage, culture, ancestry, and descent. The version of the 'people's empire' which emphasized a racial community of Britons in Australia, Canada, and New Zealand was increasingly subsumed into a wider globalized identity that also encompassed America: the idea of English-speaking peoples.

Indeed, a 'special relationship' foregrounded Britain and America, while the 'people's empire' of a racial community of Britons became 'the rest'. Like the racial community of Britons, the idea of the English-speaking peoples was racialized, excluding African-Americans and a range of black groups in empire and Britain who spoke English.

There are many different ways in which the story of the impact of loss of imperial power on national identity could be told. I have not strayed here onto the sports pages of newspapers, or the corresponding coverage produced through newsreel, radio, and television. That is a story I leave to others.[46] The story I tell about national self-representation in this period is one in which audiences in Britain were rarely shown how others saw the British nation and empire. It thus replicates the absence of other perspectives —including the perspective of the formerly colonized and their descendants—that is a key feature of the media representations discussed.

I have little to say about the non-English nations within Britain, and do not look at debates about how far the end of empire contributed to a break-up and fragmentation of British identity.[47] The terms 'English' and 'British' were often deployed interchangeably in the period, particularly by English people, and I attempt to avoid this practice. I use the term British–American relations, for example, and not the more common term Anglo-American. A number of popular representations of relations with America both before and after the Second World War focused on Scotland, even if they were made from an English perspective.[48] But my focus on Englishness and empire acknowledges the extent to which media representations of Britain, empire, and Commonwealth were Anglocentric. As Kenneth Lunn has argued, the interchangeability of the terms English and British was not merely slovenly, but expressed what he calls 'a series of assumptions about the natural right of England to speak for Britain'.[49]

In a period when Britain's imperial frontiers were dismantled, imagery of frontiers and boundaries proliferated in stories of nation. These images were very varied—geographical and territorial, national and domestic,

[46] C. L. R. James, *Beyond a Boundary* (London: Hutchinson, 1963); Mike Cronin and Richard Holt, 'The Imperial Game in Crisis: English Cricket and Decolonisation', in Ward, *British Culture*, 111–27.

[47] Tom Nairn, *The Break-Up of Britain: Crisis and Neo-Nationalism* (London: New Left Books, 1981); John Osmond, *The Divided Kingdom* (London: Constable, 1988); Keith Robbins, ' "This Grubby Wreck of Old Glories": The United Kingdom and the End of the British Empire', *Journal of Contemporary History*, 15 (1980), 81–95; Andrew Marr, *The Day Britain Died* (London: Profile Books, 2000); Richard Weight, *Patriots: National Identity in Britain 1940–2000* (Basingstoke: Macmillan, 2002).

[48] *The Ghost Goes West* (Rene Clair, 1935); *The Maggie* (Alexander Mackendrick, 1953); *The Battle of the Sexes* (Charles Crichton, 1960).

[49] Kenneth Lunn, 'Reconsidering "Britishness": The Construction and Significance of National Identity in Twentieth Century Britain', in Brian Jenkins and Spyros Sofos (eds.), *Nation and Identity in Contemporary Europe* (London: Routledge, 1996), 87.

sexual and racial. Sometimes the erosion of boundaries was welcomed. As television developed, so did a progressive story about the media's abolition of boundaries of space and time. But imagery of boundaries and frontiers often signalled fears and insecurities about collapsing and permeable boundaries—between colonizers and colonized, black and white. The idea that black people belonged in an empire under British colonial rule, current in the first half of the twentieth century, maintained a racial separation between empire and metropolis. It informed the post-war media when they defined immigration as 'our colour problem'. It is replicated in much of the literature on contemporary British history which maintains a separation between the imperial and domestic. *Englishness and Empire* chips away at those boundaries.

2

The People's Empire and the People's War

In September 1939, an early wartime cover of the *Radio Times* portrayed a country lane set in summer countryside above the caption 'There'll Always Be An England'.[1] The caption referred to the title of a recent popular song, and the image of a tranquil rural scene with sunlit cottages showed the nation that the song celebrated: 'There'll always be an England while there's a country lane'. Both the picture and the song that it illustrated produced a highly traditional image of England, drawing on ideas of the peace and beauty of rural landscapes, associated with the South. The song's refrain, linking this version of England with empire, produced an Anglocentric identity that conflated England and Britons, and an equally conservative image, characteristic of representations in the First World War, where the empire could be relied on to answer Britain's call for aid at a time of national peril:

> Red, white and blue; what does it mean to you?
> Surely you're proud, shout it aloud,
> 'Britons, awake!'
> The empire too, we can depend on you.
> Freedom remains. These are the chains
> Nothing can break.

Despite its conservatism, as Alison Light has observed, Vera Lynn's 1939 version of 'There'll Always Be An England' provided a contrast to earlier patriotic songs.[2] Unlike the more bombastic, flag-waving mood of 'Rule Britannia', it was intimate and restrained, offering a personal address to its audience— 'If England means as much to you as England means to me'. Even so, the BBC suggested in an editorial in the *Listener* in July 1940 that 'Our patriotism is not of the kind that passionately protests its love . . . To some people there was something almost indecent . . . about that lyrical affirmation, heard so much a few months ago, that "there'll always be an England".'[3]

After September 1939, conservative ideas of nation quickly shifted to a far more inclusive image that served to democratize nation: the 'people's

---

[1] *Radio Times*, 17–23 Sept. 1939.

[2] Alison Light, *Forever England: Femininity, Literature and Conservatism Between the Wars* (London: Routledge, 1991), 154.

[3] Quoted in Sian Nicholas, *The Echo of War: Home Front Propaganda and the Wartime BBC, 1939–45* (Manchester: Manchester University Press, 1996), 42.

war'. In the month after the cover of the *Radio Times* featured the English country lane, the Ministry of Information warned the BBC against a focus on 'England', and the use of 'England' and 'Britain' as interchangeable terms.[4] 'There'll Always Be An England' remained a popular song, and featured in wartime feature films like *Two Thousand Women* (1944), which showed a rendition by female British internees in Occupied France. *The Captive Heart* (1946) showed a whistled rendition by male British prisoners of war as they marched into prison camp.[5] But both these films were careful to offer a far more inclusive version of national identity than that suggested by rural landscapes and the conflation of England and Britons. Both depict groups—one female and the other male—that overcome conflicts to achieve coherence and unity, despite diversity of class, region, and different national identities within Britishness, both foregrounding Scottish characters.

The role of propaganda in showing the war effort as a 'people's war' has attracted considerable attention from historians.[6] The 'people's war' showed a community united across differences of class and gender as well as different national identities within Britishness, although Northern Ireland received scant attention.[7] Most work on this imagery has been confined to the British war effort, and the development of a corresponding version of imperial identity has received much less attention within a literature that generally separates the projection of empire from discussion of the 'people's war'.[8] Yet the imperial war effort received considerable media coverage—on radio, newsreels, and documentary film.

Of these media, newsreels reached a wide audience as regular features of commercial cinema programmes and, according to Mass Observation reports in 1940, were well liked by audiences.[9] Documentary films usually had

---

[4] Quoted in Sian Nicholas, *The Echo of War: Home Front Propaganda and the Wartime BBC, 1939–45* (Manchester: Manchester University Press, 231.

[5] *Two Thousand Women* (Frank Launder, 1944); *The Captive Heart* (Basil Dearden, 1946).

[6] See, for example, David Morgan and Mary Evans, *The Battle for Britain: Citizenship and Ideology in the Second World War* (Routledge: London, 1993); Anthony Aldgate and Jeffrey Richards, *Britain Can Take It: The British Cinema in the Second World War* (Edinburgh: Edinburgh University Press, 1994); Jeffrey Richards, *Films and British National Identity: From Dickens to Dad's Army* (Manchester: Manchester University Press, 1997); James Chapman, *The British At War: Cinema, State and Propaganda 1939–1945* (London: I. B. Tauris, 1998); Mark Donnelly, *Britain in the Second World War* (Routledge: London, 1999).

[7] Two documentary films on Northern Ireland's war effort were produced during the war. Of these, *Letter From Ulster* (Brian Desmond Hurst, 1943), concerned a 'letter' home from American GIs stationed in Northern Ireland, in a film that focused on GIs and paid scant attention to the people of Northern Ireland. See Toby Haggith, 'Citizenship, Nationhood and Empire in British Official Film Propaganda', in Richard Weight and Abigail Beach (eds.), *The Right to Belong: Citizenship and National Identity in Britain, 1930–1960* (London: I. B. Tauris, 1998), 78–9.

[8] But see Haggith, 'Citizenship', 59–88; Thomas Hajkowski, 'The BBC, the Empire, and the Second World War, 1939–1945', *Historical Journal of Film, Radio and Television*, 22 (2002), 135–55.

[9] Jeffrey Richards and Dorothy Sheridan (eds.), *Mass-Observation at the Movies* (London: Routledge and Kegan Paul, 1987), 381–423.

more limited audiences, but are interesting for any analysis of representations of empire, since they contributed to the development of themes that informed other empire propaganda, and were often targeted at audiences in Britain as well as empire. Radio programmes produced by the wartime BBC were particularly conscientious about the promotion of imperial unity and the provision of information for British, as well as empire, audiences. The BBC made considerable efforts to reach popular domestic audiences through a variety programme on empire called *Travellers' Tales* and a quiz programme called *Brush Up Your Empire*.[10] There is evidence of difficulty at the BBC in interesting a British audience in empire—one of the reasons that they began to make programmes that they hoped would appeal to a popular audience, like *Brush Up Your Empire*.[11] Even so, the extent of imperial propaganda meant that many media audiences—in Britain and empire—heard or saw both 'people's war' and imperial versions of the war effort.

The 'people's war' marked a twentieth-century high point in inclusive imagery of Britishness. The move to an image of nation that stressed national unity across class and gender difference came very early in wartime documentaries. *The First Days*—the first GPO Film Unit documentary of the war, made in 1939—made no reference to rural England.[12] Its imagery was urban, focusing on the people of London preparing for war, and the opening titles reminded the audience at the outset that 'four-fifths of our people live in cities'.

To demonstrate the spirit of the nation, collective effort was strongly emphasized, and London was constructed as a community that stood for nation. Co-operation was shown through images of people in groups, with few close-ups of individuals—and the lack of individuation was reinforced by the commentary on the effort to collect sand for sandbags, and then to shovel the sand into them, referring to people running 'to and fro like ants'. The commentary was also careful to point out that this co-operation was across class difference: 'The thousand classes of London, some from their damp basements, and some from their luxury flats come to work for the public good.'

The First Days also showed women's active role in the war effort, although the references to the early days of the war in London as a 'revolution' for women who 'had to face a new life' were accompanied by reassurance that in 'the new trappings there was the old spirit', and that 'above all endurance was the woman's inheritance'. The shots were equally reassuring on the

---

[10] Hajkowski, 'The BBC', 147–51.

[11] Hajkowski, 'The BBC'; Sian Nicholas, ' "Brushing Up Your Empire": Dominion and Colonial Propaganda on the BBC's Home Services, 1939–45', *Journal of Imperial and Commonwealth History*, 31 (May 2003), 207–30.

[12] *The First Days* (Humphrey Jennings and Harry Watt, 1939).

limits of this 'revolution', showing women cooking, serving food in a canteen, nursing, and knitting. In its focus on the unity of Londoners, standing for the unity of nation, the film also served as propaganda to recruit further volunteers for this collective, with commentary addressing the audience on the need to help the war effort, and the areas in which such help was urgently needed.

The First Days provided an early image that was subsequently extensively developed across a range of media. Togetherness was a recurrent image of a British community where diverse groups united across differences—joining in collective action, participating in sing-songs. Empire propaganda promoted a similar theme. The poster designed to advertise the imperial war effort showed a diverse community marching in unity, and its slogan was 'Together'. Both these versions of togetherness generally kept hierarchies in place. Propaganda about the 'people's war' paid tributes to the particular qualities of the working classes or women, but the class or gender systems usually escaped critique. The 'Together' poster showed troops from Canada, Australia, Britain, South Africa, New Zealand, India, and Africa united under the fluttering Union Jack of Britishness, but arranged them in a racial hierarchy, where Indians and Africans marched behind a racial community of Britons.

Like *The First Days*, much imagery of a 'people's war' focused on the home front. In contrast, the imperial war effort was usually shown on the fighting front, showing martial masculinity 'away'. Its most characteristic image—as in the 'Together' poster—was of marching troops. Representations of nation and empire nevertheless converged on common themes. A racial community of Britons was one prominent theme of empire propaganda, highlighting the role of white Australians, Canadians, New Zealanders, and South Africans as 'sons of empire'. This showed the efforts of the common people in empire, united with the common people of Britain in a fight for justice and freedom. But Indian soldiers were also acclaimed as courageous 'sons of empire' and much empire propaganda projected empire as a multiracial community. While a 'people's war' showed a homogeneous people pulling together across differences of class and gender, this version of a 'people's empire' showed a heterogeneous people pulling together across differences of race and ethnicity, united in a common cause.

Nation, Empire, and Media

In January 1940, newsreels showed Australian, Canadian, and New Zealand servicemen arriving in Britain; Newfoundland lumberjacks crossing the Atlantic to fell timber in Scotland for Britain's war needs; Indian and

Canadian troops arriving in France; New Zealanders living in England forming their own anti-tank unit; South African airmen patrolling 'the shores of the British empire in Africa'; and Australian troops parading through Sydney.[13] Some of these disparate stories—on Australians, New Zealanders, and Canadians—were brought together in early January to demonstrate 'the Empire's New Year greeting to the Mother Country'. Its greeting—sending 'its sons to join the fight'—brought with it the message that 'all the Empire stands together in the fight for freedom. Here are the faces of the sons of the Empire, they know that our battle is theirs too.'[14]

These 1940 newsreels projected an imperial identity that, like First World War imagery, emphasized a devoted empire coming to Britain's aid at a time of national peril, demonstrating love and support for the motherland. Like the refrain of 'There'll Always Be An England' they suggested automatic loyalty—'the empire too, we can depend on you'. This was also a dominant theme of a radio programme, broadcast in October 1939, called *The Empire Answers*. Taking its audience on a 'circuit of Empire' spanning four continents, the programme broadcast voices from Africa, South and South-East Asia, Australasia, the Caribbean, and Canada. All conveyed the same message: one of loyal devotion and support for Britain.[15]

While empire imagery remained conservative in the early stages of the war, one link between ideas of nation and empire was the role the media assigned themselves in bringing together a national and imperial community. Both *The First Days* and *The Empire Answers* converged on a common symbol of unity: the radio. *The First Days* offered an image that became recurrent in wartime documentaries—people listening to war news on the radio, often in a domestic setting. This provided a further element in the construction of London as a community that stood for nation. People who had never met, and were unlikely to ever meet, were shown as connected through the collective and simultaneous act of 'listening in'. In its imagery of the reception of the Prime Minister's radio broadcast announcing war, as in its imagery of people preparing for war, *The First Days* also showed a common identity across class and gender differences. Class is signified

[13] 'Australian Airmen Arrive', *British Paramount News*, 1 Jan. 1940; 'Making Themselves at Home', *Universal News*, 4 Jan. 1940; 'Australia Sends First Instalment', *British Paramount News*, 1 Jan. 1940; 'New Zealanders Arrive', *Universal News*, 4 Jan. 1940; 'Lumberjacks Cross Atlantic to Help', *British Paramount News*, 29 Jan. 1940; 'Newfoundland Lumberjacks Over Here', *Universal News*, 29 Jan. 1940; 'Indian Troops in France', *Pathé Gazette*, 18 Jan. 1940; 'Indian Troops in France', *Universal News*, 18 Jan. 1940; 'First Canadians Swell BEF Ranks', *British Paramount News*, 22 Jan. 1940; 'Canadian Commander in Chief', *Pathé Gazette*, 22 Jan. 1940; 'New Year Sees Empire Gathering of the Clans', *British Paramount News*, 4 Jan. 1940; 'Out with the Dawn Patrol', *Pathé Gazette*, 4 Jan. 1940; 'Australian War Efforts', *Pathé Gazette*, 8 Jan. 1940.

[14] 'Defenders of the Empire', *Pathé Gazette*, 4 Jan. 1940.

[15] *The Empire Answers*, BBC radio broadcast, 6 Oct. 1939. The script was published in *The Listener*, 12 Oct. 1939.

through clothing and housing as working-class men in cloth caps listen in a pub, a working-class woman in an apron listens in her kitchen, a pipe-smoking man sits beside his wireless set in a suburban domestic interior. All receive the news in calm, grave silence, and the sequence ends in further silence, against a shot of a cloudy sky. Shots of suburban streets show them completely deserted and quiet while the news is broadcast.

Visual media were thus not only used to represent the nation as a united community, but also to represent aural media bringing the nation into 'deep, horizontal comradeship'.[16] Those who viewed visual images of the home front were not sitting in a domestic setting listening to the radio but in a cinema—a location which provided a type of communal experience, and one that sometimes corresponded to experiences shown in war news and documentaries since screenings could be punctuated by air-raid sirens. Audiences could identify as part of a wider community of nation, or simply escape from home and wartime austerity and exhaustion into a place associated with glamour and leisure. Not everybody wanted to see war news and films. One woman recorded: 'Apart from *Mrs Miniver* I haven't seen any war films. I have tried to get away from it on my few visits to the cinema.'[17] Even so, the way in which images influenced subsequent memories suggests something of their resonance. Tom Harrisson notes that a young female Mass Observation volunteer in Stepney in the East End of London recorded in her diary on the day that war was declared, that she was playing the piano, and missed the Prime Minister's broadcast announcing war. However, her later memory was of a quite different scene, informed by just the kind of quiet gravity of 'listening in' portrayed in *The First Days*: 'I have the notion that this was a special kind of gathering; something a bit formal: aunts, uncles or neighbours, perhaps, all listening to the wireless, which, those days, was on almost all the time, in anticipation of more bad news.'[18]

The Empire Answers offered a word picture corresponding to the visual imagery of wartime documentaries. Where *The First Days* showed people in London hearing the announcement that Britain was at war with Germany, *The Empire Answers* focused on the role of radio in bringing together an imperial community, telling how the Prime Minister's voice was heard 'in all parts of the British world'. This simultaneity of listening was one where in 'thousands of homes' in South Africa people 'gathered around their wireless sets', families in Australia 'gathered round the fire after Sunday

[16] Benedict Anderson, *Imagined Communities: Reflections on the Origins and Spread of Nationalism*, rev. edn. (London: Verso, 1991), 7.

[17] Quoted in J. P. Mayer, *British Cinemas and their Audiences: Sociological Studies* (London: Dennis Dobson, 1948), 30.

[18] Quoted in Tom Harrisson, *Living Through the Blitz* (London: Collins, 1976), 325–6.

tea listening for news 12,000 miles away', and there were 'lights in the houses at midnight and the small hours' in New Zealand 'as the people listened to the momentous happenings in Europe'.

The programme cast the empire in the image of radio. However vast the distances, whatever the hemisphere, the season, or the time-zone, the radio's domestic setting of hearth, home, and family unites an imperial community. The familial intimacy associated with radio was also used as an image of imperial unity by George VI in wartime Christmas radio broadcasts. The idea of the King speaking from his home and of the royal family gathered round the hearth at Christmas became an analogy to what the King referred to as 'one great family' in 1941, 'the family circle' in 1942, and 'the family of the British Commonwealth and Empire' in 1943. 'Wherever you are, serving in our wide, free Commonwealth of Nations', he told his audience in the royal Christmas broadcast in 1942, 'you will always feel "at home". Though severed by the long sea miles of distance, you are still in the family circle, whose ties, precious in peaceful years have been knit even closer by danger.'[19]

Despite these homely and familial images, the empire presented problems for the idea of Britain as a tolerant and decent nation embodied in early images of a 'people's war', and it was not only Nazi propaganda that portrayed British colonial rule as oppressive. There was growing opposition in America to British imperialism in the 1920s and 1930s, fuelled by British responses to Indian nationalism. This was extended before America's entry into the war in American resistance to abandoning a policy of neutrality in order to fight a war in defence of the British empire. When Allied war aims were defined in the 1941 Atlantic Charter, they included self-determination for all nations, prompting the American Under-Secretary of State to declare that 'the age of imperialism is dead'.[20] In 1941, a report based on views expressed by Americans in letters sent to Britain that were intercepted by censors concluded that 'Few people in England have any conception of the reality of the Empire bogey in the American mind and elsewhere. The Nazi radio keeps at it all the time, and upon this topic it is effective.'[21]

Early moves to counter such views drew on what John MacKenzie calls the 'peace and economic regeneration' version of empire that had been extensively developed between the wars.[22] This emphasized that the British

---

[19] Tom Fleming (ed.), *Voices Out of the Air: The Royal Christmas Broadcasts 1932–1981* (London: Heinemann, 1981), 33–40.

[20] Quoted in Jeffrey Richards, 'Imperial Heroes for a Post-Imperial Age', in Stuart Ward (ed.), *British Culture and the End of Empire* (Manchester: Manchester University Press, 2001), 130.

[21] 'Digest of Material Based on Incoming Letters from US', Apr. 1941, PRO CO 875 11/13.

[22] John MacKenzie, 'In Touch with the Infinite: The BBC and Empire, 1923–53', in John MacKenzie (ed.), *Imperialism and Popular Culture* (Manchester: Manchester University Press, 1986), 183.

empire had not been founded on conquest or oppression, but love of liberty and justice. King George VI's Empire Day message in 1940 was heard not only in Britain—where cinema programmes were stopped to mark this radio broadcast—and throughout the empire, but was also carried by American stations.[23] The King stated: 'There is a word that our enemies use against us—Imperialism. By it they mean the spirit of domination, the lust of Conquest.' But, he countered: 'Our one object has always been peace—peace in which our institutions may be developed, the condition of our peoples improved.'[24]

Sonya Rose has argued that a restrained version of exemplary masculinity representing a home-loving, quiet reticence—what she calls 'the temperate hero'—was constructed in the Second World War in opposition to 'hyper-masculine' Nazis.[25] The King's speech produced a similarly temperate empire against the aggressive masculine conquest and aggression associated with the Nazis. The Colonial Development and Welfare Act, passed in 1940, extended this message, and gave some substance to the King's statement about improving 'the condition of our peoples'.

After 1942, this message was extended further. The fall of Singapore, Hong Kong, Malaya, and Burma to Japanese forces led to increasing pressure to present a modern empire. American criticism added to such pressure. In a widely reported speech in the wake of the surrender of Singapore, Sumner Welles, President Roosevelt's chief foreign policy adviser, reiterated that 'the age of imperialism is ended'.[26] The fall of Singapore led *The Times* to argue in an editorial that 'misguided conceptions of racial prestige and narrow obsolete interpretations of economic interest' must be surmounted 'if democracy is to have any meaning or appeal for the colonial peoples'.[27] From 1942, the word insistently used in empire propaganda to proclaim a modern empire was 'partnership'.[28]

Representations of a united nation and empire dedicated to improving the conditions of its peoples were always in tension with differences between the different groups that were represented. The idea of a united

---

[23] *Daily Express*, 25 May 1940.

[24] Ibid.

[25] Sonya Rose, *Which People's War? National Identity and Citizenship in Wartime Britain 1939–1945* (Oxford: Oxford University Press, 2003), ch. 5.

[26] Quoted in Suke Wolton, *Lord Hailey, the Colonial Office and the Politics of Race and Empire* (Houndsmill: Macmillan Press, 2000), 47.

[27] *The Times*, 14 Mar. 1942.

[28] See Rosaleen Smyth, 'Britain's African Colonies and British Propaganda During the Second World War', *Journal of Imperial and Commonwealth History*, 41 (1985), 65–82; Rosaleen Smyth, 'The British Colonial Film Unit and Sub-Saharan Africa, 1939–1945', *Historical Journal of Film, Radio and Television*, 8 (1988), 285–98; Kate Morris, *British Techniques of Public Relations and Propaganda for Mobilizing East and Central Africa During World War II* (Lewiston, NY: Edwin Mellen, 2000), ch. 4.

empire was often maintained by ignoring divisions. *The Empire Answers* represented India through the voice of Lord Linlithgow, the Viceroy, broadcasting to the Indian people, and did not mention that eight of the eleven devolved self-governing provinces, established in 1935, resigned after he had announced that India was at war with Germany without consulting them, or any other Indian.[29] Nor did it mention Eire, a member of the Commonwealth until 1948, which maintained a policy of neutrality throughout the war. In South Africa, where the war issue was highly divisive, and the decision to abandon the early policy of neutrality was opposed by many Afrikaner nationalists, the programme recorded that news that Britain was at war had 'spread like wildfire through the vast crowds gathered in the streets', and stressed unity between Afrikaners and Britons 'as members of the active citizens forces manning their posts'.[30] Such unity remained a strong theme in coverage of the South African war effort, and the commentary over newsreel images of 'South Africa's sons' mobilizing for war in the Transvaal in 1940 stated that 'Afrikaners and Britons...stand together', despite continuing opposition from nationalists who organized anti-war rallies in various parts of the Transvaal in June 1940.[31]

Representations of a progressive empire were particularly important in the context of American anti-imperialism, and the need to address American audiences was a consistent thread in the wartime projection of a temperate 'people's empire'. But the audiences for empire propaganda were highly diverse. The BBC became increasingly aware of the diversity of its audience in Britain, and concerned that jokes about 'darkies', and references to 'a black man as a scare to white children', would be found offensive. It was urged that producers should be reminded that 'there are a lot of coloured people in the country now—Africans, West Indians and Americans, and there is therefore particularly good reason to be careful not to say anything which might be interpreted as showing colour prejudice'.[32] In 1942, the monthly intelligence summary argued that people in the Middle East were not won over by images of British decency, while images of Churchill, replete with cigar, did not win over Indians whose conception of leadership involved the spiritual and symbolic.[33]

[29] Kathryn Tidrick, *Empire and the English Character* (London: I. B. Tauris, 1990), 250.

[30] *The Empire Answers.*

[31] 'Transvaal Troops on the Move', *Pathé Gazette*, 8 Jan. 1940; A. D. Harvey, *Collisions of Empires: Britain in Three World Wars, 1793–1945* (London: Phoenix, 1992), 508.

[32] Memo from Assistant Controller of Overseas Services to R. A. Rendall, 1 May 1943, BBC WAC, R34/306, Policy, Coloured People, 1941–1944.

[33] Philip Woods, 'From Shaw to Shantaram: The Film Advisory Board and the Making of British Propaganda Films in India, 1940–1943', *Historical Journal of Film, Radio and Television*, 21 (2001), 299.

In this context, the media began to recognize a need to appeal to non-white audiences to enlist support for the war effort. One strategy used was the production of programmes for specific audiences. The BBC expanded its services to empire which, before the war, had been aimed mainly at the self-governing Dominions. The service to the West Indies, for example, previously reserved mainly for special occasions such as cricket Test Matches, was now expanded with 'morale-boosting talks on West Indians and the war effort'.[34] Sometimes the specific audiences addressed were a result of racial segregation. The exclusion of West Africans from Nairobi cinemas was brought to the attention of the Colonial Office in 1941, and, on enquiry, they were informed by the Governor of Kenya that the Kenyan government censored films as 'suitable for non-Africans only'.[35] This exclusion offers a striking example of divisions imposed on audiences of British media that were simultaneously showing an empire united against the Nazi threat.

If some films were for 'non-Africans only', others were specifically addressed to black Africans. The Colonial Film Unit was set up early in the war as part of the Ministry of Information's efforts to mobilize support for the war throughout the empire. Developing propaganda in conjunction with the Colonial Office, it produced documentaries designed mainly for black Africans, and provided mobile cinema vans to take these films into rural areas.[36] The racial hierarchy underpinning ideas about audiences was evident in the assumption that, because of the visual illiteracy of their audience, these films should be slow-moving, their narrative patiently explained in commentaries.[37] In 1948, George Pearson, the chief film-maker at the Colonial Film Unit, addressed a Conference organized by the British Film Institute on 'The Film in Colonial Development' entitled 'The Making of Films for Illiterates in Africa'. He spoke admiringly of documentary technique, but 'found its leaps across time and place in pictorial narration beyond the understanding of our audiences'.[38]

The recognition of a need to address diverse audiences, to counter American anti-imperialism, and to recover from the surrender of Singapore to Japanese forces meant a continuing need to emphasize unity and loyalty. But it also meant a move to modernize imperial identity, emphasizing

---

[34] Delia Jarrett-Macauley, *The Life of Una Marson, 1905–65* (Manchester: Manchester University Press, 1998), 146–7.

[35] Sonya Rose, 'Race, Empire and British Wartime National Identity, 1939–45', *Historical Research*, 74 (2001), 230.

[36] Smyth, 'Britain's African Colonies', 77. The Colonial Film Unit's African films were not thought suitable for Indian audiences. See Woods, 'From Shaw to Shantaram', 299.

[37] See James Burns, 'Watching Africans Watch Films: Theories of Spectatorship in British Colonial Africa', *Historical Journal of Film, Radio and Television*, 20 (2000), 203.

[38] George Pearson, *Flashback: The Autobiography of a British Film Maker* (London: George Allen and Unwin, 1957), 211. I am grateful to Mike Paris for this reference.

themes of partnership and welfare. This was an image that advertised the virtues of Britain as a liberal and tolerant nation, and demonstrated common resistance to Nazi Germany by a temperate empire that was neither racist nor oppressive.

Martial Masculinity

In *From the Four Corners* (1941), soldiers from Australia, Canada, and New Zealand who meet in London are greeted by a woman who calls them 'splendid fellows' and tells them: 'How wonderful you are coming all those thousands of miles to answer the motherland's call to arms.' The woman's greeting encapsulates the dominant view of empire in the First World War: loyal and devoted, answering the call from Britain. But it is a view that makes these Second World War soldiers uneasy, and the woman, who is middle-class and middle-aged, is shown as gushing and patronizing in contrast to their plain speaking and youthful manliness. These soldiers represent the common people of the self-governing Dominions—privates not officers—on leave in Britain. They are rescued from the woman's clutches by the English film star, Leslie Howard, who takes them off to that classic institution of the 'people's war'—a pub, where they drink pints.[39]

Howard was not only a film star but also a prominent broadcaster on the BBC overseas service. His broadcasts identified the heroic qualities of a 'people's war'—'courage, devotion to duty, kindliness, humour, coolheadedness, balance, common sense, singleness of purpose . . . and idealism'.[40] In *From the Four Corners* the soldiers from Australia, Canada, and New Zealand exemplify this heroism and an idealism that links Englishness and empire. Howard disputes the woman's claim that the soldiers are answering the motherland's call, and they assent to this in characteristic plain speech—'that's a lot of hooey'. But he also disputes their own version of why they have enlisted, expressed in equally plain speech—'to kick Hitler in the pants of course . . . We hate Hitler's guts.' Howard is prone to eloquence and his voice dominates the film as he identifies their war aims for them in considerable detail. He treats them to a history lesson—a stirring story of common law and justice, freedom and democracy, taken by British pioneers to the ends of the earth. That is why they came, he tells them, to defend these values—out of idealism.

The trio of soldiers in *From the Four Corners* was one of the most characteristic representations of empire in the war, foregrounding martial

---

[39] *From the Four Corners* (Denham and Pinewood Studios, 1941).
[40] Quoted in Jeffrey Richards, *Films and British National Identity: From Dickens to Dad's Army* (Manchester: Manchester University Press, 1997), 15.

masculinity and a racial community of Britons. Howard plays himself—his status as a film star providing a short low-budget documentary with at least some star attraction. When the Australian soldier confirms this status, telling Howard he has seen him in the movies, he also identifies a more widely disseminated imperial image: 'our chaps marching through the streets... the troopship going out'.

Newsreels of troopships appeared to confirm American fears that the British were fighting in defence of their empire, as they showed imperial manhood circulating around the empire, disembarking in various theatres of war that were often imperial territory. And then they marched. *Britain At Bay* (1940)—a documentary with a commentary written and spoken by J. B. Priestley—shows a racial community of Britons, like the trio of soldiers in *From the Four Corners*, described by Priestley as 'men from the ends of the earth, from our Great Dominions in Australia, New Zealand and Canada', against shots of them marching.[41] But marching was often a metaphor for a wider imperial unity—a multiracial community that marched together. *The Empire Marches* (1941) ended with shots of imperial troops in action and the question: 'Is it not significant that men of every race, creed and colour are marching and fighting to the common end?'[42]

Martial masculinity had a long history as a prominent image of empire that focused on the soldier hero. Imagery of martial Indians had acquired considerable popularity in pre-war Hollywood films of empire, although their British officers were the main focus of attention. British officers and administrators used 'martial race theory', first developed in India, in the recruitment of imperial troops.[43] Defining which ethnic groups made good soldiers, this theory identified a martial race as naturally warlike, courageous, loyal, disciplined (when well led), and of considerable physical prowess.[44] Such imagery of martial masculinity advertised the strength and vigour of imperial manhood, and was in tension with the temperate heroism of quiet courage, but empire imagery often attempted to combine these.

Reporting of the martial masculinity of Indians and Africans lost any subtleties about distinctions between different ethnic groups, but repeatedly rehearsed the qualities of courage, loyalty, and physical prowess, especially in newsreel representations of Indian troops. Newsreel commentaries

---

[41] *Britain at Bay* (Ministry of Information, 1940).

[42] *The Empire Marches* (Universal, 1941).

[43] Anthony Kirk-Greene, ' "Damnosa Hereditas": Ethnic Ranking and the Martial Races Imperative in Africa', *Ethnic and Racial Studies*, 3 (1983), 395.

[44] Scott Worthy, 'A Martial Race? Maori and Pakeha New Zealand Soldiers of the Great War in Imperial Context', paper delivered to British World Conference II, University of Calgary, July 2003; Timothy Parsons, *The African Rank-and-File: Social Implications of Colonial Military Service in the King's African Rifles 1902–1964* (Portsmouth: Heinemann, 1999), 53–103.

claimed that there were 'no more fearless fighters in the world', called Indian troops 'hardy little men from the hills and the plains', and described them as tough as the mules—'fighters from the Punjab and the North West Frontier, men who have spent their lives in the open'.[45] *War Came to Kenya* (1942)— retitled *War Comes to Africa* for distribution in Britain—identified an Indian mounted battery as 'men of magnificent bearing and physique'.[46] Africans joined Indian warriors in the litany of martial masculinity—troops from the Gold Coast described as 'bronze giants of nature, every man strips to display muscles calculated to make Joe Louis look to his biceps'.[47] Like Indian soldiers, it was not only their bodies that were a focus of attention but their loyal allegiance as volunteers: 'They are not conscripts, but volunteers who have found the Union Jack worth living under, and worth fighting for.'

The loyalty of India to the empire/Commonwealth, exemplified by their military prowess was the major theme of media coverage of India throughout the war in imagery that was dominated by British views and British voices. 'India stands with Britain', claimed a newsreel on the 'sons of empire' in 1940 that showed the Indian mule corps serving with the British Expeditionary Force in France. Their loyalty to the King Emperor was stressed, in a compilation of images that also showed New Zealanders to demonstrate 'the youth of this great Commonwealth of nations' all answering 'the call to arms', and thus 'the unity of the British Empire'.[48] In *Defenders of India* (1941) the voices of General Auchinleck, who provides a foreword to the film, and Robert Stimson as commentator, linked 'India's stalwart troops' to a temperate 'people's empire'—marching, training, and fighting 'for the empire and reasonableness and decency'.[49] Investitures of Indians with Victoria Crosses in 1943 and 1944 demonstrated the Indian Army's 'reason to be proud of its record in this war'.[50] A 1945 story of former Indian prisoners-of-war from Germany, visited by royalty in a camp in Norfolk, acclaimed their contribution to the war effort as 'warriors of India' receiving a royal tribute for their 'heroic contribution to the Allied victory', having fought with distinction 'in the honoured tradition of fighting India'.[51]

British voices did not always tell narratives of India and, for the first time, British officers were sometimes nowhere to be seen when Indian military

---

[45] 'Indian Troops in France', *Pathé Gazette*, 18 Jan. 1940.
[46] *War Came to Kenya* (Information Office of Kenya, 1942).
[47] 'Troops from the Gold Coast', *Pathé Gazette*, 20 Jan. 1941.
[48] 'Sons of Empire', *Gaumont British News*, 18 Jan. 1940.
[49] *Defenders of India* (Indian Film Unit, 1941).
[50] 'Viceroy Presents VCs', *Pathé Gazette*, 3 Feb. 1944; 'Indians at Buckingham Palace', *Pathé Gazette*, 4 Oct. 1943.
[51] 'Former Indian POWs Cheer King', *British Paramount News*, 28 June 1945.

were shown. *Planes of Hindustan* (1940), produced for an Indian audience and narrated by its director, G. Radcliffe Genge, was careful to establish that the Indian Air Force was the only armed unit of the Crown entirely officered by Indians.[52] It also established the modernity of the Indian Air Force, showing canteen facilities, a child welfare centre, and an officers' swimming pool. *India Marches* (1941), sponsored by the government of India and the Ministry of Information, also showed Indian modernity in medicine and communications, including an exemplary postal service. Focusing on Indian military, the film shows no British, although it does pay tribute to the 'magnificent leadership of General Wavell in Africa'. Its narrator—the Indian, Z. A. Bokhari, who worked in the BBC Empire Service during the war—addresses a Western audience and educates them about India, informing them, for example, about sports in which Indians are world champions, including hockey, which 'may be an English game, but we have, so to speak, owned it for a bit'. The film ends with a long sequence of Indian soldiers marching, but this is as much a metaphor of Indian self-sufficiency as of imperial unity, and the film emphasizes Indian membership of the British Commonwealth and not the empire.[53]

The wartime representation of Indian servicemen as loyal and courageous 'sons of empire' countered the idea of Indian opposition to British rule. The government of India, as well as the Ministry of Information, the Colonial Office, the India Office, and all other bodies involved in decisions about empire propaganda on India faced a tangled web of contradictory pressures. The rise of Indian nationalism between the wars made British media more aware of the impact of their productions on Indian audiences, especially in the contexts of popular and official protests in India at empire films, including those by Hollywood.[54] When war was declared, the need to recruit Indians into the military made the impact of productions on Indian audiences a more urgent consideration.

American audiences also had to be considered. Despite Hollywood celebrations of the British empire in India, American anti-imperialism, like Nazi propaganda, portrayed British rule in India as oppressive. 'There is a great fear in certain circles of America that England will make peace with the Axis powers rather than lose India', stated one letter-writer from America to Dublin in 1942. Another letter-writer from Florida to London appealed: 'I wish you'd tell those stupid English to give India its freedom or we won't play any more. After all, if this war's being fought for liberty they'd better start in their own back yard. (That is the popular

---

[52] *Planes of Hindustan* (G. Radcliffe Genge, 1940).
[53] *India Marches* (Bombay Talkies, 1941).
[54] Prem Chowdhry, *Colonial India and the Making of Empire Cinema: Image, Ideology and Identity* (Manchester: Manchester University Press, 2000).

sentiment here, not just mine).'[55] In this context, there was a particular need to portray a 'people's empire' in India—progressive, modern, loyal.

The image of loyalty became especially important in the context of the 1942 Quit India movement, named after the resolution taken by the Indian National Congress, in July 1942, which told the British to 'purify themselves by surrendering power in India'. The mass demonstrations of the Quit India movement in 1942, in the aftermath of the arrest of the leadership of the Indian National Congress, were a serious disruption to the imagery of India that had been developed. Violent British repression of demonstrators did not exactly fit the idea of British rule in India as progressive or of a 'people's empire'. The RAF was brought in to machine-gun crowds from the air, and it was British statistics which showed that, by mid-September, police firing on rioters and clashes with troops had caused 658 Indian deaths and 'large numbers' of injuries. This compared to 11 troops killed and 7 injured.[56] An emergency Whipping Act, introduced in August, enabled whipping to be inflicted on anybody convicted of rioting.[57] American opposition was expressed in an open letter from the editors of the American magazine, *Life*, to the 'People of England' which affirmed: '*One* thing we are sure we are *not* fighting for is to hold the British Empire together. We don't like to put the matter so bluntly, but we don't want you to have any illusions...In the light of what you are doing in India, how do you expect to talk about "principles", and look our soldiers in the eye?'[58]

In this context, the martial Indian bravely serving empire became even more important to representations of India. Churchill, speaking in Parliament, claimed that the Congress Party was unrepresentative of the Indian majority, and attributed rioting to 'hooligans and agitators' and 'lawless elements'. He used India's 'martial races' to demonstrate its loyalty and paid tribute to 'the bravery of the Indian troops', adding that in two months of Quit India demonstrations, 'more than 140,000 new volunteers for the Army have come forward in loyal allegiance to the King Emperor'. He went on to praise the 'fine work of the Indian Police' in bringing the situation successfully under control.[59] A good deal of the British media followed suit. Like Churchill, they attributed the demonstrations to hooligans and agitators, who were unrepresentative of 'India's Millions'.[60]

[55] Quoted in 'An Examination of the Many Reasons for the Unfriendly Feelings of a Large Number of Americans Towards Great Britain', *Postal and Telegraph Censorship Report on The United States of America*, 11 Sept. 1942, PRO CO 875/18/11.
[56] *The Times*, 26 Sept. 1942 and 17 Sept. 1942.
[57] *The Times*, 16 Aug. 1942.
[58] Quoted in Harvey, *Collision of Empires*, 526.
[59] *The Times*, 11 Sept. 1942.
[60] 'The Trouble in India', *Pathé Gazette*, 3 Sept. 1942; *Daily Express*, 12 Aug. 1942.

Indians, while less widely represented than white Australians, Canadians, and New Zealanders, were a strong focus for images of martial masculinity. The depiction of other groups, like Maori, was sketchy. The representation of the New Zealand armed forces in newsreels focused on white soldiers, with Maori only occasionally visible as part of New Zealand contingents— inspected by the King, parading, and marching German prisoners along the road in Cassino in 1944.[61] *Maximum Effort* (1944)—a documentary targeted mainly at an audience in New Zealand, and with a New Zealand narrator—incorporated a Maori into its narrative of an RAF aircrew, also comprising Canadians and English, flying an air raid over Germany.[62] Such representations, however sketchy, served to demonstrate Britain and New Zealand as liberal and tolerant as well as unity between diverse peoples.

Representations of Africans were far more common than Maori, and they were often ascribed the qualities of warriors, but the racial hierarchy of the South African armed forces ensured that black South Africans were rarely visible. Debates about the role of black South Africans in the armed forces provoked very considerable hostility from white South Africans to the idea that they should bear arms. Throughout the war black South Africans and men of mixed parentage were seen as non-combatants. They served in subordinate roles in white fighting units to release whites for combat duty, under the command of the Non-European Army services—as guards, batmen, latrine-diggers, cooks, waiters, drivers, dispatch riders, stretcher bearers, medical aids, tailors, clerks, and typists. The highest rank open to black Africans was staff sergeant, while that for volunteers in the Coloured Cape Corps was warrant officer I.[63]

The racial segregation of the American armed forces stationed in Britain prompted some media attention, much of it critical. But there was virtually no media interest in the racial hierarchy of the South African armed forces in empire. Jan Smuts, Prime Minister of South Africa, identified South Africans as a white people in debates about the armed forces in 1940, arguing: 'I cannot conceive of anything which would have the effect of creating . . . greater quarrels and greater division among the people than the arming of coloured people or the native population of the Union.'[64] Throughout the war, the media followed Smuts in portraying South Africa as white. Its racial hierarchy occasionally emerged in images that showed Members of the Cape Coloured Corps leaving for the front, and a passing-

---

[61] See, for example, 'His Majesty Meets New Zealanders', *British Movietone News*, 11 July 1940; 'Before and After Crete', *Gaumont British News*, 30 June 1940; 'Cassino Close Up', *Pathé Gazette*, 6 Apr. 1944.

[62] *Maximum Effort* (Michael Hankinson, 1944).

[63] See Kenneth Grundy, *Soldiers Without Politics: Blacks in the South African Armed Forces* (Berkeley: University of California Press, 1983), 63–89.

[64] Quoted ibid. 66.

out parade of black African physical training instructors being inspected by the Director of the Non-European Army Services. A newsreel on white South African troops manning the front line included a shot described on the shot list as 'a huge Buck Nigger stopping a car and making the driver sign the book'.[65]

Violent British repression of Indian nationalism and South African racial policies potentially disrupted the idea of a liberal, tolerant empire that was neither racist nor oppressive. Nazi propaganda drew on the history of empire in South Africa to portray British imperialism as brutal, not temperate. *Ohm Kruger*—a Nazi propaganda film made in 1941—associated concentration camps with British imperial history rather than Nazi contemporary practice.[66] Depicting the British–Boer War of 1899–1902 in South Africa, the film focused on British concentration camps where Boer women and children were incarcerated, and on the story of Kruger's daughter-in-law, who is raped by a British soldier. His son, when visiting her in the concentration camp, is captured and hanged by the British.

This propaganda was countered in the British wartime film *The Life and Death of Colonel Blimp* (1943) through its central character, General Clive Wynne-Candy (Roger Livesey), who travels to Germany to refute German propaganda about British atrocities in South Africa.[67] Both the German charges against the British and Candy's response are left vague and, unlike *Ohm Kruger*, the film does not deal with the issue of British concentration camps, where 28,000 white Afrikaners and 14,000 black Africans had died by the end of the British–Boer war, nor with the controversy they provoked in Britain. But, less directly, the film reverses German propaganda in developing the story of Candy's long military career up to the Second World War, attributing atrocities to German militarism, in contrast to Candy's chivalric ideals.

Candy's chivalry is used to sanitize the history of empire but, as the title of the film makes clear, he is also the 'Blimp' of David Low's cartoons— comically reactionary and bigoted as well as red-faced. Low made him into a staunch imperialist, and in *The Life and Death of Colonel Blimp* his pre-1939 military career involves service not only in South Africa, but also India and Canada. The film offers a much more ambivalent version of Blimp than Low's cartoons, both mocking and celebrating what Candy represents. But it makes clear how out of touch he is with a modern world in which his military codes of honour no longer have a place. Blimp's values are consigned to the past.

---

[65] 'South Africa's Total Effort', *War Pictorial News*, 22 Dec. 1941; 'South Africa', *War Pictorial News*, 30 Mar. 1942; 'South African Troops Man Front Line', *British Movietone News*, 28 Nov. 1940.
[66] *Ohm Kruger* (Hans Steinhoff, Germany 1941).
[67] *The Life and Death of Colonel Blimp* (Michael Powell and Emeric Pressburger, 1943).

The 'people's empire' also consigned Blimp's values to the past. This was an empire of 'partnership', peace, and freedom where all peoples marched together. A racial hierarchy was less apparent in imagery of South Africa, where black South Africans were more or less invisible, than in the focus on a racial community of Britons—white 'sons of empire' who were always more prominent in imagery than those from Asian, African, or Caribbean colonies. As imperial manhood was shown circulating around various theatres of war, white 'sons of empire' moved into the metropolis, and there were numerous stories showing white Canadians, Australians, and New Zealanders, like the trio of soldiers in *From the Four Corners*, receiving a warm welcome in Britain. Emphasis on the ethnic heterogeneity of empire contrasted strongly with a white metropolis. Indians and Africans served loyally and courageously in an 'elsewhere' defined by empire and the imperial war effort—on the fighting front, thousands of miles away.

Home Fronts

In his *English Journey*, published between the wars, J. B. Priestley, reflecting on patriotism, had regretted that he was not born early enough to be called a 'little Englander'. 'Little Englander' had been a term of abuse, as Priestley noted, and used in the early twentieth century to characterize anti-imperialists, who argued that Britain should focus on domestic affairs and problems without the distractions and expense of imperial adventures. Priestley's own characterization of 'Big Englanders' had resonances of the imperialism of Colonel Blimp, as well as the upper-middle-class language of a public school elite: 'Red-faced, staring, loud-voiced fellows, wanting to go and boss everybody about all over the world, and being surprised and pained and saying, "Bad show!" if some blighters refused to fag for them.' But adopting a rather different use of the term 'little Englander' as one that he would willingly use for himself, Priestley wrote: 'That *little* sounds the right note of affection. It is the little England I love.'[68]

During the war, Priestley's radio broadcasts provided his audience with a version of a 'little England' that celebrated the common people. In contrast to the red-faced and loud-voiced 'Big Englander', Priestley spoke of a common people characterized by humour and quiet courage, by modest domestic pleasures and homely comforts, and particularly by kindliness. Identifying with those he addressed—'you and I, all of us ordinary people'—Priestley celebrated their virtues.[69] The highly popular series of

[68] J. B. Priestley, *English Journey* (London: William Heinemann, 1934), 416.
[69] J. B. Priestley, *Postscripts* (London: William Heinemann, 1940), 19.

radio messages that he broadcast on Sunday nights in 1940, entitled
Postscripts to the News, attracted an audience of some 30 per cent of the
adult population in 1940, rising to 40 per cent in 1941.[70] They offered his
audience a version of a fireside chat—the intimacy and homeliness of the
occasion reinforced by his slow delivery in a Yorkshire accent.[71] Despite the
absence of visual images, audiences were familiar with his appearance as a
middle-aged, pipe-smoking man. Indeed, there was a picture of him on the
cover of the first wartime edition of the *Radio Times*, compiled before war
was declared. The picture advertised his reading of his novel, *Let the People
Sing*, while in an inside feature he was interviewed about his work.[72]

As a quiet, pipe-smoking Englishman, Priestley personified the temperate hero. In case anybody should remain ignorant of his identity, Priestley
himself gave them constant reminders. The autobiographical details with
which he furnished his audience established a persona that merged work-
ing- and middle-class, Northern and Southern identities—his status as a
broadcaster and novelist resident in the Isle of Wight combining with his
Bradford origins, Yorkshire accent, and celebration of aspects of working-
class life. Within his *Postscripts*, he referred to himself as 'this middle-aged
civilian', and 'a civilian in the cheerful muddle of ordinary civilian life', and
to his 'after-lunch pipe'. Describing his transition from active service in
the First World War to 'a comfortable, pipe-and-slippers man', who had
decided that he would 'keep as close to cowardice as possible', he adopted a
self-description that removed him very far from the qualities of martial
masculinity. In September 1940, he told his audience: 'I speak as a comfortable pipe-and-slippers man, none of your heroes but a wary, and, you
might almost say, cowardly old soldier.'[73]

It is hard to imagine a sharper contrast to the version of nation personified by Priestley than that represented by Winston Churchill. Both were
middle-aged and ex-soldiers—Churchill served on the North-West frontier
of India in the late nineteenth century, and Priestley served in the First
World War. But Churchill was very far from seeing or presenting himself as
a man who enjoyed the comforts of middle age, still less as a 'cowardly old
soldier'. In contrast to Priestley's pipe, Churchill's major symbol was the
large cigar, suggestive of the wealth and privilege of his aristocratic origins.
His accent confirmed this, and was very far removed socially, as well as

[70] Nicholas, *Echo of War*, 244.

[71] BBC audience research found that reactions to the Yorkshire accent of Wilfred Pickles, who
was appointed as a radio newsreader during the war, were divided between 'those who welcome the
more intimate, homely atmosphere which it is thought a "regional" voice induces, and those who
prefer newsreading to be de-personalised as much as possible'. A Listener Research Report, Wilfred
Pickles as Newsreader and Regional News Readers in General, 1941, BBC WAC R9/9/5.

[72] *Radio Times*, 3–9 Sept. 1939.

[73] Priestley, *Postscripts*, 40, 61, 51, 66, 70.

geographically, from the Pennines and the North of England. Priestley spoke of the home front, and the need for a new order, and his vision of what the war was being fought for called for change to create greater social and economic equality. Churchill told of the need for resolve and sacrifice to defend and preserve existing values. He rarely spoke of the home front, and the term 'little' scarcely featured in his vocabulary. His wartime speeches were not about a common people representing kindliness, tolerance, and decency, but a great nation and empire engaged in epic struggle. Personifying the martial masculinity associated with empire, Churchill called the nation to heroic deeds associated with imperial identity.

When Churchill spoke at a Lord Mayor's luncheon in London in November 1942 he said: 'I have not become the King's First Minister in order to preside over the liquidation of the British Empire.'[74] The contrasting versions of nation personified by Priestley and Churchill were Priestley's 'little England' and the temperate hero of the home front, against Churchill's 'greater Britain' signified by martial masculinity and imperial identity on the front line. But these were versions of nation that were increasingly brought together. It was Churchill himself who noted that 'The front lines run through the factories. The workmen are soldiers with different weapons, but the same courage.'[75] Although 'little Englander' was a term that had originally been coined for anti-imperialists, Priestley's version, with its emphasis on the common people, was not incompatible with a 'people's empire'. The commentary of *Britain at Bay* (1940), written and spoken by Priestley, celebrated 'these people of ours, as easy-going and good-natured as any folk in the world' against the menace of the German paratroops and the tyranny of Hitler. But it also emphasized British willingness to fight in defence of democratic values, joined by 'men from the ends of the earth, from our Great Dominions in Australia, New Zealand and Canada', and ended with a close-up of Churchill, as Priestley spoke his words.[76] Priestley, unlike Churchill, rarely mentioned empire. But he was capable of seeing the virtues of Englishness radiating out to the wider identities of Britain and empire, envisaging 'the kindness of England, of Britain, of the wide Empire forever reaching out towards new expressions of Freedom'.[77]

Despite overlapping ideas of the home front and the front line, 'people's war' imagery found its earliest and most extensive development in relation to the home front in Britain. In contrast to the fervent patriotism invoked during the First World War, these images focused on an ability to keep going with the everyday round as a strong symbol of the people's courage. *The First*

[74] *The Times*, 11 Nov. 1942.
[75] Quoted in Angus Calder, *The People's War: Britain 1939–1945* (London: Panther: 1971), 20.
[76] *Britain at Bay* (Ministry of Information, 1940).
[77] Priestley, *Postscripts*, 18.

Days shows a sober and responsible people, responding to the war not with flag-waving, much less with panic, but with quiet order. This is an idea that resonates throughout the film, from the sequence where the announcement of war is received in grave silence, through a sequence on the first air-raid warning of the war, where images of orderly queues for air-raid shelters are accompanied by silence on the sound track, to shots of orderly preparations for war in the movement of evacuees, pets, and paintings from the National Gallery, as well as soldiers, out of London. *The Front Line* (1940), showing Dover within sight of German-occupied France, plays with the notion of 'the front' in Dover as a familiar scene of English beaches, against a different 'front line' where Dover has become an 'outpost' and a 'frontier town'. Its imagery produces the idea of quiet order and courage particularly through a focus on the idea that 'the little things of life still go on'—as the commentary records against shots of a woman feeding seagulls, people roller-skating, and women attired in a combination of bathing suits and tin hats. The film gives the last word to a woman. Coded as an ordinary housewife—wearing an apron, her hand in her apron pocket—she stands at her front door, rejecting any suggestion of leaving Dover, and then adds, 'but still, you're wasting my time, I've got my dinner to cook'.[78]

The celebration of a common people characterized by quiet courage was embodied not only in filmic imagery but also in genre. Between the wars, critics had identified the documentary movement as a distinctively national contribution to cinema.[79] It was a tradition extended during the war not only through the continued work of documentarists, but also through an increasing blurring of the boundaries, as war developed, between documentaries and feature films. Narrative-documentary techniques were adopted in many films on the war, and their strong associations with realism made them particularly suited to the idea of a sober and responsible nation, offering unsensational narratives characterized by a sense of stoicism and emotional restraint.

Feature films like *San Demetrio London* (1943) provided images that were very similar to the pre-war documentary *North Sea* (1938) and the early wartime documentary *Men of the Lightship* (1940)—all three films offering narratives conveyed in a documentary realist style.[80] In each case, the narrative concerns ships getting into difficulties—a trawler damaged in a storm and losing radio contact (*North Sea*), a lightship bombed by Nazi aeroplanes (*Men of the Lightship*), and an oil tanker shelled by a German

---

[78] *The Front Line* (Harry Watt, 1940).

[79] See Andrew Higson, *Waving the Flag: Constructing a National Cinema in Britain* (Oxford: Clarendon Press, 1995), 176–220.

[80] *North Sea* (Harry Watt, 1938); *Men of the Lightship* (David Macdonald, 1940); *San Demetrio London* (Charles Frend, 1943).

battleship (*San Demetrio London*). The focus is on an exclusively male group, celebrating male community and camaraderie. Working-class masculinity is shown as tough, strong, resourceful, but also restrained and stoical, with an emphasis on the self-composure of the men, as they remain calm within the chaos. The fact that wartime feature films depicting war were made in black and white, like documentaries, reinforced these connections with sober realism, as well as reflecting wartime austerity. As war developed, the documentary realist style earned increasing praise from critics as distinctively British. The frequent contrasts that they made between the idea of a national cinema and Hollywood reinforced the idea of national responsibility, restraint, and sobriety against Hollywood as escapist, spectacular, glamorous, sensational, and over-emotional.

While films depicting the fighting front often foregrounded men, women were prominent on the home front. Even when shown at home, waiting for news of their men, strength and courage were attributed to women. *In Which We Serve* (1942), while focusing on a homosocial world of naval service, also gives detailed attention to the courage and deaths of women in the Blitz.[81] Such images showed the transformation of home from a domestic sanctuary to a place of danger and death, eroding the idea of warfare as a masculine sphere. This erosion was even more evident in films such as *Millions Like Us* (1943), *The Gentle Sex* (1943), and *A Canterbury Tale* (1944), where women were shown abandoning domesticity to serve in aircraft factories, the services, and the land army.[82] In contrast to the traditional role of women in guarding their home, these films celebrated women who were actively involved in the war effort and, like *Two Thousand Women*, featured femisocial communities that matched the traditional homosocial images of war service.

Within the emphasis of empire imagery on martial masculinity, imperial home fronts were never widely represented, but the role of women in a racial community of Britons received some attention. Stories showed 'Canada's girl-power'—on the land, and in factories and shipyards. Australian women 'served the guns', cutting up cordite and filling mines and shells with liquid TNT, and took over from men on lifeguard duty on Australian beaches.[83] *War Came to Kenya* (1942) showed white women taking over the management of farms and the control of African labour, as well as working as nurses.

---

[81] *In Which We Serve* (Noel Coward and David Lean, 1942).

[82] *Millions Like Us* (Frank Launder and Sidney Gilliat, 1943); *The Gentle Sex* (Leslie Howard and Maurice Elvey, 1943); *A Canterbury Tale* (Michael Powell and Emeric Pressburger, 1944). For a discussion of the image of the mobile woman in wartime British cinema see Antonia Lant, *Blackout: Reinventing Women for Wartime British Cinema* (Princeton NJ: Princeton University Press, 1991).

[83] 'Canada's Girl War Workers', *British Paramount News*, 4 Sept. 1941; 'Canadian Women Shipyard Workers', *Gaumont British News*, 4 Feb. 1943; 'Women Who Serve the Guns', *War Pictorial News*, 20 Dec. 1943; 'Girl Lifeguards', *British Movietone News*, 27 Apr. 1944.

Arms From India (1941) showed a predominantly male home front where Indians equipped the forces of the empire with munitions and clothing—making steel, ammunition, rifles, cotton, woollens—emphasizing the vast production from India as the 'eighth industrial country of the world'.[84] Planning for a 1943 Empire Day BBC radio programme designed to show the empire's war effort also solicited only male speakers. Requests to New Zealand and Uganda asked for a New Zealand airman and a non-commissioned officer from the King's African Rifles, who would speak about their military experiences and—in the case of the African soldier—express 'pride in the King's African Rifles and in his service under the Crown'. But requests to Jamaica and Accra asked for a 'coloured West Indian Government servant' and a 'newly appointed African official'. The careful orchestration of their contributions was designed to show a different home front in the colonies—not one of munitions factories and shipyards, but the 'attachment of colonies to the British connection and confidence in the progressive realisation of aspirations within the framework of the British Empire'.[85]

West Indies Calling (1943) was one of the few films made during the war that united ideas of the 'people's war' and the 'people's empire' in imagery of the British home front.[86] However limited its audience in Britain, and rare the images that it portrayed, it is an important film for any account of representations of the British home front, since it disrupted the boundaries between empire and metropolis where 'home' was shown as white. Sponsored by the Ministry of Information, it was made in two versions—one for a West Indies audience entitled *Hello! West Indies*, and a shorter version with an added introduction for a British audience.[87] Both were set in a BBC studio in London and based on one of the major radio broadcasts on the BBC empire service—*Calling the West Indies*. This programme was generally organized as a party, sometimes held in London, sometimes in Glasgow and Edinburgh, with music and guests who sent messages to relatives and friends in the Caribbean.[88] In reversing the title of the radio programme, the British version of the film also reversed the direction of the messages. A narrative voice, absent from the West Indies version, was inserted at the outset to explain that 'Each week some of them broadcast messages home . . . But this evening, they are broadcasting to Britain.'

West Indies Calling takes care to show West Indian identity as multiracial with shots of white-Caribbeans, Indo-Caribbeans, and African-Caribbeans. But the film is dominated by the voices and images of black West Indians

[84] *Arms from India* (Indian Film Unit, 1941).
[85] J. Grenfell Williams to Noel Sabine, 21 Apr. 1943, PRO CO 875 19/17.
[86] *West Indies Calling* (John Page, 1943).
[87] PRO INF 6/1328.
[88] For the radio programme see BBC WAC SC 19/28; R 46/92.

who tell a narrative of both a 'people's war' and a 'people's empire' and insert themselves into this narrative. The compère, as on *Calling the West Indies*, is Una Marson, who, first arriving in Britain in 1932, had been involved in the League of Coloured Peoples, and was employed on the radio series from 1941.[89] She introduces Learie Constantine—a well-known figure to British audiences as a Trinidadian cricketer who had played in the Lancashire League before the war—Flying Officer Ulric Cross, a bomber navigator, and Carlton Fairweather. They provide the narrative voices over shots of Caribbean men employed in munitions factories in Britain, some of the 10,000 volunteers for the armed services from the Caribbean, and foresters in Scotland, recruited mainly from British Honduras. All three speakers, along with Una Marson, are positioned behind a microphone labelled 'BBC', with all the weight of authority and truth-telling that label involved, especially in wartime.

Narratives and shots of a 'people's empire' emphasize the friendships developed between people from different parts of the Commonwealth—Britons, Canadians, Caribbeans, New Zealanders—and stress the hope this offers of a 'new world that we all want to see', including a better life in the West Indies. Many images are familiar from other wartime films showing the home front and the armed services and there are numerous shots of women's active involvement in the war as nurses and soldiers. Lance Corporal Williams, introduced as a woman from British Guiana in the Royal Army Ordnance Corps, is shown retreading tyres in an army work-shop. In a context where white women's active involvement in war, especially on home fronts—in Australia, Canada, and New Zealand, as well as Britain—received attention, *West Indies Calling* provides a very rare example of imagery that includes black women's active involvement in war. It provides an equally rare example of a 'people's war' and a 'people's empire' that foregrounds black people on active service in Britain.

In telling its story of a 'people's empire' *West Indies Calling* shows Britain as a decent and tolerant nation. In inserting Caribbean people into dominant narratives, as contributors to the war effort in Britain, it studiously avoids any mention of racism. The widespread practice of colour bars throughout much of the British empire attracted virtually no public attention in Britain throughout the war.

Constantine publicized the practice of a colour bar in Britain in 1944 when he sued a London hotel that had refused him rooms that he had booked in advance in 1943. Questions on the case were raised in the House of Commons.[90] In 1943, he talked of his experience of racism in Britain in

---

[89] For Una Marson, see Jarrett-Macauley, *The Life of Una Marson*.
[90] *The Times*, 23 Sept. 1943.

a broadcast to a British audience on BBC radio. His talk was originally intended as a *Postscript*, but was rejected for this popular slot on the grounds that it was 'too controversial'. The Director of radio talks suggested that 'With a British audience I should have thought far more sympathy would be obtained if the speaker identified himself with his audience by describing . . . some of the joy of first class cricket'. However, he saw 'no reason why this script should not be accepted for a weekday if Constantine's own Ministry and the Colonial Office will pass it', and the programme went out in September 1943 on the Home Service. Rejecting the script for a Sunday *Postscript*, the Director of radio talks minuted: 'You will remember that the object of that series is to stress unity rather than diversity.'[91]

Despite its disruption of the racial boundaries between metropolis and empire and its narrative of Caribbeans on the British home front as well as on the fighting front, *West Indies Calling* emphasized unity as much as diversity. The need to boost morale and to show a united community of nation and empire offered some scope for self-representation by black Caribbeans, who speak on their own behalf, and take on the narrative voice and the role of educating their audience. This was a very different role from the one black people were generally allotted in documentaries made both before and after the war. Within the tradition of social exploration on which many documentaries drew, camera and narrative voice would offer to take the audience on a journey into unknown territory, and to unveil for them sights with which they were unfamiliar, defining their subject as a social problem. Even so, *West Indies Calling* obscured the issues that Constantine publicized elsewhere to present a wholly positive portrait of West Indians in Britain and of British–Caribbean relations. People of many backgrounds in a diverse empire were shown pulling together across differences of race and ethnicity, united in a common effort.

In 1942, a Foreign Office official, after discussion with other government departments, offered the conventional view of black people as a social problem that *West Indies Calling* challenged. He noted that 'the recruitment to the United Kingdom of coloured British subjects, whose remaining in the United Kingdom after the war might create a social problem, was not considered desirable'.[92] In the same year, the Cabinet urged that America should 'reduce as far as possible the number of coloured troops . . . sent to this country', and the Foreign Secretary, Anthony Eden, explained to the American Ambassador that the British climate was 'badly suited to negroes'.[93]

---

[91] Memorandum from the Director of Talks, G. R. Barnes, 8 July 1943, BBC WAC, Learie Constantine, Talks, File 1, 1939–62.

[92] Quoted in David Reynolds, *Rich Relations: The American Occupation of Britain 1942–1945* (London: HarperCollins, 1996), 217.

[93] Ibid.

Despite 10,000 volunteers for the armed services and the 2,000 men employed in munitions factories and as foresters from the Caribbean, the British government, under pressure from America, admitted far more black GIs than black Britons—130,000 by D-Day.[94] Schemes that recruited black and Asian Britons were regarded as a temporary expedient. Indian munitions workers were featured in newsreels and newspapers learning the skills of airplane rigging and tool making in Britain, where they were visited by the King and Queen.[95] But reporting emphasized the Indian, not the British home front, and the benefits of this scheme to India, where, once training was completed, the trainees would return to instruct workers, eventually enabling India to produce aircraft in large numbers. Generally black and Asian Britons continued to be portrayed in an 'elsewhere' defined by empire and the imperial war effort, maintaining racial boundaries between empire and metropolis.

America and Empire

After the fall of France in July 1940, *Punch* published a cartoon showing two soldiers looking out to sea. One says, 'So our poor old empire is alone in the world', and the other replies: 'Aye, we are—the whole five hundred million of us.'[96] In 1940, the imperial version of identity that stressed the automatic loyalty of a vast empire jostled with an island story of Britain at bay—the only nation still at war with Germany and undefeated. In 1943, the *Daily Express* reflected on this history: 'We frequently say that in the Battle of Britain we stood alone . . . But we were never just these little islands entirely by themselves. Canadian troops were among us. Australian troops were here. From all parts of the Empire aid flowed to us in men and goods.'[97]

Before the entry of the Soviet Union and the USA into the war in 1941, even the 'five hundred million' people of the empire did not promise victory. A need to convert the USA from its policy of neutrality and appeal to American audiences haunted many images of nation and empire produced in Britain.[98] In the context of American anti-imperialism, British media that addressed primarily American audiences showed 'these little

---

[94] See Ben Bousquet and Colin Douglas, *West Indian Women at War: British Racism in World War II* (London: Lawrence and Wishart, 1991); Marika Sherwood, *Many Struggles: West Indian Workers and Service Personnel in Britain, 1939–45* (London: Karia Press, 1985).

[95] 'Indians Train Here to Make Munitions', *British Paramount News*, 29 May 1941; 'Indians to Learn Munitions Making', *British Movietone News*, 29 May 1941; 'Royal Visit to Indian Trainees', *British Movietone News*, 2 Oct. 1941.

[96] *Punch*, 17 July 1940.

[97] *Daily Express*, 25 May 1943.

[98] For a full account of this period see Nicholas Cull, *Selling War: The British Propaganda Campaign Against American 'Neutrality' in World War II* (Oxford: Oxford University Press, 1995).

islands entirely by themselves'—the Englishness of the home front and the 'people's war'. The need to address American audiences, continuing after American entry into the war, shaped many British representations of nation and empire.

The unequal traffic in visual imagery between America and Britain, and dominance of Hollywood, meant that both British and American audiences consumed American ideas of Britishness throughout the war. The Hollywood film *Mrs Miniver* (1942), which showed an embattled but brave British home front, was the top box-office earner in Britain in 1942. It enjoyed considerable success in America, where one viewer commented: 'I am sure everyone leaves that picture with the highest regard for the British people working to win.'[99] But there were a range of British moves to redress these inequalities, targeting America with messages about the British war effort.

In the early stages of the war, with America still neutral, British propaganda addressed to Americans focused on the projection of a 'people's war'. J. B. Priestley conveyed this vision of the war not only to a British audience in his *Postscripts*, but also to an American audience in regular broadcasts on the BBC North American Service. These broadcasts reached a limited number of Americans on short-wave radio, but a film specially made for an American audience—*London Can Take It!* (1940)—reached an estimated 60 million American viewers. Like *Christmas Under Fire* (1941), it was introduced by Quentin Reynolds, the London correspondent of the American magazine *Collier's Weekly*, who announced the novelty of these documentaries as 'film dispatches' that he was sending to America and, like Priestley in his broadcasts, emphasized that he was no propagandist, but a 'neutral reporter'.[100] In providing a narrative voice that was American, Reynolds ensured that the films would remain immune from American objections to the manner in which the English spoke English. British narrators of documentaries were often identified in America as unsuitable for an American audience—with objections ranging from a style and intonation that were 'prosy', 'verbose', or 'semi-poetical', to the complete incomprehensibility of regional accents.[101]

The narrative voice of Reynolds also made his message appear American, disguising the origins of these documentaries as films from the British

[99] Quoted in 'An Examination of the Many Reasons for the Unfriendly Feelings of a Large Number of Americans Towards Great Britain', *Postal and Telegraph Censorship Report on The United States of America*, 11 Sept. 1942. PRO CO875/18/11.

[100] *Britain Can Take It!* (Harry Watt and Humphrey Jennings, 1940); *Christmas Under Fire* (Harry Watt, 1941).

[101] Reports from British Information Services, New York, 21 Mar. 1944 and 18 Sept. 1944, PRO INF 1/599; Report from Film Officer about distributing films in the US, 22 Oct. 1941, PRO INF 1/598.

Ministry of Information with British directors. The message was one of unstinting praise and admiration for the English people, focusing on an Englishness of stoicism and quiet order and courage during the devastation of the Blitz. In *London Can Take It!* Reynolds tells the story of a night of the Blitz, and the heroes of the night who are 'members of the greatest civilian army ever to be assembled'. He assures his audience that 'there is no panic, no fear, no despair in London town. There is nothing but determination, confidence and high courage among the people of Churchill's island.' In *Christmas Under Fire*—described by its director, Harry Watt, as 'an obvious tear-jerker'—England is shown besieged but undaunted and courageous, celebrating Christmas underground.[102] Reynolds's voice constantly invokes the idea of England: 'England is fighting for her life'; 'For the first time in history no bells ring in England'; There is no reason for America to feel sorry for England this Christmas—England does not feel sorry for herself; 'Today England stands unbeaten, unconquered, unafraid'. This Anglocentric commentary survived for the British distribution of the film, but *London Can Take It!* was retitled *Britain Can Take It!*, and Reynolds added extra commentary to point out that the film's portrayal of the Blitz in London was representative of what was happening in every other British city and town.[103]

One film aimed at an American audience told a narrative of both a 'people's war' and a 'people's empire'. *49th Parallel* (1941)—retitled *The Invaders* for its American release—was the only full-length feature film financed by the Ministry of Information during the war. Its story of a Nazi U-boat sunk by the Royal Canadian Air Force on the coast of Canada, and the journey made by its Nazi survivors through Canada in their attempt to get to neutral America, showed that America was not immune to the Nazi threat. To reinforce this point, it opened with an image of the line that separated America from Canada—the forty-ninth parallel of the British title. The film was very popular in Britain—the highest box-office earner in 1941—but its message to America was largely irrelevant by the time it opened there in March 1942, three months after American entry into the war.[104]

49th Parallel self-consciously portrays Canada as part of an empire that is ethnically diverse. As they attempt their escape to neutral America, the Nazi group encounter French-Canadians, English-Canadians, German-Canadians, Inuit, and First Nations. The portrayal of a multiracial

---

[102] Quoted in James Chapman, *The British At War: Cinema, State and Propaganda 1939–1945* (London: I. B. Tauris, 1998), 100.

[103] Ministry of Information, 14 Oct. 1940, PRO INF 6/328.

[104] *The 49th Parallel* (Michael Powell, 1941); Kevin MacDonald, *Emeric Pressburger: The Life and Death of a Screenwriter* (London: Faber, 1994), 166–81.

community is one in which indigenous people remain unindividuated—their function to establish that white Canadians are not racist, and to demonstrate common resistance to Nazi Germany across ethnic difference. Nazi racism and brutality against the only Inuit character who is named—Nick (Ley On)—is contrasted with his treatment by white Canadians, exemplified by Johnnie—a French-Canadian trapper (Laurence Olivier). Nick's brutal treatment at the hands of the Nazi group prompts set-piece dialogue in which white Canadians affirm the humanity of Inuit against Nazi pronouncements that they are racially as low as Negroes—semi-apes. Once Nick has demonstrated the virtues of white Canadians against the Nazis he makes no further appearance in the film.

The Nazi encounter with Philip Armstrong-Scott (Leslie Howard)—an English-Canadian—produces a further contrast between Canadians and Nazis. Armstrong-Scott is a temperate hero—one that the Nazis pronounce 'soft and degenerate through and through'. An aesthete who collects books and paintings, he is engaged in writing about the customs and culture of the Blackfoot tribe. His writings are among the books that the Nazis burn. Initially ignorant of their identity, Armstrong-Scott offers the Nazis hospitality and, for his pains, not only has his books and paintings burned, but is ignominiously bound and gagged.

A British review of *49th Parallel* worried that this representation of an English dilettante would confirm the idea of 'the Englishman as soft and decadent' which, it observed, had been developing over the past decade, especially in the USA. But it suggested that such a representation might nevertheless be good propaganda, since Armstrong-Scott was revealed as unexpectedly tough.[105] As a temperate hero Armstrong-Scott can nevertheless fight when roused, and takes his revenge against his Nazi persecutors by knocking one out with his fists. The final Canadian encountered by the last Nazi survivor produces a similar contrast between a temperate hero and hyper-masculine Nazis. Andy Brock (Raymond Massey) is a soldier, absent without leave, en route by train to neutral America. Like Howard he does not at first recognize the identity of the last surviving Nazi and offers hospitality—in his case cigarettes and drink. In return, he is held up at gunpoint. Like Armstrong-Scott, he has his revenge, showing, according to one reviewer, that 'a member of the decadent British empire can thrash a Nazi superman'.

The self-conscious portrait of ethnic heterogeneity in Canada contrasted strongly with representations of America. Most British films showed British–American relations as a friendship between white nations. Americans were not seen as part of a racial community of Britons, but they were

---

[105] *Documentary Newsletter*, Nov. 1941.

shown on terms that corresponded closely to this version of a 'people's empire' stressing common culture, heritage, and ancestry. *The Foreman Went to France* (1942) provides a classic image of 'togetherness' featuring a Welsh factory foreman (Clifford Evans) and two British soldiers (Gordon Jackson and Tommy Trinder)—one Scottish and one English/Cockney, but both privates.[106] The film shows them united in a common journey and mission to outwit Nazis, and incorporates a white American woman (Constance Cummings) into this community. *San Demetrio London* (1943) incorporates an American man (Robert Beatty) into the group of merchant seamen on the oil tanker shelled by German guns.[107] In case there should be any doubt about his nationality, he is called 'Yank' by his fellow seamen throughout the film. Set in 1940, before American entry into the war, the film shows Yank joining the ship in order to get to Britain to join the RAF. Initially an outsider, and dismissive of the British, Yank is converted to increasing respect for their qualities. In their turn the British increasingly incorporate him into the community of their 'people's war', and the film ends with the unanimous decision of the crew to present him with the ship's red ensign, that flew throughout the ship's misfortunes.

Wartime traffics in imagery between America and Britain meant that American audiences saw a British 'people's war' mainly through British productions. Although the Office of War Information encouraged Hollywood to show 'the real people of England, the workers and shop-keepers and miners', there was little enthusiasm in Hollywood for a move away from the version of Britishness that was popular with American audiences.[108] Pre-war Hollywood films set in Britain favoured a tourist version of the country, depicting castles and thatched cottages. They showed a semi-feudal social structure where the aristocracy and their wealth were prominent. In the Hollywood film *Ruggles of Red Gap* (1935), American fascination with butlers reached a high point, showing Ruggles (Charles Laughton), a British butler won by an American in a poker game, but wooed away from deference to become an ardent fan of all things American.[109] Hollywood films developed an opposition between American modernity and British tradition, exemplified by figures like Ruggles. American men were vigorous and dynamic while British men, mired in tradition, like Ruggles at the outset of the film, were potentially staid and dull.

This was an opposition which was particularly apparent when Britain was shown from the perspective of a white American, who, in the *A Yank*

---

[106] *The Foreman Went to France* (Charles Freud, 1941).
[107] *San Demetrio London* (Charles Freud, 1943).
[108] Quoted in Glancy, *When Hollywood Loved Britain*, 201.
[109] *Ruggles of Red Gap* (Leo McCarey, US 1935). I am grateful to Susan Sydney-Smith for information on this film.

at ... series, was always a youthful male. *A Yank at* ... films, beginning with
the highly popular *A Yank at Oxford* (1938), rehearsed a litany of differences
between white Americans and white Britons, leading to conflicts at the
outset that were increasingly resolved in the development of close friendship
marked by mutual admiration and respect. The series was developed during
the Second World War when *A Yank in the RAF* (1941) highlighted a
Britain of public-school educated officers and gentlemen while *A Yank at
Eton* (1942) focused on their junior counterparts.[110] The Office of War
Information was highly critical of *A Yank at Eton* for its focus on the upper
classes, and a public-school setting that, they suggested, was not 'the most
ideal means of proving British democracy'.[111]

The Office of War Information was more successful in discouraging the
Hollywood empire genre. Before America entered the war, Hollywood
continued to celebrate the British empire in imagery that had proved
popular before the war, producing films like *The Sun Never Sets* (1939)
and *Sundown* (1941).[112] But it did adapt its message, transposing stories
where British heroism was pitted against villainous slave-traders or native
rulers, intent on fomenting rebellion against British rule, into stories where
British heroism defeated Fascist villains with the same intentions. Once
America came into the war, anti-imperialism dictated that it should no
longer show its ally as an imperial power. Plans to reissue *Gunga Din*
(1939), and to produce an adaptation of Rudyard Kipling's novel *Kim*—
both films set in India—were shelved.[113] *Kim* was not made until after
Indian independence.[114]

One film about Britain produced in America, directed by Frank Capra
and designed for a specifically American audience, reversed these trends.
Know Your Ally: Britain (1944) was intended for screenings to GIs before
they set out for Britain. It goes to considerable lengths to dispel Hollywood
images of Britain, showing neither butlers nor aristocrats. Reviewing the
tourist image of Britain, to which Hollywood was generally devoted, it
introduces its audience to a different nation, juxtaposing castles and country lanes against heavy industry in Leeds, Manchester, Sheffield, and
Glasgow. Accusations of oppressive imperialism, and of Britain fighting
only to save its empire, are attributed to Nazi propaganda, and not American anti-imperialism. They are directly countered in the film, which, like
British propaganda, shows a 'people's empire'. The film uses a still of the
trio of soldiers in *From the Four Corners* and describes them as exemplars of

---

[110] *A Yank in the RAF* (Henry King, US 1941); *A Yank at Eton* (Norman Taurog, US 1942).

[111] See Glancy, *When Hollywood Loved Britain*, 199–200.

[112] *The Sun Never Sets* (Rowland Lee, US 1939); *Sundown* (Henry Hathaway, US 1941).

[113] Glancy, *When Hollywood Loved Britain*, 189–93.

[114] *Kim* (Victor Saville, US 1950).

the fighting men of Australia, Canada, and New Zealand. Its commentary echoes the history lesson that Leslie Howard had delivered in *From the Four Corners*, informing its GI audience of the freedom and democracy of the self-governing Dominions. There is no mention of the 'Quit India' movement and its violent repression by the British. Instead, the commentator notes that Britain has promised the same self-government to India.

Welcome to Britain (1943), the British counterpart of *Know Your Ally Britain*, directed by Anthony Asquith, makes an interesting contrast to the American film. Intended for screenings to GIs on arrival, it never went on general release. The opening credits announced it as 'a film presented by the War Office to US troops arriving in the UK', a message reinforced by the British General Sir Ronald Adam, featured at the outset, who calls the film 'a gift from us (the British army) to you (GIs in Britain)'. The film takes no risks with American objections to the manner in which the English speak English, deploying an American narrator—Burgess Meredith— whose voice dominates the film. But it also takes no risks with American objections to the British empire. Unlike *Know Your Ally: Britain*, where American anti-imperialism is directly confronted and refuted, *Welcome to Britain* portrays a 'people's war' and makes no mention of imperial identity.

The GI audience is a constant presence in *Welcome to Britain* as Meredith—who collaborated on the script and dialogue—turns to camera to address them confidentially, offering friendly tips on 'over here' and the pitfalls they are likely to encounter.[115] The staple theme of differences between Americans and British in the *A Yank at...* series is Meredith's major preoccupation. British coffee is awful, their beer is warm, they have a fetish about tea. They are likely to be offended by Americans who throw their money or their weight around. Meredith's voice dominates the film dispensing this advice. The American audience is given little opportunity to find British speech verbose or incomprehensible, for the British characters that Burgess meets on his travels say little. 'Some of these people are a little more reserved than some of us,' Meredith explains; 'just give them time, they'll come your way.' Sequences in which the British display temperate heroism include classic scenes of the people's war—a pub where they play 'quiet games', streets of houses reduced to rubble in the Blitz, a bomb-damaged church, a British home with damaged windows where Meredith explains about rationing. This is a Britain of the home front, including imagery of farms, coalmines, and factories.

Welcome to Britain presents a sequence where a British woman leans out of a railway carriage to shake the hands of her American travelling companions: Meredith and a black soldier, Corporal Collier. She reminds

[115] PRO INF 6/601.

Collier how odd it is that he should come from Birmingham too, and tells him that if he ever comes to 'my Birmingham', he must come and have a cup of tea with her. Although a black GI has just been shown, Meredith, in one of his many confidential asides to camera, addresses his audience as a white group to give them tips on prejudice: 'Now look men, you've heard that conversation, that's not unusual here, it's the sort of thing that happens quite a lot. Now let's be frank about it. There are coloured soldiers as well as white here, and there are less social restrictions in this country. An English woman asking a coloured boy to tea . . . Now look that might not happen at home. But the point is we're not at home. And the point is that if we bring a lot of prejudice here, what are we going to do about that?'

In this sequence, Meredith is rambling and incoherent in contrast to his usual slick delivery, and breaks off abruptly to invite an American General to speak about the rights that black Americans will have once the war is over. Censure of American racial policies was regarded as problematic in wartime Britain. The BBC felt that discussion of 'the Negro question in America' should be postponed until after the war, because of 'the overriding necessity of keeping relations sweet between Americans and British'.[116]

Even so, some British media used the racial segregation of the American armed forces to portray America as less egalitarian than Britain. The American colour bar was represented as alien to a Britain characterized by a 'heritage of tolerance and liberalism'.[117] A report in the *Sunday Pictorial* in 1943 condemned the advice given by a British vicar's wife on the treatment of black GIs stationed in Britain, which included instructions to women to move if seated next to them in a cinema, and on no account to invite coloured troops into their homes. It represented such advice as wholly untypical of British attitudes: 'Any coloured soldier who reads this may rest assured that there is no colour bar in this country and that he is as welcome as any other Allied soldier. He will find that the vast majority of people here have nothing but repugnance for the narrow-minded, uninformed prejudices expressed by the vicar's wife. There is—and will be no persecution of coloured people in Britain.'[118] This version of British–American relations that showed Britain as more egalitarian than America contrasted strongly with Hollywood productions with their emphasis on a semi-feudal Britain of aristocratic privilege. American audiences rarely consumed this contrast between a reactionary America and a liberal Britain.

[116] Memo from Controller of Home Service to Director of Talks, 21 June 1944, BBC WAC R51/92, Talks, Coloured People.

[117] *News Chronicle*, 8 May 1944.

[118] Quoted in Graham Smith, *When Jim Crow Met John Bull: Black American Soldiers in World War II Britain* (London: I. B. Tauris, 1987), 45.

Evidence of the practice of colour bars in Britain was sometimes attributed to white Americans. Identifying a change of British attitudes to black GIs in 1944, an article in the *News Chronicle* argued that it would be a mistake for Britons to defer to the reactionary attitudes of some white Americans, and so sell their heritage short.[119] In 1944, when Learie Constantine sued the hotel that had refused him a room and won the case, he raised the issue of a colour bar in Britain, but the issue of an American colour bar was also highlighted in reporting. According to the hotel manageress, Constantine had been refused the room because of the presence of white American soldiers in the hotel who would object to a black fellow-guest. A witness told the court that Constantine had 'stated the fact that he was a British subject, and that he saw no reason why Americans, who were aliens, should have any preference at the hotel over a British subject'.[120]

Constantine's claim that he should have preference over Americans as aliens was reversed in much wartime imagery. Close relationships between Britain and America were as widely represented as close relationships with the Dominions, and on the same terms—as white friendships characterized by common culture, ancestry, heritage, language.[121] Despite *West Indies Calling*, racially inclusive imagery did not generally extend to the portrayal of the British home front. Nor did it extend to the portrayal of South Africa, which was shown as a white man's country. The practice of colour bars throughout much of the British empire, notably South Africa, received little media attention, but Britain was shown as tolerant in contrast to the racism of others—including America as well as Nazi Germany. Since Britain was a white country, the issue of a colour bar did not arise, and could be represented as an alien practice introduced into Britain by the American armed forces, and black GIs. The idea of a geographic separation between metropolis and empire, white and black, underpinned the association of colour bars with America rather than Britain. Issues of racial difference belonged to empire, not metropolis, and so were largely irrelevant to metropolitan identity.

The 'people's war' and the 'people's empire' nevertheless connected ideas of Englishness and empire. The need to address diverse audiences in empire and metropolis and to counter American anti-imperialism prompted a considerable shift away from the conservative imagery of 'There'll Always Be An England' and its idea of automatic loyalty from empire. The impact of the fall of Singapore strengthened moves to portray a temperate empire

---

[119] *News Chronicle*, 8 May 1944.

[120] *The Times*, 20 June 1944.

[121] Hollywood and British films which make reference to common ancestry include *The Canterville Ghost* (Jules Dassin, 1944); *I Live in Grosvenor Square* (Herbert Wilcox, 1945); *A Matter of Life and Death* (Michael Powell and Emeric Pressburger, 1946).

through themes of welfare and partnership. The focus on the martial masculinity of a 'people's empire' gave far less attention to women, civilians, and the home front than imagery of a 'people's war', but showed the common people of Britain and the 'British world' united across vast distances in a common cause. Despite its limitations, the racial inclusiveness of empire imagery offered a message that echoed that of the 'people's war'. British imperialism bore no resemblance to Nazi imperialism and was characterized by tolerance and liberty, not conquest and aggression. Britain's decency was demonstrated not only by the kindliness and friendliness of its people, their attachment to democracy and their qualities of reasonableness and tolerance, but also by its empire.

Was the wartime 'people's empire' a narrative that engaged or enthused a British audience? Sian Nicholas, charting the very considerable efforts at the BBC to produce empire propaganda, argues that difficulties in persuading their audiences that the empire was relevant to them meant that such propaganda 'could do nothing in practice to strengthen—or in fact to slow the decline of—positive imperial feeling for the post-war world'.[122] British audiences were undoubtedly more engaged by the story of a 'people's war' than a 'people's empire', and many may have slumbered in their cinema seats during newsreel shots of 'sons of empire'. Even so, the BBC itself produced evidence that, while the 'people's empire' may not have inspired fervent enthusiasm, it commanded considerable assent. Planning a series of talks on the empire in 1943, it commissioned research which found that the majority of its audience thought that 'our colonial record is mixed, but the good exceeds the bad'. In response to questions about the meanings of the terms 'British Empire' and 'British Commonwealth of Nations', most people regarded them as geographically synonymous, but much preferred the term 'British Commonwealth of Nations' because of its more democratic implications and 'freedom from imperialistic associations'.[123] Despite an increasingly anti-imperialistic climate internationally, led by America, anti-colonialism in Britain, during and after the Second World War, was mainly confined to groups on the left who were sympathetic with the aims of colonial nationalism. Their campaigns had little popular resonance.[124]

Once the war was over, the story of a 'people's war' was eclipsed. J. B. Priestley had commanded the attention of 40 per cent of the radio audience in 1941, but it was Winston Churchill, and not Priestley, who became a cult figure in the 1950s. In contrast, the story of a 'people's empire' was extended, and enjoyed a brief moment of very considerable publicity in

---

[122] Nicholas, 'Brushing Up Your Empire', 226.

[123] See Audience Research Special Reports no. 7, Sound and General, 1943, BBC WAC, R9/9/7.

[124] For an account of these groups see Stephen Howe, *Anti-Colonialism in British Politics: The Left and the End of Empire 1939–1964* (Oxford: Oxford University Press, 1993).

Coronation year in 1953. But in the aftermath of war, the story of a 'people's empire' no longer made reference to the imperial war effort or the unity of diverse peoples fighting in a common cause. Post-war narratives of the Second World War took up imagery which, in wartime, had been characteristic of the imperial war effort: martial masculinity on the fighting front away from home. As these narratives moved from the quiet courage of a 'people's war' to the glory of a 'hero's victory', they no longer featured Indian or African troops as brave and loyal 'sons of empire', but celebrated the martial masculinity of British officers and leaders.

3

The Post-War People's Empire

At the Victory Parade in London in June 1946, marching columns took two hours to pass the dais where King George VI stood taking the salute. The display drew extensively on wartime representations of nation, empire, and British–American relations, beginning with contingents from eighteen Allied countries, headed by American troops. Next came the imperial troops that had so often been shown marching in wartime newsreels and documentary film. The parade exactly replicated the wartime poster that showed marching troops—'Together'—arranging troops into a racial hierarchy. A racial community of Britons—contingents from Canada, Australia, New Zealand, and South Africa—were followed by Indian troops. Behind them marched detachments from colonies, including those from Africa, from Mediterranean, Caribbean, and Pacific islands, and from territories in South-East Asia that had been occupied by Japan during the war. The Parade concluded with contingents that represented a 'people's war', including the women's services and civilian services.[1]

The late 1940s were a transitional moment in representations of war and empire. In its immediate aftermath, the outcome of the war was celebrated as a 'people's victory'. Newsreels of the Victory Parade praised the efforts of civilians as well as the armed forces, including miners, bus drivers, and land girls. *Pathé News* deplored the absence from the parade of 'women to represent the 13 million housewives of Britain', and paid its own tribute to their wartime work for their families—'their patience, their endurance, their courage'.[2] The theme of togetherness continued to be celebrated, as in *Passport to Pimlico* (1949), an Ealing film that showed the continuing need for a wartime sense of community in the context of post-war problems—notably continued rationing and shortages.[3] But the idea of a 'people's victory', surviving in the 1940s, was increasingly displaced in the early 1950s by imagery of a 'hero's victory'.

The correspondence between the 'people's empire' and the 'people's war' was strongly articulated in another Ealing feature film made in the immediate aftermath of war. *The Overlanders* (1946) offered an Australian

[1] W. David McIntyre, *British Decolonization 1946–1997* (Basingstoke: Macmillan, 1998), 1–2.
[2] 'Victory Parade', *Pathé News*, 10 June 1946.
[3] *Passport to Pimlico* (Henry Cornelius, 1949).

version of 'the people's war' and also celebrated a 'people's empire', showing an epic 1,500-mile journey by Australians, driving cattle across country during the Second World War.[4] Once the war was over, there was considerable development and extension of the idea of a 'people's empire' and, despite the racial hierarchy of imperial troops that marched in the Victory Parade and its traditional display of martial masculinity, much imagery of empire distanced itself from militarism and power to show a modernized imperial identity of egalitarianism. Indeed, the Victory Parade was one of the last displays of imperial martial masculinity on the streets of London. Representations of a 'people's empire' focused on themes of welfare and development, while in the media and elsewhere the empire was increasingly renamed 'Commonwealth'. The wartime slogan of 'partnership' was refined to 'equal partnership'. This was a 'people's empire' proclaimed in the *Sunday Times* in the run-up to Indian independence in 1947 as a 'Fourth British Empire of independent peoples freely associated'.[5]

By comparison with two other stories developed in the early 1950s—the story of a 'hero's victory' in the Second World War, and of a 'special relationship' with America—the story of a 'people's empire' began to look increasingly fragile. It was disrupted by its own contradictions and by the onset of colonial wars in Malaya and Kenya which showed one racial version of a 'people's empire' at war with another—a racial community of Britons represented by white settlers in Malaya and Kenya under siege from the violence of the colonized. Even so, it remained sufficiently secure to enjoy wide publicity and celebration in Coronation year in 1953.

Ania Loomba observes that 'One of the most striking contradictions about colonialism is that it both needs to "civilise" its "others", and to fix them into perpetual "otherness"'.[6] This contradiction threaded its way through post-war imagery of empire. The idea of 'equal partnership' was in tension with the racial hierarchy that was displayed at the Victory Parade and that constantly seeped into imagery of empire. 'Equal partnership' in an Indian context emphasized the willingness to grant independence as the culmination of long civilizing processes through which Britain had prepared Indians to shoulder the responsibilities of self-government. In other contexts, especially in Africa, 'equal partnership' emphasized British provision of welfare and modernizing efforts on the assumption that British rule would continue. But much imagery of Indians and Africans remained fixed into 'otherness'. The hallmarks of modernity belonged to the British—their order invoked through the theme of orderly withdrawal from India, and

---

[4] *The Overlanders* (Harry Watt, 1946).

[5] *Sunday Times*, 6 July 1947.

[6] Ania Loomba, *Colonialism/Postcolonialism* (London: Routledge, 1998), 173.

their rationality and scientific expertise associated with welfare and development in empire. Shifting representations showed Indians as fully prepared for self-government, and Africans as the beneficiaries of modernizing welfare projects. Simultaneously, they showed Indians and Africans as violent, turbulent, superstitious, or resistant and obstructive to such projects. Even the Western-educated or Westernized African and Indian was rarely endowed with the attributes of modernity, and was often given a narrative of unbelonging in empire.

Racialized imagery of a 'people's empire' was particularly evident in the continuing priority given to a racial community of Britons in Australia, Canada, and New Zealand. Once the war was over, the need to maintain and strengthen this racial community was embodied in emigration schemes from Britain that solicited white migrants. These schemes sought to maintain Britishness as a global identity that was white. In 1946, however, in a much-publicized speech in Fulton in the United States, Winston Churchill, speaking of the threat posed to world peace by Communism, argued that the prevention of another war depended on 'the fraternal association of the English-speaking peoples'. Such a fraternal association, he stated, meant 'a special relationship between the British Commonwealth and Empire and the United States'. The idea of a 'special relationship' with America—a phrase first used by Churchill in this 1946 speech—promised to maintain Britain as a world power. A racial community of Britons was increasingly subsumed into a wider global identity encompassing America—the English-speaking peoples.

The 'special relationship' with America offered a story where Britain continued to provide the world with leadership, now joined by America, both representing the values of freedom and democracy against Communism. But another more popular narrative of British national destiny expelled Americans. The British–American alliance was glowingly endorsed in films made about the Second World War as the war was ending, but faded from view in most British imagery of the Second World War that was developed once the war was over.

Americans were not the only group expelled from British imagery of the Second World War. The late 1940s was a transitional moment but, by the beginning of the 1950s, a 'people's war' was subject to very considerable revision. It is a measure of how far the idea of a 'people's victory' was displaced that so many groups that marched in the Victory Parade of 1946 were expelled from Second World War narratives. The home front and civilians faded from view. So did Indians and Africans, in an abandonment of the racial inclusiveness of some wartime imagery. Women scarcely featured in post-war narratives of the Second World War, especially British women actively engaged in war service. By the early 1950s, best-selling novels, autobiographies and memoirs, stories in children's literature and comics, as well as a burgeoning filmic genre, told a story of the Second World War that celebrated the martial masculinity of British officers and leaders.

Martin Green has argued that adventure tales in the eighteenth and nineteenth centuries were the 'energizing myth of English imperialism'.[7] Adventure tales of the Second World War in the 1950s offered a new energizing myth of nation. If wartime imagery represented a high point in inclusive imagery of Britishness, the reworking of Second World War narratives from a 'people's war' to a 'hero's war' produced a far more exclusive story. The inclusiveness of wartime imagery had been, in part, a product of the need to recruit to the war effort—women to war industries in Britain, Indians to the armed forces. The shift to an exclusive story of national greatness in the 1950s meant that Second World War imagery took over the territory which empire imagery vacated, and in the 1950s, the war film bore more resemblance to the pre-war empire genre than the post-war empire film. Empire films no longer allowed for the response recorded by a female viewer in the 1930s—'exultant pride in my own country and her achievements'.[8] In contrast, Second World War narratives, transposing manly and high-minded heroes from an imperial to a Second World War setting, offered a new myth of national destiny.

Orderly Withdrawal

Robert Stimson, reporting on the Indian Independence Day ceremony for BBC radio in August 1947, told his audience of 'the delirious moment when Lord and Lady Mountbatten arrived in state at the Constituent Assembly, to be greeted and cheered and applauded as no Englishman has ever been greeted in India before'.[9] Newsreels of the ceremony offered similar stories—their cameras focusing on the figure of Lord Mountbatten, the last Viceroy of India, and crowds cheering him. These stories were not unlike those produced by King George VI's tour of South Africa in the same year—in both cases showing or describing enthusiastic acclamation of a white British man in a white naval uniform. Independence followed a long campaign of resistance to British colonial rule in India, but the focus on the acclamation of a naval figure rendered a wholly unprecedented

---

[7] Martin Green, *Dreams of Adventure, Deeds of Empire* (London: Routledge and Kegan Paul, 1980), 3, 37, 323.

[8] Quoted in J. P. Mayer, *British Cinemas and their Audiences* (London: Dennis Dobson, 1948), 84.

[9] 'News Talk', BBC radio broadcast, 15 Aug. 1947.

occasion into something that looked reassuringly familiar: an imperial spectacle.

The theme of orderly withdrawal was carefully orchestrated. Mountbatten not only made a considerable contribution to the familiarity of the Independence Day spectacle through his uniformed appearance, but also played a large part in its planning and, in a gruelling schedule, flew from Karachi to Delhi to attend both major independence ceremonies. Robert Stimson was one of a team of reporters sent to India by the BBC, while Mountbatten instructed his press secretary to commission newsreel coverage.[10]

Film and newsreels screened in cinemas remained the most important media for the dissemination of visual imagery of empire in the late 1940s. Film versions of the Victory Parade included one made by the Colonial Film Unit for distribution in Africa.[11] Although the Victory Parade coincided with the reopening of the fledgling BBC television service in Britain that was closed in September 1939, and remained closed throughout the war, few people in Britain in the late 1940s and early 1950s had access to television. Some parts of empire and Commonwealth did not receive television until much later than Britain—1960 in New Zealand. In orchestrating newsreel coverage of the Indian independence ceremonies, Mountbatten expressed his satisfaction with the results: 'newsreel of the transfer ceremonies in Delhi arrived very expeditiously in time to be shown at the Sunday evening show on the 24th August. This was seen by a large audience who were much impressed by the excellence of the photography and the competence of the commentary.'[12]

Reports on British newsreels repeatedly invoked Mountbatten's relationship to Queen Victoria, reassuring their audiences that it was under the 'great grandson of the old Queen-Empress' that 'the transfer of power is completed'.[13] Indian independence was generally portrayed in the British media as a sign of British stability, order, and continuity, and history was invoked not only through Mountbatten, but a wide range of eighteenth- and nineteenth-century figures. Clement Attlee, the Prime Minister, speaking in the House of Commons, quoted Mountstuart Elphinstone writing in 1854. The *Sunday Times* quoted Thomas Macaulay, while the *Yorkshire Post* dated a 'people's empire' to the eighteenth century, affirming that the

---

[10] John Turner, *Filming History: The Memoirs of John Turner, Newsreel Cameraman* (London: BUFVC, 2001), 114–5. I am grateful to Mike Paris for supplying this reference.

[11] *The Victory Parade* (Colonial Film Unit, 1946). Several film versions were made including *The Victory Parade* (Castleton-Knight Productions, 1946); *Victory Parade* (H. R. Dance, Chelsea Colour films, 1946).

[12] Letter from Lord Mountbatten to Castleton-Knight quoted in Turner, *Filming History*, 120.

[13] 'Indian Story', *British Paramount News*, 21 Aug. 1947; 'India Takes Over', *Pathé News*, 18 Aug. 1947.

transfer of power had been 'since the days of Warren Hastings...the ultimate end of British endeavours'.[14] In the week before Independence Day, the *Sunday Times* portrayed a 'generous Empire' that had given India peace and unity, and was now consummating this gift by the peaceful transference of power. 'It is', the paper affirmed, 'a unique record of service by one nation to another.'[15]

The *Daily Express* was one of the few media to distance itself from this celebratory mood, and spoke of 'a great act of renunciation' by the people of Britain, and of the 'abdication' of Britain from India.[16] Four days after the independence ceremonies, it called the British coverage of Indian independence an 'orgy of self-praise' and urged that this should be brought to an immediate end, noting that 'blood flows, fires rage in the Punjab'.[17] Communal violence that preceded independence prompted a question that threaded its way through much reporting: 'Can Hindus and Muslims live peacefully together?'[18] Independence Day ceremonies coincided with violence in the Punjab where Muslims burnt down a Sikh *gurdwara* in Lahore, and Sikhs in Amritsar paraded Muslim women naked through the streets, and burned some alive.[19] The British media offered an account of 'India's Day of Joy'.[20] Robert Stimson reported from Delhi for BBC radio that 'There have been sixteen or seventeen hours now of excitement and celebration, and all I know is that I've never felt happier or prouder to be an Englishman in India'.[21]

The theme of pride in a job well done suggests how far Indian independence was understood as the culminating moment in a long history of British service to India, and the fulfilment of its mission. It was also used to demonstrate the modernity of the Commonwealth. Sir George Schuster, writing in the *Manchester Guardian*, declared that 'for all who believe in liberal ideals today must be an occasion for rejoicing'.[22] The idea of 'partnership' became almost obligatory in reporting. Robert Stimson, speaking on BBC radio about the Karachi ceremony, noted: 'Inside the Constituent Assembly...the Viceroy and Mr Jinnah sat side by side, expressing symbolically what from now on will be the equal partnership of Britain and Pakistan

[14] *Sunday Times*, 10 Aug. 1947; Sir Harold Wilberforce-Bell, 'The Situation in India', *Yorkshire Post*, 12 Mar. 1947.

[15] *Sunday Times*, 10 Aug. 1947.

[16] *Daily Express*, 19 Aug. 1947 and 26 Aug. 1947.

[17] *Daily Express*, 19 Aug. 1947.

[18] 'India Takes Over', *Pathé News*, 18 Aug. 1947.

[19] Nicholas Owen, '"More Than a Transfer of Power": Independence Day Ceremonies in India, 15 August 1947', *Contemporary Record*, 6 (1992), 441.

[20] 'India's Day of Joy', *Pathé News*, 21 Aug. 1947.

[21] 'News Talk', BBC radio broadcast, 15 Aug. 1947.

[22] Sir George Schuster, 'The Future of India: Tasks that Face the Two Dominions', *Manchester Guardian*, 15 Aug. 1947.

in the British Commonwealth.'[23] In rather more garbled fashion a newsreel commented that 'Indian dominions walk in free partnership'.[24]

The communal violence produced by the partition of India led to an estimated 180,000 deaths in the Punjab, while ten and a half million Hindus, Muslims, and Sikhs became refugees.[25] This also did little to disturb notions of British order. Violence following independence was seen not as the product of a particular historical event—partition—but as an essential characteristic of the East following, regrettably but inevitably, when Britain no longer conferred the benefits of order. Newsreels that showed looting, burning, and refugees thronging roads commented on 'an orgy of Oriental savagery'—communal warfare that was 'bitter and cruel beyond anything known to the Western world'.[26] Gandhi's assassination in January 1948 was used in the *Daily Express* as further evidence of what happened when the 'impartial rule of Britain' was abolished: 'Another black deed, senseless as it is dreadful, is added to an evil chapter.'[27] Although Indian and Pakistani independence was by far the most violent event in the history of British decolonization, the reassuring conventional imperial spectacle of 'India's Day of Joy' meant that it continued to be widely regarded as a model of orderly, dignified, and peaceful withdrawal.[28]

The theme of 'equal partnership' in the reporting of Indian independence drew on the attempts to refashion imperial identity that were evident during the Second World War. Princess Elizabeth, in her twenty-first radio broadcast to empire from South Africa in 1947, dedicated her life to the service of what she called an 'Imperial Commonwealth', but increasing attempts were made to disassociate the Commonwealth from the empire in a refashioning of language.[29] Indian independence extended this refashioning, and the language of empire and Commonwealth became extraordinarily varied and confused. Was it to be called British Empire, British Empire and Commonwealth, British Commonwealth, or simply Commonwealth? What was the distinction between Dominions and colonies?

By the time of Indian independence it was increasingly difficult to be well versed in this distinction. The term 'Dominions' had been introduced in 1907 for the self-governing settler colonies who regarded the term 'colony'

---

[23] 'Indian Independence Celebrations', BBC radio broadcast, 14 Aug. 1947.

[24] 'New Dominions Join Commonwealth', *British Paramount News*, 21 Aug. 1947.

[25] These figures are the estimates given in Owen, 'More Than a Transfer', 442.

[26] 'Delhi Riots Kill One Thousand', *British Paramount News*, 22 Sept. 1947; 'Million Flee Punjab Riots', *British Paramount News*, 11 Sept. 1947.

[27] *Daily Express*, 31 Jan. 1948.

[28] Owen, 'More Than a Transfer', 442–4.

[29] Princess Elizabeth's radio broadcast was widely reported in the press and on newsreel. See, for example, 'Princess's Birthday Message', *British Movietone News*, 24 Apr. 1947.

as inappropriate because of its associations with inferiority.[30] In July 1947, however, in the run-up to Indian independence, the Dominions Office was renamed the Commonwealth Relations Office and the Secretary of State for Dominion Affairs became the Secretary of State for Commonwealth Relations.[31] An editorial in the *Sunday Times* explained that the decision had the implicit objective of 'opening the door wide to free and equal membership in the Commonwealth for nations of different race for which the title Dominions was always inept'.[32] Even so, when India and Pakistan became independent, they were styled Dominions, and much reporting emphasized their new status as Dominions.

The move to a multiracial Commonwealth was generally uncontroversial in Britain where the distinction between Dominions and colonies was one that only 25 per cent of the sample in the Survey of Public Opinion on Colonial Affairs in 1948 could name correctly.[33] 'British Commonwealth', while sometimes used interchangeably with empire before 1945, had generally denoted a racial community of Britons in the self-governing Dominions. Since the pre-war Dominions included a country with a black majority population—South Africa—as well as indigenous populations in Canada and Australia, and Maori in New Zealand, they were more multiracial than their association with a racial community of Britons suggested. They were also places of varied white settlement, including a substantial Afrikaner population in South Africa, and French population in Canada. But the racial distinction that had generally been made before 1939 between the British Commonwealth, and an empire comprising black and brown people under colonial rule, collapsed when Pakistan, Ceylon, and Burma, as well as India, gained independence in 1947 and 1948. All except Burma became self-governing Dominions and members of the Commonwealth.

Changes in language were intended to associate the Commonwealth with modernity, democracy, and freedom as a 'people's empire'. The idea that the terminology of empire was *passé*, and that the Commonwealth had nothing to do with the empire was developed by Lord Salisbury, the Secretary of State for Commonwealth Relations—the new title for the former Secretaryship of State for Dominion Affairs. Salisbury explained in a broadcast on the European Services of the BBC in 1952 that those who thought that the Commonwealth still meant imperialism were 'sadly out of date'.[34] The

[30] S. R. Mehrotra, 'On the Use of the Term "Commonwealth"', *Journal of Commonwealth Political Studies*, 2 (1963), 1–16.

[31] W. David McIntyre, 'The Strange Death of Dominion Status', *Journal of Imperial and Commonwealth History*, 27 (May 1999), 200.

[32] *Sunday Times*, 6 July 1947.

[33] G. K. Evans, *Public Opinion on Colonial Affairs*, June 1948 (London: HMSO, 1948), 2.

[34] Central Office of Information, *Britain and the Commonwealth: A Broadcast Given in the European Service of the BBC on 7th April, 1952* (London: HMSO, 1952).

idea that the term 'empire' suggested militarism, despotism, and domination, and was inappropriate for the self-governing Dominions had a long history.[35] Wartime audience research at the BBC found that, despite ignorance of distinctions between Dominions and colonies, many people in Britain disliked the term 'empire' because of these associations.[36]

In the wake of Indian independence in October 1948, the language of empire and Commonwealth changed again, as the adjective 'British' was dropped from the term Commonwealth. When Winston Churchill voiced his concerns, Herbert Morrison branded his attitude as 'old-fashioned' and 'nineteenth century', and argued that it 'made him a menace to the unity of the Commonwealth of Nations'.[37] Even so, there remained considerable confusion over terminology. Since the decision to drop the term 'British' was made 'tacitly, without announcement' and nobody who was questioned in Parliament could confirm it had been taken, it is perhaps not surprising that the adoption of this new vocabulary was patchy.[38] Even those who knew that 'British Commonwealth' was no longer the appropriate title did not always remember to use 'Commonwealth' instead. Some even used 'empire'. Many continued to use the terms 'empire' and 'Commonwealth' interchangeably so that, for example, Viscount Kemsley interpreted 'the underlying sense of belonging together in the Commonwealth' as a sign of 'empire-mindedness'.[39] But after 1947, although not very consistently, the 'British Commonwealth' was increasingly called simply 'the Commonwealth', or 'the Commonwealth of Nations'.

Hollywood favoured a different way of modernizing empire. Between the wars most of its stories of the British empire had been set in India, providing adventure narratives that focused on martial masculinity.[40] The *Daily Express*, reviewing *Gunga Din* in 1939 under the headline 'Hollywood makes a fine job of glorifying Britain's empire', commented that 'the British empire need not worry for propaganda while Hollywood does its imperial publicity'.[41] In the early 1950s, Hollywood continued to demonstrate some interest in portraying martial masculinity in India, making epics like *King of the Khyber Rifles* (1954), focusing on an Anglo-Indian soldier.[42] But Hollywood increasingly merged the empire genre with the western. Jeffrey Richards notes that three Hollywood epics of British India—*Lives of a*

[35] Mehrotra, 'On the Use of the Term "Commonwealth"'.
[36] See Audience Research Special Reports no. 7, Sound and General, 1943, BBC WAC, R9/9/7.
[37] *The Times*, 29 Oct. 1948.
[38] Central Office of Information, *The Commonwealth of Nations* (London: HMSO, 1957), 20.
[39] Viscount Kemsley 'Belonging Together', *Sunday Times*, 9 May 1948.
[40] *Lives of a Bengal Lancer* (Henry Hathaway, US 1934); *Wee Willie Winkie* (John Ford, US 1937); *Gunga Din* (George Stevens, US 1939).
[41] *Daily Express*, 24 Feb. 1939.
[42] *King of the Khyber Rifles* (Henry King, US 1954).

Bengal Lancer (1934), *Four Men and a Prayer* (1938), and *Gunga Din* (1939)—were 'remade as cavalry westerns'—*Geronimo* (1939), *Fury at Furnace Creek* (1948), and *Soldiers Three* (1951).[43]

After Indian independence, British productions showed little interest in an Indian setting, and films and television programmes of the late 1940s and 1950s rarely featured martial masculinity in India. It was not until the late 1950s, notably with the production of *North West Frontier* by Rank in 1959, that British films revisited imperial adventure in India featuring a soldier hero.[44] *North West Frontier* followed the Hollywood model, merging an empire film with a western, and was widely acclaimed by British critics as an 'Eastern western'.[45] Indian settings did not regain popularity in British productions until the range of colonial nostalgia films and television programmes made in the 1980s which, through their focus on India, earned the label 'raj nostalgia'.[46] But although raj nostalgia still offered imperial spectacle in abundance, it moved towards a narrative of white personal and sexual relationships and an increasingly elaborate portrayal of white domestic and community life that divorced imperial spectacle from adventure.

The extent to which imagery of India was distanced from militarism and power before the late 1950s was evident in two very different films that did have an Indian setting. *Black Narcissus* (1947) was released in the year of Indian independence, and was the first film on empire to depict a white femisocial rather than a homosocial community, featuring only one white man—the British agent, Mr Dean (David Farrar).[47] *Bhowani Junction* (1956), an American–British production, while featuring martial British masculinity showed a hero—Colonel Rodney Savage (Stewart Granger)—who departed from pre-war versions of this figure. The film ends with Savage's decision to resign his commission in order to stay in India and marry the Anglo-Indian woman whom he loves.[48]

Michael Powell, who directed *Black Narcissus*, described it as 'the most erotic film that I have ever made'.[49] Powell and his co-director, Emeric

---

[43] Jeffrey Richards, 'Boy's Own Empire: Feature Films and Imperialism in the 1930s', in John MacKenzie (ed.), *Imperialism and Popular Culture* (Manchester: Manchester University Press, 1986), 157.

[44] *North West Frontier* (J. Lee Thompson, 1959). Rank also made *Harry Black* (Hugo Fregonese, 1958), the story of a tiger hunter in India. Other films set in India included *Zarak* (Terence Young, 1956) and *The Bandit of Zhobe* (1958)—both American–British productions, starring Victor Mature.

[45] *Daily Express*, 11 Oct. 1959; *News of the World*, 11 Oct. 1959.

[46] These included *Heat and Dust* (James Ivory, 1982); *A Passage to India* (David Lean, 1984); *The Far Pavilions* (ITV, 1984); *Jewel in the Crown* (1984: a fourteen-episode television serial which was adapted from Paul Scott's *The Raj Quartet*, a series of novels published between 1966 and 1975). Colonial nostalgia was also set in Africa, including *Flame Trees of Thika* (Thames television, 1981) and *Out of Africa* (Sydney Pollack, 1985).

[47] *Black Narcissus* (Michael Powell and Emeric Pressburger, 1947).

[48] *Bhowani Junction* (George Cukor, 1956).

[49] Michael Powell, *A Life in the Movies: An Autobiography* (London: Heinemann, 1986), 559, 584.

Pressburger, had never been proponents of documentary realism, but *Black Narcissus* departed further from this than their wartime productions. Documentary realism was increasingly seen as a British style against the over-emotion and hysteria associated with Hollywood, but *Black Narcissus* featured not only hysteria, but also the melodrama that was associated with women's films rather than the masculinity of the empire genre. Female hysteria also figured prominently in *Bhowani Junction*—the first film to be made about the events surrounding Indian independence. But while in *Black Narcissus* white women's encounter with India provokes their hysteria, in *Bhowani Junction* an encounter with a white man brings an Anglo-Indian woman's hysteria under control. However different, both films are obsessed with themes of order and control.

In putting white women at the centre of its story, *Black Narcissus* shows them increasingly seduced by the exotic in a colonial encounter that threatens to breach racial boundaries. The film shows a group of nuns travelling from Calcutta to the Himalayas to establish an outpost of civilization, where they intend to provide health care and education for the local people. Initially they represent modernity—bringing the benefits of Western medicine and education to local peoples and teaching local children to speak English. Their view of local people as 'like children' is endorsed throughout the film.

The nuns' sexual purity is in opposition to Eastern sexuality signified particularly by the figures of Kanchi (Jean Simmons) and the Young General (Sabu) who run away together. Kanchi is defined by her sexuality, and says nothing during the course of the film. She is constructed in opposition to the nuns—narcissistically preoccupied with her appearance, deficient in domestic virtues, and decked out in richly coloured clothes and elaborate jewellery, in contrast to the simplicity of their white habits. The Young General, like Kanchi, is resplendent in rich colours and cloth, offering a highly effeminized version of exotic Eastern masculinity. He is named 'Black Narcissus' by Sister Ruth (Kathleen Byron) after the perfume that he wears.

The idea of narcissism is central to the representation of the colonial encounter in *Black Narcissus*, While the nuns initially represent modernity and set out to bring the values of order, discipline, and rationality to local people, they increasingly resemble local people, becoming childlike, emotional, fickle, and unpredictable. Sister Philippa (Flora Robson), seduced by the beauty of the place, plants flowers in the garden instead of vegetables. Sister Clodagh (Deborah Kerr), who is the Sister Superior, becomes preoccupied with a past love affair, and begins to lose control and authority.

The collapse of racial boundaries is most apparent in the figure of Sister Ruth. The moment when she abandons her nuns' white habits, and displays her sexuality, is shown as a move towards hysteria and madness. She has named the Young General 'Black Narcissus', but is aligned with his narcissism. Surveying herself in a mirror, she decorates her mouth with bright red lipstick—and, in what is represented as a pathological transgression of gender boundaries, makes herself into a sexual offering for Mr Dean, who refuses her. Her death, plunging from a cliff, seals the failure of the civilizing mission. Racial boundaries are restored only by the nuns' departure. Although profoundly affected by their contact with the East, the nuns leave behind no trace of their presence and, as Mr Dean waves them off and the rains finally come, they are obliterated from sight. In a film released in the year of Indian independence, British withdrawal is thus coded as a female failure.

Unlike the nuns in *Black Narcissus* whose contact with the East involves a move from rationality to hysteria, *Bhowani Junction* shows female hysteria brought under control by the major British character in the film—Colonel Rodney Savage. It is Savage who provides the narrative voice for the film, telling the story of India from a British perspective. In contrast to his measured and authoritative tones, Victoria Jones (Ava Gardner), the central female character, endorses Savage's description of her as 'touchy' and 'highly-strung'. Like Kanchi in *Black Narcissus*, Victoria is played by a white actress, despite the focus of the film on her identity as a woman of mixed parentage. Unlike Kanchi, her speech is prolific, and there is very little about it that is either measured or controlled. The major theme she develops in dialogue throughout the film endorses Savage's verdict at the beginning: that since she is 'Indian with English blood or English with Indian blood', she belongs to neither side and 'won't belong anywhere when we pull out'. But while Savage outlines her crisis of belonging in measured tones, Victoria reiterates this in hysterical and often tearful outbursts: 'We can't become English because we're half Indian, we can't become Indian because we're half English, I don't belong anywhere!'

Modernity and manliness in *Bhowani Junction* is colour-coded as Victoria works out her crisis of identity in relation to three suitors. Of these, the Indian Ranjit Kasel (Francis Matthews) has the darkest skin colour, and is the most effeminate. Dominated by his mother, Ranjit asks Victoria to marry him on his mother's instructions. A second suitor, Patrick Taylor (Bill Travers), an Anglo-Indian like Victoria, attempts to act with authority, but with notable lack of success, and is a bumbling, awkward figure by the side of Savage. He lacks chivalry, drunkenly threatening to hit Victoria when she leaves him for Ranjit. Despite these failings, he redeems himself at the end of the film by an act of bravery, meeting his death as he defuses explosives on a railway line and saves many lives. In contrast to Ranjit and Patrick, the

British Colonel is courageous, authoritative, efficient, and chivalrous, and it is he who wins Victoria's hand.

Victoria's hysterical crisis of identity against Savage's control is only one opposition that *Bhowani Junction* develops between British order and Indian turbulence. Although the film represents non-violent passive resistance, India is characterized by crowded and chaotic railways and streets, and recurrent scenes of strikes, rioting, and protest demonstrations—noisy, disorderly, and often violent. Made during the Cold War, the film makes Indian villains into Communists in another example of colour-coding, where the dark skin colour of the Communist agitator Ghanshyam (Peter Illing) represents violence, brutality, and ruthlessness. British masculinity is also represented as violent in the figure of Lieutenant MacDaniel (Lionel Jeffries), who attempts to rape Victoria. Savage's authority sometimes appears brutal, especially when he orders buckets of sewage to be thrown over passive resisters lying on railway tracks. But the film goes to considerable lengths to show the necessity of his decisive action, and the result of the delays caused by the passive resisters: terrible carnage. Stern action is central to the manliness that Savage displays, and earns the respect of his Indian subordinates, as well as the love of Victoria. At the same time, he demonstrates his own love of India through his decision to resign his commission and return there.

When Savage decides to return to India, there is considerable emphasis on India as his home: an idea endorsed by his visit to the grave of his great-grandmother who died in the Indian Mutiny of 1857. British departure from India signals no crisis of British identity in a film that attributes such a crisis to Anglo-Indians. The narrative of orderly withdrawal that told of Britain successfully preparing Indians for self-government conflicted with the turbulence and violence shown in *Bhowani Junction*. But, like the communal violence that surfaced in reporting of Indian independence—and especially in its aftermath—violence was not associated with the particular history of partition, but shown as endemic to the East. Even in *Black Narcissus*, the nuns become disordered only through their contact with the East. Like reporting of the Indian and Pakistani independence ceremonies, *Bhowani Junction* shows India as the beneficiary of British order and control. As Savage's narrative voice controls the story, so Indian turbulence marks out what may follow when the British are no longer there to confer these benefits.

The theme of British order dominated reporting of Indian independence, and was also very marked in the representation of subsequent independence day ceremonies. These came thick and fast in the late 1950s and 1960s, always orchestrated to show continuity and stability, not the collapse of empire. Like former imperial spectacles, they often featured a message from the Queen, read by her representative at the ceremony—often a member of the British royal family—welcoming the newly independent nation to the Commonwealth. Even when the ceremony had been preceded by colonial war it could be described as 'brilliant' and 'solemn', as the *Sunday Times* described Merdeka Day in Malaya in 1957.[50] All this signified continuity and stability and was often portrayed as the culminating act of British rule which had long been concerned to prepare the colonized for independence. Violence might precede or follow such a ceremony, as in India and Malaya. If so, it was often understood as the eruption of a savagery to which the colonized were naturally disposed and which followed inevitably, if tragically, when the British were no longer there to keep order.

Welfare and Expertise

Frederick Cooper, writing about the Colonial Development and Welfare Act of 1940, which was renewed in 1945, observes that 'health, medicine, water supplies ... all of these issues crossed the line between metropole and colony'.[51] The development and extension of the wartime 'people's empire' and its focus on welfare and partnership corresponded closely with issues foregrounded in plans for post-war reconstruction at home. The Labour landslide victory of 1945 promised a new order focusing on the universal welfare of all citizens—its emblematic moment the foundation of the National Health Service in 1948. In the late 1940s, as a 'people's peace' was proclaimed, there was considerable correspondence between ideas of Englishness and empire.

Unlike British colonies in South Asia, which gained independence in the late 1940s, most African colonies remained under British colonial rule throughout the 1950s. In the late 1940s and early 1950s, Africa was the focus for representations of a 'people's empire' of welfare and development. Like the post-war welfare state, the post-war welfare empire made clear the need to follow expert advice in order to achieve modernity, highlighting the importance of British technical and scientific expertise in defeating the ravages of the tsetse fly, modernizing African agriculture, providing healthcare. But this moment of a 'people's empire' proved short-lived. The most publicized modernizing project in Africa begun in 1947—the groundnuts scheme—proved a disaster and a very embarrassing advertisement for British expertise. And, as reporting of Africa in the mid-1950s was dominated by news of colonial war in Kenya, any narrative of a welfare empire was

---

[50] *Sunday Times*, 1 Sept. 1957
[51] Frederick Cooper, *Decolonisation and African Society: The Labour Question in French and British Africa* (Cambridge: Cambridge University Press, 1996), 67.

increasingly displaced by a dominant narrative that showed the British under siege in empire.

The late 1940s and early 1950s was nevertheless a transitional period when the story of welfare and development in Africa was developed. *Men of Two Worlds* (1946)—a feature film that went into production during the war, but was not released until 1946—showed British expertise brought into Africa to defeat the tsetse fly.[52] *Where No Vultures Fly* (1951)—one of Rank's top box office successes in 1951—celebrated the classic landscape of the African safari, but the traditional safari narratives of exploration and big-game hunting had shifted decisively to a different form of journey in a film that told the story of a quest to preserve wildlife and the hero's struggles to establish a National Park in Kenya.[53] Reporting of the groundnuts scheme gave prominence to British technical expertise facilitating African development, with plans to modernize African agriculture by clearing and planting more than three million acres of land in East Africa over a five-year period, and an expectation of creating 32,000 jobs for Africans. In the 1948 Social Survey of Public Opinion in Britain on Colonial Affairs which showed that only 49 per cent of respondents could name one colony, 67 per cent had heard of the groundnuts scheme, while a further 63 per cent knew that groundnuts were used to make margarine and fats.[54]

The idea of British scientists defeating the tsetse fly had been championed during the Second World War as a good story for empire propaganda. As early as 1940, Gervais Huxley, head of the empire division of the Ministry of Information, drafted a script for a documentary film called 'Man Versus Fly' and sent it to the Colonial Office. He called another script on locusts 'Africa's Two Thousand Years' War'.[55] During the Second World War, these schemes came to fruition mainly on radio. Elspeth Huxley, who worked at the BBC as liaison officer with the Colonial Office and was married to Gervais, wrote a script for a Home Service programme on *War Against the Locusts*, broadcast in 1943—part of a series of three empire programmes which also included *Life of a District Officer* and *War Against Superstition*.[56]

Men of Two Worlds offered a story that followed the broad lines of Gervais Huxley's early suggestions in his draft script for 'Man Versus Fly': 'To meet the sleeping sickness menace, the white man's science so far has only one resort, to clear the whole area of every human being and leave it empty and abandoned so that the fly has no infected human to bite and

[52] *Men of Two Worlds* (Thorold Dickinson, 1946).

[53] *Where No Vultures Fly* (Harry Watt, 1951); *The Planter's Wife* (Ken Annakin, 1952).

[54] Evans, *Public Opinion*.

[55] Gervais Huxley to Noel Sabine, 21 May 1940, PRO CO 323/1754/5.

[56] Rosaleen Smyth, 'Britain's African Colonies and British Propaganda During the Second World War', *Journal of Imperial and Commonwealth History*, 41 (1985), 70; BBC WAC, Elspeth Huxley, Scriptwriter, 1943–62.

then carry the infection to others that he bites.'[57] *Men of Two Worlds* also merged the themes of the 1943 BBC radio empire programmes, focusing on a moral mission to combat an outbreak of sleeping sickness caused by the tsetse fly, led by a District Commissioner and obstructed by African superstition. Set in Tanganyika, and commissioned by the Colonial Office and the Ministry of Information, it earned considerable praise from British critics—as 'an unusual and important film about East Africa', 'a spectacular and dramatic story of Empire', and a film that 'clearly and patiently emphasises the urgent and difficult task of bringing civilisation to East Africa...a tribute to British administration in mandated territories'.[58]

The hallmarks of modernity in *Men of Two Worlds* belong to the British, but a main message of the film is conveyed through the figure of an educated and Westernized African, Kisenga (Robert Adams). Kisenga returns to Africa as a result of his recruitment as assistant to District Commissioner Randall (Eric Portman) to persuade Africans to move away from areas infested by tsetse fly and is thus a key figure in the representation of a welfare empire and ideas of 'partnership'. Robert Adams, an actor from British Guiana, who played Kisenga, had trained as a barrister and worked as a teacher. He appeared in a BBC discussion on colour prejudice in 1943 that, through a subsequent decision, was never broadcast, and criticized the depiction of Africans in films that showed 'the white man in the bush surrounded by half-naked savages. People tend to accept such things as being typical of all negroes.'[59]

Adams's critique was relevant to *Men of Two Worlds*, which developed binary oppositions between British and Africans—modernity, rationality, and welfare against primitivism, superstition, and disease. Within these oppositions, Kisenga occupies an ambivalent position. The opening sequence shows him dressed in bow-tie and suit, performing as a solo pianist at a wartime concert in the National Gallery in London, accompanied by an entirely white orchestra and choir with white conductor, and earning rapturous applause from a predominantly white audience. In a film that went into production during the war, he is thus incorporated into the idea of a 'people's war'—an acclaimed performer at a National Gallery concert was an image familiar from wartime documentaries like *Listen to Britain* (1942).[60]

---

[57] Draft script for 'Man Versus Fly', Gervais Huxley to Noel Sabine, 21 May 1940, PRO CO 323/1754/5.

[58] *Daily Sketch*, 9 July 1946; *Daily Mirror*, 18 July 1946; *Wembley News*, 6 Sept. 1946.

[59] 'Draft Announcement for Colour Prejudice Discussion', BBC WAC, R51/92, Talks, Coloured People 1943–1954.

[60] This image is used in *Listen to Britain* (Humphrey Jennings, 1942); *Diary for Timothy* (Humphrey Jennings, 1945).

But Kisenga is a very ambivalent figure in the idea of a 'people's empire'. Any message about partnership is constantly undercut as he is cursed by a witch doctor and falls into an illness caused by his superstitious belief in the force of this curse. The film explicitly explores essentialist ideas of racial difference, particularly in Kisenga's own explanation of his terror of the effects of the witch doctor's curse: 'Fifteen years in England—what's that against ten thousand years of Africa in my blood?' The project of the British, and of the film, is the defeat of the witch doctor, and the battle between the forces of progress, represented by the British, and the forces of darkness, represented by the witch doctor, becomes a battle over whether Kisenga will die or not.

While Kisenga succumbs to superstition, a main representative of scientific rationality is a British woman—Catherine Munro (Phyllis Calvert). As the doctor responsible for medical investigations and reports on the spread of disease, Munro is shown taking samples of blood from unwilling Africans to test for infection and scrutinizing slides down a microscope. She is also shown as a figure of considerable authority, speaking to large groups of Africans to explain the need to sample blood. In a sequence that suggests the work of the Colonial Film Unit in Africa, depicting Africans watching the screening of a film, Munro provides the narrative voice that explains the images and warns Africans of the dangers of sleeping sickness.

Munro is given the attributes characteristically associated with emancipated spinsters, as a formidable, forceful, and even domineering figure, as well as the emblems of the modern woman—she smokes and, on occasion, wears trousers and drinks whisky. Despite his Westernization, Kisenga represents African superstition as much as modernity. Next to Munro, he is a very fragile figure, reduced to a pitiful state when the witch doctor curses him. His voice becomes high-pitched, and he loses all the attributes of Western masculinity—crying, sweating, shaking. In showing the extent to which Munro shares the qualities of British men—authority, expertise, rationality—gender difference between Britons is made less significant in an imperial context than racial difference between Britons and their 'others'. Munro's image is aligned with District Commissioner Randall's against the Westernized African while Kisenga is constructed as effeminate and primitive in opposition to the white woman as strong and modern.

Where No Vultures Fly (1951) portrayed another aspect of a welfare empire, and received a royal command performance. Shot on location in Kenya, it produced Kenya as entertainment and spectacle offering beauty, space, and wild life—an Edenic landscape shown as 'unspoilt' for the consumption of a Western audience. 'No one', the *Daily Telegraph* commented, 'will wonder why it was chosen for this year's royal film show. It is not sordid, as so many new films are; it has a theme that almost everyone will find appealing, and the corner of the Empire where it is set is fresh, beautiful and exciting to look at.'[61]

Robert Payton (Anthony Steel) offered a new type of imperial hero—a family man who takes his wife Mary (Dinah Sheridan) and their son Tim (William Simons) with him on safari, introducing familial and domestic imagery into the adventure landscape. The family transforms the manly outdoor form of domestic life involved in camping out—a familiar image in adventure films. Tim adopts a number of African animals as pets, and uses the safari landscape as a type of adventure playground. Imperial adventure is thus made into a family story offering family entertainment. The *Daily Mail*, commenting on its selection for the 1951 royal command performance, suggested that it would have been an ideal choice if Prince Charles—then 3 years old—had attended, and called it 'a pleasant picture, especially for children'.[62]

In keeping with the film's theme of modernization, Payton proclaims a 'new Africa'. This is a notion that remains vague, consisting mainly of Payton's own determination to preserve wildlife and his confidence that Africa is still a white man's country. In a set-piece confrontation with the white villain Mainwaring (Harry Warrender)—an ivory poacher dedicated to obstructing Payton's project—it is the villain who asserts that 'Africa's finished—there's nothing in it for the white man . . . the only thing to do is to . . . get out while the going's good'. Payton retorts that Africans are 'black brothers'—a claim that is immediately endorsed when a leopard attacks him and a black African saves his life. But otherwise the film's images provide little support for the view of Africans as 'brothers'. Donna Haraway comments: 'In establishing the game parks of Africa, European law turned indigenous human inhabitants of the "nature reserves" into poachers, invaders in their own terrain, or into part of the wildlife.'[63] These are three recurrent images of Africans in *Where No Vultures Fly*.

Despite their rhetoric of equal partnership and brotherhood, both *Men of Two Worlds* and *Where No Vultures Fly* not only retain conventional oppositions between British and Africans, but give Africans narratives of unbelonging. Kisenga in *Men of Two Worlds* is attributed a crisis of identity, like Victoria in *Bhowani Junction*. His illness is not only a result of his belief that he will die because he has been cursed by a witch doctor, but also a result of Africans disowning him, because of his Westernization, as a white man. Returning to Africa in early sequences, he repeatedly refers to it as 'home', but as he becomes ill, he tells his sister: 'I thought I had two

[61] *Daily Telegraph*, 6 Nov. 1951.

[62] *Daily Mail*, 6 Nov. 1951.

[63] Donna Haraway, *Simians, Cyborgs and Women: The Reinvention of Nature* (London: Free Association, 1991), 223.

worlds—now I have none at all.' In *Where No Vultures Fly*, Robert Payton forcefully articulates a view of Africans as 'invaders of their own terrain' as the Masai tribe threaten the success of his venture by bringing in diseased cattle to spread rinderpest in the Park:

Queer lot the Masai, just as they were a thousand years ago. The only tribe that's managed to resist civilisation completely. Always on the move, living on blood and milk. I must keep their cattle out... they're rotten with disease... they'll infect my whole area in no time, and if that happens, then the veterinary department comes in and shoots everything. So I must keep them out.

The credits of *Where No Vultures Fly* named the white actors but, adopting a convention of empire films, credited black performances under the generic 'Africans of Kenya, Tanganyika and Uganda', suggesting that Africans did not perform for the camera, but played themselves—part of the landscape. The *Daily Telegraph* review praised the spectacle of majestic scenery and wildlife, and added as an afterthought: 'As for the natives, I found them all enchanting.'[64]

The use of Africans as extras in films—a backcloth to the story of modernizing projects in Africa as British crusades—provides a contrast to the representation of white women. Munro is as important a figure as District Commissioner Randall in keeping a vigil by Kisenga's bedside in the closing images of *Men of Two Worlds*. While Kisenga lies sweating and hallucinating, Munro and Randall are both cool and collected, and it is only as a result of their wisdom, succour, and determination that Kisenga survives. In *Where No Vultures Fly*, the emphasis is less on the modernity of the emancipated woman than on modern marriage and motherhood, where Mary Payton expects to be consulted about Robert's decision to 'live in the bush'. The couple provide a version of companionate marriage as, however reluctantly, Mary accompanies Robert on safari. Both films show welfare and development in terms of British benevolence where British women share the enterprise with British men. Both cast white women, rather than black Africans, as 'partners'.

In associating white women with modernity, post-war representations of Africa demonstrated some of the contradictions in claims to an empire that civilized and modernized its 'others'. Different readings of *Men of Two Worlds* suggest that the inequitable distribution of the attributes of modernity, which passed unnoticed by British critics, was a major concern of Africans in Britain. While the film was in production during the war, the Secretary-General of the West African Students' Union (WASU) protested

---

[64] *Daily Telegraph*, 6 Nov. 1951.

to the Colonial Office that it 'casts a slur on the prestige of African peoples as a whole ... is in no way suggestive of real cooperation between white and blacks' (and) ... prejudices future relations between the African peoples and the British Empire'.[65] The Colonial Office dismissed these protests, and privately considered that 'the whole attitude of mind underlying the letter from WASU seems ... to be unreal and to result from an inferiority complex'.[66]

WASU protests against the persistence of habits of mind associated with colonialism in *Men of Two Worlds* exposed the contradiction between representations that showed Britain civilizing its 'others', and at the same time fixed them into 'otherness'. The film, they protested, perpetuated the 'erroneous idea that modern progress among indigenous Africans is usually rendered abortive owing to the alleged overwhelming influence and complete domination which witch-doctors exercise over the Chiefs and people of every African community'.[67] An African writing to *The Times* read the film as one that wholly failed to modernize imperial identity. 'Is the object of the new film to boost British rule in Africa?' he asked. 'If so,' he argued, 'is it a credit to Britain to advertise to the world that after over half a century of British rule, Africa is still one vast mass of jungle and naked people living in round huts?'[68]

After 1951, the portrayal of a welfare empire in Africa as 'a credit to Britain' became increasingly problematic. The year that saw the release of *Where No Vultures Fly* also saw the disastrous failure of the groundnuts scheme. Much vaunted at the outset as a modernizing project in Africa, the groundnuts scheme was described in a Christmas Day broadcast on the BBC in 1947 as offering 'solid ground for hope, hundred of miles of jungle cleared by science and the bulldozer with a real promise of a better life for African and European'.[69] A newsreel item cast it as a white man's project, like the war against the tsetse fly in *Men of Two Worlds*, with Africans in subordinate roles: 'Battling against tremendous odds, the white man (helped by the natives) got down to the job.'[70] Some publicity which hailed Africa as 'the larder of Britain' and an 'end to food rationing' threatened a slippage from the idea of development, facilitated by British expertise, that was for the welfare of Africans to exploitation of imperial resources for the welfare of the British.[71] The scheme proved a very costly embarrassment to

---

[65] Letter from Lapido Solanke, 27 July 1943, PRO CO 875 17/6.
[66] Memorandum from T. K. Lloyd, 20 Aug. 1943, PRO CO 875 17/6.
[67] Letter from Lapido Solanke, 27 July 1943, PRO CO 875 17/6.
[68] *The Times*, 11 Sept. 1946.
[69] Quoted in MacKenzie, *Imperialism and Popular Culture*, 183.
[70] 'Groundnuts – The Facts', *Pathé News*, 24 Nov. 1949.
[71] Kate Morris, *British Techniques of Public Relations and Propaganda for Mobilizing East and Central Africa During World War II* (Lewiston, NY: Edwin Mellen, 2000), 422–4.

the British government. In 1951, it was effectively abandoned, and debts of £36 million were written off.[72]

The vision of a welfare empire in Africa was even more vulnerable to colonial war in Kenya. The image of Kenya in *Where No Vultures Fly* as idyllic and majestic spectacle, peopled by what the *Daily Telegraph* called 'enchanting natives', was quickly succeeded by representations which showed it as a savage and murderous place where no white settler could feel secure against the atavistic Mau Mau. When newsreels told the story of the massacre of Kikuyu villagers in Lari by Mau Mau in 1953, they reported that 'there's no part of the location where no vultures fly'.[73]

English-Speaking Peoples

When Winston Churchill made his widely publicized Fulton speech in the USA in 1946, and spoke of a 'special relationship between the British Commonwealth and Empire and the United States', he provided his audience with a heroic narrative of national destiny. This was the first time that the idea of a transformation of the wartime alliance with America into a continuing 'special relationship' was mooted. Churchill spoke of this 'special relationship' in the context of what he identified as the chief post-war threat to world peace: Communism. The prevention of another war, Churchill declared, was dependent on 'the fraternal association of the English-speaking peoples'.

A heroic narrative of national destiny based on the idea of the English-speaking peoples had been elaborated as early as 1867 by Sir Charles Dilke in a popular and influential book on his travels in English-speaking countries across diverse continents, based on the letters he had written home. Dilke's book, entitled *Greater Britain*, offered a detailed account of his travels in the USA, and assigned America as well as the white settler colonies an important role in the process through which 'the English race' would dominate the rest of the world. 'As the English element has given language and history to that land,' he wrote, 'America offers the English race the moral directorship of the globe, by ruling mankind through Saxon institutions and the English tongue. Through America, England is speaking to the world.'[74]

---

[72] Richard Cavendish, 'Britain Abandons the Groundnuts Scheme, January 9th 1951', *History Today*, Jan. 2001, 52.

[73] 'Mau Mau Massacre 150 Kikuyu', *British Paramount News*, 6 Apr. 1953.

[74] Sir Charles Wentworth Dilke, *Greater Britain: A Record of Travel in English-Speaking Countries During 1866 and 1867* (1st edn. 1867; 5th edn. London: Macmillan, 1870), 230.

Churchill's idea of the English-speaking peoples followed Dilke's in focusing on the importance of America, despite his rhetoric about the 'British Commonwealth and Empire'. Churchill's four-volume *History of the English-Speaking Peoples*, published between 1956 and 1958, also provided extensive publicity for a community of English-speaking peoples. But while recording the histories of Britain and America in considerable detail it had little to say about Canada, Australia, New Zealand, or South Africa.[75] As John Ramsden has shown, after he left the army in 1900, Churchill spent more time in the USA than the empire, and sometimes referred to himself as a personification of the 'special relationship' between Britain and America through his mixed parentage—an American mother and a British father: 'an English-speaking union in my own person'.[76]

Publicity for the wartime alliance with America, which reached a high point as the war was ending, also focused on Britain and America. *Know Your Ally: Britain* (1944) ends with a speech by Churchill proclaiming that Britain and America will work together 'in majesty, in justice and in peace'. In *Welcome to Britain* (1943) it is an American General who articulates this message: 'The RAF and ourselves have been fighting side by side for more than a year now. And if they let us patrol the world in the years to come as we've fought together in the war, we'll be in for a long peace.'[77] *I Live in Grosvenor Square* (1945) and *The Way to the Stars* (1945)—feature films that offered glowing endorsements of the importance of British–American alliance—were released in June and July 1945, at a moment when a post-war world had just been ushered in.[78] *A Matter of Life and Death* (1946), where the wartime British–American alliance is embodied in a romance between a British airman and an American woman, originated in a Ministry of Information proposal in 1944 for a propaganda film to improve British–American relations.[79]

Despite their glowing tributes to the British–American alliance, *I Live in Grosvenor Square* and *The Way to the Stars* suggest a range of anxieties about British–American relations, and the GI presence in Britain as the war was coming to an end. *A Matter of Life and Death* awards an American woman to a British man—a plot line that posed few problems about anxieties that GIs were 'oversexed' and stealing 'our women'. *I Live in Grosvenor Square*

[75] For an account of the reception of Churchill's *History of the English-Speaking Peoples* see John Ramsden, *Man of the Century: Winston Churchill and his Legend Since 1945* (London: HarperCollins, 2003).

[76] Ibid. 326.

[77] *Know Your Ally: Britain* (Frank Capra, US 1944); *Welcome to Britain* (Anthony Asquith, 1943).

[78] *I Live in Grosvenor Square* (Herbert Wilcox, 1945); *The Way to the Stars* (Anthony Asquith, 1945).

[79] *A Matter of Life and Death* (Michael Powell and Emeric Pressburger, 1946).

and *The Way to the Stars* however, both strayed into this thorny territory, developing romantic plots between American men and British women. They were careful not to seal the notion of British–American alliance through awarding British women to American men. Both deny the possibility of union by a common plot device: the death, on active service, of the American men.

The idea of British–American alliance may not be sealed through heterosexual union between American men and British women, but it is fervently endorsed in images of male comradeship in war. Both films are careful to represent an equal partnership—one in which British and American men jointly secure victory. At the funeral of the American dead in *I Live in Grosvenor Square*, British and Americans gather in an English village church and pay 'deep tribute' to American courage and sacrifice. A village schoolboy is told: 'Your ancestor...sailed from the port of Plymouth over three hundred years ago...And it may well be that some blood of the gallant company who sailed with him had filtered into the veins of those who gave their lives for us in this village of Exmoor.' Britons and Americans may differ, but their ties go deep—common culture, heritage, and ancestry as well as common language. The film ends with the British Major (Rex Harrison) being piloted for a parachute drop over occupied Europe by an American who tells him: 'Some day I'd like to see a bridge right across the Atlantic.'

Anxiety about American power had a long and specific history in the British film industry. In 1867, Dilke had suggested that England was speaking to the world through America, but later perceptions in the film industry suggested a reversal of former relations that made Britain a colony of America. 'So far as films go, we are now a colonial people', stated *Grierson's Film News* in 1937.[80] In 1945, Michael Balcon complained that 'it is certainly easier for a camel to go through the eye of a needle than for a British film to be shown in America'.[81] In the 1960s, Tony Garnett said: 'To be an Englishman in the film industry is to know what it's like to be colonised.'[82] Conventional oppositions between American cinema as individualist and British as communitarian were apparent in wartime propaganda, but resolved through the idea of mutual admiration and respect. British films of the 1950s that represented British–American relations, like *The Maggie* (1953) and *The Battle of the Sexes* (1960), both set in Scotland,

[80] Quoted in Margaret Dickinson and Sarah Street, *Cinema and State: The Film Industry and the Government of 1927–1984* (London: British Film Institute, 1985), 58.

[81] Michael Balcon, 'Let British Films Be Ambassadors to the World', *Kinematograph Weekly*, 11 Jan. 1945, 163.

[82] Quoted in Alexander Walker, *Hollywood, England: The British Film Industry in the Sixties* (London: Michael Joseph, 1974), 73.

continued to show American individualism but gave this no respect, and resolved differences between American and British by giving hyper-modern Americans their come-uppance.[83]

While the idea of a 'special relationship' foregrounded Britain and America, subordinating a racial community of Britons in empire, post-war emigration schemes demonstrated the continuing importance attached to such a community not only in Britain but also in Australia and New Zealand. The Australian Free and Assisted Passages Agreements, funded jointly by the British and Australian governments, came into operation in 1947. Intended to maintain the Britishness of Australia, the scheme meant that ex-service men and women were given free passages and temporary housing and assistance in finding employment in Australia, while civilians had to pay a £10 contribution to their passages. Arthur Calwell, Australia's Minister of Immigration, appeared on newsreels urging Britons to emigrate. A strong proponent of the White Australia Policy, Calwell told his audience: 'Australia believes that the world's finest export always has been and always will be men and women of British stock. We want men and women with courage and enterprise.'[84] Under this scheme, 140,000 people emigrated to Australia between 1946 and 1951. Under a similar scheme encouraging British migration to New Zealand, announced in 1947, 47,815 people emigrated between 1946 and 1951. New Zealand paid the entire cost of resettlement.[85] British migrants also departed to Canada, South Africa, Kenya, and Rhodesia.

Concerns to maintain the Britishness of Australia, Canada, and New Zealand produced a final flowering of pronatalism aimed at buttressing such a racial community with extra numbers. In 1938, Richard Titmuss worried that declining numbers might mean that Britain could not retain 'our particular status in the world, our genius for Colonisation... our leadership of the British Commonwealth of Nations'.[86] The war and its aftermath sharpened the pens of many pronatalists. In 1947, Eva Hubback worried that if Britons became too few in number, the nation would not be able to maintain its position at the centre of a great Commonwealth. She argued: 'It is largely because our own 47 and a half millions can combine with the Dominions that we are still a great Power ourselves.'

---

[83] *The Maggie* (Alexander MacKendrick, 1953); *The Battle of the Sexes* (Charles Crichton, 1960).

[84] 'Wot, no Babies!', *British Paramount News*, 10 July 1947.

[85] See Kathleen Paul, ' "British Subjects" and "British Stock": Labour's Post-War Imperialism', *Journal of British Studies*, 34 (Apr. 1995), 233–76; Stephen Constantine, 'Migrants and Settlers', in Judith Brown and Wm Roger Louis (eds.), *The Oxford History of the British Empire*, Vol. IV: *The Twentieth Century* (Oxford: Oxford University Press, 1999), 163–87.

[86] Quoted in Pat Thane, 'Population Politics in Post-War British Culture', in Becky Conekin, Frank Mort, and Chris Waters (eds.), *Moments of Modernity: Reconstructing Britain 1945–1964* (London: Rivers Oram, 1999), 117.

The need to maintain British power and influence in the world and populate the Dominions had long been a concern of those who identified women's national role as motherhood, and saw the 'supreme purpose' of white British women as 'the procreation and preservation of the race'.[87] Like other post-war imagery of a racial community of Britons, post-war publicity for emigration and pronatalism sometimes suggested a return to a pre-war imperial order. British migration to Australia was linked to 'the enterprise of Britain's early pioneers that helped to found the British Commonwealth'.[88] Royal tours of empire and Commonwealth also resumed. King George VI and Queen Elizabeth had been the first reigning monarchs to visit the Dominions in a triumphant tour of Canada just before war was declared in 1939. Their 1947 visit to South Africa, accompanied by their daughters, produced much imagery familiar from the long history of traffic between metropolis and empire/Commonwealth—investitures, race meetings, cheering crowds greeting the King, and Zulu warriors dancing for him.

Despite this conservatism, imagery of a racial community of Britons also showed a 'people's empire', highlighting traffics between the common people of Commonwealth and metropolis. When Calwell appeared on newsreel urging Britons to emigrate he assured them of a welcome in Australia because 'this is a birthright of the British people, even if they haven't a penny in their pockets'. Australian food, including gifts for hospitals and children, began arriving in Britain in December 1945 and continued to arrive in subsequent years, receiving considerable publicity.[89] In 1947 Australia gave £20,000,000 to Britain, and its High Commissioner, presenting the cheque to the British Chancellor of the Exchequer, was shown explaining that this was 'equal to a contribution of a little more than £3 for every man, woman and child in Australia'.[90] In 1948 Viscount Kemsley, writing in the *Sunday Times*, suggested that although the Commonwealth owed much to the leadership of its greatest statesmen, it owed just as much 'to the spirit of the ordinary man and woman'. As examples of such spirit he cited recent news stories: food parcels from the Dominions and Colonies, British families who were eager to start a new life in Commonwealth countries, the spirit manifested by cheering crowds greeting the Royal Family on their tours.[91]

---

[87] This was the message of J. H. Gemmell in his Presidential Address to the North of England Obstetrical and Gynaecological Society in 1903, quoted in Vron Ware, *Beyond the Pale: White Women, Racism and History* (London: Verso, 1992), 35.

[88] 'Emigrants Leave for Australia', *Pathé News*, 16 Oct. 1947.

[89] 'Australian Food for Britain', *Gaumont British News*, 10 Dec. 1945; 'Australia Sends Food, More on Way', *British Paramount News*, 14 Feb. 1946.

[90] 'Australia Gives Britain £20,000,000', *Pathé News*, 23 June 1947.

[91] Kemsley, 'Belonging Together'.

A racial community of Britons in Australia, Canada, New Zealand, and South Africa provided an alternative version of a 'people's empire' to the ideal of a multiracial Commonwealth, maintaining Britishness as a global identity but one that was white. The idea of a 'Greater Britain', associated with English-speaking peoples, provided another. Although centred on the idea of common language, the post-war version of the 'English-speaking peoples', like Dilke's, was about 'the English race' and its descendants. African-Americans and black Britons—whether in the empire or metropolis—were rarely amongst those identified as people who spoke English. Many films in the empire genre cast white actors in the parts of Africans or Indians, and where these characters had speaking parts—regardless of whether they were played by white actors—they generally spoke English. Proposals for films about the empire during the war specified that 'it would be essential to have first-class actors eg. people of the calibre of Paul Robeson, and the African characters would have to speak English (or at second best, American)'.[92] A review of *Men of Two Worlds* praised its director for his decision to make all his characters speak English.[93] Even so, there were often contrasts in films set in Africa between English-speaking as a sign of modernity, and the speech and chants of Africans as a sign of the primitive. As the witch doctor in *Men of Two Worlds* prepares to put his curse on Kisenga, he speaks in English, but Kisenga, as a Westernized African, tells him to 'hurry up with your mumbo-jumbo'.

British films of the empire genre sometimes cast African-American actors to play the part of Africans—notably Paul Robeson between the wars. In *The Proud Valley* (1939), Robeson plays a black stoker seeking work in the Welsh coal-mines.[94] But African–American actors employed by the British film industry rarely played the parts of Americans. However British–American relations were portrayed they were shown as relations between white nations, suggesting the extent to which 'English-speaking peoples' was an identity based on ideas of race, not language. In 1956, African-Americans earned prominence in imagery of the Americanization of British culture when *Rock Around the Clock* (1956) prompted riots in British cinemas.[95] An article on 'Rock 'n Roll Babies' in the *Daily Mail* commented: 'It is deplorable. It is tribal. And it is from America... It follows rag-time, blues Dixie, jazz, hot cha-cha and boogie-woogie which surely originated in the jungle. We sometimes wonder whether this is the Negro's revenge.'[96] Such

[92] 'Films about the Colonial Empire', 1940, PRO CO 875/17/1.

[93] *Liverpool Evening Express*, 31 Aug. 1946.

[94] *The Proud Valley* (Pen Tennyson, 1939). I am grateful to Will Kaufman for telling me about this film.

[95] *Rock Around the Clock* (Fred Sears, US 1956).

[96] *Daily Mail*, 5 Sept. 1956.

imagery placed African-Americans firmly outside the boundaries of modernity associated with English-speaking peoples.

How popular was the extension of the narrative of a racial community of Britons to incorporate a 'special relationship' with America and a heroic narrative of English-speaking peoples? A Gallup Poll in 1961, taken in the context of the British application to join the Common Market, and asking, 'Which of these three—Europe, the Commonwealth, or America—is the most important to Britain?', found that almost half of all respondents (48 per cent) answered 'the Commonwealth', against 19 per cent for America, 18 per cent for Europe, and 15 per cent 'don't knows'.[97] There is no way of telling how far respondents thought of 'the Commonwealth' as a multiracial community or a racial community of Britons, but this finding suggests considerable limitations to the popularity of a 'special relationship' with America or a community of English-speaking peoples that incorporated America.

Anxieties about American power were evident as the war was ending when even the most fervent endorsements of the alliance took care to show a partnership of equals. In the aftermath of war, despite all the propaganda for the wartime British–American alliance, Mass Observation material recorded much unfavourable comment about America, far outweighing the favourable. The end of Lend-Lease and news of the Marshall Plan brought a perception of America as money-lender. Many comments drew on an anti-Semitism expressed in August 1947 when the hanging of two British sergeants in Palestine by Irgun—a Zionist group—led to anti-Jewish riots in a number of British cities. One man likened America to 'Shylock, screwing the screw'. Post-war loans from America prompted comments of 'Money-lender, Shylock, Jew and *Uncle* Sam', where Uncle stood for pawnbroker.[98] American dominance was also criticized. A woman thought that 'She (America) should mind her own business and not try to dictate so much to the rest of the World'. A man stated: 'She's out to dominate the World. America is trying to do what Hitler did.'[99]

Andrew Gamble has argued that a decisive choice shaping the decline of Britain as a world power was the decision to fight Germany rather than America in two twentieth-century world wars—a decision that helped to destroy German ambitions to become the dominant world power but which established American power instead of preserving British.[100] The

---

[97] Alex May, '"Commonwealth or Europe?" Macmillan's Dilemma, 1961–1963', in Alex May (ed.), *Britain, the Commonwealth and Europe: The Commonwealth and Britain's Application to Join the European Communities* (Basingstoke: Palgrave, 2001), 97–8.

[98] Quoted in H. D. Wilcock, 'Public Opinion: Attitudes towards America and Russia', *Political Quarterly*, 19 (1948), 64–8.

[99] Quoted ibid., 64–5.

[100] Andrew Gamble, *Britain in Decline: Economic Policy, Political Strategy and the British State* (3rd edn. Basingstoke: Macmillan, 1990), 58–9.

'special relationship' with America may have bolstered the idea of British-ness as a global identity through reference to English-speaking peoples but, as the realities of power emerged, it was haunted by a sense of British subordination to America. Wartime anxieties that Britain was being in-vaded and occupied by American troops, and that Britain was dependent on America for victory, were succeeded in the immediate aftermath of war by anxieties that Britain was financially dependent on America for survival. The wide consumption of American popular culture in Britain demon-strated its popularity, but also brought intensified anxieties about the Americanization of British culture after 1945. The popularity of rock and roll, coffee bars, and horror comics was used to exemplify an invasion by American products that threatened moral decline and depravity, especially amongst young Britons.[101] The Suez debacle in 1956 decisively demon-strated American dominance, and meant that anxieties about American power were closely linked to anxieties about loss of imperial power. In this context, British–American relations, far from bolstering ideas of Britain's status in the world, were a major way in which loss or power was registered.

Dilke's nineteenth-century idea of an England that would speak through America suggested a strange ventriloquism. Increasing anxieties after 1945 about Britain's subordination to America and the Americanization of Brit-ish culture produced resentment that Britain was now being assigned the dummy's role and speaking American-English. At the same time, both a racial community of Britons and the wider identity of English-speaking peoples offered to maintain Britishness as a global identity that was white. In the Korean war of 1950–3, the English-speaking peoples were united— Australia, Britain, Canada, New Zealand, and South Africa all sending troops to fight in the international force set up under the US General MacArthur. Commonwealth contingents lost 7,000 men during the Korean war.[102]

But the most popular heroic narrative of national destiny developed in the 1950s was not that of the English-speaking peoples representing the values of freedom and democracy against Communism. It was a narrative that looked back to a famous victory in the Second World War. As it developed from the early 1950s, this narrative continued, from time to time, to incorporate a racial community of Britons, but no longer featured Americans, paid glowing tributes to the British–American alliance, or showed a partnership between Americans and British in securing victory,

---

[101] See Dick Hebidge, *Hiding in the Light* (London: Routledge, 1988), Ch. 3.

[102] For an account of the representation of the Korean war on British cinema and television newsreel, see Howard Smith, 'The BBC Television Newsreel and the Korean War', *Historical Journal of Film, Radio and Television*, 8 (1988), 227–52.

however equal. Wartime films that celebrated the British–American alliance had no counterparts in the 1950s.

The People's Empire and the Post-War Second World War

Scholars of a literary genre of imperial narratives in the eighteenth and nineteenth centuries have argued that imperial adventure came under considerable strain by the late nineteenth century, and was buried in the mud of Flanders Field.[103] Patrick Brantlinger detects an elegiac quality in late Victorian and Edwardian imperial literary adventure, as Britain's power declined, while John McClure suggests that imperialism was beginning to be identified as the enemy of romance by the close of the nineteenth century, as global modernization robbed empire of mystery.[104] Many scholars date the demise of the adventure hero to the Western Front of 1914–18, when the immobilization, dismemberment, and slaughter of trench warfare wrote the obituary of active masculinity in quest of military glory.[105] After 1918, Martin Green argues, 'the adventure of imperialism had lost intellectual and moral credibility'.[106]

Dating the death of imperial adventure is nevertheless a complex process, and scholars who have looked at visual rather than literary texts have traced the history of an important new site for consumption of imperial adventure narratives in Britain after 1918: the cinema. As Alison Light notes, some literary texts, like E. M. Forster's novel *A Passage to India*, first published in 1924, began to imagine imperial experience as 'an extension of domestic or private life'.[107] But the 1930s empire genre in film showed action, not domesticity. Typically celebrating a homosocial world and adventure heroes

---

[103] Green, *Dreams of Adventure*; Patrick Brantlinger, *Rule of Darkness: British Literature and Imperialism, 1830–1914* (Ithaca: Cornell University Press, 1988); John McClure, *Late Imperial Romance* (London: Verso, 1994). For a critique of what he calls 'the end-of-adventure arguments', which, he suggests, concentrate on 'serious' and 'literary' forms at the expense of popular narratives, see Graham Dawson, *Soldier Heroes: British Adventure, Empire and the Imaginings of Masculinities* (London: Routledge, 1994), 171–2.

[104] Brantlinger, *Rule of Darkness*, 42; McClure, *Late Imperial Romance*, 11–12.

[105] There is an extensive literature on the impact of the First World War on ideals of masculinity and femininity. See, for example, Bernard Bergonzi, *Heroes' Twilight: A Study of the Literature of the Great War* (London: Constable, 1965); Paul Fussell, *The Great War and Modern Memory* (Oxford: Oxford University Press, 1975); Robert Wohl, *The Generation of 1914* (London: Weidenfeld and Nicolson, 1980); Elaine Showalter, 'Rivers and Sassoon: The Inscription of Male Gender Anxieties', in Margaret Higgonet (ed), *Behind the Lines: Gender and the Two World Wars* (New Haven: Yale University Press, 1987), 61–9; Alison Light, *Forever England: Femininity, Literature and Conservatism Between the Wars* (London: Routledge, 1991); Susan Kingsley Kent, *Making Peace: The Reconstruction of Gender in Interwar Britain* (Princeton NJ: Princeton University Press, 1993).

[106] Green, *Dreams of Adventure*, 323.

[107] Light, *Forever England*, 212.

who discovered and demonstrated their manhood on the frontier, it defined British masculine adventure against the world of domesticity and women.

There are readings of particular films made in the 1930s that suggest the increasing fragility of the adventure narrative, arguing that 'an overwhelming sense of masculine loss' associated with the First World War resonated in an exposure of the inadequacy of English imperial masculinity.[108] But most film historians have seen the empire genre between the wars—to which Hollywood made such a substantial contribution—as one which continued to celebrate British masculinity and was highly successful in promoting an imperial world-view.[109] Marcia Landy argues that it translated expansionism, colonization, and commerce into a 'spectacle of benevolence', featuring high-minded heroes taking up the white man's burden.[110] Empire films remained popular at box-offices in Britain in the 1930s, their mass consumption suggesting that imperial adventure and imperial ideas of national destiny continued to be important to imaginings of Britishness.

In 1946, *The Overlanders*, directed by Harry Watt, offered an exciting adventure story set in Australia—one that foreshadowed post-war developments in the empire genre. The film made Chips Rafferty, who played the part of Dan McAlpine, into Australia's first international film star. It shows Dan embarking on an epic 1,500-mile journey, driving cattle across country to prevent their slaughter as part of a 'scorched earth' policy prompted by the threat of Japanese invasion of Australia. It is Dan's voice that tells the story of the journey and describes himself as a 'plain cattleman'. Those who join him are united across differences of gender and ethnicity in their determination to complete the journey, and include a Scottish sailor (Peter Pagan), a white Australian family including three women—Bill and Ma Parsons and their two daughters (John Hayward, Jean Blue, Daphne

[108] See the discussion of *The Four Feathers* (Zoltan Korda, 1939) in Kathryn Dodd and Philip Dodd, 'Engendering the Nation: British Documentary Film, 1930–1939', in Andrew Higson (ed.), *Dissolving Views: Key Writings on British Cinema* (London: Cassell, 1996), 45–6. Sarah Street has also noted that the contradictions of imperialism began to surface in empire films of the 1930s, and argues that in *The Drum* (Zoltan Korda, 1938) contradictory themes, sounds, and images 'emphasise the sense of imperial insecurity which pervaded the 1930s', *British National Cinema* (London: Routledge, 1997), 43–6.

[109] This is the view taken in Jeffrey Richards, '"Patriotism with Profit": British Imperial Cinema in the 1930s', in James Curran and Vincent Porter (eds.), *British Cinema History* (London: Weidenfeld and Nicolson, 1983), 245–56; Richards, 'Boy's Own Empire'; Marcia Landy, *British Genres: Cinema and Society 1930–1960* (Princeton: Princeton University Press, 1991), ch. 3; Ella Shohat and Robert Stam, *Unthinking Eurocentrism: Multiculturalism and the Media* (London: Routledge, 1994); Lola Young, *Fear of the Dark: 'Race', Gender and Sexuality in the Cinema* (London: Routledge, 1996); Jeffrey Richards, *Films and British National Identity* (Manchester: Manchester University Press, 1997), Part I. John MacKenzie's important criticism of the view that empire was discredited after 1918 explores the popular culture of the period, including film. See *Propaganda and Empire: The Manipulation of British Public Opinion* (Manchester: Manchester University Press, 1984).

[110] Landy, *British Genres*, 97.

Campbell, and Helen Grieve)—and Jackie, an aboriginal man (Clyde Combo).

In celebrating Australian heroism and endurance, *The Overlanders* could be read as a tribute to Australian 'mateship' drawing on the popular Australian narrative of tough white men in a frontier society whose virility distinguishes them from white men in the mother country. Unlike 'mateship', however, which traditionally excluded women and aborigines, *The Overlanders* incorporates an aboriginal man and white women. Harry Watt had directed a range of documentaries in Britain during wartime that portrayed a 'people's war'. *The Overlanders* resembles these not only in its documentary realism and focus on a collective group, but also in attributing qualities characteristic of a 'people's war' to Australians: the volunteer spirit through which they get involved in such an epic journey, their tolerance, friendliness, and humour, and their ability to improvise, calm in the face of crises. But the dangers that they face are not bombs, but crocodiles and stampedes. As an Australian version of the 'people's war' *The Overlanders* showed a home front that was very different from the blackout and the Blitz, involving vast open spaces and an epic cattle drive that made the film into an Australian western.

The Overlanders foreshadowed many of the developments in the empire genre in the late 1940s and 1950s. Like Dan McAlpine, the post-war heroes in this genre resembled the temperate heroes of the 'people's war'—civilians and often family men who were sometimes joined by heroines. *The Overlanders* was the first film of an Ealing trilogy on Australia. *Eureka Stockade* (1949), the second in the trilogy, showed the 1854 revolt of gold-miners in Australia against colonial authoritiy and their demands for citizenship rights. *Bitter Springs* (1950), the last in the trilogy, was a pioneering drama, showing a family of white settlers in Australia, and was distinguished by a liberal view of aboriginal claims for land rights and the conflict between Europeans and aborigines over rights of access to water.[111] *Where No Vultures Fly* not only featured a family on safari, but also carefully established the credentials of Robert Payton as 'third-generation East African'. Its sequel, *West of Zanzibar* (1954), featured the same hero.[112] *The Seekers* (1954), set in New Zealand, focused on a family of early white settlers and their conflicts with Maori.[113] *The Planter's Wife* (1952) and *Simba* (1955) depicted colonial war in Malaya and Kenya through a focus on civilians rather than military, extolling the courage not only of the rubber planter and the farmer, but also their wives.[114]

---

[111] *Eureka Stockade* (Harry Watt, 1949); *Bitter Springs* (Ralph Smart, 1950).
[112] *West of Zanzibar* (Harry Watt, 1954).
[113] *The Seekers* (Ken Annakin, 1954).
[114] *The Planter's Wife* (Ken Annakin, 1952); *Simba* (Brian Desmond Hurst, 1955).

The Overlanders also foreshadowed an increasing tendency for the empire genre to merge with the western following Hollywood models. Hollywood empire films in the 1930s had merged British and American versions of adventure genres, often casting American actors in the role of British heroes, and claiming the manly virtues they portrayed, however indirectly, for white Americans. This merging of British and American identities in a process of Americanization of British adventure narratives was also apparent in the resemblance between Hollywood empire films and westerns, due in part to the practice of shooting both genres in Lone Pine, California. Jeffrey Richards observes that when *Lives of a Bengal Lancer* (1935) was produced there in 1934, Gary Cooper played the leading role, replacing the original choice—the British actor, Henry Wilcoxon—whom the director found 'authentic but dull'. Cooper was advised to think of the film 'as a western set in India'.[115] A number of British films made after 1945 also followed the advice offered to Gary Cooper. *Bitter Springs* as well as *The Overlanders* was a western set in Australia, *Diamond City* (1949) and *The Adventurers* (1950) in South Africa, and *The Seekers* in New Zealand.[116] By drawing on the western, the empire film could offer visuals that resembled a common image of adventure consumed in Britain by the mid-1950s, not only in cinema, but through the import of westerns by the new commercial television companies.[117]

In drawing on the Hollywood western, *The Overlanders* offered an unusual image of the Second World War at a time when few war films were being made. In the late 1940s, attitudes in Britain to the recent war were complex and ambivalent and the peace was associated not only with the expansion of the welfare state, but also with austerity, difficulty, national exhaustion, and decline. Continuing and sometimes intensified rationing and shortages together with bankruptcy and dependence on American loans did not appear to be the hallmarks of a great victory.

Opponents of the Labour government portrayed continued rationing and controls as measures that cheated the people of the fruits of victory. In the context of financial crisis in 1947, the *Daily Telegraph* noted 'a grim irony in the reflection that in the third year of peace a victorious country is condemned to revert to a war-time footing in respect alike of the necessities and amenities of life'.[118] The *Daily Express* put the blame firmly on the government: 'The nation that used to be proud and strong... suffers a new humiliation from its rulers. For do not doubt it—the cuts and restrictions ...are...the result of wrong thinking and wrong policy on the part of the

---

[115] See Richards, 'Boy's Own Empire', 145.
[116] *Diamond City* (David MacDonald, 1949); *The Adventurers* (David MacDonald, 1950).
[117] Dawson, *Soldier Heroes*, 236–7.
[118] *Daily Telegraph*, 28 Aug. 1947.

group of men in power.'[119] *Picture Post*, running a special edition on the financial crisis in April 1947, made the housewife into the emblematic figure of hardship, weariness, and disappointment with the victory. Mrs Jones, they reported, while knowing nothing of economics and caring less, was finding her job much harder than before the war—harder even than during the war: 'Yes, her prevailing mood is one of profound disappointment. We won the war. We expected an easier time. Why is it so much worse? Why are we so short? She finds there is less food for the family ...that there are less goods in the shops...She is fed up with queuing ...And she hates the rudeness, the drabness she meets everywhere.'[120]

By the early 1950s, Second World War narratives increasingly removed the war from associations with weariness and disappointment to celebrate elite British martial masculinity winning a famous victory—moving from the idea of a 'people's war' and a 'people's victory' to a 'hero's victory'. Narratives of the Second World War in the 1950s, especially in film, have been the subject of considerable recent literature. Much of this notes what Malcolm Smith calls a 'marked disjuncture' from the wartime 'people's war'.[121] Neil Rattigan suggests that 1950s war films, subtracting from wartime myths the very thing that had formed their basis—the notion of a 'people's war'—are concerned 'with putting the "people" back in their place'.[122] John Ramsden observes that 'War films of the 1950s do not celebrate the union of classes and regions...rather they tend to revert to the stock officers-as-heroes and other-ranks-as comic-figures that was more characteristic of films of the 1930s'.[123] Christine Geraghty describes a move 'from a representative group of individuals with whom the audience can identify to an elite group whom the audience is invited to admire'.[124] Michael Paris argues that 'Overall, the war is reduced to a series of exciting and heroic adventures undertaken by middle-class males'.[125]

Much of this literature is also in agreement on the groups and images that were expelled in the production of this 'hero's war'—the working classes, the home front, civilians, domestic imagery, women, and especially British

---

[119] *Daily Express*, 28 Aug. 1947.

[120] *Picture Post*, 19 Apr. 1947.

[121] Malcolm Smith, *Britain and 1940: History, Myth and Popular Memory* (London: Routledge, 2000), 120.

[122] Neil Rattigan, 'The Last Gasp of the Middle Class: British War Films of the 1950s', in Wheeler Winston Dixon (ed.), *Re-viewing British Cinema 1900–1992* (Albany, NY: State University of New York Press, 1994), 148–50.

[123] John Ramsden, 'Refocusing "The People's War": British War Films of the 1950s', *Journal of Contemporary History*, 33 (1998), 56.

[124] Christine Geraghty, *British Cinema in the Fifties: Gender, Genre and the 'New Look'* (London: Routledge, 2000), 187.

[125] Michael Paris, *Warrior Nation: Images of War in British Popular Culture, 1850–2000* (London: Reaktion, 2000), 227.

women actively involved in war.[126] The move towards a more exclusive racial image receives little attention. Jackie, the aborigine in *The Overlanders*, provided a late example of an attempt at some racial inclusiveness in imagery of the imperial war effort. White Australians, Canadians, and New Zealanders—always the main focus of wartime imagery—continued to be shown from time to time. But, once the war was over, the part played by Africans, Caribbeans, Indians, and Maori was generally forgotten.

There is less agreement in this literature on matters of genre. James Chapman suggests that the Second World War film—exploring codes of masculine behaviour and dramatizing a potent national myth—is 'the British equivalent of the western'.[127] Graham Dawson suggests that Second World War adventure recoded the desert and the jungle of imperial adventure as an Alpine castle or German-occupied countryside of France or Italy, so that 'colonial adventure found itself subsumed into this larger field of heroic, national memory'.[128] Richard Weight combines these views, suggesting both that 'war films can be seen as British westerns', and that they 'mimicked colonial epics in style'—although he adds that 'the similarity ends there'.[129]

These views on British cinema and genre are not necessarily conflicting. The pre-war empire genre, as Marcia Landy argues, had provided the closest British counterpart to the Hollywood western, through its theme of conflict between savagery and civilization. She notes, however, that 'the British film does not exalt the rugged self-made individual'. Rather 'the British hero is exemplary of the values of his class . . . a representative of the best of the British public schools'.[130] In so far as the 1950s Second World War film reworked the pre-war empire film, it could also be seen as a counterpart to the western. But what these arguments fail to note is the opposite trajectories taken by the war and empire film in the 1950s.

These opposite trajectories were marked particularly by imagery of martial masculinity which, fading from the empire genre, became a major focus of the Second World War narrative and its prolific imagery of uniforms and martial displays—especially in the air. Like the pre-war empire story, these were narratives about public-school educated men,

---

[126] The only films that focused on women were *Odette* (Herbert Wilcox, 1950) and *Carve Her Name with Pride* (Lewis Gilbert, 1958). For an account of the transitional texts of the late 1940s and the expulsion of women from Second World War narratives see Wendy Webster, 'Reconstructing Boundaries: Gender, War and Empire in British Cinema, 1945–1950', *Historical Journal of Film, Radio and Television*, 23 (2003), 43–57.

[127] James Chapman, 'Our Finest Hour Revisited: The Second World War in British Feature Films Since 1945', *Journal of Popular British Cinema*, 1 (1998), 72.

[128] Dawson, *Soldier Heroes*, 229.

[129] Richard Weight, *Patriots: National Identity in Britain 1940–2000* (Basingstoke: Macmillan, 2002), 345–7.

[130] Landy, *British Genres*, 97–8.

exemplifying the values of their class, who found, demonstrated, and proved their manhood in a homosocial world. As Smith notes, 'family life and femininity are marginalized in pursuit of the quest'.[131] Thus the incorporation of women and civilians into empire films coincided with an increasing expulsion of such figures from the Second World War narrative. Although the same actors were cast in empire and war genres, it was in the war genre that they were required to play military heroes—Jack Hawkins commenting that 'I played enough senior officers to stock the entire Ministry of Defence'.[132] In 1953, when Jack Hawkins topped the *Motion Picture Herald* poll for a number of performances, it was for roles as senior officers in the war films *Malta Story* (1953) and *The Cruel Sea* (1953), but for his performance as a civilian—a rubber planter—in the empire film *The Planter's Wife*.[133]

All these developments are apparent in shifts in the prisoner-of-war genre. *The Captive Heart* (1946)—the first prisoner-of-war film in the genre, released in the immediate aftermath of war—situated its story in a transitional moment between war and post-war, showing the early release of some of the prisoners and their homecomings to a Britain where the war was coming to an end.[134] The film developed characteristic 'people's war' imagery—careful to emphasize an inclusive British identity incorporating Scottish and Welsh characters, urban as well as rural locations, and other ranks as well as officers. In its representations of women and home, however, it marked a shift in imagery of the 'people's war'. Women were shorn of most associations with war-work, and shown as passive figures who had spent the war at home, patiently waiting for their men to return. The home front, once a place of danger and death, was now represented in opposition to the hardships of the prisoner-of-war camp—a haven which the prisoners long to see. Subsequent films in the prisoner-of-war genre— including high box-office earners like *The Wooden Horse* (1950) and *The Colditz Story* (1955), both based on best-selling books—moved to a narrative of a homosocial world and of escape attempts portrayed as daring adventure, foregrounding officers.[135] As Marcia Landy comments, they offered 'no space for fantasies of home'.[136]

A prisoner-of-war film that ran counter to this trend was set in empire. *A Town Like Alice* (1956) develops imagery of a 'people's empire', with

[131] Ibid. 122.
[132] Quoted in Ramsden, 'Refocusing "The People's War"', 43.
[133] Sue Harper and Vincent Porter, 'Cinema Audience Tastes in 1950s Britain', *Journal of Popular Cinema*, 2 (1999), 72. *Malta Story* (Brian Desmond Hurst, 1953); *The Cruel Sea* (Charles Frend, 1953).
[134] *The Captive Heart* (Basil Dearden, 1946).
[135] *The Wooden Horse* (Jack Lee, 1950); *The Colditz Story* (Guy Hamilton, 1954).
[136] Landy, *British Genres*, 176.

opening sequences that show Jean Paget (Virginia McKenna) initiating a
welfare project in Malaya, and her friendships with local women who join
her in celebrations of the opening of the well she has funded in a Malayan
village.[137] Like *The Overlanders*, the film merges a 'people's empire' with a
'people's war' as the action then moves back in time to show Jean's wartime
experience in Malaya, focusing on a group of British women, including
Jean. Taken prisoner when the Japanese invade, the film shows the women
successively stripped of the privileges of white womanhood, spending the
war on a long march around Malaya, involving exhaustion, suffering, and
death. In its focus on women, the film represents a diverse group including
officers' wives, but it is Jean, who is an unmarried secretary, who increasingly takes up a position of leadership and, by the time they arrive at the
Malayan village, acts as the spokesperson for the group.

Jean is prepared to abandon the privileges of white womanhood in order
to survive, and persuades the other women to do the same. She is distinguished from them by her decision to abandon European clothes, and dress
in clothes which symbolize a 'people's empire'. Given to her by a local
woman, they reinforce the theme of her friendship with local women with
which the film begins. A 'people's empire' as well as a 'people's war' is further
developed through the romantic plot between Jean and Joe Harman (Peter
Finch), an Australian man who is also a Japanese prisoner. He introduces
himself to Jean as a 'stockman', conjuring for her a vision of the vast expanses
of Australia, like those represented in *The Overlanders*. Like Dan McAlpine
in the *Overlanders* Joe is given attributes that characterized 'the people's war':
friendly, good-humoured, with a strong ability to improvise. In foregrounding Australian men and British women, the film pays little attention to
British men, who appear briefly at the beginning of the film. Although also
captured by the Japanese, British men are separated from the women and
children immediately, and make no further appearance. Thus, as in *Black
Narcissus*, themes of British failure, humiliation, and defeat are represented
through females.

In providing a version of a 'people's war' as well as a 'people's empire'
A Town Like Alice aligns images that were otherwise widely separated by the
mid-1950s. The Victory Parade in 1946 had displayed pride in victory
through contingents representing martial masculinity in empire, but a
'people's war' at home, including women's and civilian services. Most
1950s imagery reversed this, representing Britain and not empire through
martial masculinity and expelling women and civilians. Empire imagery of
the late 1940s and 1950s increasingly celebrated the efforts of ordinary
citizens, offering some democratization of imperial identity. The Second

---

[137] *A Town Like Alice* (Jack Lee, 1956).

World War narrative told a far more exclusive story that focused on a male elite. This narrative earned criticism from reviewers in film magazines and in the quality press, which saw it as old-fashioned, socially conservative, and cliched. But it provided a more popular narrative than stories of a 'people's empire'. At the box-office it was the second most popular genre after comedy. *The Dam Busters* was the top box-office earner in Britain in 1955, *Reach for the Sky* in 1956, *Bridge Over the River Kwai* in 1958, and *Sink the Bismarck!* in 1960.[138]

Second World War narratives took up many of the themes of pre-war imperial films showing exciting adventure, soldier and seamen heroes—now joined by airmen—and homosocial worlds where men demonstrated courage, endurance, and humour away from home. The war narrative became a vehicle for the celebration of the virtues of the old imperial hero—active, resourceful, manly, courageous, but also high-minded and self-sacrificing, and associated with the traditional values of a middle- or upper-class, public-school educated gentleman. The idea of heroic British masculinity was transposed from an imperial to a Second World War setting. This was an image that enlarged and dignified ideas of Britishness, and associated national strength with white British masculinity to offer a heroic and masculine narrative of national destiny and a new energizing myth of nation.

---

[138] Ramsden, 'Refocusing "The People's War"', 62–3.

4

Coronation Britain

In Coronation year a 'people's empire' was widely endorsed as highly significant for national identity throughout the British media. The most fervent endorsement came from Queen Elizabeth II herself, speaking to an audience in Britain and empire/Commonwealth on radio. This was the culminating moment in the narrative of a 'people's empire'. Despite the disaster of the groundnuts scheme and ongoing colonial wars in Malaya and Kenya, the image of an empire/Commonwealth rejoicing at the crowning of the Queen elaborated the wartime idea of unity between diverse peoples. Such rejoicing was a dominant theme of the Coronation story, and the 'people's empire' celebrated in Coronation year was commonly identified as a multiracial community—now routinely named 'Commonwealth'. Embellished and popularized through new heroes, the Coronation story of empire/Commonwealth was one of youth, optimism, and unity.

The Coronation procession in 1953, like the Victory Parade of 1946, represented the Commonwealth and empire through a display of martial masculinity. Contingents marched from all parts of the empire and Commonwealth. Reviews praised *A Queen is Crowned*—the most popular film at box-offices in 1953—for its shots of 'soldiers from Pakistan, Ceylon and from the Colonial territories marching proudly and spendidly with the New Zealanders and Australians in the brotherhood of Empire'.[1] But most imagery of empire in Coronation year, while drawing on the idea of 'brotherhood' and partnership, did not show martial masculinity, and the popular heroes of a 'people's empire' were characterized by their friendliness and smiles.

By 1953, the Second World War was being refashioned into a symbol of national greatness, but late 1940s perceptions—shaped by continued austerity, rationing, difficulties on the home front, and national bankruptcy—lingered in Coronation coverage. Violet Markham, broadcasting on BBC radio, and reflecting that 'with the end of the war... a great weariness has fallen on the nation', wanted to 'have done with unworthy murmurs that we, with our great past and great traditions, are now a second-class power'.[2]

---

[1] *A Queen is Crowned* (J. Arthur Rank Organisation, 1953); *Sunday Express*, 7 June 1953.
[2] Violet Markham, 'The New Elizabethan Age', *The Listener*, 28 May 1953.

The Times even went so far as to refer to 'the barrenness of the victory so far'.[3] The idea that a 'new Elizabethan age' might restore the nation had begun as early as 1947 when, on the occasion of Princess Elizabeth's wedding, Arthur Bryant had noted that 'the reign of the first Elizabeth was one of conscious national youth and vigour' and contrasted this with 'our war-weary, shabby, austerity-stifled epoch'.[4] The Festival of Britain in 1951 had advertised a sense of national recovery and renewal, and this theme was even more prominent in Coronation year.[5] The Coronation was widely interpreted as marking a moment of release from the shabbiness and dreariness of post-war austerity, and a sense of national rejuvenation after the exhaustion of the Second World War.

Imagery of empire and Commonwealth figured prominently in the idea of national rejuvenation and modernity. Despite the traditional display of martial masculinity in the Coronation procession, the Coronation 'people's empire' was represented as marking a decisive break with traditional imperial identity. The most striking definition of the modernity of Commonwealth came from Queen Elizabeth herself. At the end of Coronation year, she broadcast her radio Christmas message to the Commonwealth from Auckland, New Zealand—the first Christmas message spoken by a monarch from outside the metropolis. In 1947, on her first royal tour with her parents to South Africa, she had dedicated her life to the service of what she called 'our great Imperial Commonwealth'. In 1953, she reiterated that dedication but in different language. It was to what was described in her speech as 'an entirely new conception' that she offered herself. The Commonwealth, she stated, 'bears no resemblance to the Empires of the past'. She defined it instead as a 'world-wide fellowship of nations, of a type never seen before', in which 'the United Kingdom is an equal partner with many other proud and independent nations, and ... is leading forward yet other still backward nations to the same goal'. The final words of her broadcast were: 'To that one conception of an equal partnership of nations and races, I shall give myself heart and soul every day of my life'.[6]

The theme of rejuvenation and renewal was popularized not only through Queen Elizabeth II's youthfulness, but also through the heroes of Coronation year. The timing of news that men had reached the summit of

---

[3] *The Times*, 3 June 1953.

[4] Arthur Bryant, 'Throne and People', *Sunday Times*, 16 Nov. 1947

[5] For the Festival of Britain, see Becky Conekin, '"Here is the Modern World Itself": The Festival of Britain's Representations of the Future', in Becky Conekin, Frank Mort, and Chris Waters (eds.), *Moments of Modernity: Reconstructing Britain 1945–1964* (London: Rivers Oram, 1999), 228–46; Becky Conekin, *The Autobiography of a Nation: The 1951 Festival of Britain* (Manchester: Manchester University Press, 2003).

[6] Tom Fleming (ed.), *Voices Out of the Air: The Royal Christmas Broadcasts 1932–1981* (London: Heinemann, 1981), 74.

Everest, which appeared in the press on Coronation morning, reinforced a mood of celebration that emphasized youth and optimism—what the *Daily Mail* called 'the cock-a-hoop, confident Britain'.[7] The news associated the Commonwealth with youthful adventure, and provided it with a new hero: Edmund Hillary. In her first Christmas broadcast as Queen before her Coronation Elizabeth had spoken of the need to 'keep alive that courageous spirit of adventure'—a spirit which, she averred, 'still flourishes in the old country and in all the younger countries of our Commonwealth'.[8] The conquest of Everest fulfilled these hopes. As the *Daily Express* noted: 'Everest was conquered by a New Zealander. What could be more joyfully appropriate than such a reminder that the spirit of old Britain has spread through the whole of the young Commonwealth?'[9] In October 1953, the Queen attended the first performance of a film featuring this adventure landscape—*The Conquest of Everest*—accompanied by her husband, the Duke of Edinburgh, who was patron of the expedition. The film began with scenes of her Coronation, with cheering crowds juxtaposed against images of newspaper headlines acclaiming the 'crowning glory' of the Everest news. 'On June 2 everything was new and exciting', the commentary announced. 'Britain had won a new victory.'[10]

Celebration of the Everest triumph was not confined to a racial community of Britons represented by the figure of Edmund Hillary. Media images of a 'people's empire' in 1953 self-consciously strove to show a multiracial empire. Tenzing Norgay, who reached the summit of Everest with Edmund Hillary, also became a popular and celebrated figure. Tenzing—or 'Sherpa Tenzing' as he was often called in the media—was not born in the empire/ Commonwealth, but he was sometimes claimed, like Hillary, as a Commonwealth hero. The publicity for Tenzing, although often ambiguous and racialized, was used to exemplify an 'equal partnership of nations and races'. Queen Salote of Tonga—a British protectorate in the South Pacific— visiting London to take part in the Coronation procession, also attracted considerable publicity, which, like that for Tenzing, was ambiguous and racialized. As a Queen, her credentials as heroine of a 'people's empire' were less obvious than Hillary's or Tenzing's, but she became a highly popular figure celebrated particularly for her friendliness. The main story developed around her was of how she braved the rain in an open carriage in the Coronation procession, and both her height—six foot, three inches—and her smile as she waved to the crowds were prominent features of this story. The *Daily Mirror* described the 'tremendous roar of approval' given by the

[7] *Daily Mail*, 2 June 1953 and 10 June 1953.
[8] *Illustrated London News*, 3 Jan. 1953.
[9] *Daily Express*, 3 June 1953.
[10] *The Conquest of Everest* (Countryman Films, 1953).

rain-drenched crowd to the equally wet Queen of Tonga as the 'high-point of the procession'.[11]

At the centre of all this imagery was Elizabeth, acclaimed as 'A Young Queen for a Young Commonwealth'.[12] A biography, broadcast on BBC television just before the Coronation—*The Second Elizabeth*—included shots of readings of the proclamation of Elizabeth as Queen in cities throughout the Commonwealth, and of her speech as Princess Elizabeth from Cape Town in 1947, in which she dedicated herself to the Commonwealth.[13] In turn, imagery of the Commonwealth rejoicing at her Coronation demonstrated the Commonwealth's dedication to its Queen. Everest itself was seen as a gift to the Queen—'the last untopped piece of earth ... laid at Her Majesty's feet' and a symbol of a manly frontier spirit which embellished her crown.[14] Imagery of world-wide rejoicing and people flocking to pay tribute showed London at the centre of a world stage. The Commonwealth promised to maintain Britishness as a global identity through transforming its imperial dimension.

Media, Nation, and Modernity

The Coronation could be regarded as a notable example of the type of cultural representation by which Benedict Anderson has argued that people come to imagine a shared experience of identification with the nation.[15] The publicity which it received beforehand, the procession and ceremony on Coronation Day, and the aftermath of the ceremony, including viewings of *A Queen is Crowned*, all mobilized a wide variety of symbols and images of nationhood. Much of Britain, especially London, was turned into what would later be known by a term of American origin—'theme park'. The theme was Britishness, and there was very little about the occasion that did not make reference to ideas of national tradition and culture, marking what was perhaps the most fulsome celebration of British heritage in the history of the twentieth century.

People participated in this collective ritual in different ways, transforming the highly rehearsed ceremony in Westminster Abbey into a mass ceremony, which was widely understood to embody a collective celebration of the entire nation. In Britain there were street parties, bonfires, fancy-dress

---

[11] *Daily Mirror*, 6 June 1953.

[12] *Manchester Guardian*, 28 May 1953; *Daily Mail*, 2 Apr. 1953.

[13] *The Second Elizabeth* (BBC television, 1953).

[14] *Daily Mail*, 2 June 1953.

[15] Benedict Anderson, *Imagined Communities: Reflections on the Origin and Spread of Nationalism* (London: Verso, 1983).

parades, tugs-of-war, open-air feasts, carnival processions, and amateur dramatics, including productions of Edward German's *Merrie England*.[16] In the Commonwealth, celebrations included Zulus doing traditional dances.[17] Millions arrived in a much-decorated London to camp out on the streets, sometimes for several days, to catch a glimpse of the Coronation coach. But a major form of participation was viewing media images, and especially television. Through reporting the Coronation, the media became involved not only in representing the nation, but also self-representation that demonstrated their own claims to speak for the nation. Producing imagery of a unified nation and Commonwealth, they cast themselves in a key role in the creation of such a community, projecting their importance in enabling people to participate. They commonly described the Coronation as 'a historic event', but often focused on their own modernization of the spectacle.

The idea of a modernity distinguished by speedy and efficient communication that was beginning to erode boundaries of space and time was promoted by the documentary movement between the wars. The GPO Film Unit produced numerous films, notably *Night Mail* (1936), showing an exemplary postal service.[18] In demonstrating the efficiency and speedy delivery of post, telegrams, and wireless messages, these films emphasized the Post Office's continuing programme of modernization, and the way in which it bound the nation together.[19] Other films celebrated the modernity of aeroplanes in pioneering speedy and efficient communication between diverse peoples in a world-wide empire.[20]

The modernity of new systems of communication were also assigned an important role in promoting a shared imperial identity in royal radio broadcasts. When King George V made the first royal Christmas broadcast in 1932—six days after he had opened the Empire Service of the BBC—his opening words acknowledged that it was through 'one of the marvels of modern Science' that he was able 'to speak to all my peoples throughout the Empire'. He went on to suggest that it was 'a good omen that Wireless should have reached its present perfection at a time when the Empire has been linked in closer union', and express his confidence in its 'immense possibilities to make that union closer still'. In 1933 he claimed that 'science has practically abolished time and space in our dealings with one another'.[21]

---

[16] See, for example, *Manchester Guardian*, 26 May 1953; *Daily Express*, 28 May 1953.

[17] These celebrations were shown on *Her People Rejoiced* (BBC television, 16 May 1953).

[18] *Night Mail* (Harry Watt and Basil Wright, 1936).

[19] *North Sea* (Harry Watt, 1938); *A Midsummer Day's Work* (GPO Film Unit, 1939); *Nine for Six* (GPO Film Unit, 1939).

[20] See, for example, *Wings Over Empire* (Stuart Legg, 1939); *They Flew Alone* (Herbert Wilcox, 1941).

[21] Fleming, *Voices Out of the Air*, 11–12.

This was a message reiterated by Princess Elizabeth—later Queen Elizabeth II—in her 21st birthday radio broadcast to empire and Commonwealth, made from South Africa in 1947. Creating an image of imperial unity, she acknowledged that it was radio that enabled her to do so. It was, she said, 'through the invention of science I can ... make my solemn declaration with a whole Empire listening. ... I declare before you all that my whole life, whether it be long or short, shall be devoted to your service and the service of our great Imperial Commonwealth to which we all belong.'[22]

In Coronation year, the modernity of new systems of communication was represented principally by television and the live television broadcast of the occasion—the first of its kind. Initially resisted by the Queen's advisers, the live television broadcast represented a considerable break with tradition, and became a prominent part of the Coronation story. It prompted a large increase in the sale and rental of television sets in the run-up to the ceremony, and was watched by over twenty million people in Britain.[23] The wartime emphasis on radio constructing a unified community, bringing together people in different settings and from different classes through the common and simultaneous act of 'listening in', was supplanted by imagery of television. In the *Listener*, Christopher Salmon suggested that 'Something extraordinary, which may perhaps even have been unique, happened in England last week ... The people involved themselves. Through their television sets they found means, on that day, themselves to participate in the service, and commonly, very commonly I am told, those who were watching were moved to tears ... We were all one.'[24] Newspapers also sang the praises of television coverage, the *Daily Mail* commenting that 'The result was a magnificent instantaneous reproduction of the event in more than 20,000,000 homes. For the first time the people really took part in the ceremony—and thus for the first time witnessed its real glory.'[25] The limitations of 1950s visual technology meant that there could be no corresponding story of simultaneous viewing throughout a world-wide Commonwealth.

If television was symbolic of modernity, other media advertised their credentials to compete. At the most recent previous Coronation—the crowning of King George VI, Queen Elizabeth II's father, in 1937—newsreels had been allowed to film the service for the first time, and had been able to claim 'the most solemn and sacred pictures ever taken by a

---

[22] Princess Elizabeth's radio broadcast was widely reported in the press and on newsreel. See, for example, 'Princess's Birthday Message', *British Movietone News*, 24 Apr. 1947.

[23] Conekin, *Moments of Modernity*, 2; Ben Pimlott, *The Queen: A Biography of Elizabeth II* (London: Harper Collins, 1996), 207.

[24] Christopher Salmon, 'The Trumpets Have Sounded', *The Listener*, 11 June 1953.

[25] *Daily Mail*, 4 June 1953.

newsreel . . . inside the Abbey, the supreme moment'.[26] Now, superseded by television, Pathé advertised its use of 'the largest telephoto lens in the world' as well as 'a zoom lens costing £1,000' against shots of banks of cameras and cameramen. *A Queen is Crowned*, while offering its audience a profoundly traditional representation of nation, nevertheless offered this in Technicolor against television's black and white. Its publicity emphasized the speed with which negatives were rushed from camera sites to Technicolor laboratories. While the Coronation procession moved slowly and consisted entirely of people in carriages, on horses, or on foot, media images moved fast. Americans were shown receiving a still picture of the event on their television screens within seven minutes—'as quickly as the television age would allow'—and film arriving within nine hours of the crowning.[27] Only seven and a half hours after the nineteen television cameras had recorded the Coronation ceremony, the television films were on the last lap of their air journey to Canada, via Labrador.[28]

Symbols of modernity jostled with symbols of tradition in an extraordinary mixture of ideas. The coincidence of Queen Elizabeth II's name combined with her youth led to much heralding of a 'new Elizabethan age', enabling ideas of modernity to be linked with history. The conquest of Everest was immediately incorporated into this image: 'new and exciting', but linked to past glories and history. Newspaper reports declared the expedition 'an Elizabethan performance' which 'set the standards for this Elizabethan reign', compared Colonel John Hunt, its leader, to Sir Francis Drake bringing a tribute of glory to his sovereign, and heralded the expedition as 'an epic achievement gloriously in line with the adventurings of the first Elizabethans'.[29] But there was also emphasis on the role of advanced technology in producing success, and *The Conquest of Everest* depicted equipment being tested in wind tunnels in preparation for the expedition, as well as scientific experiments conducted in the rarefied atmosphere of Everest.

In this to and fro between modernity and tradition the media, while associating themselves with modernity, offered an otherwise intensely conservative and traditional representation of nation. The actorly voice of Laurence Olivier as the narrator of *A Queen is Crowned* was highly appropriate for the message of the film, conveying the heritage of Shakespeare and

---

[26] Quoted in Rosalind Brunt, 'The Family Firm Restored: Newsreel Coverage of the British Monarchy 1936–45', in Christine Gledhill and Gillian Swanson (eds.), *Nationalising Femininity: Culture, Sexuality and British Cinema in the Second World War* (Manchester: Manchester University Press, 1996), 141.

[27] *Daily Mail*, 3 June 1953.

[28] Kenneth Munro, 'Canada as Reflected in her Participation in the Coronation of her Monarchs in the Twentieth Century', *Journal of Historical Sociology*, 14 (Mar. 2001), 27.

[29] *Daily Express*, 2 June 1953; *The Times*, 2 June 1953.

the English theatre. The film opened with images of seascape and coastline, castles and villages, as Olivier's narrative voice spoke lines from Shakespeare's *Richard II*—'This royal throne of kings, this sceptr'd isle | This earth of majesty, this seat of Mars...This blessed plot, this earth, this realm, this England'. As Olivier moved to speak in praise of 'this England', the film moved to rural scenes of thatched cottages, country churches, villages, and lanes. While there was careful attention to the inclusion of different national identities within Britishness, this was also through traditional imagery, with shots of castles that the commentary named as Balmoral Castle in Scotland, and Caernarvon Castle in Wales, and mention of 'the Ulstermen' and 'the Channel Islanders'.

Reporting of the Coronation constantly threatened to show a nation that was mired in tradition, hierarchy, and deference. Every prop, from St Edward's Crown and the Coronation Chair, through the orb, spurs, and Sovereign's ring, to the ampulla and spoon used for the anointing, was solemnly picked over in the media. Every aspect of Coronation history was explained before, during, or after the ceremony. In *A Queen is Crowned* Olivier's narrative voice reverently explained the significance and history, among much else, of the heraldic symbols, the five swords of state, and the iconography of the Battle of Britain on the window of Westminster Abbey. Men began to appear in London, and other major cities, in a wide variety of historical costumes, usually involving wearing tights. The British media associated men's fancy-dress displays with the dignity and ancient origins of the British constitution. *A Queen is Crowned* showed them speaking 'the proclamation words (that) echo out of the history of this land'. The *Illustrated London News* showed a close-up of a man's leg, clad in tights, to illustrate the wearing of the garter on the left leg, below the knee.[30] Only the *Daily Express* hinted at flamboyance, noting that the men who attended the Coronation service in Westminster Abbey would be 'dressed to kill', decked out in 'all the familiar feminine eye-catchers—buttons and bows, satin and full jewels and feathered hats'.[31]

Broadcasters were also bound up with the values of tradition, hierarchy, and deference. Television cameras were highly deferential, observing what the Head of Television Outside Broadcasts later described as the 'unwritten law' that at royal events 'cameras should not encroach closer than 30 feet to members of the Royal Family'.[32] The anointing of the Queen—widely

---

[30] *Illustrated London News*, 30 May 1953.

[31] *Daily Express*, 25 May 1953. For the history of British men's enthusiasm for elaborate and expensive uniforms, and the shift of style from 'peacock male' to 'sombre man of action', see Linda Colley, *Britons: Forging the Nation 1707–1837* (London: Vintage, 1996), esp. 197–200.

[32] Letter from Peter Diamond, 6 Oct. 1960, BBC WAC T14/1, 932/1 Churchill, Commercial Television.

considered the most spiritual moment of the occasion—was not disclosed to television viewers. The narrative voice of Richard Dimbleby, providing the commentary for the long religious service in Westminster Abbey, was reverential. When he was asked to do the commentary on the radio broadcast, Dimbleby took the view 'that television will be one of the big "stories" of the Coronation, and for his career's sake he would like to be in on it'.[33] Dimbleby was right. But although the story of television's modernization of the spectacle earned wide publicity, Dimbleby claimed that 'we as a nation have done ourselves a profound service by showing to the world how unchanging are the traditions and pride which are our foundations'.[34]

When Dimbleby died, Huw Wheldon wrote: 'He was the voice of the BBC on thousands of occasions, and on hundreds...I think he was the voice of the nation.'[35] Through his television commentary Dimbleby earned a considerable reputation as a national and Commonwealth figure. In London, *The Times* remarked upon 'the debt the television audience owed to Mr Richard Dimbleby's quiet, lucid and dignified explanation of much that might otherwise have perplexed them'. In New Zealand, the *Auckland Star* hailed 'Dimbleby's genius for rising to the event' and suggested that 'his accounts...fully deserved the tremendous world-wide audience he was accorded'.[36]

The BBC had considerable discussion about appropriate commentators for the occasion, on radio as well as television, attempting to offer a variety of narrative voices incorporating Commonwealth figures. The controller of television programmes, announcing plans to include Australian and Canadian commentators, added that 'a woman would not be inappropriate, but she would have to take her place in the commentary line as a commentator and not just as a fashion expert'. One female commentator joined the television team—Mary Hill—while the radio team had two women: Jean Metcalfe and Audrey Russell. A year before the ceremony, as the BBC made preparations, programme controllers also suggested that 'we should invite each of the principal Dominions to send us their No. 1 commentators to help with the broadcast...It would be a good Commonwealth gesture.'[37] The Home sound programme, broadcast simultaneously to

---

[33] Memo from Head of Outside Broadcasts, 5 Jan. 1953, BBC WAC T14/841 TV Outside Broadcasts, Queen Elizabeth II Coronation, Artists, Commentators and Speakers.

[34] Richard Dimbleby, 'My Coronation Commentary', in Leonard Miall (ed.), *Richard Dimbleby by his Colleagues* (London: BBC, 1966).

[35] Huw Wheldon, 'What Can We Do Except Mourn Him', in Miall, *Richard Dimbleby*, 167.

[36] Quoted in Jonathan Dimbleby, *Richard Dimbleby: A Biography* (London: Hodder and Stoughton, 1975), 245, 249.

[37] Memo from Acting Controller Television Programmes, 3 June 1952, BBC WAC T14/841 TV Outside Broadcasts, Queen Elizabeth II Coronation, Artists, Commentators and Speakers.

Commonwealth countries, British forces overseas, ships at sea, and English-speaking listeners throughout the world, incorporated a number of Commonwealth figures, including men from the Canadian and Australian Broadcasting Corporations and Willy Richardson, a black Trinidadian who was producer on the BBC Overseas Service.

While television leant the occasion modernity, it also borrowed claims to tradition from its broadcast. A comment in the *Sunday Times*—that this was 'television's finest hour', when the BBC had 'magnificently vindicated the noble idea of a public service' and 'behaved with impeccable taste and dignity'—suggested how successfully the BBC spanned the divide between tradition and modernity.[38] Sylvia Peters, opening the television broadcast, attributed tradition not only to the monarchy but also to television: 'it is surely the greatest moment in television history as we take you out into the heart of London to these memorable events'. The notion of television history was somewhat precarious in 1953—the small fledgling service had been shut on the outbreak of war and did not reopen until 1946. In conjuring with this notion, however, Peters's introductory comments suggested the extent to which the BBC used the Coronation to enhance its own prestige and, in the process, began to claim television as a historic institution. Despite its own youthfulness, television became a sign of a virtuous nation associated, like the Queen, with national unity and devotion to public service.

The persistent emphasis on heritage and history at home contrasted with a general consensus that the Commonwealth was new. *The Times* suggested: 'If the sense of Empire, which was so great at Queen Victoria's golden jubilee...was absent from Queen Elizabeth the Second's Coronation—it had vanished in a breathing space of Time shorter than that of Queen Victoria's own reign—a feeling of Commonwealth and community had taken its place.'[39] Coronation year became the moment of the Commonwealth, and a 'feeling of Commonwealth' was endorsed throughout the media. The *Daily Telegraph* stated that 'This is not the end of the empire as some observers would have us believe: rather it is its fulfilment'.[40]

The term 'empire' was increasingly abandoned, although there remained some confusion about the exact relationship of Commonwealth to empire.[41] An article by Lord Elton in the *Daily Mail* in Coronation year not

---

[38] *Sunday Times*, 7 June 1953.
[39] *The Times*, 3 June 1953.
[40] *Daily Telegraph*, 28 May 1953.
[41] The language of 'colonial' and 'colonialism' was also increasingly abandoned in the 1950s. *The Colonial Review* changed its title to *Overseas Quarterly* in March 1958. The Committee and Institute for Colonial Studies at Oxford University substituted the word 'Commonwealth' for 'Colonial' in its title in 1956. See Richard Symonds, *Oxford and Empire: The Last Lost Cause?* (London: Macmillan, 1986), 290.

only embodied such confusion, but also commented on it. Explaining to readers 'the new character of the Empire', he proceeded to discuss the Commonwealth. He confessed his difficulties in naming the subject of his article: 'We are none of us even any longer quite certain what to call it. Empire? British Commonwealth? Commonwealth?'[42] Some remained wedded to the language of empire, notably the *Daily Express*, its staunchest champion. But even the *Express* registered the changes, commenting on the day before the Coronation: 'In Empire Parliaments— beg pardon. False start. So difficult to keep out these naughty words like "Empire". The Commonwealth Parliaments...'[43] Moreover the *Express* shifted into a liberal discourse of a community of equal nations, albeit in the language of 'empire': 'In a joyful sense, indeed, it is true that Britain is in decline—for the other members of the Empire bulk larger in it every year. Britain is already no better than an equal among other vigorous people. She can have no prouder or happier place in the world than that status of equality.'[44]

Despite the contrast between heritage and history at home against a new Commonwealth, there was considerable correspondence between ideas of nation and empire in Coronation coverage. The *Manchester Guardian* commented that 'The Coronation ceremony has become an expression of national community and a symbol of the international community of the Commonwealth'.[45] Diverse peoples at home and away were cast in the role of loyal and devoted subjects of the Queen. Even on-going colonial wars in Kenya and Malaya did little to disrupt the idea of loyalty and unity. They were a constant feature of news in the British media in 1953. On Coronation Day itself, a brief item, submerged in the focus on celebrations, noted that 54 Mau Mau terrorists had been killed, 16 wounded, and 21 captured in Kenya.[46] In the weeks leading up to the Coronation, stories about contingents from empire and Commonwealth disembarking in Britain to take part in the Coronation procession contrasted with stories about British troops of the East Yorkshire Regiment learning the art of jungle warfare in Malaya.[47] Earl Mountbatten was shown reviewing Australian and New Zealand servicemen on their way to take part in the Coronation procession and assuring them of the 'warm, family welcome that awaited them in the Mother Country'. Bill McConville, a Pathé news cameraman, reported a different reception when he flew to Nairobi, saw Mau Mau suspects 'being

---

[42] *Daily Mail*, 2 Apr. 1953.
[43] *Daily Express*, 1 June 1953.
[44] Ibid.
[45] *Manchester Guardian*, 30 May 1953.
[46] *Daily Express*, 3 June 1953.
[47] See, for example, 'Canadian Coronation Contingent Arrives', *British Movietone News*, 14 May 1953; 'Coming for the Coronation', *British Movietone News*, 25 May 1953; 'Troops Learn Jungle Craft', *Pathé News*, 14 May 1953.

checked prior to interrogation', and reported that 'you could feel the tension as soon as you set foot off the plane'.[48]

Malaya and Kenya were nevertheless incorporated into the image of a united empire. Newsreels showed craftsmen in Kuala Lumpur preparing illuminated addresses expressing the loyalty of the people of Malaya to the Queen.[49] Black Africans in Kenya were shown decorating their villages with Union Jacks to celebrate the Coronation, and sampling drinks from Coronation mugs. The commentary emphasized that 'these people, troubled though they may be, hold an abiding loyalty for their sovereign', and concluded that 'In Kenya, as throughout the Empire, the people rejoice in Her Majesty's Coronation'.[50]

Diverse peoples at home and away were also cast in the role of spectators of a display of expensive, highly-rehearsed, elaborate, and lavish spectacle. The live television broadcast was widely welcomed in the press as offering democratization of royal pageantry. The Queen would be crowned in the sight of many of her people, not just an elite audience in Westminster Abbey. But the most prominent image shown on television was the Queen's progress through London streets closed to all other traffic, dressed in all her Coronation finery and jewellery, and waving to the assembled crowds from a gilded state coach. While the 'people's war' and 'people's empire' of wartime propaganda marked a high point in inclusive imagery of Britishness in the twentieth century showing 'the common people' as the core of national values, this was displaced in Coronation year by a focus on the uncommon—a nation and empire headed by the royal family, and flanked by peers, baronets, and knights.

Despite all the lavish display, moral seriousness was common to all media. Such seriousness was not only seen as appropriate to the occasion but as a defining characteristic of the nation: one that was sober, responsible, and mature, as demonstrated by a rich and proud history, and by the willingness to make the transition from empire to Commonwealth. Expressed in the language of service and dedication and the reverential voices of commentators, such seriousness excluded all levity. When the *Manchester Guardian* published a cartoon by David Low that identified the Coronation as 'a £1,000,000 spree', it not only produced one of the very few critical comments on the occasion in the British media, but a furore among its readers. The majority were hostile to the cartoon's message. 'Your humour', commented one reader, 'has belittled the wonderful spirit of service and

---

[48] 'Mountbatten Reviews Anzacs on Way Here', *British Paramount News*, 7 May 1953; 'Assignment Mau Mau', *Pathé News*, 7 May 1953.

[49] 'Malayan Coronation Address', *Pathé News*, 25 May 1953; 'Malaya Celebrates the Coronation', *Universal News*, 22 June 1953.

[50] 'Kenya Ready for Coronation Day', *Pathé News*, 1 June 1953.

dedication and the inspiring unity of all the people who rejoiced together.'
Another claimed that 'This was no spree but a unique and inspiring
experience. If the example of Her Majesty in dedicating herself to a life of
selfless devotion to duty and service...can be followed by all in these
islands and the Commonwealth there will be no need to entertain doubts
about the future or to regret the past.'[51]

The idea of a united nation and empire/Commonwealth as a media
audience, scattered across millions of homes but simultaneously participating in the Coronation, was confined to radio. Limitations in 1950s visual
technology meant that the television broadcast could not be seen live in the
Commonwealth. But in a year when the traffic in imagery between metropolis and Commonwealth reached a post-war high point, there was
prolific representation of simultaneous rejoicing. *Her People Rejoiced*,
shown on BBC television, celebrated the Commonwealth's homage to the
Queen, featuring shots of Fiji, the West Indies, Canada, New Zealand, and
South Africa, and North Borneo tribesmen wearing a medallion of the
Queen.[52] Stories showed the movement of people, loyal addresses, and gifts
from empire and Commonwealth to London. In a reverse movement in
November 1953, Elizabeth began a six-month tour of empire/Common-
wealth and became the first reigning monarch to set foot in Australia and
New Zealand. This produced further publicity for a united nation and
Commonwealth, extending the traffic in imagery. Scenes of cheering
crowds in London in June 1953 were succeeded by scenes of cheering crowds
in Bermuda, Jamaica, Fiji, Tonga, and New Zealand in November and
December and, in 1954, by cheering crowds in Australia, Ceylon,
and Commonwealth countries in Asia, Africa, and the Mediterranean.
The dominant image was of rejoicing in a world-wide Commonwealth.

Family Feelings

When the *Sunday Times* reproduced the text of Elizabeth's Christmas radio
broadcast from Auckland, New Zealand in December 1953, it added a
leading article on her tour of Commonwealth and empire entitled 'Family
Feelings'. The tour, it suggested, was 'a sign of the strange unity-in-diversity
that characterises the modern Commonwealth, its family oneness, though it
is scattered across the globe'.[53]

The idea of the 'family oneness' of an empire and Commonwealth united
by 'family feelings' was a staple of royal radio Christmas broadcasts, but in

[51] *Manchester Guardian*, 8 June 1953; 5 June 1953.
[52] *Her People Rejoiced*, BBC television, 16 May 1953.
[53] *Sunday Times*, 27 Dec. 1953.

Coronation year it acquired more concrete meaning through new heroes of a 'people's empire'. The Everest triumph brought a range of popular heroes, but attention focused especially on the two men who reached the summit: Edmund Hillary and Tenzing Norgay. Queen Salote of Tonga was also regarded with considerable affection, attracting publicity not only when she visited London for the Coronation, but also when Queen Elizabeth visited Tonga in December 1953. Tenzing and Salote were characterized particularly by their smiles. Tenzing, newspaper comment suggested, was 'always smiling'.[54] When Queen Salote left Britain to return to Tonga in July 1953, a farewell article, headlined 'The Smile Goes Home Tomorrow', stated that it was a smile which 'came 17,000 miles, shone for 52 days' and 'won the heart of London'.[55]

By comparison with the speed with which imagery of the Coronation was disseminated to the Commonwealth and empire, visual imagery of the Everest expedition was slow to arrive in London. At first Edmund Hillary's presence on the summit dominated the news of the Everest triumph reported in New Zealand and Britain. In the *Auckland Star* the headline was: 'New Zealander Climbs Everest—Edmund Hillary with a Porter and All's Well'. The paper reported that 'Aucklander Edmund Hillary, of Papakura, has conquered Everest. With him was Tensing Norkay, the expedition's leading porter, a member of the Sherpa tribe of Nepal.'[56] The *Daily Express* offered the same message in rather different terms: 'Briton First on Roof of the World'.[57] The slippage between 'New Zealander' and 'British' in identifying Hillary was not confined to the British media. The Prime Minister of New Zealand, Sidney Holland, speaking at a time when more New Zealanders offered 'British' than 'New Zealander' when asked about their nationality, reinforced this when he praised the tenacity, endurance, and fortitude of the climbers as 'a symbol that there are no heights or difficulties which the British people cannot overcome'.[58] His praise was symptomatic of a general tendency to use ideas of a British and a Commonwealth triumph interchangeably.

Hillary's triumph evoked 'family feelings' in the *Daily Mail*, which noted: 'We in this island share the pride our kith and kin in New Zealand

[54] *Daily Mail*, 3 June 1953.

[55] *Evening News*, 7 July 1953.

[56] *The Auckland Star*, 2 June 1953. Tenzing Norgay's name was spelt in a variety of ways in different reports. With the exception of quotations, I have adopted the spelling which Norgay himself preferred, having been advised by lamas that this was the best rendering of his name. See Tenzing Norgay in collaboration with James Ramsey Ullman, *Tiger of the Snows* (New York: G. P. Putnam, 1955), 6. John Hunt also adopted this spelling because of Tenzing's preference. See John Hunt, *The Ascent of Everest* (London: Hodder and Stoughton, 1953), p. ix.

[57] *Daily Express*, 2 June 1953.

[58] James Belich, *Paradise Reforged: A History of the New Zealanders from the 1880s to the Year 2000* (London: Allen Lane, 2001), 320.

must feel in their son's superb accomplishment, for we are of one family, as the great ceremony in London today demonstrates.' In attributing victory to a racial community of Britons, the *Mail* explained that the expedition, 'though British led and organised, is in personnel an Empire expedition, and the peak has been won by a young New Zealander, Edward [*sic*] Hillary, accompanied by the intrepid Sherpa Tensing'.[59] While Hillary was sometimes claimed as a British hero, the increasing acknowledgement of Tenzing's role, as in the *Mail*, often claimed him for the empire or Commonwealth.

Tenzing was not born in the Commonwealth, although he had lived in India for a number of years before the successful ascent of Everest. Peter Hansen suggests that, while born in Tibet, he did not think of himself as Indian or Nepali or Tibetan and had no conception of national identity.[60] In Nepal and India he was heralded as the hero of Everest, and images showed Hillary as a subordinate dangling pathetically on the end of a rope, with Tenzing leading the way and reaching the summit first.[61] It was in this context that Colonel Hunt, broadcasting on radio Nepal to acknowledge the 'traditionally full and essential part' that Sherpas had played, acclaimed Tenzing as the 'greatest Sherpa of all time'.[62] In Britain, however, Hunt expressed delight that Hillary and Tenzing, 'representing, in a sense, members of the Commonwealth, had been successful in getting to the top. It was only right and proper.'[63]

Sherpas had traditionally been cast in the role of porters, not climbers. Much reporting, drawing on conventions of adventure narratives, continued to construct an opposition between 'climbers' and 'porters', and it was not only the *Auckland Star* that cast Tenzing in the latter role.[64] In British coverage the terms 'Sherpa' and 'porter' were used interchangeably and also differentiated from 'climbers'. *The Times*, for example, noted that 'The climbers of these expeditions rely upon their Sherpas for most of the mundane necessities of life in the hills...On Everest...Sherpa duties include the carriage of stores to high altitudes.'[65] As Tenzing observed:

[59] *Daily Mail*, 2 June 1953.

[60] Peter Hansen, 'Confetti of Empire: The Conquest of Everest in Nepal, India, Britain, and New Zealand', *Comparative Studies in Society and History*, 42 (2000), 312–13.

[61] *The Times*, 22 June 1953.

[62] *The Times*, 18 June 1953.

[63] Quoted in Peter Hansen, 'Coronation Everest: The Empire and Commonwealth in the "Second Elizabethan Age"', in Stuart Ward (ed.), *British Culture and the End of Empire* (Manchester: Manchester University Press, 2001), 63.

[64] The subordination of Tenzing Norgay, along with other Sherpas, was not confined to representations. In Katmandu, 'climbers' slept in the British Embassy, while Sherpas' sleeping-quarters were in a former stable in the grounds of the Embassy, and Norgay considered going to a hotel as a form of protest. See Norgay, *Tiger of the Snows*, 210.

[65] *The Times*, 11 June 1953.

'many people seem to think...the name "Sherpa"...means simply "mountain porter"—or at best "mountain guide"—in the Himalaya. It means nothing of the kind...In reality, Sherpa is the name of a mountain tribe...to which I belong.'[66]

The claims in India and Nepal that Tenzing had reached the summit first brought him increasing attention in the British media. In July 1953 the *Daily Express* published 'Tenzing's Own Story' denying such claims over four days—a story which they were keen to establish had been dictated by Tenzing and accurately translated.[67] A photograph of Tenzing standing on the summit of Everest became the defining visual image of the expedition. When Hillary reached the summit, he took out a camera and subsequently recorded:

I...clumsily opened it with my thickly gloved hands. I clipped on the lenshood and ultra-violet filter and then shuffled down the ridge a little so that I could get the summit in my viewfinder. Tenzing had been waiting patiently, but now, at my request, he unfurled the flags wrapped around his ice-axe and standing on the summit held them above his head. Clad in all his bulky equipment and with the flags flapping furiously in the wind, he made a dramatic picture, and the thought drifted through my mind that this photograph should make a good one if it came out at all.[68]

The photograph did come out. It provided the only visual image of a man at the top of Everest which the expedition yielded. Tenzing recorded: 'I motioned to Hillary that I would now take his picture. But for some reason he shook his head; he did not want it.'[69] Hillary recorded a different version of this moment: 'I didn't worry about getting Tenzing to take a photograph of me—as far as I knew, he had never taken a photograph before and the summit of Everest was hardly the place to show him.'[70] Hillary, the white New Zealander on a British expedition, had 'shuffled down the ridge a little' to produce an image of a Sherpa—traditionally cast on mountaineering expeditions in the subordinate role of 'porter'—standing at the summit of the highest mountain in the world.

The photograph of Tenzing was not very explicit about national or personal identity. Tenzing's face and body were covered in an oxygen mask and heavy clothing, while no less than four flags fluttered on his ice-axe—those of Britain, Nepal, India, and the United Nations. But, as the

---

[66] Tenzing Norgay Sherpa, *After Everest: An Autobiography by Tenzing Norgay Sherpa as told to Malcolm Barnes* (London: Allen and Unwin, 1977), 32.

[67] *Daily Express*, 1, 2, 3, and 6 July 1953.

[68] Edmund Hillary, *High Adventure* (London: Companion Book Club, 1956), 239–40.

[69] Norgay, *Tiger of the Snows*, 250. This book was published in Britain as *Man of Everest: The Autobiography of Tenzing* (London: Reprint Society, 1955).

[70] Hillary, *High Adventure*, 240.

'triumph of Everest' photograph, it by no means showed him as a porter and contributed to an increasing acknowledgement of his role that effectively dismantled traditional distinctions between 'climbers' and 'porters'. It formed the frontispiece of John Hunt's book on *The Ascent of Everest*, which was first published in November 1953, and reissued in December, and January 1954. It was used in magazine stories about the expedition, and retained its currency in New Zealand television broadcasts in the run-up to the millennium when celebrations of Hillary's role in the Everest expedition were illustrated by this still.[71] It provided the opening visual in the film of the *Conquest of Everest*, while the announcement of the arrival of men on the summit—the climax of the film, accompanied by dramatic music—was represented by the same still.

The Conquest of Everest was a classic example of a 'people's empire' text in Coronation year, pervaded by a sense of optimism about Britain while at the same time striving to dismantle racial hierarchies. 'Full prominence', one reviewer commented, 'is given to the contribution of the Sherpas.'[72] The film's closing images intercut shots of Hillary and Tenzing, Commonwealth men and Sherpas, to acknowledge their equal partnership. As Hillary and Tenzing are shown descending to base camp, they are greeted by Colonel Hunt, the leader of the expedition, who falls on each of them in turn, taking them into his arms in warm embraces. The camera moves to a group of Sherpas in front of a tent, as the narrator reminds us that 'Sherpas and British alike, all had their share in this'. Equal attention is then given to Hillary and Tenzing, as they are shown in turn in close-up, and the narrator tells us that one was 'born in New Zealand, the other born under Everest'. The idea of the expedition as a team effort of British, Commonwealth, and Sherpa men is invoked again as the camera, showing a group posing for photography—most of them Sherpas—moves along a row of faces, while the narrator identifies them as 'the men who paved the way to victory'. The final image is of Tenzing and Hillary standing side by side and gesturing upwards to the mountain.

Despite these attempts to acknowledge equal partnership, a residue of the distinction between European climbers, distinguished by technical expertise, and Sherpa porters survives to undercut this. Many images in the film show Sherpas climbing up the mountain, but their first meeting with members of the expedition is described in the commentary as 'climbers' meeting 'Sherpas who will carry their loads on the mountain'. Janet Smith's comment in a review of the film—that its success lay in the way in which the 'little figures' effortfully toiling up the mountain were figures 'to whom

[71] See, for example, *Illustrated London News*, 27 June 1953.
[72] *Daily Telegraph*, 22 Oct. 1953.

we could give names and personalities'—disregarded Sherpas, who, with the notable exception of Tenzing, were barely given either.[73] British and Commonwealth members of the team were named on the commentary as they were shown in close-up—eating, climbing, cutting steps in the ice, fitting oxygen masks. Apart from Tenzing, Sherpas were rarely individuated through close-up shots or named. The credits of the film reflected this practice, naming all the British and Commonwealth team and 'Tensing Norkay Sherpa' and, at the end of this list, crediting 'the team of 35 Sherpas'.

In *The Conquest of Everest*, the audience is given various briefings by Colonel Hunt with images of climbing frequently interrupted by diagrams of the route to the summit, a finger pointing out the various obstacles to be encountered, and Hunt's authoritative voice explaining the strategy for conquest of the mountain. On the BBC television programme, also called *The Conquest of Everest*, Hunt performed a similar role, describing the ascent of Everest against a scale model of the mountain.[74] But in the film it is Hillary's voice that narrates the final journey to the summit, providing a much more informal commentary. While the representation of Hillary and Tenzing in terms of national identity and Commonwealth membership was shifting and volatile, both had impeccable credentials as heroes of a 'people's empire'. In contrast to the tradition of British climbers, dominated by public-school educated, middle- and upper-middle-class gentlemen, Hillary, as many stories pointed out, was a bee-keeper in New Zealand. Newspaper comment gave him the qualities of the 'Everest men' more generally: 'unpretentious, unconscious of greatness or courage, horrified by formality, embarrassed by acclaim'.[75] At the end of 1953 the *Daily Mirror*, acclaiming Tenzing as one of 'the heroes of the year', paid this tribute: 'No words, nothing but Tenzing's world-famous grin can express the triumph we all felt when news of the unsurpassable exploit spread across Britain on Coronation morning.'[76]

While making Tenzing into a figure with whom Britons could identify and, like *The Conquest of Everest*, striving to portray an equal partnership between Tenzing and Hillary, the description of Tenzing in the *Daily Mirror*—as Edmund Hillary's 'tough little Sherpa companion'—bore traces of representations of martial Indians in the Second World War.[77] Tenzing's toughness as well as his smile was often noted in the media along with his stature—'little' by comparison with Hillary, who was six foot, four inches.[78]

[73] Janet Smith, 'Filming Everest', *Sight and Sound* (Jan.–Mar. 1954), 139.
[74] *The Conquest of Everest*, BBC television, 14 July 1953.
[75] *Daily Express*, 24 June 1953.
[76] *Daily Mirror*, 23 Dec. 1953.
[77] Ibid.
[78] See, for example, *Daily Mail*, 2 June 1953 and 3 June 1953; *Daily Express*, 26 June 1953.

The preoccupation with physicality was common to representations of Queen Salote of Tonga, who also attracted a great deal of attention for her stature and her smile. In a period when it was assumed that women should be shorter than men, and casting practices on stage and screen confirmed this difference, Queen Salote was almost as tall as Hillary, and much taller than most men at the Coronation.

Imagery of both Tenzing and Salote in the British media was volatile and shifting, with a tendency to represent them differently in the contexts of 'home' and 'away'. A farewell story about Salote's departure from Britain in July encapsulated all the main aspects of the imagery that had developed around her: 'Smiling Queen Salote, 6ft 3in friendly Queen of the Friendly Islands, was saying her farewell today... She laughed her way into London's hearts as she sat in her open carriage in the pouring rain on Coronation Day.'[79] In the same week that the media said farewell to Salote, they welcomed the victors of Everest to London through an idea of 'homecoming' that claimed the expedition as a British venture, but scarcely fitted either of the two men who had reached the summit of the mountain.[80]

In a Himalayan context Tenzing was increasingly incorporated into a story of white men's adventure. But the media showed him as out of place in London, representing him as a childlike figure—an image in which Sherpas had been conventionally cast—with much comment on his bewilderment and the fact that he wore two wrist-watches, one on each wrist.[81] In contrast, while Salote's smile and stature were the dominant features of her image during her London visit, she was also given some of Elizabeth's dignity, with emphasis on her royal lineage and heritage. Farewells described her both as 'unmistakably regal, every inch a queen' and as 'the Queen with a thousand years of royal lineage behind her'.[82] Like Elizabeth, she made an extensive tour of Britain after the Coronation, although Salote's tour incorporated visits to Ireland, and the Pope in Rome. Reporting of her tour emphasized the adulation with which she was received as 'the people waited, sometimes for hours in the rain, just to catch a sight of this

[79] *Star*, 3 July 1953.

[80] 'Everest Heroes Home', *Pathé Sound News*, 6 July 1953.

[81] For the history of representations of Sherpas, see Sherry Ortner, *Life and Death on Mount Everest: Sherpas and Himalayan Mountaineering* (Princeton: Princeton University Press, 1999). Imagery of Tenzing and Everest has received considerable scholarly attention. See Gordon Stewart, 'Tenzing's Two Wrist-Watches: The Conquest of Everest and Late Imperial Culture in Britain 1921–1953', *Past and Present*, 149 (1995), 170–97; Peter Hansen, 'Debate: Tenzing's Two Wrist-Watches: The Conquest of Everest and Late Imperial Culture, 1921–1953: Comment', *Past and Present*, 157 (1997), 159–77; Peter Hansen, 'Confetti of Empire: The Conquest of Everest in Nepal, India, Britain, and New Zealand', *Comparative Studies in Society and History*, 42 (2000), 307–32; Peter Hansen, 'Coronation Everest: The Empire and Commonwealth in the "Second Elizabethan Age"', in Ward, *British Culture*, 57–72.

[82] *Evening News*, 7 July 1953; 'Queen Salote Bids Farewell to Britain', *British Paramount News*, 13 July 1953.

captivating woman'.[83] Preoccupation with her face, while dominated by her smile, also recorded her skin-colour as 'soft brown velvety', while farewell tributes hailed her as a woman 'in whose face shines the very essence of motherhood'.[84] The American 'mammy' image of black women—nurturing, desexualized, motherly, and usually large-breasted—had little currency in Britain, but there were perhaps suggestions of it in the way that Salote was portrayed.

It was in making the journey from Everest to Kathmandu to London that Tenzing also made a journey away from an identity as intrepid hero to bewildered child. In the case of Salote, it was her return to Tonga that involved her incorporation into a fantasy of happy brown people, living in a 'paradise of simple plenty'.[85] When Elizabeth visited Tonga on her post-Coronation royal tour of the Commonwealth, newspapers reminded their readers of Salote's celebrity earlier in the year, suggesting that 'everyone in Britain with a TV set knows Salote...a brown giantess'.[86] Salote's smile and stature were now made emblematic of a people who were exoticized as happy and above all big—an island 'entirely inhabited by beaming brown giants'.[87] The dominant image of the Commonwealth signifying world-wide rejoicing at the Coronation became a scene of frenzied acclamation: 'The two queens, Elizabeth and the massive, 6' 3" Salote sat side by side on a dais. The crowds went wild with joy—singing, cheering, waving, shouting. Native drums beat louder and louder.'[88]

Considerable levity surrounded this publicity, focusing on the idea of 'Tongan size'. Newspapers commented that 'The kingdom of Tonga may be the smallest in the world, but the people here have the biggest appetites in the universe'.[89] Newsreels showed the feast Salote served—sucking pigs, duck, and chicken—and commented that this was supplemented, 'lest anybody felt peckish, by lobsters and fish, breadfruit and melon, bananas and island vegetables', while those who performed at the 'cabaret' 'had their little lunch late'.[90] Salote's son, the Prime Minister of Tonga, was described as 'a good-natured 20-stone chap with a grin like a slice of melon'.[91]

This levity about Tongan size and appetite made a strong contrast to the emphasis on the spirituality of the Coronation, the selfless devotion and dedication attributed to Elizabeth, and the intense seriousness that

[83] *Evening News*, 7 July 1953.

[84] *Evening News*, 7 July 1953; 'Queen Salote Bids Farewell to Britain', *British Paramount News*, 13 July 1953.

[85] 'Tonga and New Zealand Fete Queen', *British Paramount News*, 31 Dec. 1953.

[86] *Daily Express*, 19 Dec. 1953.

[87] Ibid.

[88] *Sunday Chronicle*, 20 Dec. 1953.

[89] *Daily Mail*, 21 December 1953.

[90] 'Tonga and New Zealand Fete Queen', *British Paramount News*, 31 Dec. 1953.

[91] *Daily Express*, 19 Dec. 1953.

surrounded her. Even in London Queen Salote was treated with a certain levity. The *Sunday Express* composed a poem inviting her to 'linger longer', which rhymed with Queen of Tonga.

> Linger longer, Queen of Tonga,
> Linger longer wiv us.
> Longer while the English summer
> Gives us all the shivvas.
> While the summer east winds blow
> And shake our English livvas.[92]

On the day of the Coronation, a joke about Salote circulated, sometimes attributed to Noel Coward, and sometimes to an anonymous member of the crowd. Someone asks about the identity of the man who shares Salote's carriage in the procession. Like most men he is much smaller than Salote. The reply is 'her lunch'.

The language of smiles was one in which Queen Salote's beam denoted cheerfulness, her son had a 'grin like a slice of melon', and Tenzing had a 'world-famous grin'. The friendliness with which both Queen Salote and Tenzing were received in the British media represented the idea of an affectionate British public, and may have corresponded to some version of the Commonwealth and the 'family feelings' by which it was characterized. But in a year when the intense seriousness of everything connected with the Queen and her Coronation was reverently explained—among other narrative voices—by Richard Dimbleby and Laurence Olivier, the affection extended to Tenzing and Queen Salote did not dismantle a racial hierarchy in which, quite simply, neither was taken very seriously. A joke linking Elizabeth with cannibalism was beyond imagination.

America and Commonwealth

'*A Queen is Crowned* has no equal in Hollywood or anywhere else', effused a reviewer in the *New York Daily Tribune*. 'Its golden coach, sleek horses, plumed Guardsmen, lavish decor, milling spectators, solemn rites, gleaming relics, velvet-and-ermine peers, and beribboned Royalty look like a Cecil B. De Mille dream world.'[93] In noting the film's resemblance to Hollywood spectacle, the comment was at odds with the moral seriousness that characterized most self-representation in the British media. Such self-representation did not include the idea that Britain mounted Hollywood spectacle—on screen or on the streets of London.

---

[92] *Sunday Express*, 14 June 1953.
[93] *New York Herald Tribune*, 9 June 1953.

When Richard Dimbleby reflected on the Coronation, he made a contrast between American dynamism and British tradition that reversed Hollywood representations of British–American relations. Hollywood's version of Britishness, preoccupied with aristocracy, hierarchy, and traditional institutions, portrayed Britain as picturesque, quaint, staid, or moribund, contrasted explicitly or implicitly with American dynamism. In Dimbleby's account, however, this was a contrast that provoked considerable envy among Americans: 'Visitors from abroad who were in London on Tuesday were envious of everything they saw, and none more so than the Americans—a race of such vitality but so lacking in tradition—who know that they must wait a thousand years before they can show the world anything so significant and so lovely.'[94]

Dimbleby's concern with the reception of the Coronation by Americans was shared by much of the British media. Although British–American relations were by no means such an important theme in Coronation reporting as the modernized imperial identity signified by the Commonwealth, they were the next most widely covered international story, and featured far more prominently than British relations with Europe. Coronation year produced an array of contradictory narratives about British–American relations, and even those stories that endorsed the 'special relationship', emphasizing friendly and familial ties between Britain and America and common culture and ancestry, generally displayed anxiety about Britain's declining prestige and subordinate place in such a relationship.

Dimbleby's contrast between American vitality and British tradition, and his judgement that Americans were envious of British heritage, were widely echoed in the mainstream British media. Whether they were in London as tourists, visitors, or official guests, or at home watching broadcasts, or writing articles for American publications, Americans were portrayed as conforming, more or less closely, to what the *Daily Mail* reported as the 'bubbling enthusiasm' of Mr Raymond C. Appleyard of New York visiting London for the Coronation, and the verdict he had 'boomed' on the occasion: 'the British are the greatest people in the world'. His countrymen at home, the *Mail* suggested, might not be quite so carried away, but they could not help but be impressed, since they would see the whole thing on 'video'.[95]

Many of these stories drew on the idea of English-speaking peoples, showing America, like Commonwealth countries, as youthful in contrast to the 'old country', and invoking the common origins and ancestry of Britons and Americans. The *Daily Mail*, under the headline 'The Family Sends

---

[94] Dimbleby, 'My Coronation Commentary', 83.
[95] *Daily Mail*, 3 June 1953 and 4 June 1953.

Loyal Greetings', published a number of 'special messages' from Commonwealth Premiers. A message from Harry S. Truman, former President of the
United States, asserting that 'the two nations have been friends for more
than 135 years', appeared at the bottom of the same page, incorporating
America into the 'family'.[96]

Although the Coronation symbolized a main difference between Britain
and the American Republic, this was discounted in reporting in which
Americans were made to resemble Commonwealth citizens as loyal subjects
of the Crown. The *Daily Express* referred to the numbers of Americans
visiting London for the occasion as a 'Transatlantic pilgrimage', and reinforced this metaphor in its comment that 'Their attitude to the Queen is
more like that of loyal and devoted subjects than of inquisitive tourists out
to see a show'. It also developed the theme of familial ties, in which
Americans were portrayed as of British origin:

The roots of millions of Americans are here in these islands. When the Coronation is
over, many will set forth to see the villages and country towns where their ancestors
lie buried. There is a common heritage, in the soil and traditions of Britain, which
will withstand any malicious efforts which may be made to split Britons and
Americans asunder.[97]

American devotion to the monarchy, as well as envy of British heritage, was
portrayed in a cartoon on the following day, showing an American woman
admonishing her husband: 'Stop, Elmer, stop! You're dreaming that un-
American dream again.' Both are sitting with Coronation souvenir programmes on their knees, and Elmer's dream is of a Coronation procession,
with Union Jacks and Coronation coach outside 'Manhattan Palace', and a
banner which reads: 'Long Live Her Majesty, Queen Elizabeth of USA'.[98]

This story of American envy was used to counter anxieties about declining British prestige, especially as reflected in American attitudes to Britain.
Raymond C. Appleyard's verdict on the British as 'the greatest people in the
world', reported in the *Daily Mail*, was put in opposition to that of an
American reporter who, before the Coronation, had written of Britain as a
nation of lazy loafers (a verdict with which the *Mail* did not always
disagree). On this occasion, the paper argued that 'Everest has given the
lie to this falsehood', and that the Coronation, as vouched for by Mr
Appleyard's enthusiasm, 'could only spring from the heart and soul of a
country alive and vibrant with energy and tradition'.[99] Other Americans
journalists were recruited by the British media to affirm the Coronation as a

[96] *Daily Mail*, 29 May 1953.
[97] *Daily Express*, 25 May 1953.
[98] *Daily Express*, 26 May 1953.
[99] *Daily Mail*, 4 June 1953.

symbol of Britain's rejuvenation. Malcolm Muir, an American writer for *Newsweek*, in a particularly fulsome tribute in the *Daily Telegraph*, noted not only that the Coronation provided 'new insight into the mastersprings of Britain's greatness', and that 'we who come from a relatively young country can now better understand why England is so proud of her traditions', but also that 'what has taken place . . . is a sweeping and evidently deep-rooted rebirth of the spirit of England'.[100]

Anxieties about British–American relations were a recurrent theme in Coronation year. Controversy over the use of American security checks on a British civil servant working at the United States Air Force depot in Burtonwood was fuelled by the idea—apparent when American troops were stationed in Britain in the Second World War—that Britain was being subjected to an American 'invasion'. A Trade Unionist commented: 'We are not as yet an occupied country; we are not a subjugated people, and we will not be treated as such by the Americans or anybody else.'[101] Attacks on Britain by Senator McCarthy meant that only two weeks before the Coronation a BBC radio broadcast was referring to 'the rift in Anglo-American relations', and 'transatlantic name-calling'.[102] The preparations for the Coronation provided opportunities to mend this rift, and it was American journalism, reported in the British media, that claimed: 'The Coronation is doing more to cement British–American friendship than any single occurrence since the unpleasantness of 1776.'[103] A view of Britain as sober and restrained against the hysteria of McCarthyism was supported by some Americans, who wrote to British newspapers to acknowledge that 'we do have our puerile and barbarous demagogues' and to ask for patience.[104] Stories of ardent American admiration for the Queen and the Coronation ceremony, like stories of hysterical McCarthyism, produced Britain as a mature nation in opposition to America—this time through the idea of American envy of its heritage and history.

The idea of Britain as a mature and responsible nation was produced against America once more in the aftermath of the Coronation, in widespread condemnation of American practices. Reports that the ceremony, as shown on American television, had been interrupted by commercial breaks placed American behaviour in a very different category from that of loyal and devoted subjects of the Queen. To make matters worse, one of the commercial breaks had featured a baby chimpanzee called J. Fred

---

[100] *Daily Telegraph*, 4 June 1953.
[101] *Manchester Guardian*, 21 May 1953.
[102] Clifton Utley, 'The Rift in Anglo-American Relations', *The Listener*, 21 May 1953.
[103] *Daily Telegraph*, 2 June 1953.
[104] *Manchester Guardian*, 22 May 1953.

Muggs—a star of American commercial television—who had been asked his opinion of the Coronation.

Protests at the appearance of J. Fred Muggs represented this exchange between Britain and America as an encounter between high moral serious-ness and the apotheosis of tastelessness. In some accounts, the chimpanzee had even interrupted the most solemn moment of the occasion: the anoint-ing of the Queen, while another break had included a comment from an American suggesting that the Coronation was 'a psychological device to bolster the somewhat shaky empire'.[105] The *New York Times* was quoted extensively in the British media to condemn American practices: 'These were programmes that transgressed the boundaries of good taste again and again . . . The Corporation's [BBC's] magnificent achievement . . . even sur-vived the tasteless embellishments and outrageous behaviour of some of the American networks. Tuesday was British television's day, not America's.[106] Questions raised on the issue in the House of Lords demonstrated how seriously it was regarded. In reply, the Postmaster General represented the incident as a brief hiccough in an otherwise positive story where the Coronation was 'a great source of emotional union and understanding between our two peoples'.[107]

This story once again made the media central to ideas of national life and national identity, showing the British media as sober and responsible in contrast to America's tasteless commercialism. In the same way that the documentary realist style in film earned praise from critics as distinctively British against Hollywood escapism and sensation, an idea of British national television was now produced in contrast to American practices. In a British context the live television broadcast was a marker of progressive modernity. In an American context, the commercial television broadcast became a sign of modernity gone awry. The idea of sober and responsible coverage by the BBC, appropriate to the dignity and solemnity of the occasion, suggested the extent to which lavish display had been successfully sanctified.

In December 1953 a speaker in an Oxford Union debate about the introduction of commercial television in Britain helped to defeat a motion in its favour by introducing his audience to a picture of a baboon, and recalling J. Fred Muggs, the American Coronation chimpanzee.[108] There was some irony in the fact that affirmations of the impeccable taste of British television in contrast to American practices coincided with proposals

---

[105] *Daily Express*, 9 June 1953.
[106] *The Times*, 8 June 1953. American condemnation was also reported in *Daily Mail*, 8 June 1953 and 9 June 1953; *Daily Express*, 10 June 1953.
[107] *The Times*, 17 June 1953 and 24 June 1953.
[108] *Daily Express*, 15 December 1953.

to introduce commercial television in Britain. Opponents of its introduction, like the speaker at the Oxford Union, used the American story to support their case in debates that articulated long-standing fears of the Americanization of British culture, and pointed up the danger of importing American practices into Britain.

Letters in the *Manchester Guardian* referred to the American broadcast exemplifying the 'vulgar disruption of a solemn religious ceremony', and 'the disgusting level of taste to which the domination of business can bring normally intelligent people', while a leading article in the newspaper suggested: 'The contrast between the BBC's treatment of the Coronation and the American has shaken much opinion that, on grounds of theory, was not averse from competition.'[109] Meanwhile advocates of commercial television argued that it would operate to higher standards in a British context.[110] Trading on the taste for American popular culture in Britain, the *Daily Express* simultaneously paid its dues to high moral seriousness, quoting American sources condemning the broadcast as tasteless, and made J. Fred Muggs a minor celebrity in British as well as American popular culture, unfolding his story for the entertainment of their readers.[111] Two years later, in September 1955, commercial television broadcasting began in Britain, and imported many programmes from America.

The volatility of ideas of British–American relations in Coronation year suggests how far anxieties about national decline were registered through perceptions about American power. Was British prestige waning? This question haunted claims of an avid American audience for the Coronation, filled with envy. An American audience for British films had often been seen as desirable because of the huge box-offices American popularity could deliver. But now the popularity of the Coronation in America was used to bolster national pride. It showed that Americans were eager to learn how 'the ancient forms and ceremonies of British history can embody a message for the present time, and become a living witness of the ideals of Commonwealth and Empire'.[112] It demonstrated a British 'come-back' in America, where 'in one week we have won back the full confidence and respect which had been dissipated during the lean years'.[113] Was British power waning? This question also surfaced. In some contexts, the Commonwealth served as a counterbalance to the idea of American power—Leo Amery claiming in Coronation year that its natural resources were far

---

109 *Manchester Guardian*, 11 June 1953 and 15 June 1953.
110 See, for example, the letter columns of the *Manchester Guardian*, 11–20 May 1953.
111 The story of J. Fred Muggs was run in the *Daily Express* from 9 to 13 June 1953.
112 *Manchester Guardian*, 30 May 1953.
113 *Daily Mail*, 10 June 1953.

greater than those of the United States.[114] In other contexts, the idea of English-speaking peoples and the 'special relationship' with America, couched as an 'equal partnership', provided reassurance. The *Daily Mail*, worrying about how Britain could be saved from 'relegation to the category of a second-rate power', took comfort in the idea that 'we appear ready and able again to assume the responsibilities which in the post-war years we seemed so willing to slip off our tired shoulders'. It added that 'Our leadership must be shared jointly and equally with America'.[115]

Ben Pimlott has characterized the mood of Coronation year as one of 'anxious optimism'.[116] Anxieties may have surfaced in conflicting stories about British–American relations, but the Commonwealth was a source of very considerable optimism. Its Coronation homage and loyalty—barely disrupted by colonial wars in Malaya and Kenya—placed Britain at the centre of a world stage. Everest could be claimed as a British or Commonwealth triumph, depending on the context. The willingness to discard traditional imperial identity in favour of a multiracial community of equal nations became a marker not only of liberality and tolerance but also of modernity, and was embellished and exemplified by imagery of a 'people's empire'. The *Daily Express*, the most ardent champion of empire, even went so far as to suggest that 'At no time in British history has she enjoyed the moral prestige which the Commonwealth, including Britain, now commands'.[117] The Commonwealth promised to maintain Britishness as a global identity. For a brief moment, it was celebrated, popular, and widely regarded as important to the future.

[114] *Daily Express*, 25 November 1953.
[115] *Daily Mail*, 6 June 1953.
[116] Pimlott, *The Queen*, 202.
[117] *Daily Express*, 4 June 1953.

5
Colonial Wars

In 1948 an internal memorandum in the BBC commented that the general effect of news about empire highlighting 'sensational and often unfortunate events' might well be, over a long period, to create the impression on listeners 'that the Empire is in a sorry mess'. The writer of the memorandum —J. Grenfell Williams—pointed to a number of 'sensational and unfortunate events' that were likely to create such an impression— 'insurrection in Malaya, a riot in the Gold Coast, a labour disturbance with shooting in British Guiana, a claim for British Honduras'.[1] He could not have predicted the pervasiveness of news of colonial wars in the British media throughout the 1950s. This was a traffic in imagery that threatened to disrupt ideals of equal partnership and a multiracial Commonwealth and to displace them with a wholly different narrative: that of an Englishness threatened not only within empire, but by empire.

By the mid-1950s, scarcely a week went past without listeners—and increasingly viewers—of BBC news hearing of anti-colonial resistance, and British counter-insurgency activity. The war in Malaya (1948–57), that Grenfell Williams noted as one sensational event creating the impression of an 'empire in a sorry mess', coincided with other colonial wars—in Kenya (1952–6) and Cyprus (1954–9). The war in Kenya was particularly widely reported in newspapers and newsreels during the 1950s and represented in a range of feature films. Audience research at the BBC in 1956, undertaken before Suez, found that perceptions of a decline in Britain's position in the world often cited 'trouble spots throughout British territories' as well as 'the fact that every little nation seems to think it can cock a snook at us'.[2]

Colonial war stories maintained the idea of a geographical separation between white and black where racial problems and conflict belonged elsewhere—thousands of miles away. They nevertheless came nearer to home than most other colonial stories because of their threat to the lives

---

[1] J. Grenfell Williams, 12 July 1943, BBC WAC R51/91/5, Talks, Colonies and Dominions, 1947–1954.

[2] 'Pre-broadcast Study of the Public's Awareness and Evaluation of Changes in Britain, both in the Way of Life at Home and in her Position in the World', 1956, BBC WAC R9/10/3 Audience Research, Special Reports, Television. 1956.

of Britons. Much reporting of colonial wars in Malaya and Kenya focused on the fate of white civilians—of whom, in Kenya, 32 were killed by Mau Mau by comparison with 1,819 African civilians.[3] Much reporting in the British media also appealed to the idea of a racial community of Britons— white settler communities that were under siege from the violence of the colonized. Since colonial wars received far more media attention than other forms of anti-colonial resistance, violence was registered as part of the end of empire. But most stories attributed violence to the colonized rather than the counter-insurgency efforts of the British. Indeed, the dominant image of colonial war in Kenya was one of atavistic, bestial violence by Mau Mau.

Colonial wars were a staple theme of empire stories before 1945 when, together with the safari and the mountaineering expedition, they provided narratives of British adventure, their central figure of the adventure hero, and his brave masculine exploits in conquest, exploration, and discovery.[4] Characteristically such stories showed a British civilizing mission, where the British acted to protect 'good' and loyal native peoples, against the insurrection of 'bad' natives, and conflicts were resolved through the restoration of British political and military order. In the nineteenth and early twentieth centuries, the adventure landscape was important to the traffic in images between metropolis and empire. Discoveries made on expeditions needed acknowledgement at home for recognition and were reported through a scientific paper read to a learned body like the Royal Geographical Society.[5] Trophies from safaris were taken or exported to the metropolis to be displayed on walls and floors or—through the work of taxidermists—in metropolitan museums. Popular entertainments and museums sometimes displayed 'natives' as another form of 'trophy'.[6] Imperial identities depended on the exchange between metropolis and empire, as the notion of home was enlarged and dignified through its connections with heroic deeds in far-away places, while these heroic deeds awaited acclamation at home to be legitimated.

---

[3] Brian Lapping, *End of Empire* (London: Granada, 1985), 425–6.

[4] For a discussion of the connections between hunting, mountaineering, and masculinity, see John MacKenzie, 'The Imperial Pioneer and Hunter and the British Masculine Stereotype in Late Victorian and Edwardian Times', in J. A. Mangan and James Walvin (eds.), *Manliness and Morality: Middle-Class Masculinity in Britain and America 1800–1940* (Manchester: Manchester University Press, 1987), 176–98; Peter Hansen, 'Albert Smith, the Alpine Club, and the Invention of Mountaineering in Mid-Victorian Britain', *Journal of British Studies*, 34 (1995), 300–24.

[5] The role of the Royal Geographical Society in providing recognition for mountaineers' ascents is discussed in Peter Hansen, 'Vertical Boundaries, National Identities: British Mountaineering on the Frontiers of Europe and the Empire', *Journal of Imperial and Commonwealth History*, 24 (1996), 48–71.

[6] See, for example, John MacKenzie, *Propaganda and Empire: The Manipulation of British Public Opinion 1880–1960* (Manchester: Manchester University Press, 1984), 97–120; Annie Coombes, *Reinventing Africa: Museums, Material Culture and Popular Imagination in Late Victorian and Edwardian England* (New Haven: Yale University Press, 1994); Ella Shohat and Robert Stam, *Unthinking Eurocentrism: Multiculturalism and the Media* (London: Routledge, 1994), 107–9.

During the Second World War the British media generally obscured divisions and conflicts within empire sufficiently to maintain the dominant image of a diverse but united empire, pulling together against a common enemy. Divisions and conflicts were also obscured at the Coronation, but Coronation year nevertheless produced a good deal of news of 'trouble spots'. It opened with a widely reported story of Kitty Hesselberger and Dorothy Raynes-Simson. Attacked in the sitting-room of their Kenyan bungalow, they had killed three Mau Mau, and wounded a fourth. Their courage and resourcefulness were widely celebrated. The *Illustrated London News* pictured them on its cover with their boxer dog as 'three against Mau Mau', while they were acclaimed in the *Daily Mail* as 'the two bravest women in Africa'.[7] The year ended with a rather different Kenyan story when Captain Gerald Griffiths was court-martialled on charges of shooting Africans in the back. Denying these charges at his trial, he nevertheless found no difficulty in admitting that five shillings was paid in his company to each man who killed a Mau Mau terrorist, and that a scoreboard recording the kills was pinned up at his company's headquarters.[8]

These contrasting stories—one foregrounding masculinity and the other femininity—both involved reworkings of empire imagery. The story of Captain Griffiths's trial suggested the way in which colonial wars were understood as a type of safari, where insurgents became a form of savage wildlife to be tracked and killed. In contrast, the story of Kitty Hesselberger and Dorothy Raynes-Simson reworked a theme that was prominent in narratives of the Indian Mutiny/First War of Independence of 1857.[9] Like these nineteenth-century narratives, it focused on the violence of insurgents and their violation of British domestic sanctuaries representing a domesticated version of empire through female figures. However, where women in narratives of the Indian Mutiny had been represented mainly as passive victims of violation, with some emphasis on rape, Hesselberger and Raynes-Simson were shown as intrepid women who could defend them-selves with guns. Colonial wars in Malaya and Kenya produced no stories that alleged the rape of white women.[10]

Unlike Coronation imagery of world-wide rejoicing, there was little in exchanges of imagery of colonial wars between metropolis and empire that could be acclaimed in Britain. Narratives that reworked the safari threa-tened to show masculine adventure demonstrating British violence and

---

[7] *Illustrated London News*, 17 Jan. 1953; *Daily Mail*, 5 Jan. 1953.

[8] *Daily Express*, 27 Nov. 1953.

[9] For these narratives, see Alison Blunt, 'Embodying War: British Women and Domestic Defilement in the Indian "Mutiny", 1857–8', *Journal of Historical Geography*, 26 (2000), 403–28.

[10] For the way in which the Indian Mutiny was remembered as a barbaric and sexual attack on white women, see Jenny Sharpe, *Allegories of Empire: The Figure of the Woman in the Colonial Text* (Minneapolis: University of Minnesota Press, 1993).

brutality rather than heroism. They were discouraged by the Colonial Office, and a dominant narrative of colonial wars, especially in feature films, moved towards a concern with home fronts and with women. The classic frontier hero of imperial imagery became an increasingly embattled figure in stories that showed white men pinned down in domestic settings, their capacity for action eroded as they defended their homes alongside women. A dominant narrative of colonial wars depicted the British under siege.

When Kitty Hesselberger and Dorothy Raynes-Simson were attacked in their sitting-room, most reporting quoted their comment that their attackers 'came silently like panthers with incredible swiftness'.[11] The siege narrative not only produced imagery of Englishness under threat, but also undermined the modernized imperial identity represented by a multiracial Commonwealth. It showed two versions of the 'people's empire' at war with one another—a racial community of Britons represented by white settlers in Malaya and Kenya against the savage violence of the colonized. Like the safari narrative, the siege narrative evoked the bestiality of the colonized, who were shown in colonial war films like *The Planter's Wife* (1952), set in Malaya, as denizens of the jungle, and in *Simba* (1955), set in Kenya, as primitive savages.[12]

Representations of colonial wars in the 1950s have attracted little attention by comparison with Second World War narratives. Yet *The Planter's Wife* was one of Rank's biggest box-office successes in 1952.[13] The casting of Claudette Colbert, an American star, as heroine fitted government concerns to bring British efforts against Communism in Malaya to American attention, and the Rank publicity release expressed the hope that the film would 'help make the American people as a whole more aware of the part Britain is playing against Communism in the Far East'.[14] At the same time, such casting was also intended to secure commercial success for the film, in both Britain and America, reflecting Rank's designs on the American market, as well as its concern to challenge Hollywood's dominance of British box-office receipts. The choice of Jack Hawkins to play the male lead in *The Planter's Wife* was probably an important factor in its box-office success in Britain. In the year after its release he was voted the most popular male star in Britain, while Dirk Bogarde, who played

---

[11] See, for example, *Daily Express*, 5 Jan. 1953.

[12] *The Planter's Wife* (Ken Annakin, 1952); *Simba* (Brian Desmond Hurst, 1955).

[13] Vincent Porter, 'Methodism Versus the Market Place: The Rank Organisation and British Cinema', in Robert Murphy (ed.), *The British Cinema Book* (London: British Film Institute, 1997), 126.

[14] Quoted in Susan Carruthers, *Winning Hearts and Minds: British Governments, the Media and Colonial Counter-Insurgency 1944–1960* (London: Leicester University Press, 1995), 112.

the male lead in *Simba*, had displaced Hawkins as most popular male star in Britain by 1955.[15]

Like *Men of Two Worlds* (1946), these films drew on a traditional repertoire of racial imagery, but made domestic order and harmony key signs of 'civilization'—'away' as well as at 'home'. Continuing to portray Britain's 'others' in an 'elsewhere' defined by empire and characterized by exoticism, primitivism, or barbarism, empire films provided one of the most important sources of visual imagery of racial difference in Britain in the 1950s. Despite Commonwealth migration to Britain in this decade, immigration was not widely represented visually.[16] A number of black people in Britain in the 1950s discovered that white British reactions to them were informed by imagery of colonial wars. Beryl Gilroy, who came to Britain from British Guiana after the Second World War, comments that the memory of the Mau Mau, always linked with atrocity stories, lingered on long after the Kenyan war was over. She was asked, 'Are you a Mau-Mau lady?'[17] The 15-year-old daughter of a family in Liverpool, who was born in England and had never travelled outside it, was told in a shop to 'go back to Mau Mau land'.[18]

Racial imagery in empire films not only maintained the idea of racial boundaries between empire and metropolis, but also increasingly developed themes about the unbelonging of the colonized in empire. British policies involved much displacement of the colonized. In Malaya, families were separated and communities destroyed when their villages were burnt down by the British as a form of 'punishment' for aiding or harbouring terrorists, and refusing to co-operate with the security forces. In Kenya, thousands of Kikuyu men were forcibly detained, their settlements were razed, and 'secure villages' constructed for women, children, and the elderly.[19] By the end of 1955, over a million people had been resettled in Kenya in nearly 900 'villages'.[20] British feature films, however, showed displacement and family separations not as a consequence of British policies, but of the violence of the colonized.

The incorporation of white women, and the modification of the masculine adventure story, with its imagery of conquest, power, and action, by the

[15] See Andrew Spicer, 'Male Stars, Masculinity and British Cinema 1945–1960', in Murphy, *The British Cinema Book*, 144–53. Dirk Bogarde also starred in *The High Bright Sun* (Ralph Thomas, 1965), a colonial war film, set in Cyprus.

[16] Of the few films of the 1950s that featured blacks in the metropolis, *Pool of London* (Basil Dearden, 1950) showed a black seaman as a transient visitor, while *Sapphire* (Basil Dearden, 1959) associated black migrants with crime and low-life. Television documentaries provided a main visual image of immigration as a social problem. See Chapter 6.

[17] Beryl Gilroy, *Black Teacher* (London: Bogle L'Ouverture Press, 1976), 121.

[18] *Daily Mirror*, 15–17 Mar. 1955.

[19] See Lapping, *End of Empire*, chs. 3 and 9.

[20] John Newsinger, 'A Counter-Insurgency Tale: Kitson in Kenya', *Race and Class*, 31 (1990), 65.

introduction of familial, romantic, and domestic imagery, meant that home, family, and community were constructed as white. Whites enacted and resolved their conflicts and divisions through relationships to colonized men, but the colonized were associated with family and relationships mainly through their connections with whites. A new figure appeared in the filmic adventure landscape—the native child or baby who was motherless and orphaned, and cared for by whites. This child demonstrated white capacity for family and community against the incapacity of the colonized. Home, family, and community thus became much more important as markers of difference between colonizers and colonized. As white women were increasingly incorporated into imagery of empire, the development of a narrative of unbelonging for the colonized was reinforced by the continuing absence of colonized women from most imagery.

The siege narrative of colonial wars in the 1950s took a different trajectory from Second World War narratives, which increasingly expelled the home front, civilians, and women. The incorporation of white women in colonial war films conformed to developments in the 1950s empire genre more generally, and produced a more intimate sense of British identity in empire than pre-1945 films that showed homosocial communities of soldiers or administrators. In empire, white women could symbolize national weakness and vulnerability, or intrepidity and courage. But they also gave narratives of colonial wars a more liberal register, suggesting British commitment to welfare, development, and peace-keeping—a moral endeavour undertaken in very difficult circumstances. Despite these gestures towards a 'people's empire', colonial war narratives produced a very different image from the wartime 'people's empire'. Diverse peoples were no longer united against a common enemy. Instead a racial community of Britons was under siege in empire.

The Safari

The safari provided a recurrent image of an imperial adventure landscape in the nineteenth and early twentieth centuries. It was a landscape of vast expanses, rich in wildlife, offering an image of Edenic cornucopia, but one that involved a journey into territory that was dangerous as well as exotic. The taming and conquest of the wild was an important image of white manliness, and although a cast of local labour was often employed—both to support expeditions, and as 'extras' in films that represented them—they were never associated with adventure. As 'porters' they made a common journey, carrying loads as well as performing a wide range of other tasks, including cooking and serving food, pitching tents, tracking, and bearing hunters' trophies back to camp. In this domestic role they substituted for women. Safaris sometimes employed local women, but the emphasis on such expeditions as masculine meant that there was increasing reluctance to employ women porters after the 1890s.[21]

Increasingly the loads that porters carried included cameras. Photography was widely used in the nineteenth and twentieth centuries to produce images of safaris, and the conventions of picturing the big-game hunt portrayed the white man, and sometimes the white woman, dominating and taming nature.[22] The hunter was shown above a dead animal prone on the ground, sometimes with a foot on its neck, sometimes sitting on it. After 1918, as emphasis on preservation of wildlife developed, the photograph not only provided pictorial evidence of the trophy, but became itself a trophy, with safaris mounted in order to 'shoot' animals with cameras.[23] The quest for safari photographs and film produced a small sub-genre of safari literature, where film-makers described the hazards of their expeditions, as well as the majesty of the wildlife they had shot with cameras.[24]

Kenya was strongly associated with wildlife and the adventure of the safari, and most pre-1952 filmic images established the idea of Kenya through shots which showed the landscape, as it was described in *Where No Vultures Fly* (1951), as 'teeming with wild animals, free and unafraid'. By 1953, the major image of Kenya was one of fear, showing a savage and murderous place where no white settler could feel secure against the atavistic Mau Mau. But the theme of Kenya as safari landscape did not disappear, and in some contexts produced the Mau Mau as a form of savage wildlife to be tracked and killed. George Adamson, like the fictional Robert Payton in *Where No Vultures Fly*, was a game-park warden in Kenya. Adamson was later celebrated for his role in preserving wildlife, and especially lions, together with his wife Joy Adamson. *Born Free* (1966)—a film based on an account of Elsa, the lioness, by Joy Adamson—received a royal command performance, like *Where No Vultures Fly*.[25] In 1953, however, Adamson had a different safari on his mind. He recorded in his diary:

Started off this morning with full safari. Found the gang had headed SE. Followed up. Off saddled and away again about 3.00 pm. Found another boma recently

[21] For the employment of women as safari porters, see Kenneth Cameron, *Into Africa: The Story of the East African Safari* (London: Constable, 1990), 23–4, 75.

[22] James Ryan, *Picturing Empire: Photography and the Visualisation of the British Empire* (London: Reaktion, 1997), ch. 4.

[23] For a discussion of 'preservation' and 'conservation' policies see MacKenzie, 'The Imperial Pioneer and Hunter', 183–6; John MacKenzie, *The Empire of Nature: Hunting, Conservation and British Imperialism* (Manchester: Manchester University Press, 1988).

[24] See, for example, Cherry Kearton, *In the Land of the Lion* (London: Arrowsmith, 1929); Stirling Gillespie, *Celluloid Safari: Filming Big Game from Cape to Cairo* (London: Blackie, 1939).

[25] *Born Free* (James Hill, 1966).

vacated, part of freshly killed ox and a little posho (maize flour). Hard ground, difficult spooring... Sent 5 men along the west side of the stream to look for tracks, while the main safari took the eastern side... After about 2 miles Kikango killed a Mau Mau.[26]

Adamson was recruited, with his game scouts, to help the police and Home Guard in the campaign against the Mau Mau.[27] His adaptation of the language of hunting—safari, tracking, spooring—was a more general feature of how the war was perceived in Kenya. The Colonial Office, following complaints that operations against the Mau Mau were being portrayed as a game hunt, became concerned about the sporting and hunting metaphors used in Kenyan press releases.[28] But, as the trial of Captain Gerald Griffiths demonstrated, this was an idea of the war in Kenya that had wide resonance among the military. In 1953, Fenner Brockway, a leading figure in the anti-colonialist left in Britain, and a Labour MP, noted that the Devonshires' regimental journal depicted the campaign 'as though it were a hunt for game'.[29] Frank Kitson, a district military intelligence office in Kenya, later recorded that 'one cannot savour the full thrill of the chase until one hunts something which is capable of retaliation'.[30] In Malaya, as in Kenya, the army drew up league tables of killings. John Newsinger, analysing military memoirs of British soldiers who served in the colonial war in Malaya, comments that they tell 'a story of colonial warfare waged by young white men in an exotic locale against an alien foe: the very stuff of the imperial imagination'.[31] A number of these memoirs explicitly portray the conflict as a hunt for a particularly dangerous kind of game, where the trophies returned to camp were not elephants' tusks, but human ears and hands.[32]

The safari narrative, when transposed onto colonial wars, portrayed anti-colonial resistance in terms of bestiality, but also showed British responses to insurgency as brutal and violent. When Fenner Brockway alleged, in the wake of the court-martial of Griffiths, that British troops regarded the campaign as a safari, the British press moved to condemn such attitudes. *The Times*, for example, differentiated between the legitimacy of stern pursuit of Mau Mau and the illegitimacy of 'the atmosphere... of an afternoon's shoot or a pig-sticking match'.[33] However, there was generally

[26] Quoted in Adrian House, *The Great Safari: The Lives of George and Joy Adamson* (London: Harvill, 1993), 205–6.

[27] Ibid. 203.

[28] Carruthers, *Winning Hearts and Minds*, 152.

[29] Quoted ibid. 174.

[30] Quoted in Newsinger, 'A Counter-Insurgency Tale', 67.

[31] John Newsinger, 'The Military Memoir in British Imperial Culture: The Case of Malaya', *Race and Class*, 35 (1994), 48.

[32] Ibid 58.

[33] *The Times*, 22 Dec. 1953.

scant attention to British atrocities in the British media, by comparison with those of insurgents. Susan Carruthers shows the muted response in Britain to a series of photographs published in the *Daily Worker* in 1952, the first of which showed a British marine holding up the head of a Chinese insurgent in Malaya. No other newspaper reproduced the photographs, and the story was not taken up by other media.[34] Government investigations found that this was a practice sanctioned by the military on the grounds that it allowed identification of enemy dead, and the Cabinet ordered that hands must be cut off, not heads.[35] In contrast, atrocities by insurgents were a main focus of many colonial war films and news stories. A newsreel on the Lari massacre in Kenya in 1953, for example, warned viewers that the story contained 'harrowing scenes', but stated that 'British Pathé News believe that only by showing them can the situation be brought into its true perspective'. It depicted burnt corpses, and shots of African children in hospital, including a close-up of a child's burnt face.[36]

Although the Colonial Office discouraged the use of safari metaphors for British military action in Malaya and Kenya, some feature films were less inhibited about making connections between colonial wars and big game hunts. *Safari* (1956)—a British–American production—began with the image of the violation of a domestic sanctuary by the Mau Mau, and their murder of a white child.[37] The father of the murdered child—Ken Duffield (Victor Mature)—is a white hunter who is hired to take a British aristocrat and his wife on safari. The story of how he tracks and kills Mau Mau in revenge for his son's death is thus merged with the story of the big game hunt.

In using a contemporary colonial war to embellish the safari adventure story of a journey into exotic and dangerous territory, *Safari* drew on the Hollywood film *Mogambo* (1953), which starred Clark Gable as Victor Marswell, the American white hunter hero.[38] Like Duffield, Marswell is hired to take a British man and his wife on safari. His journey involves the rescue of a wounded British official who has been attacked by Africans—providing an obscure reference to the African territory depicted as a British colony where there is anti-colonial resistance, while suggesting that this is a domain where American power now holds sway. Through the figure of Marswell, *Mogambo* constructs American masculinity as resourceful and courageous, for Marswell not only saves the lives of the British official, but those of both main British characters. By the time these British characters—

---

[34] Carruthers, *Winning Hearts and Minds*, 110–11.
[35] Lapping, *End of Empire*, 172.
[36] 'The Mark of the Mau Mau', *Pathé News*, 11 May 1953.
[37] *Safari* (Terence Young, 1956).
[38] *Mogambo* (John Ford, US 1953).

Donald and Linda Norberry (Donald Sinden and Grace Kelly)—appear, Marswell has mastered the natural world through hauling wild animals from a trap, as well as making a sexual conquest through his encounter with an American woman, Eloise Kelly (Ava Gardner). As he tells Eloise to try and behave decorously when the British arrive, Britishness is already coded as potentially stuffy and out of place in a safari landscape. This is confirmed when the first words that the British man utters are: 'I've got the beastliest ringing in my ears.' Shortly afterwards he faints.

White women are important characters in *Mogambo* and *Safari*, both of which show white hunters forming liaisons with the wives of the British men they take on safari. Incorporating white women and romantic plots into British empire imagery offered a way not only of modernizing narratives, but also of modernizing the empire genre, through reference to Hollywood models. Increasingly, in their attempt to produce exciting adventure, these films merge the imperial adventure landscapes of safari and colonial war. This was a development also apparent in the Hollywood film *Something of Value* (1957) on the Kenyan war.[39] A central image in this film is the violation of domestic sanctuaries as British women and children are threatened and murdered in their homes by Mau Mau. But its central character—Peter McKenzie (Rock Hudson)—is a white hunter who is shown on safari both with his black African friend, Kimani (Sidney Poitier), and later with his white wife, Holly (Dana Wynter), on honeymoon. After the Mau Mau attack on his home Peter undertakes a different safari, when he helps the police to track the Mau Mau in the forest and ambush their hide-outs. Since Peter is peace-loving and denounces racism, and since part of his purpose in tracking Mau Mau is to restore his friendship with Kimani—by now their local leader—the film produces an image which manages to associate white hunters recruited to kill Mau Mau with white benevolence. However, through an opposition between Peter and Joe Matson, a white farmer who is aggressively racist and warlike, the Hollywood film, unlike British films on Kenya, also shows the torture of Mau Mau detainees.

Despite the extent to which colonial wars could be merged with safari narratives, a consistent aspect of most British imagery was the representation of violence and brutality as attributes of the colonized. It was the Hollywood film *Something of Value* that showed the torture of Mau Mau detainees, prompting Peter to suggest: 'We're not such a big jump away from being savages ourselves are we?' Stories of British violence only acquired some prominence in the media in 1959, when it was revealed that 11 Kikuyu detainees at Hola detention camp had died as a result of

[39] *Something of Value* (Richard Brooks, US 1957).

beatings, while many more were seriously injured, and that the deaths had originally been blamed on 'infected water'. They prompted Enoch Powell to criticize his government: 'We cannot say, "We will have African standards in Africa, Asian standards in Asia and perhaps British standards here at home."'[40] While torture at Hola produced widespread condemnation in Britain, British representations rarely suggested any collapse of the boundaries between whiteness and savagery. When they did show white violence this was generally represented as necessary for the maintenance of order, the protection of the vulnerable, or self-defence, against the bestial violence of the colonized.

Little England

'In Malaya', the *Daily Mail* noted in 1953, 'three and a half years of danger have given the planters time to convert their previously pleasant homes into miniature fortresses, with sandbag parapets, wire entanglements, and searchlights.'[41] The image of the home as fortress and a juxtaposition of the domestic with menace and terror was central to many British media representations of colonial wars in Malaya and Kenya in the 1950s. The repertoire of imagery deployed in the *Daily Mail* for the 'miniature fortress' in Malaya was extended to Kenya, where it noted wire over domestic windows, guns beside wine glasses, the charming hostess in her black silk dress with 'an automatic pistol hanging at her hip'. A newsreel report showed Mrs Joan Severn at home in Nairobi with a gun by her side as she read her children a bedtime story.[42] Imagery of violence in colonial wars often converged on a common theme: the threat to an Englishness symbolized by the idea of home.

In contrast to stories that merged contemporary colonial wars with the safari, these images conjured up a 'little England' in empire under threat. Here men were not engaged in expansive adventure, exploring vast territory. They were pinned down in domestic settings, their action confined to the perimeters of their bungalows or homesteads. In place of imagery of the manly outdoor life involved in camping, the focus was on domestic interiors in imagery that was characterized by a moral seriousness absent from the colonial war/safari story.

The domestication of the frontier is particularly apparent in the elaboration of domestic detail to signify Englishness. In newspaper reports of Dorothy Raynes-Simson and Kitty Hesselberger killing three Mau Mau in

---

[40] Quoted in Carruthers, *Winning Hearts and Minds*, 267.
[41] *Daily Mail*, 26 Jan. 1953.
[42] 'Assignment Mau Mau', *Pathé News*, 7 May 1953.

Kenya, photographs and text reconstructed the moment of attack—the women in their lounge, one cracking a Christmas nut against a background of Christmas cards arranged on the mantelpiece, both close to the radio listening to the nine o'clock BBC news.[43] These scenes of domestic order became images of Englishness under siege. The *Daily Express* commented on the Kenyan interior: 'The house is warm with the comfort of good books and nice things—if you don't brood on the bullet hole under the old Dutch clock. This could be Carshalton instead of No Woman's Land.'[44] The *Daily Mail* noted the 'warm Kenya sun beating down on a lovely English-looking garden...It might have been Worcestershire or Herefordshire in deep summer. The Mau Mau terror has been poised to strike at their homestead—any British homestead—for months. They were not afraid.'[45] Newspaper reports of the murder of a Kenyan farmer and his doctor wife credited them with building 'a little corner of Somerset in the foothills of the Aberdare mountains', and juxtaposed the 'huge panga knives' used by their attackers against 'their English-looking lawn'.[46]

In the early twentieth century, the idea of 'little England' was often associated with hostility to empire, and 'little Englander' was a term used for those who supported the idea that Britain should focus on domestic concerns and spurn involvement with foreign adventures. It was in the context of anxieties about national weakness, provoked by the British–Boer war (1899–1902), that G. K. Chesterton, in a symposium of papers by the Patriots' Club, advocated a return to 'our ancient interest in England' as opposed to 'our quite modern and quite frivolous interest in everywhere else', in tracing the 'error in our recent South African politics'.[47]

An emphasis on 'little England' was associated with fears of national decline, and developed between the wars, when colonial rule was contested, particularly through the Irish War of Independence and the rise of Indian nationalism. This was a period when, as Chris Waters observes, 'Britons were reinvented as members of an essentially unassuming nation, a quiet, private and ordinary people defined by their modesty, kindness to others, loyalty, truthfulness, straightforwardness and simplicity.'[48] Before 1939,

[43] See, for example, *Daily Express*, 5 Jan. 1953; *Daily Mail*, 5 Jan. 1953; *Illustrated London News*, 17 Jan. 1953.

[44] *Daily Express*, 7 Jan. 1953.

[45] *Daily Mail*, 5 Jan. 1953. Some newspapers reported that Dorothy Raynes-Simson was South African, but this did not disrupt the connections made between images of a peaceful home and garden and Englishness.

[46] *Daily Mail*, 26 Jan. 1953.

[47] Quoted in Martin Wiener, *English Culture and the Decline of the Industrial Spirit 1850–1980* (Cambridge: Cambridge University Press, 1981), 60.

[48] Chris Waters, '"Dark Strangers" in our Midst: Discourses of Race and Nation in Britain, 1947–1963', *Journal of British Studies*, 36 (1997), 211. See also Alison Light, *Forever England: Femininity, Literature and Conservatism Between the Wars* (London: Routledge, 1991).

however, although used as an anti-imperialist image, 'little England' also coexisted with notions of imperial identity, and could be invoked to characterize white settler communities creating English homes and gardens in Kenya or Rhodesia.

In imagery of colonial wars, these homes and gardens became a symbol of embattled Englishness. *The Planter's Wife* is framed by sequences of violence against British planters' homes in Malaya. Beginning with shots of 'bandits' crawling on their bellies from the night-time jungle, killing a planter as he emerges in pyjamas from his bungalow, and then setting fire to it, the film ends with a long sequence of another planter's bungalow under siege on the following night by 'bandits', who cut the barbed wire, occupy the sandbagged parapets, and shoot the searchlights. The main theme of *Simba* is similarly the threat to white homes, families, and settlement in Kenya from the Mau Mau. At the outset of the film, there is the promise of a white romantic plot, as Allan Howard (Dirk Bogarde), on a visit to his brother from England, is met at Nairobi airport by Mary Crawford (Virginia McKenna). But their arrival at Allan's brother's farm is disrupted by the sight of police outside, and they enter a domestic interior reduced to chaos by a Mau Mau attack, where Allan's brother has been murdered.

This juxtaposition of the happy anticipation associated with familial and domestic imagery against murder and chaos—the promise of brothers' reunion, as well as romance, against the devastation of the Mau Mau attack—is characteristic of a film that sets the ideas of white home, family, and community against African violence. The film ends with a scene of conflagration as this farm, now run by Allan, is attacked by a black mob. Although the army arrives in the nick of time to save the day in *The Planter's Wife* and *Simba*, neither film shows much confidence that the British can continue to maintain control for very long.

The domestic world on which such images focused was also ambivalent—one which marked the civilization of the British against those who resisted their rule, but which also threatened to feminize British masculinity. In newspaper reports where civilians were the focus of interest, there was an elaboration of domestic detail which suggested male vulnerability as well as female. Pyjamas frequently figured as a sign of unpreparedness for attack, as in reports from Kenya where men were killed 'eating their New Year's Day dinner in pyjamas and dressing gown' and 'in pyjamas, taking his nightly last look round with his 32-year-old wife'.[49]

Feature films took up this imagery. Like *The Planter's Wife*, *Simba* opens with the murder of a white man in pyjamas. It shows an expansive

[49] *Daily Express*, 3 Jan. 1953 and 26 Jan. 1953.

landscape, familiar from *Where No Vultures Fly*, where an African man is riding a bicycle along a path in daylight. Dismounting to investigate cries for help, and propping his bike against a tree-stump, he discovers the white man, lying seriously wounded on the ground. Instead of ministering to him, the African proceeds to butcher him. The hero of *The Planter's Wife* is first shown in his bedroom, wearing pyjamas, awakened from sleep by a telephone call—the police checking on his safety—introducing both the notion that his home is under threat and the domestic setting in which he is pinned down during the main action of the film, defending it against attack. As a man of action, he is nevertheless closely associated with this domestic world as he turns the bungalow into a military fortification, and it is this bungalow which is the scene of battle. It is perhaps in an attempt to align him more closely with the traditional adventure hero of imperial films—whose struggles and conquests were in vast territory—that he is shown at daybreak, crawling under the barbed wire which surrounds his home in an attempt to save his rubber trees from attack. However, even in this sequence, he is still in sight of the bungalow.

In Kenya a particular symbol of threat to homesteads was the disloyal servant—an image, like the violated domestic sanctuary, that had been prominent in narratives of the Indian Mutiny.[50] In a Kenyan context, the fear was that servants might be members of the Mau Mau or let them into the employer's home. The distinction between different black masculinities represented in *Simba*—the tamed and domesticated 'houseboys' and the atavistic and murderous Mau Mau—is blurred by white anxieties about whether 'houseboys' will betray them. These are anxieties which are shown as justified. There remains a distinction between loyal and disloyal servants since the film shows an attack on a white farm where some servants let the Mau Mau in, while others are themselves murdered. Mary's mother, whose husband is killed in this attack, has defended her servants against charges of possible disloyalty by arguing that they are 'one of the family', reinforcing the idea of an intimate betrayal.

Richard Dyer has noted the rigid binarism around which *Simba* is organized, where white stands for modernity, reason, order, and stability, and black for backwardness, irrationality, chaos, and violence.[51] But it is also worth noting that stability and order are represented mainly through images of home, so that treachery is associated with the domestic, not the political or military. The master/mistress and servant relationship stood for the wider authority and control of white over black, as well as the idea that black men could be tamed. This scene of white domestic order invaded by

[50] See Graham Dawson, *Soldier Heroes: British Adventure, Empire and the Imagining of Masculinities* (London: Routledge, 1994), 91.

[51] Richard Dyer, 'White', *Screen*, 29 (1988), 49.

black violence through treachery from within could be read as a particularly telling instance of the violation of a domestic sanctuary signifying loss of imperial power.

Domestic order not only became a central image of Englishness, but also frequently the only resolution narratives offered to the conflicts they portrayed. *The Times*, reviewing *Simba*, wondered whether there was something distasteful in making a record of the violence and bloodshed in Kenya and 'tacking on to that record a conventional film love story'. Reviewing *The Planter's Wife*, it commented: 'the film is sensible enough not to pretend that, because husband and wife kiss and make up, all is well in Malaya'.[52] The imperial adventure, although occasionally incorporating themes of heterosexual romance, had formerly been resolved mainly by the restoration of British military and political order. Now, as these comments suggest, domestic order not only became a central image of Englishness, but also the resolution to war narratives. *The Planter's Wife* explores the impact of colonial war in Malaya through the damage it has done to the relationship between Liz and Jim Frazer (Claudette Colbert and Jack Hawkins). The main sign of this damage—Liz's decision not to return to Malaya if she goes back to England to take their son to boarding school—is part of her recognition of the breakdown of their marriage as a result of the war. As she acts to save her marriage and stay by Jim's side, the movement of the film is towards a reconciliation between husband and wife, and the final image—where they stand together happily united on a station platform, waving farewell to their son, who is being taken back to England by friends, and not by Liz—seals the notion of reunion. But the wider conflict in Malaya remains unresolved.

The image of the plucky white British woman, staying on despite the danger, was common to media representations of colonial wars in this period. The *Daily Mail* celebrated a planter's wife in Malaya in 1948: 'Mary...will not leave her husband because his labourers are watching for the first signs of weakness in the master's bungalow. Her departure would be so construed and could panic the coolies who are openly anti-Communist and fearful of the Communist-led guerrillas.'[53] The idea of the strong and intrepid female in empire had been mobilized by women to insert themselves into narratives of nation in a range of Victorian and Edwardian writing, and imperial adventure featuring heroines had been produced in literature for girls, although not in the British empire film genre.[54] Imagery of colonial

---

[52] *The Times*, 19 Sept. 1952.
[53] *Daily Mail*, 16 Aug. 1948.
[54] For explorations of colonising women's attachment to imperial identity as one amongst a complex range of responses to empire, see Margaret Strobel, *European Women and the Second British Empire* (Bloomington: Indiana University Press, 1991); Nupur Chaudhuri and Margaret Strobel (eds.), *Western Women and Imperialism: Complicity and Resistance* (Bloomington: Indiana University Press, 1992); Inderpal Grewal, *Home and Harem: Nation, Gender, Empire and the Cultures of Travel*

wars drew on two connected images: the adventurous and pioneering imperial woman, and the formidable and forceful emancipated woman.

The armed British woman, shooting to kill, however taboo in a Second
World War context, was a recurrent image of female courage in colonial
wars, and female violence where white women killed non-white men
became a sign of strength rather than pathology. In *The Planter's Wife*, Liz
shoots a 'bandit' in the compound of her bungalow against the background
of domestic animals and washing-line, drawing a gun from the folds of her
dress. Later, when her home is attacked at night, she is behind a machine-
gun. But Liz stands for vulnerability as well as courage and, after she has
killed the 'bandit' in the compound, she swoons and is taken up in the arms
of Jim, who carries her into the bungalow. When Kitty Hesselberger and
Dorothy Raynes-Simson were attacked in the sitting-room of their Kenyan
bungalow and shot three Mau Mau, there was some comment on their
vulnerability as well as heroism—their friends as well as themselves 'all
living alone and all middle-aged or old'.[55] But news reports also compared
them both to the heroines of westerns and to male heroes of the Second
World War: 'If you are a woman of Kenya out on the lonely farms in the
black zones you wear slacks all day, you have a holster on your hip, and you
look like the heroine of a Western film . . . Britain! Do you remember the
way you reached out in love and praise to the men of Arnhem, embattled
and faithful? Today give your hearts to the women of Kenya. They are
surrounded by menace but they do not budge.'

Return to England represented retreat—in the language of the popular
press, 'scuttling'. In *The Planter's Wife*, although Jim agrees to let Liz stay
on, she also successfully persuades him to 'take some leave'. In *Simba* the
notion of return is also coded as 'taking leave' as Mary's father is shown
telling his wife about his plans to do so over their midday meal, just before
he is murdered in a Mau Mau attack. Neither film portrays a return,
celebrating instead the courage of those who stay on.

Domesticated images of colonial wars work to show an Englishness that
is shared by white settlers in empire and white English in metropolis.
Increasingly it is England that stands for order against empire—a safe
haven away from the violence of colonial wars. 'A year in England—

(London: Leicester University Press, 1996); Clare Midgley (ed.), *Gender and Imperialism* (Manchester: Manchester University Press, 1998). For the incorporation of girls and women into imperial
adventures in literature for girls, see Kathryn Castle, *Britannia's Children: Reading Colonialism
Through Children's Books and Magazines* (Manchester: Manchester University Press, 1996); Richard
Phillips, *Mapping Men and Empire: A Geography of Adventure* (London: Routledge, 1997). For
representations of the intrepid imperial female in the post-1945 period, see Wendy Webster,
'Elspeth Huxley: Gender, Empire and Narratives of Nation, 1935–64', *Women's History Review*, 8
(1999), 527–45.

[55] *Daily Express*, 7 Jan. 1953.

Peace!' Mary's mother pronounces in *Simba* when her husband tells her of his plans to get in a manager for the farm. England itself is imagined as a domestic sanctuary, against empire and former empire.

Moral Strength

'Are we being weak?' is a question posed by Allan Howard in *Simba*. His question is prompted by the death of his brother, David, at the hands of the Mau Mau: 'Was David just hiding weakness with a whole lot of ideals?' Allan is aware that David, like Mary, was the friend of Peter Karanja (Earl Cameron)—the Westernized doctor who is the central black African character in the film. He is also aware that David, Mary, and Karanja all shared liberal views on race. Allan's question associates weakness with these interracial friendships and liberal views. His use of 'we' suggests one version of a 'people's empire'—a racial community of Britons—constructed in opposition to another: a multiracial community.

Allan's question receives no clear answer in *Simba*, but the connections it expresses between ideals of Commonwealth, notions of weakness, and struggles over the meanings of white masculinity were common to many representations of colonial wars. Emphasis on stern action against insurgents in Malaya and Kenya threatened to portray a hyper-masculine Britain engaged in oppressive and brutal action, as in the safari narrative. Emphasis on a 'little England' under siege threatened to show a feminine nation—weak and vulnerable.

White settler communities in Malaya and Kenya also raised the question of weakness when they voiced demands for stern action and a show of military strength. 'Get Tough or Get Out of Malaya', the *Daily Mail* headlined the demands of planters and tin-miners in Malaya, who, it reported, regarded British colonial administrators as 'disciples of optimism and inaction' who were 'letting Malaya slip away when a real show of strength could keep it more unified'.[56] Through such demands white settler communities presented themselves as defenders of the nation against a feminized metropolis that was betraying the cause of empire.

Demands for stern action looked back to authoritarian versions of empire—British power, militarism, manliness, and the values of hierarchy and obedience. In 1952, there was considerable publicity for new 'get tough' policies in both Malaya and Kenya. The appointment of General Sir Gerald Templer as the new High Commissioner in Malaya was widely seen, and often welcomed in the British media, as a sign that Britain would

---

[56] *Daily Mail*, 16 Aug. 1948.

get 'tough'—stressing his 'brilliant record as a tough fighter', and his 'tough policies', like cutting food rations to villages that had supplied food to 'bandits'.[57] The *Daily Express*, praising Templer's impact on the war at the end of 1952, connected this with the reputation of a major icon of strong masculinity and leadership, attributing to Winston Churchill the decision 'that Britain was not going to scuttle from Malaya'.[58]

In the same year there was also considerable publicity for the stern measures taken in Kenya, which included 'collective punishment' for Mau Mau attacks on white civilians—mass evictions, the forcible detention of suspected Mau Mau in compounds behind barbed wire, and public executions. A mobile gallows, built by the Public Works Department, ensured that prisoners could be executed in their home districts and, by the end of the war, over 1,000 rebels had been hanged.[59] There was some anxiety in London about the scale of executions. Winston Churchill advised that 'care should be taken to avoid the simultaneous execution of any large numbers of persons', to avoid the impression of brutality and mass executions.[60] But, when 'shows of strength' were justified as a response to the vulnerability of white settlers—both male and female—the metropolis could be represented as masculine in relation to white settler communities.[61]

Many representations of colonial wars emphasized British moral rather than military strength, incorporating aspects of a 'people's empire'—welfare and peace-keeping—into their stories. In *Simba*, moral strength is represented particularly in the figure of Mary Crawford, Her work, although similar to that of Catherine Munro in *Men of Two Worlds*, bringing the benefits of Western medicine to Africans, is represented as prompted by her concerns for Africans, emphasizing her compassion rather than her expertise or authority. Within a film that is concerned to represent a variety of white attitudes to Africans, it is Mary who speaks for a position broadly in line with the Commonwealth ideal of a multiracial family of nations. Moreover, she acts as an assistant to Karanja—and in many ways her image is aligned with Karanja's rather than with a British man.

In *Windom's Way* (1957), moral strength is represented through the hero, Doctor Windom (Peter Finch), who also brings the benefits of Western medicine to local people, and is among the most exemplary figures ever to

[57] 'Templer Gets Malaya Job', *Pathé News*, 21 Jan. 1952; 'Templer Gets Tough', *Pathé News*, 3 Apr. 1952.

[58] *Daily Express*, 2 Dec. 1952.

[59] Newsinger, 'A Counter-Insurgency Tale', 70.

[60] Ibid.

[61] 'Collective punishment' was justified in some reports as an appropriate response to the murder of Commander Meiklejohn and the serious wounding of his wife in their Kenyan home. But news stories also reported charges of British brutality, connected not with the policy of 'collective punishment', but its implementation — women and children rounded up by dogs, and men carried off in chains. See *Daily Express*, 25 and 26 Nov. 1952; *Daily Mail*, 27 Nov. 1952.

appear on British screens.[62] His is a benevolence that knows no limits: completely self-sacrificing, utterly dedicated to the welfare of local people. *Windom's Way*, set on an island somewhere in 'the East', depicts a post-colonial situation on this island where the British no longer rule. It was generally understood as a film about Malaya and was released in the year of Malayan independence.

The film begins by offering a spectacle of benevolence, showing Windom surrounded by devoted villagers. Their childlike gratitude is apparent in the opening sequence when the camera follows Windom into a local house where he delivers a baby and places it in its mother's arms. It is an image of a benevolent father-figure later reinforced by the local mayor, who, in a ceremony welcoming Windom's wife to the island, calls Windom 'our beloved Doctor', and declares 'our affection for the doctor who has done so much to bring health and happiness to this village'. Like Mary, Windom speaks for a liberal position, opposing the sacking of a local plantation worker—Jan Vidal (John Cairney)—and, as the plantation troubles escalate, treating wounded strikers who have been fired on by police. Like Mary, he embodies multiracialism through his medical work—assisted by Anna Vidal (Natasha Parry)—a local woman who is Windom's head nurse and Jan's sister, and is devoted to Windom.

Despite suggestions of closeness between Mary and Karanja, Windom and Anna, the romantic plots in both *Simba* and *Windom's Way* are between whites. 'Miscegenation'—usually envisaged as relationships between white women and black men—was a major theme of immigration discourse in the period, expressing the fear of a collapse of boundaries between black and white. But although a number of British films, including empire films, showed interracial romances and sex between white men and non-white women, the portrayal of white women in empire films—long subject to censorship—did not venture into the territory of interracial romance, maintaining the boundaries between colonizers and colonized.[63] Karanja may be aligned with Mary in terms of their shared liberal perspective on race, their shared medical work, and their friendship, but he functions in the plot as a character through whom Mary and Allan work out their emotional conflicts, and finally resolve them.

While *Simba*, as well as *The Planter's Wife*, shows white communities beleaguered through the threat posed by the violence of the colonized, in

---

[62] *Windom's Way* (Ronald Neame, 1957).

[63] British films of empire that showed relationships between white men and non-white women included *The Seekers* (Ken Annakin, 1954); *Outcast of the Islands* (Carol Reed, 1951). A number of Second World War films of the 1950s also showed such relationships, including *The Purple Plain* (Robert Parrish, 1954); *The Black Tent* (Brian Desmond Hurst, 1956); *The Wind Cannot Read* (Ralph Thomas, 1958). I am grateful to Mike Paris for providing these references.

Windom's Way there is more emphasis on the community of the local inhabitants, which initially is shown as simple, innocent, and in need of Windom's guidance, protection, and leadership. Their own mayor is endearing, but comically ineffectual. With no trace of irony the film shows Windom explaining to the authorities the villagers' need for 'independence' as he acts as their spokesperson and mediator. Windom's way is, however, defeated. Portraying a civil war erupting in a post-colonial context, the film depicts a local community destroying itself, in a movement that is represented from Windom's perspective as one from childlike simplicity to violence.

Both Mary's and Windom's liberal positions are constructed sympathetically within films that gesture towards multiracialism. Windom's position is shown in opposition to the casual brutality of the white British plantation owner, Patterson (Michael Horden), who has ordered Jan's sacking, called in the police, and who tells Windom, 'This is the East, not Harley Street.' In *Simba* Mary's position is shown sympathetically through Allan's increasing respect for it. Initially, Allan's attempts to avoid weakness are expressed through his suspicion and hostility towards Karanja. This hostility brings him into conflict with Mary, who tells him: 'You're beginning to hate Africans aren't you?' But the film moves to show Allan's increasing regard for Karanja and, in the final sequence of the film, Mary and Allan come together over the body of Karanja, ministering to him as he lies dying in Mary's arms. Mary and Allan provide a white substitute family for Karanja, while the *Pietà*-like tableau of Mary holding Karanja's dead body provides a Christian resonance to the image.

Karanja, like Kisenga in *Men of Two Worlds*, represents a version of masculinity that had previously received little attention in British empire films—the Westernized or Western-educated African. Richard Dyer suggests that he embodies the possibility of blacks becoming like whites, and that the anxiety surrounding this possibility is the foundation of *Simba's* narrative.[64] If a fear of the collapse of boundaries between black and white characterized representations of Westernized men, however, this is resolved in *Simba* by giving Karanja a narrative of unbelonging. Like *Men of Two Worlds*, which attributes a crisis of identity to Kisenga when he is disowned by other Africans as a white man, *Simba* attributes a crisis to Karanja. Karanja's father disowns his son: 'He's not my son. He's a white man.' A sense of unbelonging in both black and white worlds is articulated by Karanja when he speaks about whites to Mary: 'Nobody quite trusts me—you know that', and when he speaks of Africans to Mary and Allan as he is dying: 'They didn't listen.' Unlike Kisenga, however, Karanja is

---

[64] Dyer, 'White', 51.

associated neither with primitivism nor effeminacy, but with the moral strength of courage and independence.

When Mary and Allan come together over Karanja's body, they are surrounded by devastation. Karanja's death is at the hands of the Mau Mau, led by his father. His death at the hands of fellow-Africans marks the defeat of his position by primitivism. The group formed by Mary, Allan, and Karanja are surrounded by the wreckage of Allan's farm, burnt by the mob. Similarly in *Windom's Way*, the position that Windom represents is defeated. As the plantation troubles escalate, the 'good native' is consigned to the past and all those who represent innocence and devotion to Windom are killed. Jan's defection to the rebel army is shown as a betrayal of Windom's trust, and Jan himself provides a chilling image of this movement, telling Windom: 'We shall now fight for our freedom with cold steel.' Powerless in the face of these developments, Windom is held captive by the rebel army, which kills the local mayor. As the film ends he is chastened by his discovery of the folly of involvement in local politics, and local people are on the brink of violent war. The lesson that Windom learns is that local people must be left to fight it out, and the best that can be done is to provide medical aid to treat the worst casualties.

The final image of *Windom's Way* shows Windom's wife Lee (Mary Ure) cradling a local boy—Kosti (Kurt Sigenberg)—in her arms. Like other colonial war films, *Windom's Way* offers reconciliation between Windom and Lee as its only resolution. In early sequences, Windom is convinced of their incompatibility, seeing Lee as a sophisticated and fun-loving woman who brings an expensive and prolific wardrobe to a remote island. But Lee's increasing willingness to care for local children is used in the film as a sign of her growing maturity. In an early sequence, Kosti explains to Lee that since his parents are long since dead, Windom has adopted him: 'Doctor my father now. You be my mother Lady Doctor.' In the final image of the film, Lee has taken on the role of mother. When Windom resolves to leave the island, it is Lee who dissuades him. Her argument about the value of his medical work affirms their reconciliation.

Children were new figures in the empire filmic genre, providing emotive images of Britons caring for the colonized. The Hollywood film, *Something of Value*, ends with an image of Peter carrying Kimani's baby son in his arms, resolving that he will take him home, where his sister can raise him with her children. This extends the theme of interracial friendship that runs through the film and echoes the circumstances of Peter's own childhood, for his own close and enduring friendship with Kimani was forged when, on his mother's death, Peter had been reared by Kimani's mother. Kimani's son, however, has been orphaned as a result of British violence.

British films never attribute the displacement of children, or their family-less state, to British violence. *Simba* like *Windom's Way* ends with an image of a child, focusing on a close-up of his face. Early sequences are careful to establish that Joshua is a victim of Mau Mau violence—familyless, aban-doned, and wandering aimlessly around Allan's farm because, as Allan's servant tells him: 'He belongs to nobody. No family at all Bwana. Mau Mau kill all of them.' As Joshua walks towards the form of family group that is offered by the figures of Mary, Allan, and Karanja, this is an image that also acts as a final reminder of African incapacity for family and community. Joshua's image has been read in different ways—Richard Dyer suggests that he symbolizes 'the only possible hope for the future', while Christine Geraghty sees him as 'the symbol of the uncertain future', used in the film 'to restore a liberal position that has been thoroughly defeated'.[65] Like Karanja, he is a victim not of British but of African violence. This final image, as well as Karanja's death, tended by Mary and Allan, contrasts white capacity for relationship and community with black incapacity.

Images of white couples caring for local children showed a continuing moral role for the British despite the limitations of their power, emphasiz-ing moral rather than military strength. They spread a patina of multi-racialism over the idea of moral strength. But it is a thin patina within imagery that generally constructs a benevolent racial community of Britons against the violence of the colonized—one that provides a hierarchical, paternalistic image where whites act as parents to the colonized. Multi-racialism was rarely portrayed as moral strength and might serve as a sign of weakness.

The first programme of a BBC television series entitled *We the British, Are We in Decline?* (1956) explicitly portrays colonial wars as signs of weakness. Indian independence, which, by the mid-1950s, had become a model of orderly withdrawal, is shown in the programme as 'retreat with dignity', taking place 'in an atmosphere of friendship and goodwill', against shots of the Indian and Pakistani Independence Day ceremonies. This is contrasted with shots of colonial wars in Cyprus, Malaya, and Kenya, described as 'ignominious retreat'. The narrative voice of Christopher Mayhew comments on how strongly British rule and influence is now challenged, suggesting that 'the mere fact of fighting sets back our prestige in world affairs, and is attacked as colonialism by our enemies'. These shots of Cyprus, Malaya, and Kenya become symbols of loss of power, national decline, and a sign of Britain on the defensive, especially when compared to the rise of the Soviet Union and the United States.[66]

---

[65] Ibid. 53; Christine Geraghty, *British Cinema in the Fifties: Gender, Genre and the 'New Look'* (London: Routledge, 2000), 126.

[66] *We The British Are We in Decline?*, BBC Television, 24 Apr. 1956.

In its investigation of whether Britain had declined as a world power, *We the British* tells a narrative of empire and loss of imperial power, and makes no use of ideas and images of the Second World War, or of the Cold War. Reporting of colonial wars sometimes identified insurgents in Malaya as Communists and the war as 'anti-Red', and there were also attempts to connect the Mau Mau with Communism. Even so, those who fought the British in Malaya were as likely to be labelled 'bandits' as Communists. *We the British* locates colonial wars within the history of empire rather than the contemporary Cold War.

The programme nevertheless maintains an emphasis on British moral strength associated with the Commonwealth. Moving from what it calls 'the pessimist's picture', identifying colonial wars as signs of 'ignominious retreat', it puts the case for considering the transition from empire to Commonwealth as a sign of Britain's continuing moral and political strength and finds grounds for considerable optimism in the Commonwealth. Defining a country's political and moral strength as the 'ability to give a lead and be followed because people respect it', it suggests that many British people, looking at Britain's position in the world from this perspective, would deny that Britain was in decline because of 'our immense moral influence in the Commonwealth'. Professor Carrington, who was Professor of Commonwealth Relations at the Royal Institute of International Affairs, rehearses this view, defining the Commonwealth as 'quite a different kind of thing' from empire—characterized by co-operation and free exchange and discussion, not power. This vision of co-operative harmony was very far removed from imagery of anti-colonial resistance and British counter-insurgency activity.

In showing colonial wars as signs of 'ignominious retreat' and national weakness *We the British*, like Allan's question in *Simba*, exposes some of the tensions involved in representations of colonial wars. 'Get tough' policies could support the idea of British military strength against the suggestion, voiced particularly by white settler communities in Kenya and Malaya, of a weak and feminized metropolis. But, like the safari narrative, they threatened to associate Britishness with brutality. An emphasis on moral strength, despite a patina of multiracialism, drew on a traditional repertoire of racial imagery, constructing Britishness against a racial 'other'.

The idea of moral strength, attributing benevolence to the British, also drew on traditional ideas about a civilizing mission, but, as decolonization gathered pace, this was in the context of an increasing sense of loss of power. *Simba*, released in 1955, portrays a time on the cusp between British resolve to stay on and maintain colonial rule and the end of empire. In *Windom's Way*, Windom moves from confidence that he can influence events to a realization of impotence in a film that shows the British as increasingly powerless. As civil war erupts in a post-colonial context, violence can no longer be contained by British rule. Both films suggest a benevolent role that outlasts empire—one where the British continue to take responsibility for medical welfare and attempts at peace-keeping. But they also suggest that decolonization is a disaster for local people, plunging them into chaos and violence.

North West Frontier

North West Frontier (1959) could be regarded as the culmination of many of the developments in colonial war films of the 1950s. It features women and children as prominent characters, focuses on a white community under threat, and incorporates domestic imagery, including tea-drinking ceremonies, a parasol, and the feeding of a baby. The violence of the colonized is a major theme, but its British soldier hero is dedicated to peace-keeping. Its heroine is shown as nurturing and benevolent, but also emancipated and independent, and she kills the villain with a gun. The film ends with the hero and heroine coming together to care for an Indian baby—walking into the distance, carrying a baby-basket.

Despite its Indian setting, reviews of *North West Frontier* made more reference to America than to the British empire. The *Sunday Times* saw the film as an amalgam of the empire genre and the western—'a bit of *The Drum* and *Lives of a Bengal Lancer* and *The Four Feathers*...a dash of *Stagecoach*'.[67] Most other reviews were clear about which genre predominated, naming the film 'an Eastern Western' and a 'mighty and exciting epic Wild Western'.[68] The *Daily Mail* thought that 'this north-western eastern can claim to be the first genuine British Western'.[69] The reviewer in the *Star* considered the film 'one of the best Westerns I remember'.[70] In making a western, many reviewers judged that the British film industry had successfully staked a claim to match or outdo Hollywood. The *Daily Telegraph* thought that 'even by Hollywood standards this Rank film is spectacular'.[71] According to the *News of the World*, it showed that 'anything Hollywood can do, they (the producers) can do as well'.[72] The *Daily Herald* announced that 'the sensational thing about *North West Frontier* is that it proves we can

---

[67] *Sunday Times*, 12 Oct. 1959.
[68] *Daily Herald*, 9 Oct. 1959; *Daily Express*, 9 Oct. 1959. Both these reviews called the film an 'Eastern Western'. *News of the World*, 12 Oct. 1959.
[69] *Daily Mail*, 9 Oct. 1959.
[70] *Star*, 8 Oct. 1959.
[71] *Daily Telegraph*, 10 Oct. 1959.
[72] *News of the World*, 12 Oct. 1959.

make epics too', and enthused: 'at last we have beaten Hollywood at its own game'.[73]

The power of American models and the American market to shape the empire genre in film is particularly striking in *North West Frontier*. Hollywood films of the British empire had increasingly merged the genre with westerns, and many post-1945 British films had followed suit. But *North West Frontier* was distinctive as a British empire film widely acclaimed in Britain for its Americanization of the genre. Its director, J. Lee Thompson, had dreamed since childhood of being 'an *American* film director', and moved to Hollywood in the early 1960s.[74] Its makers—Rank—had announced a policy of only producing films that had international entertainment value in 1956 and, in their determination to get films into the American market, had established Rank Film Distributors of America in 1957 to bypass the American distributors.[75] The casting of Lauren Bacall as the heroine, in the role of an American female caught up in a British imperial adventure, was part of this determination, providing the film with the glamour and modernity associated with Hollywood.

Despite the attention to American models and markets, *North West Frontier* is also concerned to translate British rule in India in the Edwardian period into a version of the 'people's empire' of welfare and peace-keeping. Although it depicts colonial war, this is set in the past—ostensibly in 1905—and in India, which had gained independence in 1947. The focus of the story is a British attempt to get a 6-year-old Hindu prince—Kishan (Govind Raja Ross)—to safety, away from Hindu–Muslim conflict, by taking him out of the war-zone on a train. This attempt is led by Captain Scott (Kenneth More), the soldier hero and man of action, but one who is committed to the view that the soldier is there not to kill but to keep order.

Other colonial war films of the 1950s featured the care of young children by white civilians, but Scott's guardianship of Kishan makes him the first soldier hero in the empire genre to engage in childcare. The theme of British welfare is reinforced by an opposition between Scott and Van Leyden (Herbert Blom). Van Leyden is a strong opponent of British imperialism and, as the story unfolds, is revealed not only as a man of mixed parentage—a Dutch-Indonesian Muslim—but also the villain of the film, intent on murdering Kishan, and threatening the lives of all those on the train. The sequence where he is positioned behind a gun justifying his intention to kill Kishan to other passengers is intercut with shots of Scott promising Kishan that he will teach him how to be an engine-driver. The *Manchester Guardian* commented that the representation of Scott

---

[73] *Daily Herald*, 9 Oct. 1959.

[74] Steve Chibnall, *J. Lee Thompson* (Manchester: Manchester University Press, 2000), 278.

[75] See Porter, 'Methodism Versus the Market Place', 129.

embodying 'amiable toughness' and 'unprecedented urbanity' made him 'an Imperialist very much to the modern taste'.

A benign nostalgic image gives *North West Frontier* a light mood, and its soldier hero is capable of considerable light-heartedness even in the face of repeated attacks by Muslims on the train. His lusty singing of the Eton boating song is taken up by the sound-track, so that renderings of the song, like these attacks, punctuate the dangerous journey. Another central character—the steam-train—reinforces this benign nostalgia. The train is called *Empress of India*, but affectionately known as Victoria by its driver. It needs careful attention at all times to coax it into life, and is represented as ancient even in the Edwardian period in which the film is set.

Steam-trains were increasingly becoming objects of nostalgia in Britain in the 1950s, as railway lines—especially small branch lines—were closed under modernization schemes and diesel trains were introduced. Films like *The Titfield Thunderbolt* (1952) celebrated the efforts of a village community to save its branch line from small-time crooks bent on closing it, and endowed steam with romance against prosaic coaches and cars.[76] The crooks in the film are coach-owners and their advocacy of modernity is associated with watching westerns on television as they dream up their schemes to vandalize the railway. In *North West Frontier* such nostalgia, far from being produced against the western, is incorporated into it. Victoria occupies the place of John Ford's *Stagecoach* (1939) as hordes of Indians, mounted on horseback, descend to attack it, and are successfully beaten off.[77]

By placing Victoria at the centre of its imagery, *North West Frontier* evokes the atmosphere of popular children's stories of the 1950s where other brave little engines undertook dangerous and difficult journeys. Victoria, like Thomas the Tank Engine and Henry the Green Engine in the popular series by the Reverend W. Awdry, is anthropomorphized. Its driver, Gupta (I. S. Johar), as well as Captain Scott, addresses it/her, pats her, and praises her. Gupta claims that 'Victoria talks to me, I understand her language'. Scott calls her 'the old girl'. Gupta comments on one of her many eccentricities—a habit of whistling unprompted—'she shouts too much when she is happy'. With such a central character the empire is necessarily benign.

The British and especially their steam-trains win the affection of faithful Indians, especially Gupta, the engine-driver. But although *North West Frontier* superimposes modernized imagery of welfare and peace-keeping onto a story of Edwardian colonial war in India, it makes little attempt to provide a multiracial image. Neither of the Indian soldiers under Scott's

[76] *The Titfield Thunderbolt* (Charles Crichton, 1952).

[77] Earlier examples include *The Overlanders* (Harry Watt, 1946); *Diamond City* (David MacDonald, 1949); *Bitter Springs* (Ralph Smart, 1950); *The Seekers* (Ken Annakin, 1954).

command has a speaking part, while Gupta is a character from the 1930s empire genre—faithful and comic. Steve Chibnall notes that the actor I. S. Johar who played Gupta had been imprisoned by the British after the Second World War.[78] Even so, Johar made something of a speciality of comic renderings of Indianness in the British empire genre of the late 1950s, providing a similar performance in another Rank film—as Bapu, Harry Black's faithful bearer, in *Harry Black* (1958).[79] Within a context where so much attention is given to American models and audiences, there is no move to give the colonized history or identity. Despite its light-hearted elements, moral strength and seriousness in *North West Frontier* belongs to the British, not to the Indians.

This moral seriousness is provided by discussions of war and empire, which punctuate the film as much as attacks by marauding Muslims and renderings of the Eton boating song. The party on the train is international, comprising not only Van Leyden, Gupta, and the Indian soldiers under Scott's command, but also Mr Bridie (Wilfred Hyde-White), secretary to the British governor, Lady Windham (Ursula Jeans), the wife of the British governor, Mr Peters (Eugene Deckers), a continental European arms dealer, and Catherine Wyatt (Lauren Bacall), Kishan's American governess. Of these, Lady Windham is perhaps the strongest supporter of the imperial project, declaring in the face of criticism that 'Half the world mocks us, and half the world is only civilized because we have made it so'. While the film does not wholly endorse this verdict, its benign atmosphere ensures that critics of the British empire win no arguments. Whatever they may say, their actions do them little credit. Van Leyden's ambition to kill Kishan hardly recommends his views on the empire, which are ardently anti-British.

The most serious moment of the film takes on an end of empire resonance. The train halts at a station, and the outcome of Hindu–Muslim conflict is shown—a massacre of people who had been on a refugee train fleeing the communal violence. As first Scott and then Wyatt step down on to the station platform to inspect the scene, it is represented from their perspective. The camera lingers on the image. Scott steps over bodies piled up on the station platform. There is a close-up of a blood-soaked body. The camera moves to bodies hanging out of carriage doors and windows. As Scott returns to the train, Wyatt insists on making her own investigation, against Scott's advice, to find out whether anyone is still alive. She steps over piles of bodies, and goes inside first one carriage, and then another to find tiers of bodies inside. Her gleaming white dress is set against the scenes of carnage. There is scarcely any movement, except for vultures circling. There

[78] Chibnall, *J. Lee Thompson*, 210.
[79] *Harry Black* (Hugo Fregonese, 1958).

is virtual silence on the sound track, disturbed only by the sound of insects buzzing, and the cries of vultures. The image resonates with the communal violence and massacres prompted by Indian partition in 1947.

As Wyatt emerges from the scene of massacre, she provides a distinctly maternal figure for an adventure landscape, cradling an Indian baby in her arms. Her independent action is endorsed by Scott, who admits that he was wrong about the possibility of survivors of the massacre. Her rescue of the Indian baby provides an obscure reference to Indian motherhood, as she tells her fellow passengers: 'He was completely hidden. The mother had covered him with her body.' It is through this baby that Indian communal violence brings the British passengers and the American woman together. Most do not have family connections—Wyatt is a widow, Mr Bridie lives alone, Scott is a soldier—and they represent a range of different attitudes to the imperial project. But they are connected by their horror at the violence of Indians and their consequences. Lady Windham tells Wyatt: 'That was a very courageous thing to do, my dear.' Mr Bridie provides the baby with a basket, and together they improvise a feeding device out of one of Windham's gloves. Scott names the baby 'Young India'. Although British military and political order is restored at the end of the film, when Scott successfully delivers the passengers to a place of safety and completes his mission by handing over Kishan to his guardians, the final image shows Scott emerging from the train, putting one arm around Wyatt and the other around the baby-basket. The erasure of the figure of the colonized woman, who is present in the film only in Wyatt's words, demonstrates Indian incapacity for community, and white connectedness.

Mr Peters and Van Leyden stand outside this connectedness. But Wyatt is incorporated into a distinctively imperial community, comprising not only Scott, the imperial soldier hero, but also the British governor's wife and his secretary. With Scott, Wyatt provides joint guardianship of Kishan's welfare as well as that of the Indian baby. When Van Leyden overcomes the British soldier hero in a fight on the carriage-roof, it is Wyatt who takes a gun and kills him—so saving Scott's life. This demonstration of common cause with the British against opponents of empire is extended in the final image. Scott and Wyatt carry the baby-basket together. America joins Britain in shouldering the white man's burden.

As an Americanized film of empire, *North West Frontier* thus paradoxically counters fears of Americanization through its plot line. Initially sceptical about the British and their empire, Wyatt is inclined to see them as ninnies who spend all their time drinking tea. The film shows her conversion from this view, her incorporation into the British community on the train, and her developing respect for the British, and particularly for Scott's vitality and resourcefulness. Wyatt produces not only a sense of American admiration for the British, but also a sense of the imperial project as a joint British–American endeavour. There is no evidence that *North West Frontier* was ever shown in India but, had it been, it seems likely that its imagery would have been as offensive to Indians as that in *The Drum*, which, when released in Bombay in 1938, had caused protests which brought the city to a virtual halt for more than a week.[80] Indians had also protested at Hollywood films that celebrated the British empire in the 1930s and 1940s, but by 1959, as Britain's imperial frontiers collapsed, Hollywood was no longer producing such films. If Britain wanted admiration from Americans, it had to portray this in its own productions.

North West Frontier nevertheless extends many developments in the colonial war film of the 1950s. Like other films it emphasizes ideas of welfare but, in transposing aspects of a 'people's empire' onto a story set in the early twentieth century, it is devoid of any elements of multiracialism. The construction of British order against the violence of the colonized is its most insistent theme. Kenneth More's narrative voice informs the audience at the outset that India is 'a country of many religions' where 'men find many reasons for killing each other'. Like the British, loyal Indians are appalled by such violence. At the scene of the massacre, Gupta tells Scott: 'You know Sahib, sometimes I want to get hold of my people, all my people, and beat their heads together to put a little sense into them.' Only Van Leyden remains a stern critic of the British, attributing the massacre to their policy of setting Muslim against Hindu—dividing in order to rule. But when Van Leyden meets his death at Wyatt's hands and falls from the train into the desert sand, a mounted Muslim Indian rebel, representing the cause Van Leyden champions, stops short only for a minute, registering the body with indifference, and does not dismount.

As colonial wars ended and decolonization gathered pace, the dominant narrative of an orderly and peaceful withdrawal, exemplified particularly by Indian Independence, jostled with another rather different narrative: one which showed decolonization as a disaster for the former colonized. An opposition between British order and disorder in former British colonies could work to suggest empire as a historical burden for the British that had mercifully been lifted, or as a blessing bestowed on people who were naturally disposed to the violence that erupted once the British departed. In either case these narratives displaced anxieties that colonial wars were a sign of an empire in a 'sorry mess'. As empire became a subject of memory and nostalgia, it was claimed as British history and British heritage. In *North West Frontier* the scene of the massacre, and Wyatt's discovery of the Indian

---

[80] Prem Chowdhry, *Colonial India and the Making of Empire Cinema: Image, Ideology and Identity* (Manchester: Manchester University Press, 2000), 28–46.

baby, provides an emotive image of the appalling consequences of the violence of the colonized, evoking memories of the end of empire in India and the communal violence prompted by partition. Scott drives the point home: 'Have a good look and see what happens when the British aren't around to keep order.'

6
Immigration

In 1964, responding to a BBC request for suggestions on radio programmes about the Commonwealth, the Assistant Head of Talks had difficulty in identifying a Commonwealth subject acceptable to the Light Programme audience. He wrote: 'The Commonwealth hardly evokes popular passion, except in a form very near the knuckle: coloured immigration.'[1]

The comment suggests the close link between ideas of Commonwealth and immigration by 1964, and their common focus on the reversal of the colonial encounter through black and Asian migration to Britain. Although the writer feels it necessary to specify that the popular passion the Commonwealth evokes is about 'coloured immigration', these terms had also become closely connected by 1964—almost synonymous. Despite the substantial migration of white Europeans to Britain in the post-war period, as well as some migrant whites from the Commonwealth, the terms 'immigration' and 'immigrant' generally denoted black and Asian persons. In turn, the term 'immigration' was closely connected to the idea of a 'colour problem'—a phrase that was widely used in the British media from the mid-1950s, and which generally needed no explanation to clarify that it signalled a domestic context. Through these series of connections, the Commonwealth, previously associated with a world-wide community—the 'people's empire' of a racial community of Britons, or the 'people's empire' of a multiracial family of nations—acquired a wholly new meaning: domestic problem.

Kathleen Paul has argued that this series of connections was made chiefly by the government. She challenges the government's own self-representation, and the subsequent support this has been given in historiographical interpretations—the view that liberal politicians caved in to the clamour of an illiberal public for immigration control, and were forced to legislate to restrict immigration through the Commonwealth Immigrants Act of 1962 and its successors.[2] Reversing this story, she argues that the government fostered an unfavourable public atmosphere for colonial migrants and, from March 1954, began a deliberate campaign to sway public opinion in

---

[1] Memorandum from Assistant Head of Talks, 12 Mar. 1964, BBC WAC R 51/783/1, Talks, Commonwealth.

[2] Kathleen Paul, *Whitewashing Britain: Race and Citizenship in the Postwar Era* (Ithaca: Cornell University Press, 1997), especially ch. 6.

favour of immigration control. In the British media, immigration control remained a contested issue before 1962. But the series of connections that linked the terms 'Commonwealth', immigrant', 'coloured', and 'domestic problem' was prominent not only in the right-wing press, but in a range of media representations that were anxious to establish their liberal credentials. Within a range of positions adopted, from right-wing to liberal, most converged on two common themes. They identified Commonwealth immigrants as 'the colour problem', while at the same time voicing their strong commitment to maintaining Britain as decent and tolerant.

The idea that Britain had a 'colour problem' was potentially in tension with the idea of its liberality and tolerance. 'Colour bars' and 'colour problems', while sometimes associated with empire, had rarely been connected with a domestic context before 1945. There was some media coverage of a 'colour problem' in seaports like Cardiff and Liverpool, where African and Indian seamen settled, and in 1925 the Coloured Alien Seamen Order effectively converted many African and Indian seamen into aliens by stipulating that they must register as aliens unless they could produce documentary proof that they were British subjects.[3]

Despite this, a 'colour problem' was generally seen as alien to Britain—a view registered strongly in wartime through responses to the US forces stationed in Britain. BBC audience research on 'Changes in the State of British and Public Opinion on the USA' in 1944 reported that the colour bar, as practised by US forces, was widely condemned: 'It should be remembered that it is only within the last two years that many people have actually seen the colour bar in operation, and this has made a profound impression in some quarters . . . The attitude of white American troops to their coloured compatriots was mentioned only to be condemned and used as evidence against the reality of American democracy.'[4] The association of colour bars with the USA was strengthened by events in the 1950s— notably white violence against blacks in Little Rock, Arkansas in 1957.

The new meaning of Commonwealth as domestic problem produced a number of investigations—by sociologists, journalists, television documentary-makers—which attempted to resolve the tension between British liberality and tolerance and a domestic 'colour problem'. Shaped by a tradition of social exploration, these investigations advertised their liberal credentials: one where explorers, drawing attention to social problems, often presented themselves as people with a mission, who could play an educational and campaigning role—engaging the audience's conscience in the idea that

---

[3] See Laura Tabili, *We Ask for British Justice: Black Workers and the Construction of Racial Difference in Late Imperial Britain* (Ithaca: Cornell University Press, 1994).

[4] 'Changes in the State of British and Public Opinion on the USA', 7 Feb. 1944. BBC WAC, Audience Research, R9/9/7.

reform was needed. In the nineteenth and early twentieth centuries, social explorers produced books, reports, journalism, and photography based on their journeys into the unknown in empire and at home.[5] From empire, they brought back accounts and images of fabulous, exotic, or savage peoples, and strange customs, food, clothes, religions. From home, they brought back accounts of the urban poor, involving journeys into another type of 'dark continent'.

Accounts of the white urban poor in the metropolis produced a pattern of associations between class and race, deploying a repertoire of racial imagery which linked 'darkest England' and 'darkest Africa'. Ann Stoler notes that 'strong parallels were made between the immoral lives of the British underclass, Irish peasants, and "primitive Africans" by the eighteenth century, crescendoing in the early nineteenth century when the influx of the Irish amounted to an urban invasion'.[6] Such parallels were explicit in late nineteenth-century literature of social exploration. William Booth called his account of a journey into the East End of London, published in 1890, *In Darkest England and the Way Out* after the title of Henry Stanley's *In Darkest Africa*, and described what he found there as 'colonies of heathen savages in the heart of our capital'.[7] Both in empire and at home in this period, social exploration was often characterized by the language of darkness and the abyss—explorers describing a journey into a hellish nightmare. The urban crowd was associated with fears of unrest and disorder in the metropolis.[8] This pattern of analogies linked topics otherwise divided—class close to home and race belonging to empire. But post-war social exploration of the 'colour problem' made race central to questions about home. Immigrants took the place formerly assigned to the urban poor while the urban working classes, far from being shown as 'heathen savages', were used to represent order and belonging.

Bill Schwarz has suggested another way in which the language of empire came home after 1956. Reviewing the history of white settler communities in empire, he traces a range of connections between empire

---

[5] For the history of social exploration photography see James Ryan, *Picturing Empire: Photography and the Visualisation of the British Empire* (London: Reaktion, 1997).

[6] Ann Stoler, *Race and the Education of Desire: Foucault's History of Sexuality and the Colonial Order of Things* (Durham, NC: Duke University Press, 1995), 125. See also Susan Thorne, '"The Conversion of Englishmen and the Conversion of the World Inseparable": Missionary Imperialism and the Language of Class in Early Industrial Britain', in Frederick Cooper and Ann Stoler (eds.), *Tensions of Empire: Colonial Cultures in a Bourgeois World* (Berkeley: University of California Press, 1997), 238–62.

[7] Peter Keating (ed.), *Into Unknown England 1866–1913: Selections from the Social Explorers* (London: Fontana, 1976), 150.

[8] See Anne McClintock, *Imperial Leather: Race, Gender and Sexuality in the Colonial Contest* (London: Routledge, 1995), 118–22.

and metropolis.[9] Amongst these is the convergence of the language of white settler communities in empire—especially in Rhodesia—and white opponents of immigration in the metropolis, as both identified themselves as beleaguered, vulnerable, and embattled: 'With immigration, the colonial frontier came "home". When this happened, the language of the colonies was reworked and came with it . . . two inter-related sentiments slowly cohered, unevenly and partially. First, whites were coming to imagine themselves as historic victims; and second—commensurably—blacks were believed to be acquiring a status of supremacy.'[10]

Such connections are also apparent in common themes developed in stories of white settler communities embroiled in colonial wars and stories of white communities in Britain where immigrants were settling. Both were shown as beleaguered and vulnerable. Both converged on a common theme: the violation of domestic sanctuaries. The homes and gardens in Kenya that became a symbol of embattled Englishness were replicated in imagery of immigration which focused on internal frontiers—families, homes, streets, neighbourhoods—where the nation was under siege from 'blacks next door'.

Stories of colonial war and immigration made domestic order central to Englishness, setting the idea of white homes against the incapacity of the colonized/immigrants for familial and community life. Both foregrounded the white woman as the guardian of domestic boundaries. The intrepid imperial woman who stood on guard with guns had no counterpart at home, where the white woman was not only the guarantor of boundaries but also a potential entry point for national weakness. 'Would you let your daughter marry a Negro?' was a question raised across a range of media.[11] If black and Asian migration to Britain brought a fear of the collapse of boundaries between colonizers and colonized, black and white, it was particularly through the breaching of this internal frontier that such a collapse was imagined.

As the language of empire came home, it produced an Englishness that was increasingly defined in opposition to empire/Commonwealth. Whether the language of empire shaped social investigations of the 'colour

[9] Bill Schwarz, '"The Only White Man In There": The Re-Racialisation of England, 1956–1968', *Race and Class*, 38 (1996), 65–78; Bill Schwarz, 'Black Metropolis, White England', in Mica Nava and Alan O'Shea (eds.), *Modern Times: Reflections on a Century of English Modernity* (London: Routledge, 1996), 182–207; Bill Schwarz, 'Reveries of Race: The Closing of the Imperial Moment', in Becky Conekin, Frank Mort, and Chris Waters (eds.), *Moments of Modernity: Reconstructing Britain 1945–1964*, (London: Rivers Oram, 1999), 189–207.

[10] Schwarz, 'The Only White Man In There', 73.

[11] Trevor Philpott, 'Would You Let Your Daughter Marry a Negro?', *Picture Post*, 30 Oct. 1954; Colin MacInnes, 'A Short Guide for Jumbles to the Life of their Coloured Brethren in England', in Colin MacInnes, *England: Half English* (London: MacGibbon and Kee, 1961, first published 1956), 25; *Daily Express*, 18 July 1956.

problem' or produced convergence between stories of colonial wars and immigration, it was often used to tell a story of nation as 'little England'. In wartime 'little England', like the 'people's empire', had stood for liberality and tolerance—its decent people continuing with the everyday round was a strong symbol of their quiet courage. Stories of colonial wars and immigration set 'little England' in opposition to a multiracial Commonwealth, emphasizing a domesticated identity—Englishness, not Britishness—exclusive, intimate, private, and white.

Sexual Boundaries

In 1946, the *Lancashire Daily Post* published a letter from an anonymous woman in Ashton-in-Ribble who signed herself 'Annoyed'. She wrote:

What is the real objection to Polish soldiers? I have met several of these men and found them both courteous and interesting and yet any girl showing them politeness and consideration is subject to much unpleasant gossip. How can we in Britain hope to lead the world in peace and build up international goodwill while we continue so to distrust the foreigner in our midst?[12]

The letter identifies a gulf between ideas associated with Britain as a decent and tolerant nation and an anti-alienism that is expressed particularly in 'unpleasant gossip' about white British women's relationships with foreign men. But the men in question are not Commonwealth immigrants, but Polish soldiers who stayed on in Britain when the war was over.

The letter from 'Annoyed' suggests some of the hostility encountered by Poles in Britain after 1945. During the Second World War Beverley Nichols, writing in the *Sunday Chronicle*, had seen Polish men bringing 'new colour and romance to the North', and reported 70 Polish–British marriages.[13] But after the war Polish–British marriages attracted local hostility. The British wife of a Polish man might be told to 'go and live in Poland', while what Nichols had identified as the romance of Polish men was often given a more hostile label: 'Casanova'.[14] Such anti-alienism was forcefully expressed in the *Daily Mirror* in 1948. It carried stories of European Volunteer Workers in Britain (EVWs)—who arrived as a result of a government scheme, initiated in 1946, to recruit people to employment in Britain from displaced persons camps in Germany and Austria. Its editorial was headlined 'Let Them Be Displaced'. 'In taking in Displaced

---

[12] *Lancashire Daily Post*, 10 Dec. 1946.

[13] Quoted in Sonya Rose, *Which People's War? National Identity and Citizenship in Wartime Britain* (Oxford: Oxford University Press, 2003), 257.

[14] Andrew Nocon, 'A Reluctant Welcome? Poles in Britain in the 1940s', *Oral History*, Spring 1996, 81.

Persons wholesale', the paper argued, 'we have had a bad deal. Too many are living or working in some dubious way. Some, no doubt are in the Black Market. They live on our rations—and live very well. They add to our discomfort and swell the crime wave. This cannot be tolerated. They must now be rounded up and sent back.'[15]

The anti-alienism identified by 'Annoyed', and expressed by the *Daily Mirror* in its editorial, was in conflict with the official view of post-war European migrants to Britain which, unlike official views of Commonwealth migrants, identified them not as a domestic problem but as 'suitable immigrants'. Although mainly wanted as flexible and mobile workers, they were also viewed as 'suitable immigrants' because, unlike black men arriving in Britain, they were not associated with the threat of miscegenation.

The Polish Resettlement Act of 1947 was designed to facilitate the resettlement of Poles who had served in the Polish Armed Forces in exile in Britain during the Second World War. Other Polish people arrived as a result of the government's EVW scheme. Having ended the war as refugees, for a variety of reasons—some as a result of a flight westwards to escape the advance of Russian forces, and others as a result of German occupation and subsequent deportation to Germany as enforced workers—people from displaced persons camps were named 'European Volunteer Workers' on recruitment to the British labour market. EVWs were predominantly from Eastern Europe and included a range of nationalities—Ukrainian, Yugoslavian, Estonian, Latvian, and Lithuanian, as well as Polish. However, few Jewish people were amongst those recruited. As Tony Kushner's work has shown, 'In the late 1940s, the British state placed Jewish survivors in the displaced persons camps at the bottom of its desirability lists at a time when it was recruiting labour from this source on a massive scale.'[16]

It was the labour shortage for the programme of post-war reconstruction that prompted these schemes to recruit immigrants and refugees to work in a range of areas where it was difficult to recruit indigenous labour—agriculture, mining, and textiles in particular. The government also recruited Italian men and women to work in mining and textiles, while employers recruited them to make bricks.[17] In the late 1940s road-signs in Bedfordshire, a main centre of brick-making, were in Italian as well as English, acknowledging the numbers that had arrived there since the war. Most immigrants under these schemes were formally aliens under the Aliens

---

[15] *Daily Mirror*, 20 July 1948. I am grateful to Mark Whittaker for providing this reference.

[16] Tony Kushner, 'Remembering to Forget: Racism and Anti-Racism in Postwar Britain', in Brian Cheyette and Laura Marcus (eds.), *Modernity, Culture, and 'The Jew'* (Cambridge: Polity, 1998), 233.

[17] See Terri Colpi, *The Italian Factor: The Italian Community in Britain* (Edinburgh, Mainstream, 1991).

Act of 1905 and its successors, and covered by their provisions, as, for example, in the requirement to report to the police when they changed occupation or address. By 1950, the number of aliens in Britain, at 429,329, had almost doubled from the 1939 total of 239,000. In 1961, just before the passage of the Commonwealth Immigrants Act designed primarily to restrict black and Asian migration from the Commonwealth, the number of aliens resident in Britain— predominantly white Europeans—was larger than the number of those who had arrived from the Caribbean and the South Asian subcontinent.

Irish people—the largest group of post-war migrants to Britain—were never classified as aliens, and so excluded from these figures. Those from Northern Ireland were British—an identity that some strongly contested. Those from the Republic of Ireland continued to be treated as though they had remained in the Commonwealth, even though, once the Republic left the Commonwealth in 1949, they were no longer formally British subjects. Subsequently they were exempted from the restrictions of the Commonwealth Immigrants Act in 1962. Another European group who came to Britain in substantial numbers in the 1950s—Cypriots—were from a country that was still a British colony, and so they too were excluded from the figures for aliens. Cypriots were not always seen as uncontestably white, and studies of immigration in the 1960s variously defined them as 'white Commonwealth immigrants' and as 'coloured Commonwealth citizens'.[18] Irish immigrants, although encompassed in the official view of Europeans as 'suitable immigrants', faced a wide range of exclusions. A common experience remembered by many migrants to Britain in the late 1940s and 1950s—both black and Irish—is the sign on housing for private rental that announced: 'No coloureds, no Irish'. This four-word sign demonstrates some of the complexities of the history of post-war migration, and the multiple racisms involved.

It is significant that the letter from 'Annoyed' criticizing anti-alienism was published in a regional newspaper in Lancashire, which, as a centre of the textile industry, was a county where many EVWs and some Italians were recruited. European migration to Britain was rarely a controversial topic in the national media. In Yorkshire, also a centre of the textile industry, EVWs received some coverage—the *Yorkshire Post* lauding the efforts of EVW women in the spinning department of a Yorkshire textile mill in 1948 whose 'eagerness to help forward the output drive is an example to the rest of us'.[19] *The Times*, which had described EVWs as 'suitable immigrants' in an editorial in 1947, commented on the success of the EVW scheme in

[18] Wendy Webster, *Imagining Home: Gender, 'Race' and National Identity 1945–64* (London: UCL Press, 1998), p xviii.

[19] *Yorkshire Post*, 30 Jan. 1948.

1948 in terms similar to the *Yorkshire Post*—good workers contributing to the output drive.[20]

The view of Europeans as 'suitable immigrants' was widely proclaimed officially. The Royal Commission on Population in its 1949 Report used this phrase to characterize not only EVWs as 'the main source of immigrants under the present schemes', but also the possibilities of immigration from Holland and Italy, as well as continued immigration from Ireland.[21] EVWs were described in a 1947 parliamentary debate as 'ideal immigrants', and as 'first-class people, who if let into this country would be of great benefit to our stock', whose love of freedom signalled 'the spirit and stuff of which we can make Britons'.[22] They were 'suitable' in part because they were a flexible source of labour that could be directed into particular industries where there were labour shortages. As aliens employed on a contract basis, EVWs who refused to accept the job they were allocated could be deported. But their value to Britain was recognized when the Minister of Labour told the House of Commons in November 1948 that 'this is a settlement of a permanent character: these people came here working their passage to British citizenship'.

The possibility that EVW men might intermarry with white British women was canvassed as a positive aspect of EVW recruitment, recommended in a parliamentary debate in 1947 in these terms:

We are suffering from the falling birth-rate of the late 20's and 30's and have no fewer than 200,000 numerically surplus women. I believe that is an unfortunate sociological factor . . . On the assumption that we should take mainly single men, there are the strongest possible reasons for having an infusion of vigorous young blood from overseas at the present time.[23]

Polish men, staying on in Britain under the Polish Resettlement Act, were also seen as offering a vigorous addition to British stock.[24] Under the Resettlement Act, many Polish men were reunited with their Polish wives, while others married a variety of European migrant women, and EVWs married each other or other migrants, in a variety of partnerships: Italian–Irish, Ukrainian–Polish, Italian–Ukrainian.[25] But despite the concerns of 'Annoyed' about 'unpleasant gossip' over white British women's relationships with Polish men, intermarriages between Polish and British, of which

---

[20] *The Times*, 10 Feb. 1947 and 13 Jan. 1948.

[21] Royal Commission on Population (1949) *Report*, Paras. 328, 342 (London : HMSO, Cmd. 7695).

[22] Quoted in Diana Kay and Robert Miles, *Refugees or Migrant Workers? European Volunteer Workers in Britain 1946–1951* (London: Routledge, 1992), 54.

[23] *Hansard*, 29 Feb. 1947, Col. 758.

[24] Robert Miles, *Racism After 'Race Relations'* (London: Routledge, 1993), 159.

[25] Colpi, *The Italian Factor*, 146.

4,000 were recorded at the end of the war, attracted little official concern or coverage in the national media.[26]

The absence of media interest in such marriages was in strong contrast to the identification of intermarriage between black and white as a central feature of the 'colour problem', and a strong focus on miscegenation in media coverage of black migration to Britain. Fears about miscegenation had surfaced in various contexts in the first half of the twentieth century. A newspaper headline in 1906—'tainting the race'—referred to the employment of Chinese seamen and the resulting settlement of Chinese communities in London and other ports, and spoke of the results of interracial mixing between Chinese men and English women as 'swarms of half-bred children to be seen in the district'.[27] The Chief Constable of Cardiff's proposal of a legal ban on miscegenation in 1929, modelled on the South African Immorality Act, referred to the employment of African and Indian seamen, and resulting settlement in ports like Cardiff and Liverpool.[28] Although interracial sex was never made illegal, fears of 'tainting the race' were extended during the Second World War as black British and American soldiers served in Britain.[29]

In the 1950s, such fears intensified—the *Daily Telegraph* suggesting in 1958 that 'what most of us instinctively recoil from is miscegenation'.[30] As Bill Schwarz observes: 'In the England of the 1940s and 1950s the language of miscegenation was the central issue in terms of white perceptions of race, defining the boundaries of England and signifying the inviolate centre which could brook no impurity.'[31]

The 'inviolate centre' which defined the boundaries of England was a white British woman. White men's relationships with black women were rarely a focus of attention. Characteristic questions were those posed by *Picture Post* in 1954: 'Would you let your daughter marry a Negro?', by Colin MacInnes in 1956: 'What of these tales of coloured men corrupting our young girls?', and by the *Daily Express* in 1956: 'Would you let your daughter marry a black man?'[32] All the marriages shown on the ITV documentary *Black Marries White: The Last Barrier* (1964) were between

[26] Sheila Patterson, 'The Poles: An Exile Community in Britain', in James Watson (ed.), *Between Two Cultures: Migrants and Minorities in Britain* (Oxford: Blackwell, 1977), 224.

[27] See John Gabriel, *Whitewash: Racialized Politics and the Media* (London: Routledge, 1998), 58.

[28] See Paul Rich, *Race and Empire in British Politics* (Cambridge: Cambridge University Press, 1990), 130.

[29] See Marika Sherwood, *Many Struggles: West Indian Workers and Service Personnel in Britain* (London: Karia Press, 1985); Ben Bousquet and Colin Douglas, *West Indian Women at War: British Racism in World War II* (London: Lawrence and Wishart, 1991).

[30] *Daily Telegraph*, 2 Sept. 1958.

[31] Schwarz, 'Black Metropolis', 197.

[32] See note 11.

white women and black or Asian men.[33] The presenter of *Mixed Marriages* (1958), an ITV television programme, began with a comment, not a question: 'I think if we were honest with ourselves, that we'd admit it'd be a bit of a shock if we were told that our sister or daughter was gong to marry a coloured man.'[34] In *The Negro Next Door*—a documentary on the ITV television series *This Week*—a white woman in Leeds interviewed for the programme reversed the usual direction of the question, posing it to the narrator, Desmond Wilcox. 'Would you like to see your oldest daughter marry a coloured man?' she asked.[35]

The white woman at the centre of such comments carried a range of meanings: the guardian of national boundaries, the point of entry for national weakness. The classic question—'Would you let your daughter . . . ?' was mainly designed to tease out necessary limitations to white liberal credentials. The white woman who posed the question to Desmond Wilcox in *The Negro Next Door* (1965) answered the question for him, since he remained silent, affirming her discovery of such limitations: 'You would not. I'm reading your face like a book. No, you would not.' Mr Wentworth-Day, introduced as a parliamentary candidate on *Mixed Marriages*, was anxious to deny any liberal credentials. Wentworth-Day asserted that he would strongly advise his daughter against marrying a coloured man, attributed mixed marriages to 'downright sex', and stated that 'no first-class nation can afford to produce a nation of mongrels'. The presenter of the programme—Daniel Farson—distanced himself from this answer. But Farson also distanced himself from another response in the programme from Lord Altrincham, who advocated mixed marriages—an advocacy that, in another context, extended to the suggestion that Queen Elizabeth II's children should make interracial marriages. Farson labelled Altrincham's contribution to the programme another 'extreme view'.[36]

Mixed Marriages was a television programme in the ITV 'People in Trouble' series. Whatever credentials white men claimed through their answers to the questions about their daughter marrying a negro, miscegenation was always presented as a problem. Farson's own verdict demonstrated liberal credentials which had limitations: 'One can be too enlightened about this subject. In fact, I can't honestly say that I am in favour of mixed marriages.' Radio broadcasts offered a range of items on interracial marriages which always identified them as problems.[37] In 1956 a question

---

[33] *Black Marries White: The Last Barrier* (Associated Rediffusion, 1964).

[34] *Mixed Marriages* (Associated Rediffusion, 1958).

[35] *The Negro Next Door* (Associated Rediffusion, 1965).

[36] Ben Pimlott, *The Queen: A Biography of Elizabeth II* (London: HarperCollins, 1996), 312.

[37] See, for example, 'Is this Your Problem?' An Interview with an Indian Man 'Wishing to Marry an English Girl', BBC radio broadcast, 27 Oct. 1955; 'Family Affairs: Discussion on Problems that Partners in Mixed Marriages are Likely to Meet in Britain', BBC radio broadcast, 27 Jan. 1958;

posed on the *Brains Trust* programme was: 'Does the Brains Trust approve of the power invested in magistrates to override parents' wishes and grant permission for a daughter (underage) to marry. Especially should the daughter wish to marry a coloured man.'[38]

Louise Bennett, the calypso performer, has called post-war migration to Britain from colonies and former colonies 'colonisation in reverse'.[39] Stuart Hall writes of the 'tremendous paradox involved', in a context where 'the very moment Britain finally convinced itself it had to decolonize, that it had to get rid of the colonies, the colonized began flooding into England'. But, as the focus on miscegenation suggests, 'colonisation in reverse' also produced a reversal of the familial imagery characteristically used for peoples of the empire and Commonwealth. In royal Christmas broadcasts, the idea of the royal family gathered round the hearth at Christmas was habitually used as an analogy to what Elizabeth II called, in her 1954 broadcast, 'our Commonwealth hearth' with its 'far larger family'.[40] By 1954, the rhetoric of Commonwealth as an equal partnership of races and nations made it clear that this 'larger family' was multiracial.

The idea of family and hearth with its connotations of belonging obtained only when the family stayed outside the boundaries of the metropolis. Their passage to Britain disrupted the idea of a racial separation between metropolis and empire where black people belonged in an empire under British colonial rule. Black and Asian people, making this passage to Britain from the Commonwealth, also made a transition from 'our Commonwealth hearth' to the identity of dark strangers who did not belong in Britain. Although formally British subjects, they were viewed as aliens, while those who were formally aliens, and especially EVWs, were seen as having greater claims to belong. Celebration of a multiracial family, widely used as a metaphor for the Commonwealth, did not extend to a British context, least of all to interracial marriages.

'This Colour Problem of Ours'

Has Britain a Colour Bar?—a BBC television documentary made in the Special Enquiry series in 1955—opens with the narrative voice of Robert Reid, who tells the audience: 'Not for the first time in our history we have a

'Member of the Family: Item on a Coloured Wife who is not Accepted by her Husband's Family and is Considered Responsible for his Death', BBC radio broadcast, 24 June 1962.

[38] *Brains Trust*, BBC radio, 14 Oct. 1956.

[39] Claudia Jones, 'The Caribbean Community in Britain', in Kwesi Owusu (ed.), *Black British Culture and Society: A Text Reader* (London: Routledge, 2000), 49.

[40] Tom Fleming (ed.), *Voices Out of the Air: The Royal Christmas Broadcasts 1932–1981* (London: Heinemann, 1981), 75.

Colonial problem on our hands, but it's a Colonial problem with a difference. Instead of being thousands of miles away and worrying other people, it's right here, on the spot, worrying us.'[41] By the mid-1950s, the Commonwealth was beginning to be associated with the alien not only because it was the source of 'dark strangers' arriving in Britain, but also because such migrants were seen as the cause of a 'colour racial problem' that was otherwise alien to the metropolis. The 'us' that the BBC identified as worried about 'our Colonial problem' when it was no longer thousands of miles away offered a version of nation, as well as of the audience that the BBC addressed, which not only excluded Commonwealth immigrants but was defined against them.

In identifying what it calls 'this colour problem of ours' *Has Britain a Colour Bar?* shifted attention from the title of the programme. Its identification of immigrants rather than colour bars as the problem it addressed was characteristic of post-war social exploration, including television documentaries, and especially those which were concerned to establish strong liberal credentials. Despite some attention to an investigation of white racism in Britain, Reid defined 'this colour problem of ours' as 'the problem arising out of the increasing numbers of coloured people who've settled in this country having come to find work here'. The programme equated the 'immigrant' with black and Asian migrants, not only ignoring European migrants in Britain but also eliding differences between migrants to Britain from diverse continents—Africa, Asia, and the Caribbean—into a common 'they'. It elided differences between whites in Britain into a common 'us', all worried about the 'colour problem'. It thus defined the nation against the figure of the black immigrant.

In the strong bond the programme established between the narrators of the programme and the audience addressed, *Has Britain a Colour Bar?* drew on the conventions of social exploration. The bond between the audience and the narrator of nineteenth- and early twentieth-century social exploration in empire had been primarily racial, with writers like Henry Stanley offering accounts of a journey into unknown and uncharted territory in Africa which introduced the strange peoples of Africa to an audience assumed to be white. The bond between the audience and narrator of social exploration into 'darkest England' had been primarily one of class. The middle-class explorer offered accounts of his or her journey into the world of the urban poor, unveiling sights with which the audience were assumed to be as completely unfamiliar as they were with 'darkest Africa'. Many interwar filmic documentaries that portrayed the white working classes in Britain drew on this convention—their narrative voice addressing a

---

[41] *Has Britain a Colour Bar?*, BBC television, 31 Jan. 1955.

middle-class audience assumed to be unfamiliar with the world they were shown.[42] *Has Britain a Colour Bar?*, which investigated the 'colour problem' in Birmingham, not Africa, nevertheless adopted the conventions of imperial social exploration, establishing a racial bond between the narrator and the audience addressed, bound together by a common concern about 'this colour problem of ours'. The idea that a programme called *Has Britain a Colour Bar?* might be watched by black people in Britain does not surface.

The documentary also drew on social exploration in its images of strange customs and religions. In his opening commentary, Reid announces a question that the programme will explore: 'How do they (black and Asian migrants) fit in to our ways and standards of life, coming, as they do, from places where customs, standards of life, are much different, and, very often, lower than our own?' Reid is no social explorer, and after reminding the audience of the realism of documentary— 'all the people you're going to see tonight are real people, not actors'—he hands over to Renee Cutforth, whose task is to investigate 'what sort of problem does the presence of these people raise in that city' (Birmingham)?

Shown arriving by train to embark on his journey, Cutforth's exploration involves the discovery of strange customs in the heart of Birmingham. Muslims are shown chanting in a mosque and eating curry, which, Cutforth states, 'has a very strong and very un-English smell'. Jamaicans are shown in a pub, knocking on the counter—the normal way, Cutforth states, to get service in Jamaica, but one that is not approved in English pubs. 'Well, let's face it,' Cutforth says, 'they are different. They look different and they behave differently. . . they sound different and their tastes in matters of food are different.'

Has Britain a Colour Bar? earned praise particularly for the 'slice of life' it offered—for its 'thoroughness and boldness', as 'a kind of journalism that for sharpness of impact is out on its own', and as 'first class recording of our history in the making' that was 'candid about colour'.[43] It also earned praise from the *Daily Sketch* for its 'scrupulous fairness' as 'the BBC balanced each blow against the West Indians with a defence of them'.[44] The documentary does not altogether ignore the question of racism in Britain that its title poses. It denies a colour bar but, interviewing a number of white people in Birmingham, finds considerable evidence of what it calls 'colour prejudice' as practised by employers, trade unionists, and estate agents. Its general argument follows the broad lines sketched in by Peter Stone, researching background information as a 'Birmingham diary' in 1954: 'at the national, official level there is no colour bar whatever, but at the local, personal tacit

[42] See, for example, *Housing Problems* (Arthur Elton and Edgar Anstey, 1935).
[43] *Daily Mail*, 1 Feb. 1955; Daily *Express*, 1 Feb. 1955.
[44] *Daily Sketch*, 1 Feb. 1955.

level there is a hell of a lot'.[45] Cutforth's report from Birmingham ends by identifying 'colour prejudice' as a 'very ugly thing', suggesting that 'the cure is up to the ordinary people of this country'.

In developing this argument, the programme establishes its liberal credentials, drawing on a tradition of social exploration to convey its concern with social problems and its aim to play an educative and campaigning role—engaging the audience's conscience in the idea that 'a cure' is needed. It shows the 'problems' that it identifies, structured in the rough outline treatment around six categories—arrival, employment, housing, crime, miscegenation, and overcrowding. But it is also concerned to establish liberal credentials through an emphasis on the idea that such problems are not primarily racial. In summing up, Reid draws a distinction between what he calls the 'slice of life' the programme offers—showing bias, prejudice, and fear—and 'the people who are endeavouring to push these sort of things on one side and to look at this, not as a problem wholly as one of colour, but as something which is primarily due to the fact that these immigrants have ways and lives—ways and standards of life which are so different to our own'. The people who take this approach clearly included the programme makers, whose analysis stressed the difference between 'our ways' and 'theirs'. Through its focus on immigration as a social problem, and its suggestion that the proper perspective on the issue is to regard it as cultural rather than racial, the programme reinserts a view of a decent and tolerant Britain into a discussion which also identifies colour prejudice in Britain as a 'very ugly thing'.

Has Britain a Colour Bar?, while dominated by the voices of whites, and especially the narrators, included some black voices. Many reports about the 'colour problem' that drew on social exploration recorded only white voices. Like Renee Cutforth, Tom Stacey set out for Birmingham. In 1961, he reported on conditions in Smethwick for the *Sunday Times*, quoting information and complaints from local whites to support his observations of the domestic practices of Pakistanis.[46] Elspeth Huxley's account of her journey, made in 1963, and published in *Punch*, mediated the complaints and observations of white neighbours, especially in Brixton, London, on their experiences of 'blacks next door'.[47] Sheila Patterson also made a journey to Brixton in 1963 to write a sociological study which she called *Dark Strangers*. Like Huxley, she structured her account around the expectations of white Brixtonians, noting the failure of West Indians to conform to these. Pearl Jephcott, writing a sociological study of Notting Hill, London, and

---

[45] Documentaries, Special Enquiry, Colour Bar 1954–1955, BBC WAC T4/55.

[46] Tom Stacey, 'Smethwick's Little Asia', *Sunday Times*, 30 July 1961.

[47] Elspeth Huxley, *Back Street New Worlds: A Look at Immigrants in Britain* (London: Chatto and Windus, 1964; first published in *Punch*, 1963).

describing the basement homes in which West Indians lived, quoted the comment of a health visitor: 'terrible place for a baby'.[48]

These diverse journeys were all into working-class areas of Birmingham and London, but their narrators were no longer concerned to observe the white working classes, or to liken them to 'colonies of heathens and savages'. Instead, the white working classes were themselves informants about black and Asian migrants whose information was characteristically used to support the observations of the narrators. Explorers were thus not only closely bound to the audience they addressed, but also to the white working classes whose complaints they mediated. The two nations of rich and poor of earlier social exploration at home were transformed into one nation that united white explorer, audience, and working-class informant, defined against the black 'stranger'.

Not all social exploration of the 'colour problem' excluded black voices or used the observations of the white working classes to support its findings. *The Colony*, a BBC television documentary made in 1964, focuses on the lives of Caribbean immigrants in Birmingham.[49] It opens with the voice of a woman talking about the difficulty of placing certain children for adoption against shots of Birmingham. She starts with the difficulties of placing 'the handicapped child, the mentally retarded child', and moves on to the difficulties of placing a 'big section amongst coloured and half-caste children'. It is only when the camera moves from Birmingham to a close-up of the speaker that she tells the audience: 'I feel very deeply about this because I'm coloured myself.' This opening, setting up expectations of a white voice which are then confounded, sets the agenda of the documentary. The woman's voice is followed by the words of a black male worker, shown working in a foundry, and these are repeated later in the programme, providing its refrain:

Sometimes we think we shouldn't blame the people because it's we who have come to your country and troubled them. On the other hand, we think if they in the first place had not come to our country and spread the false propaganda, we would never have come to theirs. If we had not come, we would not be the wiser. We would still have the good image of England, thinking that they are what they are not. And the English would be as ignorant of us.

The programme ends with a tour around a stately home where a black family are part of a party being shown the great drawing-room and the state bedroom. Into this account of English history and heritage, the black woman in the family party inserts the story of slavery.

---

[48] Pearl Jephcott, *A Troubled Area: Notes on Notting Hill, London* (London: Faber and Faber, 1964), 84.

[49] *The Colony*, BBC television (Philip Donnellan, 1964).

The Colony reverses the conventions of post-war social exploration in television documentaries and newspapers. In place of their accounts of a 'colour problem' where white narrators mediate the observations and complaints of local whites, it offers an account of a white problem by black speakers who interrogate Englishness. There is no narrator. With one exception, only black voices speak. Speakers are credited by name at the end of the programme: the signalman, the bus-conductor, the nurse, the teacher, and the preacher, in credits that give their Caribbean island of origin: St Kitts, Jamaica, Barbados. Even so, the programme retains a white perspective, preoccupied with West Indians' relationship to England. When speakers talk about Jamaica as 'farming country' and its breadfruit trees and banana trees, the camera is concerned to point the contrast with England— their words spoken against shots of urban Birmingham: streets of small terraces, railways, buses. The one white speaker is a teacher in a school, who asks his colleague: 'What would you suggest that West Indians can bring to this country?' It is in answer to a question from an unseen questioner that a speaker says: 'An Englishman is a hell of a lot more tolerant than any other Europeans. You're a tolerant race of people, you're a friendly people.'

In its use of black speakers addressing a white audience, *The Colony* reproduces aspects of the wartime documentary *West Indies Calling* (1943), where black speakers play an educative role, informing their audiences about the Caribbean contribution to the war. Unlike *West Indies Calling*, however, and despite the speaker who characterizes Englishness through tolerance, this information includes the diagnosis of a white problem in Britain. *The Colony* marks out the extent to which documentary was seen as the most appropriate form for portraying immigration and reproduced its characteristic concern with documentary realism and the establishment of liberal credentials, but it also demonstrates how rarely this form was employed to show a white problem. Like *Has Britain a Colour Bar?*, most investigations deflected attention from white racism. Characteristically the media presented all aspects of Commonwealth immigration as problems, and focused on a 'colour problem' imported into the metropolis through the breaching of racial boundaries between metropolis and empire/Commonwealth—the product of increased numbers of black and Asian people in Britain.

Domestic Order

Following the white riots in Nottingham and Notting Hill in 1958, the *Daily Telegraph* reported sights and sounds in the heart of England to which 'we are totally unaccustomed'. Its editorial, commenting on events in

Nottingham in August, suggested that they came 'as a considerable shock to the tranquil, tolerant British public... The cry of "lynch the blacks" has been heard in the streets of Nottingham.'[50] The shock registered in these comments is about alien practices in England but, unlike the account of Birmingham in *Has Britain a Colour Bar?*, what is alien is white. Even so, with no trace of irony, following the white riots in Notting Hill in September, the newspaper entitled its editorial: 'Our Colour Problem'.[51]

The white riots produced disturbing evidence about Britain, threatening its reputation for liberality and tolerance. The *Manchester Guardian* reported of Notting Hill, London: 'It comes as a shock to hear the ugly phrase "lynch him" on English lips in an English city. But it must be reported that these words were used not once but a dozen times yesterday afternoon.'[52] The *Daily Telegraph* still conjured 'the tranquil, tolerant British public'—a marker of British decency. But any story of British tolerance was increasingly disrupted by its reports that the language of 'lynching' was used on English streets.

The language of lynching was associated particularly with the Southern States of the USA, and the white riots drew comparisons with Little Rock, Arkansas where, in the previous year, there was white violence against blacks. The disturbing evidence about Britain thus not only threatened Britain's self-representation as a liberal and tolerant nation, but also a collapse of the construction of British tolerance against the USA and South Africa. The Notting Hill riots took place in the same week that saw Hendrik Verwoerd, formerly Minister for Native Affairs with responsibility for enforcing apartheid, become Prime Minister of South Africa— giving the question of white violence against blacks in Britain particular saliency. The *Daily Mail* worried about Britain's reputation abroad: 'Attempts will be made to show that Nottingham and Notting Hill are synonymous with Little Rock and Cape Town.'[53] An editorial in the *Daily Telegraph* shared these concerns, but moved to deny their legitimacy: 'There is absolutely no comparison between what is happening here and developments in South Africa and the Southern States of America ...'[54]

The white riots of 1958 brought disorder to the heart of England, but accounts of 'our colour problem' continued to give considerable attention to domestic order as symbolized by English homes. In 1958, English streets were places of white violence, but social explorers made them places of quiet order. Elspeth Huxley's articles in *Punch* produced the 'quiet street' and

[50] *Daily Telegraph*, 26 Aug. 1958.
[51] *Daily Telegraph*, 2 Sept. 1958.
[52] *Manchester Guardian*, 2 Sept. 1958.
[53] *Daily Mail*, 5 Sept. 1958.
[54] *Daily Telegraph*, 2 Sept. 1958.

'privet hedge' as emblems of the Englishness threatened by immigrants. West Indians in particular, she noted, disrupted English quiet and order by playing loud music and keeping late hours at weekends. They also violated domestic boundaries, leaving yards and front steps filthy and windows unwashed. Huxley used images of 'a man who lies in bed every weekend with his feet sticking out of the window', and of 'the way they keep their hats on indoors'. Characteristically these are not her own observations—she is mediating the complaints of what she calls 'Brixtonians'.[55] Sheila Patterson's account of West Indians in Brixton also focused on domestic boundary-markers—clean lace curtains, clean windows, neat house fronts, washed front steps—that stood for what she called 'our ways—a conformity to certain standards of order, cleanliness, quietness, privacy and propriety'. She noted that 'no immigrant group has in the mass so signally failed to conform to these expectations and patterns as have the West Indians'.[56]

The idea of an English home and family under siege was used in the early twentieth century by advocates of immigration controls, particularly against Jews. 'Not a day passes but English families are ruthlessly turned out to make room for foreign invaders', William Gordon, MP for Stepney, stated in 1902 in the House of Commons, advocating the control of Jewish immigration to Britain. 'Out they go to make room for Rumanians, Russians and Poles . . . It is only a matter of time before the population becomes entirely foreign.'[57] From 1905 a series of Aliens Acts were directed primarily against preventing further Jewish immigration to Britain. In the 1950s, much social exploration of the 'colour problem' produced similar siege narratives and, like colonial war imagery, portrayed immigration as a threat to an Englishness symbolized by the idea of home.

Colonial war imagery showed the violation of English domestic sanctuaries in empire, elaborating domestic detail to signify Englishness. Social exploration of immigration in the 1950s and 1960s also made home a symbol of embattled Englishness, mobilizing imagery of 'little England' to signify the nation that was threatened. Like colonial war imagery, this version of national identity constructed both family and home as white. In this context, domesticated versions of Englishness proliferated and internal frontiers received attention not only as homes, streets, and neighbourhoods, but as more specific domestic boundary-markers—front doors, letter-boxes, windows. In investigating immigration as a domestic problem, much social exploration focused on the heartland of the domestic: English homes.

[55] Huxley, *Back Street*, 46–7.

[56] Sheila Patterson, *Dark Strangers: A Sociological Study of the Absorption of a Recent West Indian Migrant Group in Brixton, South London* (London: Tavistock, 1963).

[57] Quoted in Steve Cohen, 'Anti-Semitism, Immigration Controls and the Welfare State', *Critical Social Policy*, 13 (1985), 74.

Simple oppositions between white domestic order and black domestic barbarism are complicated in both *Sapphire* (1959) and *Flame in the Streets* (1961)—the latter a film version of the BBC television drama *Hot Summer Night* (1960).[58] Both films had strong liberal credentials and were shaped by the white riots in Notting Hill in 1958. *Sapphire*, voted best British film of the year by the British Film Academy in 1959, was originally publicized as a 'film about race riots' and there was criticism of the decision to shoot it in Notting Hill as 'tactless'.[59] *Flame in the Streets*, also set in London, drew on the events of Notting Hill more extensively. Both films register disturbing evidence about Britain, showing English streets not only as places of quiet order, but also as places of white violence against blacks.

In the aftermath of Notting Hill, imagery of street violence gave films topicality. The action of *Flame in the Streets*, contained within Guy Fawkes Day, is set against the background noise of fireworks, as bangers are thrown and rockets go up, reinforcing a pervasive sense of tension. In the workplace white men abuse black. In the streets white teddy boys attack black men, disrupting the community bonfire party, and end by pushing a black man into a lighted bonfire, badly injuring him. Despite its publicity, the focus of *Sapphire* is on a murder investigation, and the only sequence that shows white violence—an attack on a black man by a gang of teddy boys—avoids depicting this directly, showing the attack as a play of shadows on a brick wall.

In both films, the topicality of street violence, focusing on males, is balanced by attention to a contrasting place—the respectable working-class home, shown as a place of privacy and order where women guard domestic boundaries. This is portrayed in both films as a white domain inhabited by families that span three generations, but one in which conflicts arise when miscegenation threatens white order. In *Sapphire*, tensions build in the Harris family when they become suspects in a police investigation into the murder of Sapphire, who had passed as white and was pregnant by David Harris (Paul Massie). In *Flame in the Streets*, conflict in the Palmer family is provoked when Kathy (Sylvia Syms) announces that she plans to marry Peter Lincoln (Johnnie Seka)—her black teacher colleague. 'Would You Let Your Daughter Marry a Negro?' one newspaper headlined its review.[60]

The question, as always, signals the possibility of limitations to white liberal credentials. The white home in both films is also a domain of white racism. In *Flame in the Streets*, Jacko Palmer (John Mills) is a shop steward who successfully opposes white members of the trade union who want to deny Gabriel Gomez (Earl Cameron) promotion to a supervisory job on the grounds that 'the men don't want to take orders from spades'. But Jacko's

[58] *Sapphire* (Basil Dearden, 1959); *Flame in the Streets* (Roy Baker, 1961).
[59] *Daily Express*, 10 Oct. 1958; *The Times*, 11 Oct. 1958.
[60] *Evening Standard*, 22 June 1961; *Evening News and Star*, 22 June 1961.

liberal credentials are sorely tested by his daughter's plans to marry Peter, suggesting that such liberalism stops short at the gate of the family home. His wife, Nell (Brenda de Banzie), has no liberal credentials and her response to her daughter's plans prompts much of the action of the film. She tells Kathy: 'I'm ashamed of you, when I think of you and *that* man sharing the same bed. It's filthy. Disgusting...I want to be sick. You can't wait can you? You're no better than the whores in the high street.' In *Sapphire*, racism is also the attribute of a white female guardian of the home and provides the final solution to the murder of Sapphire when David's sister Millie (Yvonne Mitchell) betrays her guilt in a hysterical outburst of racist invective. White working-class homes in both films are thus characterized not only by the neat house-fronts and privet hedges identified by Huxley and Patterson, but by the hysterical racism that both films attribute to white women. Like English streets, English homes can be places of white violence as well as quiet order.

Despite their revelations about the white working-class home, these films leave in place a central contrast between white and black life, where family and home are emblems of white Englishness. Both show journeys of social exploration. Like television documentaries, their liberal credentials are affirmed particularly in their attempts to promote understanding of social problems through serious treatment. Most reviews identified *Sapphire* as a mixture of detective narrative, thriller, and 'social problem' film.

This merging of genres means that the investigation of Sapphire's murder concerns Sapphire's identity as much as that of the murderer. It takes the police investigators—Superintendent Hazard (Nigel Patrick) and Inspector Learoyd (Michael Craig)—into a black world: slum territory marked by dirty windows, overflowing dustbins, and peeling walls. As they cross the threshold into the domestic interior inhabited by Johnny Fiddle (Harry Baird)—a black murder suspect—they enter scenes of dirt and chaos where they find a knife and blood-stained shirt. In *Flame in the Streets*, Nell's outburst prompts similar findings about black life. Kathy leaves home to go in search of Peter. Her attempt to find the room where Peter lives in multi-occupied housing makes her into a voyeur, standing on the threshold of black domestic interiors, surveying scenes into which she has intruded. She finds peeling wallpaper, stained walls, washing hanging from the ceiling, a black man in bed with a black woman who invites Kathy to join them. Black life in both films—always shown from the perspective of the white investigator or voyeur—lacks any of the credentials of a home.

Sapphire plays with the idea of a black world that is colourful, rhythmic, and sexual against a white world that is constrained and repressed. The investigation, reversing the journey made by Sapphire when she learned to pass as white, takes the police from white respectability into a world of black music, dancing—linked to sexuality—drinking, gambling, and fights. As they probe Sapphire's past, the police move from the International Club for students—described by a black character as 'one of those get together, let's be brothers places'—where there is music but also table-tennis, to the black club, Tulips, where there is only 'the beat of the bongos'. They move on to Johnny Fiddle's dilapidated and sleazy room, and then to a similar room inhabited by Horace Big-Cigar whose fight with Johnny accounts for the blood-stains on Johnny's shirt, and where he now drinks and gambles with his friends.

A particular focus of *Sapphire* on people of mixed parentage who pass as white produces a recurrent verdict from many characters: 'you can always tell'. While essentialist views are problematized by a number of white characters, the film endorses these through its imagery. The sequence in the black club, Tulips, shows that, whatever their skin colour, people who are 'black' will always respond to the beat of the bongo. The police encounter Sapphire's own sexuality early in the investigation of her death, discovering that Sapphire wore tweeds to pass as white, but beneath this she wore red taffeta. They encounter her sense of life throughout the investigation as witnesses identify her as a woman who loved dancing and was always laughing.

Against this colour and life, the film ends with the discovery of a white murderess who is sexually repressed. The film attributes Millie Harris's violence against Sapphire to her unhappy marriage and jealousy of Sapphire's sexuality and sense of life. Nell's racism in *Flame in the Streets* is also linked to notions of the neurotic housewife as liable to hysteria because of sexual repression—a review commenting that 'The longings of which she accuses poor Kathy are really her own long-suppressed desires in an unhappy marriage'.[61] Both films thus add a new dimension to the opposition between white and black life. Drawing on popular psychology, they make domestic order signify sexual repression and hysteria that can lurk beneath the surface of the most respectable white working-class home.

Despite the contrast between white respectability and black life, both films are careful to incorporate respectable black males—Sapphire's brother Dr Robbins (Earl Cameron) in *Sapphire* and Peter Lincoln in *Flame in the Streets*. But Peter lives in a room in the dilapidated multi-occupied house that, like Johnny Fiddle's room in *Sapphire*, stands for black domestic life, while Dr Robbins is shown in a domestic interior only when he enters the white working-class home of the Harris family. As in colonial war films, there is no representation of black family relationships. Black women feature in the background, but say nothing. Black men's relationships with white women provide their only connection to family and home.

---

[61] *Evening News and Star*, 22 June 1961.

The use of family and home as emblems of white life is strengthened by the ending of both films, which show reconciliation within the Harris and the Palmer families. White female hysteria is brought under control in the restoration of a patriarchal order. The resolution of the murder mystery in *Sapphire*, and the identification of white female guilt, means that David is reconciled with his father, whom he had suspected of murdering his girlfriend. *Flame in the Streets* offers reconciliation between white husband and wife as its only resolution.

Flame in the Streets undercuts its association of Nell with hysteria through the detailed attention given to her point of view in her conflict with Jacko. As she tells him that he had no time for her, treated her like part of the fixtures, turned the front room into an office, even made love to her as though he were taking a quick drink, Jacko is reduced to tears. Jacko demonstrates his determination to make amends and reunite the family when he accepts Nell's instructions to go and find Kathy and bring her home. As he fulfils his mission and Kathy comes home bringing Peter with her, white violence erupts on the streets, and Gabriel Gomez is pushed into a bonfire by white teddy boys. The fate of Gomez, the conflict on the streets, as well as the central problem which the film poses—whether Kathy can bring Peter home and incorporate him into white family life through marriage—all remain unresolved. As Peter crosses the boundary of the Palmer home for the first time, and Jacko brings Nell downstairs to meet him, the film ends on an uneasy image. Jacko and Nell are on one side of the family hearth, Kathy and Peter on the other, in a shot that is angled to show them separated by the whole width of the room. Whatever the future, however, Jacko and Nell have been reunited. Like colonial war films, *Flame in the Streets* offers reconciliation between husband and wife and restoration of white domestic order as its only resolution, heightening its use of family and home as emblems of white life, and of Englishness.

It is significant that the home and family used as emblems of Englishness in *Flame in the Streets* is white, urban, and working-class. As in social exploration of the 'colour problem', this symbol of Englishness was not the pastoral but the urban or suburban—the quiet street. Writing in the nineteenth-century tradition of social exploration, Henry Mayhew had commented on the London poor in 1851 that as 'vagabonds and outcasts' they lacked 'hearth and rootedness . . . sacred symbols to all civilised races'. Other nineteenth-century writers developed his notion of the urban poor as rootless, portraying them as 'wandering hordes' and 'nomadic tribes'.[62] But in post-war investigations of the 'colour problem', it was the urban

---

[62] Quoted in Stoler, *Race and the Education of Desire*, 128. For a discussion of this imagery, see Ian Baucom, *Out of Place: Englishness, Empire and the Locations of Identity* (Princeton: Princeton University Press, 1999), 55–62.

working classes who were used to represent the values of the hearth against immigrants.

In *Flame in the Streets* such rootedness is suggested in the detailed portrayal of the Palmer family, across the generations, and in the character of Jacko, who still lives in the house where he was born and takes on the mantle of his father—a founder of the trade union—in his work as a shop steward. In contrast, none of the black characters in the film is endowed with family connections. Patterson's and Huxley's accounts of their social exploration in Brixton produced a similar idea of white working-class rootedness—their contrast between neat English house-fronts and the domestic barbarism of immigrants embedded in an opposition between immigrants, and what Patterson calls 'residents' and Huxley calls 'Brixtonians'.[63] In contrast to such rootedness, immigrants were characteristically represented as transient, rootless, and adrift. *Pool of London* (1950) and *A Taste of Honey* (1961) showed black sailors on the point of moving on to another port. Colin MacInnes's novel, *City of Spades* (1957), like *Sapphire*, showed blacks inhabiting a world of prostitution, illicit drinking, gambling, drugs, and violence.[64] Post-war social exploration, assigning to immigrants the place that nineteenth-century social exploration had given to the urban poor, showed them as 'dark strangers', 'wandering hordes', and 'alien races' in the metropolis. It made race central to questions about home.

The Commonwealth and Immigrants

In 1964, *The Times* published an anonymous article by 'A Conservative', which called the Commonwealth 'a gigantic farce' and urged Britain to renounce 'the relics of world empire'. Its author portrayed the Commonwealth as a threat to Britain: 'To have our laws so far out of relation with realities', he argued, 'was the cause of the massive coloured immigration in the last decade which has inflicted social and political damage that will take decades to obliterate.'[65] The article, and its central proposition—that the Commonwealth was no longer of any importance to Britain—generated fierce debate in the letter-columns of the newspaper. Responding to the attack, an editorial in *The Times* celebrated the Commonwealth as 'the greatest effort at a multi-racial society of nations the world has seen. Multi-racialism is mankind's only way forward to universal peace and, on a world scale, the only way in which Britain leads.'[66]

---

[63] Patterson, *Dark Strangers*, 98; Huxley, *Back Street*, 47.

[64] *Pool of London* (Basil Dearden, 1950); *A Taste of Honey* (Tony Richardson, 1961).

[65] 'Patriotism Based on Reality not on Dreams', by 'A Conservative', *The Times*, 2 Apr. 1964.

[66] *The Times*, 4 Apr. 1964.

The article, subsequent letters to *The Times*, and the response in the editorial, suggest the extent to which the Commonwealth and its importance to Britain was at issue in the 1960s, and the significance of questions of race and immigration in attempts to define a post-imperial identity. In the early 1960s, these issues generated considerable debate in the popular press as well as in *The Times*. Immigration policy and the introduction of the Commonwealth Immigrants Act of 1962, the bid to join Europe in 1961–3, and a commitment to maintaining the idea of Britain as a liberal and tolerant nation produced a wide range of narratives, often contradictory, about Britain and the Commonwealth, and Commonwealth immigration.

In claiming that the Commonwealth gave Britain moral leadership, the editorial in *The Times* continued to celebrate the multiracial ideal that had been widely vaunted in Coronation year to support the idea of British liberality and tolerance. In the 1950s, this view was supported by immigration policy—claimed as a further exemplification of a liberal and tolerant Britain that kept an 'open door', offering unrestricted right of entry to citizens of the empire and Commonwealth. Henry Hopkinson, Minister of State for Colonial Affairs, commented in 1954 that 'In a world in which restrictions on personal movement and immigration have increased we still take pride in the fact that a man can say *civis Britannicus sum* whatever his colour may be, and we can take pride in the fact that he wants and can come to the Mother country'.[67]

The public image of an 'open door' policy, projected by government ministers like Henry Hopkinson, was partly a matter of concern about the impact that the introduction of restrictions on Commonwealth immigration might have on colonial and Commonwealth governments. The credentials for these government claims were often policies and ideas produced, at least in part, by concerns not to offend or anger colonies and former colonies, strengthen colonial nationalist movements, or damage Commonwealth unity. Privately, however, British governments were concerned to find means, short of legislation, to restrict black and Asian immigration. The Labour government set up a secret committee in 1950 to review further means by which to check the immigration of coloured people from British Colonial Territories. The committee of ministers set up by the Conservative government in 1955 to look at the possibility of immigration controls was also secret—Anthony Eden, the Prime Minister, denying in Parliament that any controls were envisaged. Part of its remit was to review how controls could be justified, not only in Britain, but also to 'the Commonwealth countries concerned'.[68]

[67] Quoted in Kenan Malik, *The Meaning of Race: Race, History and Culture in Western Society* (London: Macmillan, 1996), 21.
[68] Ibid. 20.

Most media images of racial tolerance were directed not at Common-wealth governments but at an audience at home, and their projection of a liberal and tolerant Britain was shaped by the long history of such self-representation and the need to avoid comparisons with America and South Africa. In 1955, before the white riots, Robert Reid in *Has Britain a Colour Bar?* had referred to the suggestion that the government should restrict immigration. He ended the programme on a note of warning about the critical world audience waiting to see 'how we're going to tackle this colour problem of ours in this country' and the need for common sense to ensure that Britain came out of the situation with credit, and 'setting an example to the rest of the world'.

Proposals to restrict immigration occupied an important place in media debates about the white riots of 1958, prompting considerable unease and ambivalence about the impact of legislation on the idea of Britain's liberality and tolerance. The issue of legislation was often prominent in media definitions of Britain's difference from the USA and South Africa. Rebutting suggestions of any resemblance between Nottingham and Notting Hill in Britain and Little Rock and Cape Town in the USA and South Africa, the press made much of legislation: 'It needs to be reiterated that the difference is that here, there is no discrimination before the law', the *Daily Mail* argued.[69] 'They [South Africa and the Southern States of America] want a colour bar, we do not. Their governors, legislature, police and public opinion support it, ours oppose it', argued the *Daily Telegraph*.[70]

Would legislation to restrict Commonwealth immigration undermine claims about British liberality and tolerance? This was a question that received contradictory answers, and the importance of maintaining Britain's reputation for tolerance was urged by both supporters and opponents of restrictions. After the riots, a letter-writer to the *Manchester Guardian*, commenting on 'ugly episodes in Nottingham and Notting Hill' that 'have brought the colour problem to our own doorstep', opposed restrictions on immigration, arguing that 'we will leave ourselves without an answer to Messrs. Talmadge and Verwoerd'.[71] An editorial in the *Observer* argued that restriction 'would be a shameful admission that the problem is too difficult for us to solve and that a multi-racial society is impossible'. Writing in the *Daily Mail*, Christopher Hollis, a former Tory MP, invoked 'our long tradition of hospitality to immigrants', arguing that this should not be abandoned 'as a result of the hooliganism of a few Teddy boys'.[72]

---

[69] *Daily Mail*, 5 Sept. 1958.
[70] *Daily Telegraph*, 2 Sept. 1958.
[71] *Manchester Guardian*, 3 Sept. 1958.
[72] *Daily Mail*, 5 Sept. 1958.

Maurice Edelman, a Labour MP, also writing in the *Daily Mail*, invoked a British tradition of liberality and tolerance to mount a very different argument. In an article headlined 'Should We Let Them Keep Pouring In?' he used this tradition to legitimate restriction: 'It is precisely to preserve that long tradition briefly interrupted by the ugly violence of irresponsible thugs that the Government must act now.'[73] On this view, far from making Britain comparable to South Africa, as the letter-writer to the *Manchester Guardian* suggested, restrictions were necessary to ensure that Britain remained tolerant.

Britain's bid to join Europe in 1961–3 further complicated debates about the importance of the Commonwealth to Britain. Findings of the Gallup Poll taken in the context of the British application to join the Common Market in 1961—where 48 per cent of respondents said that the Commonwealth was 'the most important to Britain' against 19 per cent for America, 18 per cent for Europe, and 15 per cent 'don't knows'—suggested a very different view of the Commonwealth from the verdict of the anonymous Conservative writing in *The Times* in 1964: 'gigantic farce'.[74] The only public opinion poll conducted in the period 1955–60 on the Common Market had found that the majority of respondents had never heard of it, and that a large proportion of those who had believed that Britain was a member.[75] Polls taken in 1961 demonstrated much more awareness of Europe, reflecting increasing coverage in the media in the context of Britain's application for membership. Gallup's polls on Europe were consistent in demonstrating a concern with the Commonwealth. Another poll in September 1961 found that 49 per cent of respondents thought that unsatisfactory arrangements for Commonwealth interests were a 'very important' obstacle to joining, while another 29 per cent thought them an 'important obstacle'. In response to a question in a poll in 1962 asking whether any difficulties were so overriding that they should prevent Britain from joining, 39 per cent answered 'the Commonwealth'.[76]

The British application to join the Common Market marked the beginning of a turn to Europe that, in 1952, Lord Salisbury, the Secretary of State for Commonwealth Relations, had ruled out on the grounds that 'the survival of the British Commonwealth and our membership of it must be the corner-stone alike of our Foreign and Imperial policy'.[77] It coincided

---

[73] *Daily Mail*, 2 Sept. 1958.

[74] Alex May, '"Commonwealth or Europe?" Macmillan's Dilemma, 1961–1963', in Alex May (ed.), *Britain, the Commonwealth and Europe: The Commonwealth and Britain's Application to Join the European Communities* (Basingstoke: Palgrave, 2001), 97–8.

[75] Jeremy Moon, *European Integration in British Politics 1950–1963: A Study of Issue Change* (Aldershot: Gower, 1985), 153.

[76] May, 'Commonwealth or Europe', 97–8.

[77] Broadcast on European Services of the BBC, 7 Apr. 1952.

with the first legislation to restrict immigration from the Commonwealth. The government's greater willingness to publicly advocate immigration control in 1962, like its unwillingness to do so in the 1950s, was connected with Britain's relationship to the Commonwealth and the turn to Europe. As criticism of the Commonwealth became more common, and its importance to national identity and interests faded, government concerns about Commonwealth reactions to British policy on immigration also faded.

Both the application to join Europe and the Commonwealth Immigrants Act were contested issues in the British press, and produced a complex array of narratives about Britain and the Commonwealth and questions of race. Many opponents of British entry to Europe argued that joining meant abandonment or betrayal of the Commonwealth. Some supporters of the application were anxious to deny the notion of abandonment, but others argued that clinging to an out-of-date Commonwealth identity prevented Britain from modernization in pursuit of its real interests. Narratives surrounding the Commonwealth Immigrants Act developed along similar contradictory lines. Like opponents of the application to join Europe, opponents of the Act portrayed British policy threatening the Commonwealth. An editorial in *The Times* argued: 'The damage, emotional, economic and political, which it is likely to do the already fragile fabric of Commonwealth can hardly be exaggerated.'[78] Some supporters of control, like the anonymous Conservative writing in *The Times*, argued that the Commonwealth damaged Britain.

Public concerns about the impact of European membership on the Commonwealth suggest considerable limitations to the currency of its new meaning as 'domestic problem'. It is impossible to know how many of the 48 per cent of respondents who recorded in 1961 that the Commonwealth was more important to Britain than America or Europe were thinking about a multiracial community or a racial community of Britons. In 1962, Harold Macmillan, the Prime Minister, suggested that it was the latter. Worrying about the potential damage of 'sentiment towards the Commonwealth' to the European membership bid, he wrote that such sentiment 'is really centred on the old Commonwealth countries'.[79]

In media coverage, those who developed the narrative of abandonment of the Commonwealth often focused on a racial community of Britons. An article opposing European membership by Field Marshal Montgomery in the *Daily Mirror* in 1962 spoke in defence, not of a multiracial Commonwealth, but of the British race. 'I stand for the British Commonwealth with the Queen at its head', Montgomery declared. 'The British race to which we

---

[78] *The Times*, 15 Nov. 1961.
[79] Quoted in Stuart Ward, 'Worlds Apart: Three "British" Prime Ministers at Empire's End', forthcoming.

belong', he argued, was 'united by close ties of blood, speech and religion the world over'. He urged Britain as the 'Mother of Nations' to 'gather her children about her to the call of common kindred . . . Let her grasp the hand of her children and draw them closer to her—rather than desert them.'[80]

Other stories about the impact of Britain's application to join the Common Market on the Commonwealth also highlighted a racial community of Britons. In 1962, a BBC television programme on the issue was entitled *Commonwealth Crisis: Britain and the Old Dominions*.[81] The programme began with images of Coronation day, and the narrative voice of Robin Day, who wrote the commentary as well as narrating it. Day described the roar of the crowds, welcoming Commonwealth contingents. The welcome they extended, he suggested, was particularly warm to 'the men of the "Old Dominions" proudly representing their free and sovereign nations . . .' The programme then cut to shots of Edward Heath in Brussels, where, Day explained, 'Britain is negotiating to join the European Common Market' and 'the future of the Commonwealth is in the balance'. Subsequent sequences of the programme extended this implicit identification of the future of the Commonwealth with the 'Old Dominions', showing Day interviewing Australians, Canadians, and New Zealanders about the impact of Common Market membership.

The multiracial Commonwealth celebrated by *The Times* in response to the anonymous Conservative nevertheless continued to enjoy support, and was sometimes associated with the idea of a multiracial Britain. The Bishop of Liverpool, speaking in the House of Lords in 1965, suggested that 'a multiracial society may be necessary if we are to be the centre of a multiracial Commonwealth'.[82] In a radio talk broadcast on the Third Programme in 1964, S. C. Leslie suggested that it was through the Commonwealth that 'Britain herself may find the revitalising national purpose and motive that the affluent society shows so little sign of generating'. His talk linked the Commonwealth ideal with a multiracial Britain: 'She (Britain) is already a multi-racial community, and she is so in the name of the Commonwealth. She is hastening slowly, on grounds of prudence, but the principle itself is not in question.'[83] Lord Altrincham, speaking on a BBC television programme on the 1962 Commonwealth Conference, defined a multiracial Commonwealth in opposition to a racial community of Britons. Racial equality only existed when Commonwealth Prime Ministers dined at Buckingham Palace, he said, while the Commonwealth

[80] *Daily Mirror*, 4 June 1962.
[81] *Commonwealth Crisis: Britain and the Old Dominions*, BBC television, 4 Sept. 1962.
[82] Lords *Hansard*, 10 Mar. 1965, Col. 1028.
[83] S. C. Leslie, 'While the Watchdogs Sleep', *The Listener*, 6 Feb. 1964.

Immigrants Act, like the immigration policies of Australia and Canada, undermined it.[84]

The range of views in the media about Britain and the Commonwealth, Commonwealth immigration, and racial politics in Britain contrasted with an increasing consensus about apartheid in South Africa. While the white riots of 1958 and proposals to restrict Commonwealth immigration put the idea of Britain as liberal and tolerant under strain, the condemnation of apartheid re-established liberal credentials. In the Second World War, public discussion that was often highly critical of racial segregation of the US armed forces contrasted with silence about racial segregation of the South African armed forces. But increasingly after the election of Daniel Malan's Nationalist party in 1948, and the establishment of the apartheid policy he advocated during the election campaign, South Africa, like the Southern States of the USA, was widely condemned in the British media for its racist policies. In 1950, BBC radio, planning a series of programmes on the colour bar, suggested that 'we should get a South African Nationalist to take part in the last programme, to speak for apartheid...It will not only make our effort more honest, which is the main thing, but will ensure against any protest by the South African Government.'[85] By 1960, as Howard Smith has shown, the BBC was quite clear that it did not have to be neutral about apartheid.[86]

Condemnation of apartheid was sharpened by the shootings at Sharpeville in 1961 when white South African police used automatic weapons against black South Africans demonstrating against the pass laws, killing 67 and wounding almost 200. After Sharpeville, Richard Dimbleby, introducing the flagship BBC television current affairs programme *Panorama*, compared the events there to 'places like Guernica and Lidice, Belsen and Hola and Little Rock'.[87] In 1965, Sir Hugh Greene, Director General of the BBC, referring to the BBC's high standards of impartiality, claimed that there were some respects in which it was not neutral or impartial, and that these included 'racialism'. As Smith comments, this clearly included the policy of the South African government.

The move to condemn apartheid was made throughout the British media. Although by no means always enthusiastic about the campaigning activities of the Anti-Apartheid movement in Britain, such condemnation, especially after Sharpeville, was consistent and unqualified. Even though

---

[84] *The Commonwealth in London*, BBC television, 17 Nov. 1962.

[85] Memorandum from Prudence Smith, 27 Jan. 1950, BBC WAC, R51/92, Talks, Coloured People 1943–1954.

[86] Howard Smith, 'Apartheid, Sharpeville and Impartiality: The Reporting of South Africa on BBC Television 1948–1961', *Historical Journal of Film, Radio and Television*, 13 (1993), 251–98.

[87] Quoted ibid. 253.

South Africa remained in the Commonwealth until 1961, its policies formed a strong contrast to the multiracial Commonwealth championed by Britain. Right-wing as well as liberal newspapers were anxious to deny any comparison between white violence against blacks in Nottingham and Notting Hill and developments in South Africa.

The anonymous 'Conservative' whose verdict on the Commonwealth in *The Times* in 1964 generated such fierce debate distanced himself from concerns to maintain a public image of racial tolerance. The article was written by Enoch Powell—an important figure in attempts to shift the meaning of Commonwealth from world-wide community to domestic problem in the 1960s. This was a significant moment in a long journey Powell made from an intense attachment to imperial identity—one where the shock of the news of imminent Indian independence had proved so severe that 'I remember spending the whole of one night walking the streets of London trying to come to terms with it'.[88] The empire, he had claimed in the same year, 'is the structure on which we are dependent for our very existence'. In his 1951 electoral address to constituents he had insisted that 'I BELIEVE IN THE BRITISH EMPIRE. Without the Empire, Britain would be like a head without a body.'[89] In his 1964 article this story of the crucial importance of the empire to Britain has become a story of the Commonwealth threatening Britishness.

Lord Elton made a similar journey. His views were less widely publicized than Powell's, but he was a frequent broadcaster, General Secretary of the Rhodes Trust between 1939 and 1959, and Vice-President of the Empire Day movement—renamed Commonwealth Day in 1958, and afforded dwindling attention in the media. In 1945, in a book entitled *The Imperial Commonwealth*, he proclaimed the British Empire as 'a living example of what in the new age the world will need most—the peaceful and enduring association of free nations within a world community'.[90]

By Coronation year, Elton had transferred his enthusiasm to the Commonwealth. Unlike Powell, he welcomed the transition from empire to Commonwealth. He praised the multiracial character of the Commonwealth as 'unique', and proclaimed it 'the first world association of white and coloured peoples, the first genuine bridge between West and East, a living symbol of the brotherhood of man', and as a main symbol of a vigorous nation, which might well prove 'the chief hope for the future of

---

[88] Quoted in Simon Heffer, *Like the Roman: The Life of Enoch Powell* (London: Weidenfeld and Nicolson, 1998), 115.

[89] Quoted in Humphrey Berkeley, *The Odyssey of Enoch: A Political Memoir* (London: Hamilton, 1977), 52; Heffer, *Like the Roman*, 169.

[90] Lord Elton, *Imperial Commonwealth* (London: Collins, 1945), 522.

the world'.[91] In 1965, in a book, entitled *The Unarmed Invasion* that provided a survey of what he called 'Afro-Asian Immigration', he repudiated this vision. The book demonstrated the series of connections through which the Commonwealth acquired its new meaning of domestic problem. Elton, focusing on 'the immigration of coloured folk', discussed 'the problems to which colour gives rise', and called them 'the gravest social crisis since the industrial revolution'. Immigration, Elton argued, 'already... threatens to bring about changes far-reaching and wholly unplanned in the character of Britain as we have known it'.[92] His story of the Commonwealth as a symbol of a vigorous nation became a story of its threat to the nation.

A commitment to maintaining a British reputation for liberality and tolerance meant that Powell's and Elton's views were far more likely to be condemned in the national media than endorsed. Much of the press stopped short at supporting proposals for immigration control, let alone the proposals for repatriation that Powell and Elton championed. In 1968, Powell's infamous 'rivers of blood' speech in Birmingham was widely condemned, and he was immediately sacked from the Shadow Cabinet by Edward Heath, leader of the Conservative party.

A concern across a range of media representations to advertise liberal credentials nevertheless produced stories, like those told by Powell and Elton, which continually made the chain of connections that linked 'Commonwealth', 'immigrant', 'coloured', and 'domestic problem'. In their strong commitment to maintaining Britain as decent and tolerant the media defined the nation against America and increasingly against South Africa. But in the context of the other main theme on which they converged—the 'colour problem'—they defined the nation against black and Asian immigrants. The nation that the media addressed was white—in titles like *The Negro Next Door*; in questions like 'Would you let your daughter marry a Negro'?; in references to 'our ways' defined against those of immigrants, and notably in the recurrent references to 'our colour problem'.

The many unstable and volatile narratives about the Commonwealth in the early 1960s suggest the importance of questions of race in attempts to define a post-imperial identity. The 1962 Commonwealth Immigrants Act could be regarded as a watershed in the wider history of racial politics in Britain, as the first legislation to restrict migration from the Commonwealth to Britain, targeted at black and Asian migrants, and establishing, for the first time, that British passport holders could be excluded from the right of entry. It marked the beginning of a series of Acts that increasingly

[91] Lord Elton, 'A Tremendous Past, and—I Believe that We Have a Tremendous Future', *Daily Mail*, 2 Apr. 1953.

[92] Lord Elton, *The Unarmed Invasion: A Survey of Afro-Asian Immigration* (London: Geoffrey Bles, 1965), 7–8.

tightened and racialized immigration legislation, and virtually ended primary black migration to Britain.

While the Immigration Acts enshrined racial inequality, another group of laws—the Race Relations Acts of 1965, 1968, and 1976—sought to reduce racial discrimination and promote racial equality. The Race Relations Acts pointed to Britain as a liberal and tolerant nation, but the Immigration Acts marked the idea of limitations to tolerance. Opponents of immigration who saw black migrants as alien invaders increasingly mobilized the idea of a tolerant and decent nation to identify the Britain that they threatened and to legitimate immigration control.

'Colonization in reverse', collapsing the idea of a racial separation between metropolis and empire, produced a focus on internal frontiers in England: domestic and sexual boundaries. When Enoch Powell made his 'rivers of blood' speech, he drew on the conventions of social exploration of the 'colour problem' to establish a strong bond between himself as speaker and his audience, bound together by a common fear and anger about immigration. In mediating the complaints of white working-class informants, Powell also extended these conventions—claiming to speak for the nation. Telling his audience about a 'middle-aged, quite ordinary working man employed in one of our nationalised industries' who had said that 'in this country in 15 or 20 years time the black man will have the whip hand over the white man', Powell claimed to represent what 'thousands and hundreds of thousands are saying and thinking'. Mediating the complaints of a white woman, he said: 'I am going to allow just one of those hundreds of people to speak for me.' Powell represents his own voice as that of the white nation.

In his focus on the white woman's complaint, Powell drew on imagery which had gained wide currency in the British mainstream media in the 1950s, telling a familiar story of the violation of domestic sanctuaries. Domestic order, guarded by the woman, is disrupted by immigrants. They turn her 'quiet street' into 'a place of noise and confusion'. They threaten the boundaries of her home—pushing excreta through her letterbox, breaking her windows. This is a story about nation that foregrounds a white woman, and evokes powerlessness and vulnerability at home in a quiet English street. Like colonial war imagery, Powell domesticates frontiers, depriving them of any association with expansiveness and enterprise, virile and active masculinity. The violation of a domestic sanctuary becomes a symbol of a nation under siege.[93]

Siege narratives turned the narrative of a 'people's empire' as a multiracial family upside-down. In empire, stories of colonial wars defined a racial

---

[93] J. Enoch Powell, 'Speech at Birmingham, 20 April 1968', in John Wood (ed.), *Freedom and Reality* (London: Batsford, 1969), 213–19.

community of Britons against their racial 'others' and showed them at war with one another. In Britain, stories about 'the colour problem' invoked national identity as quiet, private, intimate, domestic, and white—Englishness, not Britishness. As the Commonwealth acquired its new meaning of domestic problem, its promise of maintaining and modernizing a globalized British identity and its claim to demonstrate Britain as a tolerant and decent nation clashed with a very different story: Englishness was threatened by empire, by Commonwealth, and by their legacies—not only in empire, but at home.

7

Elegies for Empire: The Romance
of Manliness

In January 1965, on the day following Winston Churchill's funeral, an editorial in the *Observer* entitled 'Estimating Churchill' singled out his quality of 'exceptional manliness', declaring that this was 'a matter of profound rejoicing'.[1] It identified two episodes from Churchill's career that demonstrated such manliness. One was his opposition to the British government's policy of appeasement of Nazi Germany in the late 1930s. The other was his leadership of Britain in the Second World War, and especially in 1940 when Britain had stood alone: 'He possessed the manliness to fight a war with vigour if it was demanded of him and to impart an offensive spirit to others.' The *Observer* was unusual in identifying the late 1930s as a key moment in Churchill's greatness—most tributes focused on 1940 as Churchill's 'finest hour'. But its verdict on Churchill as vigorous and exceptionally manly was widely endorsed throughout the media in tributes and obituaries. They honoured Churchill as a man of action: an exemplar of martial masculinity.

The developing cult of Churchill in the 1950s demonstrated continuing investment in the Second World War as a symbol of national greatness.[2] The week of his funeral consolidated what had become a widely held consensus about the history of his leadership in the Second World War as the story of 'how he...led the nation to one of the most overwhelming victories in history'.[3] This story displayed all the key elements of a romance of manliness, focusing on the homosocial world that Churchill had inhabited, developing a quest plot, and showing the fulfilment of a male destiny through victory over all external obstacles and enemies. Such a romance formed a strong contrast to the romantic love story that focused on relations between men and women, developed a romantic and domestic plot resolved through heterosexual

---

[1] *The Observer*, 31 Jan. 1965.

[2] For a discussion of the cult of Churchill, and how far he contributed personally to the development of this cult, see John Ramsden, *Man of the Century: Winston Churchill and his Legend Since 1945* (London: HarperCollins, 2003).

[3] *Daily Telegraph*, 25 Jan. 1965.

union, and showed what Carolyn Heilbrun has called 'the female life of prime devotion to male destiny'.[4]

Martin Francis, writing about Churchill's post-1945 career, suggests that his 'extravagant patrician personality fitted uneasily into a political culture that prioritised self-restraint'.[5] Francis traces what he calls 'the imperatives of restraint' to nineteenth-century developments, including traditions of imperial service that 'cultivated a notion of heroism based on moral imperative and controlling the passions' and Edwardian celebrations of the 'stiff upper lips of imperial heroes'.[6] Susan Kingsley Kent traces the genesis of a rather different version of imperial masculinity from the mid-nineteenth century. The Indian Rebellion of 1857, and the Morant Bay uprising in Jamaica in 1865, she suggests, produced a shift from ideals of masculinity embodied in the evangelical Christian gentleman of liberal sentiments—moral seriousness, earnestness, rationality—to a strong demand for men of action.[7]

In the 1950s, Second World War narratives, expelling women and civilians, had put martial masculinity at the centre of their stories.[8] Churchill's funeral was a culminating moment in this process. Churchill had been a politician throughout the Second World War and not a soldier, but tributes identified him as the man who had led his people to a famous victory: a great warrior. Many 1950s narratives transposed the high-minded, dedicated, and self-sacrificing version of the imperial hero onto a Second World War setting, but Churchill was celebrated primarily as a vigorous man of action. Tributes that identified his 'exceptional manliness' suggested the continuing appeal of a version of the imperial and war hero that eschewed self-restraint.

Both the high-minded hero and the man of action were very far removed from 'a new man' who attracted considerable attention in the late 1950s. As discussed by Mark Abrams in a radio broadcast in 1959, the life of a 'new man' was centred on the home.[9] The idea of a domestic man who represented a quiet, decent, private, and inward-looking Englishness had been developed between the wars, and provided some basis for J. B. Priestley's celebration of the virtues of the common people during the war, and his

[4] Carolyn Heilbrun, *Writing a Woman's Life* (London: Women's Press, 1989), 26. For narrative forms of adventure see Graham Dawson, *Soldier Heroes: British Adventure, Empire and the Imagining of Masculinities* (London: Routledge, 1994), 52–66, 178–88.

[5] Martin Francis, 'Tears, Tantrums and Bared Teeth: The Emotional Economy of Three Conservative Prime Ministers, 1951–1963', *Journal of British Studies*, 41 (July 2002), 358.

[6] Ibid. 359.

[7] Susan Kingsley Kent, *Gender and Power in Britain, 1640–1990* (London: Routledge, 1999), 202–28.

[8] See Chapter 3.

[9] Mark Abrams, 'The Home-Centred Society', *The Listener*, 26 Nov. 1959.

representation of himself as a quiet pipe-smoking Englishman who had decided that he would 'keep as close to cowardice as possible'.

By the late 1950s, the 'new man' had acquired a range of new activities, associated with a 'new England' of affluence and consumption, of which a major symbol was the television aerial. His skills ran to DIY, as well as gardening, and he occasionally dried the dishes. He spent a great deal of his time watching television. He was a central figure in 'companionate marriage', where there was an emphasis on a new equality of relationship between husband and wife, variously conceived as companionship, teamwork, or role sharing.[10] As part of such a relationship, he sometimes pushed a pram at weekends. No longer the overbearing patriarch, he treated his children to guidance rather than bullying, while his relationship with his wife included awakening her to the possibilities of sexual pleasure, and then coaxing her into an experience of 'sex fulfilment'.

All these versions of masculinity prompted ambivalence in the late 1950s and 1960s. The 'new man' earned some approval as a progressive figure, but nobody attributed manliness to him—much less manliness that was a matter of rejoicing—and considerable ambivalence surrounded the possibility that he embodied a feminization of national life. Concerns were expressed particularly about the decline of working-class community that he represented, as he became apolitical, participated less in public life of all kinds—whether in trade unions or public houses—and turned to passive spectatorship of television, immured in the home.[11] Heroic versions of masculinity associated with the empire and the Second World War were honoured at Churchill's funeral, but they were increasingly identified as outmoded, and widely criticized, lampooned, and satirized. In a period when masculine self-expression began to be vaunted, contesting the value assigned to self-restraint, the stiff-upper-lip hero earned particular scorn as an absurd anachronism. This left modern masculinity defined mainly by what it was not, in a rejection of deference and moral seriousness. It was a rejection that did little to supply the modern man with positive attributes, and did not generally extend to any critique of the history of imperialism or the Second World War.

Stuart Ward has suggested that both the 'Angry Young Man' movement and the satire boom of the late 1950s and early 1960s attacked the present for failing to live up to an imperial past, providing laments 'for the material and political substance that had once underpinned a more exalted image of

[10] Janet Finch and Penny Summerfield, 'Social Reconstruction and the Emergence of Companionate Marriage', in David Clark (ed.), *Marriage, Domestic Life and Social Change* (London: Routledge, 1991), 7.

[11] Wendy Webster, *Imagining Home: Gender, 'Race' and National Identity, 1945–64* (London: UCL Press, 1998), 69–75.

the "British world"'.[12] The extent to which the 'Angry Young Man' was widely hailed as a distinctively modern voice and became something of a cult figure in the late 1950s and early 1960s suggests how far he offered a version of a modern post-imperial masculine identity not only against the 'new man', but also against an older generation of male heroics.

As working-class realism developed in films, the 'Angry Young Man' was associated particularly with Northern working-class masculinity, and promised to resolve the ambivalence surrounding both the heroic and domestic versions of masculinity—rejecting in equal measure high-mindedness, restraint, duty, deference, and domestication, while at the same time representing a youthful rebelliousness of toughness, aggression, and vitality. An 'end of empire' theme nevertheless figured prominently in what came to be seen as the foundational text of the 'Angry Young Man' movement— John Osborne's *Look Back in Anger*. Britain's dwindling international status was also a prominent theme of the satire boom of the 1960s where the etiolated masculinity of an older generation of politicians, and especially Harold Macmillan, Prime Minister between 1957 and 1963, became a main target of ridicule.

Look Back in Anger was set somewhere in the Midlands, but much 'Angry Young Man' literature, as well as the films of the British 'New Wave' that were often based on novels, relocated a masculine nation in the North of England, removing their anti-heroes from associations with notions of the effete and effeminate South.[13] When Ian Smith spoke of a masculine nation against an effete metropolis, he sited it rather further from the metropolis— in Rhodesia. In early 1965, Smith—the leader of the right-wing Rhodesian Front movement who became Prime Minister of Rhodesia in 1964— attended Winston Churchill's funeral. Late in the same year, in order to preserve white supremacy in Rhodesia, he proclaimed Rhodesia's independence from Britain through the Unilateral Declaration of Independence. By 1966, the *Sunday Times* was reporting his claim that 'If Sir Winston Churchill were alive today, I believe he would probably emigrate to Rhodesia—because I believe that all those admirable qualities and characteristics of the British that we believed in, loved and preached to our children, no longer exist in Britain'.[14]

In neatly reversing the notion of Britain as the heartland of empire, and representing Rhodesia as the bastion of a racial community of Britons

---

[12] Stuart Ward, '"No Nation Could Be Broker": The Satire Boom and the Demise of Britain's World Role', in Stuart Ward (ed.), *British Culture and the End of Empire* (Manchester: Manchester University Press, 2001), 108.

[13] See Alan Sinfield, *Literature, Politics and Culture in Postwar Britain* (Oxford: Blackwell, 1989), 60–85.

[14] *Sunday Times*, 6 Nov. 1966.

against a multiracial Commonwealth, Smith positioned himself as a true defender of the nation against the metropolis. Claiming Rhodesia as the heartland of empire—a place to which Churchill would now emigrate— Smith also claimed the imperial identity associated with Churchill as one which was now represented by Rhodesia rather than by Britain.

By the year of Churchill's funeral, British rule over an empire that in 1945 had still encompassed India was virtually at an end—although, as Smith's rebellion in Rhodesia demonstrated, this did not always mean the end of white rule. Smith's verdict that imperial identity no longer had much currency in Britain was one that was widely articulated in the late 1950s and 1960s. But even though imperial figures were often identified as *passé* and sometimes ridiculed, they continued to resonate in British culture. The satire directed at them suggested the extent to which imperial identity was at issue in attempts to usher in a modern nation. The 1960s also produced a final flowering of imperial heroism in the filmic empire genre which, like *North West Frontier* (1959), was imbued with nostalgia but also modernized imagery and was produced primarily for an American market. While 1950s empire films had feminized the genre, 1960s films returned to stories of a homosocial world.[15] They offered modernization particularly through drawing on psychology to suggest a dark side to heroism, producing some critique of imperial history and flawed heroes, but also extending a fascination with such heroism for a Western audience into a post-imperial era. This produced a contradictory story: one that both offered a romance of manliness but simultaneously—informed by knowledge of the end of empire—registered its loss. As Churchill's funeral demonstrated, when a romance of manliness was transposed onto the Second World War it told not of loss of empire but of a famous victory.

Imperial Masculinity and the Second World War

On the commercial television broadcast of Churchill's funeral, the voice of Joseph C. Harsch, an American journalist and broadcaster, paid tribute to Churchill.[16] Speaking over shots of the river procession up the Thames to the steam-train that would take Churchill on his last journey from London, Harsch reflected that

Before the days of Winston Churchill, many an American saw Britain as a selfish imperial taskmaster... During the Churchill era that image has been transformed.

---

[15] *Death Drums Along the River* (Lawrence Huntington, 1963) offered a remake of *Sanders of the River* incorporating a romantic plot but was not popular at box-offices.

[16] *The State Funeral of Sir Winston Churchill* (Peter Morley, ITV, 1965).

Today the word 'Britain' brings up memories of the great Churchill speeches, the bravery and pride of standing alone, the pledge to fight, even in the streets. Thanks more to Winston Churchill than to any other man we Americans who once thought of Britain as rapacious, insolent and domineering now think of Britain as sturdy, brave and above all honourable. Americans here with you today are proud.

In offering his tribute, Harsch was careful not to offend a British audience that he called English. 'No American', he said, 'would wish to deny or detract from the possessive pride of Englishmen in the greatness of this man.' He made no reference to Churchill's American mother and did not claim Churchill as an American hero. But he did identify Churchill as 'the first foreigner Americans could respect and trust, the first foreigner who to us did not seem a foreigner, but even one of us'.

In making Churchill 'one of us', Harsch provided some Americanization of Churchill's story, erasing his imperial identity. Churchill's late nineteenth-century military career included service with the 4th Hussars on the North-West Frontier and the 21st Lancers at Omdurman in the Sudan. As a journalist, reporting on the British–Boer war of 1899–1902, Churchill was taken prisoner by the Boers, but escaped. His political career included service as Indian Secretary in the 1880s, when he annexed Upper Burma, and later as Colonial Under-Secretary and Colonial Secretary. In the 1930s, he opposed concessions to Gandhi on Indian independence. He called Gandhi 'a seditious Middle Temple lawyer... posing as a fakir', and objected to him striding 'half-naked up the steps of the Vice-regal Palace ... to parley on equal terms with the representative of the King-Emperor'.[17] During the Second World War, he was Prime Minister when the leading supporters of the 'Quit India' movement, including Gandhi, were arrested, the movement violently repressed by the British, and the RAF brought in to machine-gun demonstrators from the air. In 1947, he opposed the Indian Independence Act. In the 1950s, he was Prime Minister when mobile gallows were introduced in Kenya to execute insurgents. Yet Harsch made him appear as a figure who had fully supported wartime American anti-imperialism.

In contrast to Harsch's comment, British voices in the media wove Churchill's imperial identity into their praise of him. Harold Macmillan's tribute, broadcast on BBC television, identified a constant strand in an otherwise varied career—'his love of Britain, of the Empire, his pride in its glorious past, his confidence in its future'.[18] The *Daily Telegraph* spoke of his 'unflagging praise for the glory and greatness of Britain (which he often

[17] Quoted in Nicholas Owen, '"More Than a Transfer of Power": Independence Day Ceremonies in India, 15 August 1947', *Contemporary Record*, 6 (1992), 437.

[18] Harold Macmillan's tribute, BBC WAC, T14/1, 948/1 Churchill, Sir Winston, Death tributes.

referred to as Britannia), and of the British Commonwealth (which he was not afraid to call the Empire)'.[19] Even American tributes noted his imperial identity—Dwight D. Eisenhower praising Churchill as 'the embodiment of all that was best of the British Empire . . . a man of great courage, indomitable will'.[20]

The celebration of Churchill as a vigorous man of action also bore traces of imperial identity, praising his force of character, and offering a version of heroism that was buccaneering and romantic. According to the *Daily Telegraph*, Churchill's vitality had found expression in physical adventure, expressing his passion for courage and peril, and his love of 'the razor's edge'. He had been 'endowed at birth with two or three times the normal human allowance of vitality', and proved that 'his country has . . . a secret vigour and a pulse like a cannon'.[21] The *Daily Express* suggested that his life was 'a testimonial freshly written to the immortal vigour of the British stock'.[22] In a televised discussion of memories of Churchill the historian, Alan Bullock, asked to talk about Churchill as a historian, called him a 'great man of action', and argued that his actions had sprung from his feeling for history and of his own place in it, while his feeling for history had also influenced his actions. Harold Macmillan referred to his life as 'a great romance . . . of adventure and hazard, for he was never afraid to take risks'.

While these tributes invoked the romance of Churchill's life, they also set it in the past. When Bullock spoke of Churchill as 'a man cast in the heroic who loved the heroic gesture and . . . rode into action', he identified the First World War as a moment when the great heroic gestures, words, and characters of the nineteenth century had gone out of fashion. Churchill, Bullock stated, was a hero in 'an anti-heroic age'. In the same discussion Lady Violet Asquith suggested that Churchill had 'reinstated the great heroic qualities'.[23] When Jo Grimond, the leader of the Liberal party, spoke of the 'romance of Churchill's life' and 'its buccaneering quality' as demonstrated by his adventures in Africa, he suggested that there were elements of nostalgia in admiration for him, since his was a life that 'differs so much from our own'.[24]

The idea of a romantic past of great heroic gestures, with its resonance of imperialism, was unyoked from any reference to the Commonwealth. The almost complete absence of references to the Commonwealth at a funeral celebrating a widely admired national figure is striking. In Coronation year,

[19] *Daily Telegraph*, 25 Jan. 1965.
[20] *National Geographic*, Aug. 1965.
[21] *Daily Telegraph*, 25 Jan. 1965.
[22] *Daily Express*, 25 Jan. 1965.
[23] 'Memories of Sir Winston', *Panorama*, BBC television, 25 Jan. 1965.
[24] Jo Grimond's tribute, BBC WAC, T14/1 948/1 Churchill, Sir Winston, Death Tributes.

the idea of Britain as a moral nation was strongly associated with a Commonwealth conceived as a multiracial community of equal nations, and celebrated as an entirely new conception, marking a decisive break with an imperial identity seen as belonging to the past. Churchill's funeral reversed this process, associating national greatness mainly with the Second World War but also with Britain's imperial past, while more or less ignoring the Commonwealth. Reporting of the arrival of a wide range of international visitors for the funeral, and the international reach of the television broadcast had echoes of imperial identity. The idea that London occupied the centre of a world stage—if only briefly, and for the last time—was prominent in reporting, but this made no particular mention of the Commonwealth.

Commonwealth contingents—prominent both in the Victory Parade of 1946 and in the Coronation procession in 1953—did not march in the procession for Churchill's funeral. The insistent identification of 1940 as Churchill's 'finest hour' celebrated the courage of a nation, personified by Churchill, that had stood alone. A *Punch* cartoon in 1940 had noted that this small island story was considerably expanded by the addition of 'our poor old empire'—comprising five hundred million people.[25] Narratives of the Second World War in the 1950s became racially exclusive, but they sometimes incorporated some of these 'five hundred million'—white Australians, Canadians, and New Zealanders. The victory celebrated at Churchill's funeral in 1965 more or less erased the imperial war effort.

At the Coronation, commentators from the Commonwealth had contributed to British broadcasts, especially on radio. Commonwealth voices were almost completely absent from British broadcasts of Churchill's funeral. One of the very few gestures towards a Commonwealth identity was an invitation from Hugh Greene, Director General of the BBC, to Sir Robert Menzies, Prime Minister of Australia, to broadcast a tribute.[26] However, programme planners for the BBC coverage had broached the idea of an American voice much earlier, in September 1963, suggesting that either the President or Dwight D. Eisenhower should be approached. In the event, tributes from Eisenhower and Menzies had an equal place in the coverage of the funeral day, while on the commercial television broadcast Harsch provided the American tribute.[27] John Ramsden notes that the verdict in the *Washington Post*—that an 'Anglo-US theme' had dominated the day—was due, in part, to Churchill's own stipulations about his funeral.

[25] *Punch*, 17 July 1940.
[26] Letter from Hugh Greene to Sir Robert Menzies, 26 Jan. 1965, BBC WAC, T14/1 948/1, Churchill, Sir Winston, Death Tributes.
[27] Memorandum from Anthony Craxton, 18 Sept. 1963, BBC WAC, T 14/1 928/1, Churchill, Sir Winston, General.

Churchill wanted American and British flags to fly side by side along the procession route, and the 'Battle Hymn of the Republic' as well as 'Land of Hope and Glory' to be included in the music for the service.[28]

The traffic in imagery between Commonwealth and metropolis, which had reached its post-1945 high point in Coronation year, was no longer regarded as of any particular significance. As early as 1958, plans were made at the Colonial Office to distribute prints of an eight-minute biographical film to British colonies—*In Memoriam: Winston Spencer Churchill*—to be shown in the event of Churchill's death.[29] There was no corresponding interest in portraying the Commonwealth as part of world-wide mourning to a British audience. Imagery of world-wide rejoicing in Coronation year focused on the Commonwealth and empire, but imagery of world-wide mourning at Churchill's funeral focused especially on America.

It was the Queen who made one of the few positive references to the Commonwealth in her message to Lady Churchill, stating that 'the survival of this country, and the sister nations of the Commonwealth . . . will be a perpetual memorial to his leadership, his vision, and his indomitable courage'.[30] Anti-Commonwealth opinion, however, was more widely expressed and, since the funeral had resonances of Britain's former imperial identity, much of this focused on the sense that the Commonwealth had little to contribute to the central theme of the funeral week—national greatness. It drew on an increasingly common idea that a main problem with the Commonwealth was that it was a pale shadow of the empire, providing an illusory sense of a global identity as some consolation for loss of imperial power. In the week of Churchill's funeral, Bernard Levin, reflecting on how Britain's greatness in the past had rested on an empire that was now at an end, suggested that the idea of Commonwealth 'has no meaning at all if viewed from the perimeter instead of the centre', and was confident that 'Britain's future leads to Europe'.[31] Colin MacInnes suggested that 'His (Churchill's) death may finally liberate us from . . . our daft illusion that the Commonwealth is the Empire he admired and sought, impossibly, to sustain'.[32] At the end of 1965, James Morris, advocating the turn to Europe, described the Commonwealth as a 'dim intermittent vision of universal niceness' and a 'sop to self-esteem'.[33]

John Ramsden has shown that the late 1940s was a transitional period in the narrative of Churchill, as in other Second World War narratives, when

[28] Ramsden, *Man of the Century*, 326.
[29] PRO INF C166.
[30] *Daily Express*, 25 Jan. 1965.
[31] Bernard Levin, 'Now Here are the New Laurels We Can Win', *Daily Mail*, 2 Feb. 1965.
[32] Colin MacInnes, 'The Week He Died', *Sunday Telegraph Supplement*, 31 Jan. 1965.
[33] James Morris, 'Going into Europe', *Encounter*, Dec. 1965, 57.

accounts of wartime Britain made scant reference to Churchill's leadership, and his defeat at the polls in 1945 was widely viewed as the end of his career.[34] The developing cult of Churchill in the 1950s began to tell a different story, contributing significantly to the eclipse of a 'people's war' and the shift to an exclusive image, focusing on élite white martial masculinity—making a great leader the personification of national greatness. The cult showed no sign of fading in the early 1960s when the BBC made an epic television series about Churchill's war leadership: *The Valiant Years*.[35] It reached its high point in the week of Churchill's funeral.

In funeral week, the idea that Churchill *was* Britain recurred in a number of tributes—ranging from that of Patrick O'Donavan in the *Observer*, to Dwight D. Eisenhower, speaking during the broadcast of the funeral on BBC television. Eisenhower claimed to speak for millions of Americans who had served in the Second World War when he said that 'Winston Churchill *was* Britain—he was the embodiment of British defiance to threat, her courage in adversity, her calmness in danger, her moderation in success'.[36] But a more insistent tribute to Churchill contrasted with the wartime inclusion of different national identities within Britishness. In the 1950s, Churchill was increasingly seen as 'the greatest living Englishman' and on his death he was acclaimed variously as 'the greatest Englishman of all time', 'the greatest of all Englishmen', or simply 'the greatest Englishman'.[37] *The Times* obituary referred to him, rather more circumspectly, as 'the Greatest Englishman of his time', while the draft of Sir Alec Douglas-Home's tribute, broadcast on BBC television, continued—somewhat inappropriately—to refer to him as 'the greatest living Englishman'.[38]

The funeral was also a culminating moment in the process through which, in celebrating a romance of manliness focused on the Second World War, women were expelled from imagery. Like Commonwealth contingents, the women's services had marched in the Victory Parade of 1946 and the Coronation procession in 1953. They did not take part in the funeral procession. Although the women's services were present at St Paul's Cathedral where the funeral service was held, only one woman participated in the march—a representative of the Westerham Branch of the British Legion.

---

[34] Ramsden, *Man of the Century*, 77–8.

[35] *The Valiant Years* (Jack Le Vien, BBC television, 1961).

[36] Patrick O'Donavan, 'Requiem that Rejected Death', *The Observer*, 31 Jan. 1965; Dwight D. Eisenhower's tribute, BBC WAC, T14/1 948/1 Churchill, Sir Winston, Death tributes.

[37] Field-Marshal Viscount Montgomery, 'Goodbye Dear Friend', *Sunday Times*, 31 Jan. 1965; Poem by Avril Anderson, read at the end of the BBC coverage of the funeral on television; *Sunday Express*, 31 Jan. 1965.

[38] *The Times*, 25 Jan. 1965; Draft of Sir Alec Douglas-Home's tribute, BBC WAC, T14/1 948/1, Churchill, Sir Winston, Death Tributes.

The voices publicly celebrating Churchill's life were those of a white male elite. Rebecca West, noting the almost complete absence of women from the funeral procession, suggested that there was something appropriate about this, given Churchill's opposition to women's suffrage and the fact that he 'lived in such a male world'.[39] The associations of Churchill's life with high politics, the armed forces, and empire were part of the male world he had inhabited, where a female presence or voice would have been considered an oddity or intrusion. The associations of Churchill's life with heritage and history involved a further male world where the female voice had little authority. It included historical works by Churchill, which produced a similar deference and praise from male historians to that of television commentators on the history his life represented. British national history, and particularly its imperial, military, and political history, was generally written as the history of white male elites, and largely a white male elite preserve. The BBC broadcast ended with a poem written for the occasion and sent in by Mrs Crabtree, whose *nom de plume* was Avril Anderson, and who had lectured to the armed forces in Northern Ireland during the Second World War, on behalf of the War Office. Her poem, however, was read by the voice of Richard Dimbleby.[40]

When Churchill did a screen test for a television party political broadcast in 1954, he expressed regret that he had to 'sink to this level' but recognized that he must move with the times. Subsequently, he ordered the film to be destroyed.[41] In the to and fro of ideas of modernity and tradition in Coronation year, the live television broadcast was a symbol of modernity. But even though Churchill himself saw television as modern, the BBC coverage of his funeral was associated with tradition, and a reputation for covering great national occasions which, by 1965, BBC television considered firmly established. One BBC official went so far as to suggest that 'Somehow the Corporation herself comes to our help in times of a national crisis, to show us out of her tradition, what we ought to do'.[42]

Like the Coronation, the funeral was treated with intense moral seriousness in the British media. The selection of voices for broadcasts, although excluding Commonwealth and female voices, otherwise produced a choice that echoed the coverage of the Coronation. Richard Dimbleby was the sole commentator throughout the funeral broadcast on the BBC, while on commercial television Brian Connell's voice as commentator was joined by that of Laurence Olivier, who had narrated the script of *A Queen is*

[39] Rebecca West, 'The Roots of His Greatness', *Sunday Telegraph Supplement*, 31 Jan. 1965.

[40] Avril Anderson's poem is in BBC WAC, T14/1 928/2, Churchill, Sir Winston, General.

[41] Synopsis of Churchill's 1954 screen test, British Film Institute Catalogue.

[42] Memorandum from Dr Ronald Falconer, Religious Broadcasting Organiser, Scotland, 26 Jan. 1965, BBC WAC, T14/1 928/2, Churchill, Sir Winston, General.

Crowned. The voices of commentators were reverential, conveying a sense of solemnity and dignity, and the moral seriousness of the history that Churchill represented. The actorly voices used on commercial television, including Paul Scofield, who read extracts from Churchill's speeches, reinforced the sense of a historic occasion conjuring up associations of the heritage of English literature, Shakespeare, and the English theatre.

Television was credited with the production of national unity, as it had been at the time of the Coronation. The idea that this was 'TV's finest hour'—a verdict that had been produced at the time of the Coronation—was reiterated not only in reviews, but also within the BBC, where those involved in the broadcast were congratulated on producing 'television's finest hours'.[43] Television coverage, reviewers suggested, meant that 'viewers were caught up in the ritual mood', making 'us all partakers in a great unifying ritual of the race' and creating 'a moving sense of unity between all of us, bound together by a common focus on a naval gun carriage and its momentous burden'.[44]

It was a mood that infected some of those working on the BBC broadcast. Richard Dimbleby wrote: 'There was also about it a strange spirit of unity which I felt from the very beginning and this, I think, permeated everyone in the whole outside broadcast team. It was almost as though we were back again with Churchill in wartime with everyone determined to do the very best he [*sic*] could.'[45] Some reviewers were even-handed about the rival television networks, Maurice Wiggins writing that 'BBC or ITV—they were equally servants of the people, the hero and the occasion'.[46] At the BBC, however, commercial television was scarcely included in the idea of 'television's finest hours'. In early plans for BBC coverage, begun in August 1958 and called 'Operation Hopenot', and then 'Standard Ceremonial Procedure'—later merged as 'SCP-Operation Hopenot' to 'avoid confusion'—an assumption had been made that commercial television would take a feed from the BBC.[47] Claims about the BBC's importance to national life were promoted through the idea that it had stronger credentials than commercial television to cover a national occasion, emphasizing the significance of its codes of deference and the likelihood that they would be violated by commercial rivals. The BBC could be relied on not to 'crowd

---

[43] *Bolton Evening News*, 1 Feb. 1965; Message from Peter Dimmock, 2 Feb. 1965, BBC WAC, T14/1 929/1 Churchill, Winston, Appreciations and Congratulations.

[44] *The Observer*, 31 Jan. 1965; *Sunday Times*, 31 Jan. 1965; *Northern Echo*, 1 Feb. 1965.

[45] Letter from Richard Dimbleby to Peter Dimmock, 3 Feb. 1965, BBC WAC, T14/1 929/1, Churchill, Winston, Appreciations and Congratulations.

[46] Maurice Wiggins, 'Through Television the Whole Nation Was There', *Sunday Times*, 31 Jan. 1965.

[47] Memorandum from Peter Dimmock, 17 Feb. 1963, BBC WAC, T 14/1 928/1 Churchill, Sir Winston, General.

the coffin', and to keep their cameras more than thirty feet away from the royal family at all times, ensuring a production that did not stray into being 'tasteless'.[48] In the event, the BBC were delighted to report that while half the total population of Britain had watched the funeral, 80 per cent of these viewers had watched the BBC.[49]

Preparing for broadcasts as Churchill was dying, the BBC ruled that *Not So Much a Programme, More a Way of Life*—a satire programme launched in 1964—should not be broadcast either on the day of death, or the following day.[50] The moral earnestness and deference appropriate to Churchill's funeral clashed with an increasing identification of such values as outmoded in the 1960s satire boom. From the mid-1950s, what Martin Francis calls a 'culture of restraint', strongly associated with moral seriousness, as well as the values of regularity and discipline, was increasingly displaced in areas as diverse as child-care and consumption by a concern with self-expression and personal choice.[51]

The high-minded hero and his codes of duty and honour also became the target of considerable levity across a range of media, including film, radio, and television. In the *Goon Show*—a radio comedy that ran in various series from June 1952 to January 1960—Major Denis Bloodnock (Peter Sellers), an ex-India army man, late of the 'Third Disgusting Fusiliers', is corrupt, cowardly, seedy, and impoverished, prone to embezzlement and fraud, marching off with regimental funds.[52] In *Carlton-Browne of the FO* (1959), the emphasis is on the hugely incompetent upper-class imperial figure. The British imperial administration has granted independence to the islanders of Gaillardia, but omitted to inform the British representative on the island. The Foreign Office official in charge of 'miscellaneous territories' (Terry-Thomas) has a name that signals the blundering ineptitude of his attempt to sort this out—Cadogan de Vere Carlton-Browne. The comedy is reinforced by the decrepit, doddery, enfeebled masculinity embodied in the British representative on the island, and Carlton-Browne's best efforts to inform him of independence are hampered by the need to bellow down an ear-trumpet to a man of considerable age, who suffers from gout.[53] Later films, like *Carry On Up the Khyber* (1968), set in India, derived comedy

[48] Draft of letter from Peter Dimmock, Head of Television Outside Broadcasts, to J. McMillan, Associated Rediffusion Ltd., 6 Oct. 1960, BBC WAC T 14/1 932/1 Churchill, W (Sir) and Commercial Television.

[49] BBC Press Release, 4 Feb. 1965, BBC WAC, T 14/1 928/2, Churchill, Sir Winston, General.

[50] Memorandum from Planning Manager, 22 Jan. 1965, BBC WAC T14/1 942/1, Churchill, Winston, Programme Planning.

[51] Martin Francis, 'The Labour Party: Modernisation and the Politics of Restraint', in Becky Conekin, Frank Mort, and Chris Waters (eds.), *Moments of Modernity: Reconstructing Britain 1945–1964* (London: Rivers Oram), 152–70; Francis, 'Tears, Tantrums, and Bared Teeth'.

[52] Spike Milligan, *The Goon Show Scripts* (London: Woburn Press, 1972), 105, 185.

[53] *Carlton-Browne of the FO* (Jeffrey Dell and Roy Boulting, 1959).

from casting characters wholly lacking the appropriate upper-class credentials as imperial officials. In case anybody should miss the point, this was also signalled through comic names in a film that installed Sir Sidney Ruff-Diamond (Sid James) as imperial governor, and Lady Ruff-Diamond (Joan Sims) as his wife.[54]

Much levity also surrounded Second World War heroics. Comedies of National Service life in the post-war army celebrated the subversion of traditional values by working-class soldiers, whose behaviour had more to do with codes of skiving and fiddling than duty and honour. A failure to live up to ideals of heroism, as well as a complete disregard for such ideals, is set against the Second World War film in *Private's Progress* (1956).[55] Soldiers on National Service on a skive attend a matinée at a local cinema, which is screening the wartime film of naval heroism—*In Which We Serve*. They lounge in their cinema seats, locked in amorous embraces with girlfriends or sleeping the afternoon away.

Subversion of official versions of heroism that focused on the working classes had a considerable history, but in the early 1960s young men who themselves had public-school backgrounds extended this mockery to their own training in duty and honour in shows and television programmes associated with the satire boom. Jonathan Miller, a member of the original *Beyond the Fringe* cast, blamed weaknesses in English satire on 'the smug courtesy of the public school sixth-former, neatly adjusted to the demands of loyal service in a growing Empire'. But, he added with some satisfaction, 'The sturdy sterling figure of the school prefect is at last becoming an object of ridicule'.[56] Kenneth Tynan reminded 'aspiring prole satirists' in 1961 that 'the tone, background and terms of reference of *Beyond the Fringe*, the sharpest London revue I have ever seen, are entirely middle class'.[57] 'The Aftermyth of War', a sketch in *Beyond the Fringe*, parodied the Second World War film, featuring one young man flocking to join 'the Few' who is told, 'I'm sorry, there are far too many'. Another is told to lay down his life: 'We need a futile gesture at this stage. It will raise the whole tone of the war. Get up in a crate, Perkins, pop over to Bremen, take a shufti, don't come back.'[58] *Private Eye*, the satirical magazine founded in 1963, made the cult of Churchill one of the targets of its first issue, and took to calling Churchill 'the greatest dying Englishman'.[59] More generally, the satire movement

---

[54] *Carry On Up the Khyber* (Gerald Thomas, 1968).

[55] *Private's Progress* (John Boulting, 1956).

[56] Jonathan Miller, 'Can English Satire Draw Blood', *The Observer*, 1 Oct. 1961.

[57] Kenneth Tynan, 'The Breakthrough that Broke Down', *The Observer*, 1 Oct. 1961.

[58] Roger Wilmut, *From Fringe to Flying Circus: Celebrating a Unique Generation of Comedy 1960–1980* (London: Book Club Associates, 1981), 16–17.

[59] See Humphrey Carpenter, *That Was Satire That Was: The Satire Boom of the 1960s* (London: Victor Gollancz, 2000), 160–1.

made much comedy out of the idea of British impotence in a post-imperial world, as represented by elite men who fail to realize that their power has dwindled.[60]

After Suez, some Second World War films began to distance themselves from the values associated with the genre, although often with considerable ambivalence, offering their audiences narratives in which duty and honour could be read as problematic and outmoded. *The Bridge On the River Kwai* (1957)—a British–American film made with American finance, directed by David Lean and produced by Sam Spiegel—was the most notable example of such films.[61] Andrew Spicer associates its popularity in Britain with a mood of disillusionment, following Suez, which 'helped to undermine the credibility of the national greatness which the officer hero incarnated'.[62] But while some contemporary reviewers noted its critique of British officers, others read it through the conventions of the imperial and war genres as an exciting adventure, and a tribute to British heroism.

It is notable that, in a British–American production, made with American finance, the verdict that traditional British martial heroism is outmoded and problematic is voiced within the film most explicitly through its American character—Commander Shears (William Holden). Moreover, these values are explicitly linked to an imperial world-view and a history of service in empire through the figure of Colonel Nicholson (Alec Guinness). The film is at pains to construct an opposition between the American Shears's modern sensibility—sceptical, irreverent, and individualist—against the British Nicholson's discipline, self-control, and stoicism. This American–British contrast is expressed particularly through physicality. Shears rarely wears much clothing. He concedes a uniform when occasion demands, but for the most part is bare-chested. British officers wear uniform at all times. Even when confined to 'the oven' by the Japanese commander of the prisoner-of-war camp in the Burmese jungle where the film is set, Nicholson keeps his shirt on. At the moment when the Japanese commander of the camp—Colonel Saito (Sessue Hayakawa)—tells Nicholson that he has won their battle over whether British officers can be required, in contravention of the Geneva convention, to do manual labour, building the bridge over the River Kwai for the Japanese, Nicholson buttons the shirt up. Nicholson's dedication to discipline and control precludes all sensual pleasure, and none of the British figures is attributed sexuality.

---

[60] Ward, 'No Nation Could Be Broker'.

[61] *The Bridge Over the River Kwai* (David Lean, 1957).

[62] Andrew Spicer, *Typical Men: The Representation of Masculinity in Popular British Cinema* (London: I. B. Tauris, 2001), 43.

Shears's self-expression extends to the pleasures of alcohol, tobacco, and heterosexuality.

The contrast between Shears's modernity and Nicholson's traditional British martial masculinity is connected to Nicholson's devotion to imperial service. Once Nicholson has effectively taken over command of the bridge-building, his determination to do a good job matches Saito's determination to build the bridge on time. It is informed by an imperial world-view as Nicholson resolves to 'teach these barbarians a lesson in Western methods and efficiency that will put them to shame. We'll show them what the British soldier is capable of doing.' Nicholson is convinced of the superior skills of his officers in building the bridge which he attributes to their experience in building bridges all over India. He tells Saito not only of his long period of military service, but of his love of India. His determination to build the bridge well offers a version of imperial masculinity as highly problematic, for Nicholson increasingly resembles Saito, enlisting his officers to do manual labour, and sick prisoners to help—the very points of his original dispute with Saito. The parallel is articulated by Major Clipton (James Donald), who, as a British Medical Officer, acts as a moral centre for the film. He pronounces them both 'Mad!!' It is Clipton too who queries whether the British must build the bridge so well, pointing out to Nicholson that 'what we're doing could be construed as collaboration with the enemy, perhaps even as treasonable activity'. Nicholson dismisses this idea.

Shears extends his irreverence about British officers after he has escaped from the camp—a plot that contrasts to most British prisoner-of-war films where the British escape attempt is the usual focus. Recruited to blow up the bridge that Nicholson is intent on building by another British officer— Major Warden (Jack Hawkins)—Shears identifies Warden as yet another Briton wedded to rule-bound tradition. He tells Warden in a set-piece speech: 'You and that Colonel Nicholson, you're two of a kind, crazy with courage. For what? How to die like a gentleman, how to die by the rules. When the only important thing is how to live like a human being.' As leader of the commando raid on the bridge, Warden is nevertheless a man of action. Shots of the commando unit hacking its way through the jungle to blow up the bridge, killing Japanese soldiers who discover them, and stalking a surviving Japanese soldier through the jungle, merge war and empire genres.

Shears's criticisms of British officers, while developing an opposition between American masculinity as modern and individualist against British deference to hide-bound traditions, do not make Shears into the hero of the film. His own code—playing by no rules, and surviving not through honour, but his own resourcefulness—includes impersonating an officer, and planning to get a discharge from the US Navy. *The Bridge On the River*

Kwai can be read as an anti-war film that opposes all versions of masculine heroics. This is certainly the verdict with which the film ends. Its final words are given to Major Clipton after Shears, Nicholson, and the youthful Canadian apprentice to martial masculinity, Lieutenant Joyce (Geoffrey Horne), have all met their deaths and the bridge is finally blown up. Clipton's verdict—'Madness! Madness!'—seems to encompass every aspect of war. It apparently extends to all national versions of martial masculinity represented in the film. On this reading, *The Bridge On the River Kwai* disrupts the conventions of the prisoner-of-war and empire genres on which it draws to produce an anti-romance of manliness.

The Bridge On the River Kwai was the most popular film at British box-offices in 1958. Was this because audiences, in the aftermath of Suez, welcomed its critique of masculine heroics linked to ideals of imperial service? Did they appreciate Shears's irreverence about British martial masculinity? There is no way of knowing. Reviewers, however, produced very different readings of the film. Some noted the anti-war theme or the resemblance between Saito and Nicholson.[63] Others reviewed it as another film in the burgeoning genre of British war films that celebrated British heroism.[64] The reviewer in the *Financial Times* praised the first half of the film as 'infinitely the finer, emphasising as it does, most movingly, the heroism of British soldiers under intolerable conditions'. But he did not see the second half of the film as less fine because it critiqued masculine heroics. Rather he regretted the shift from 'heroism' to 'heroics' which made the film into 'simply a superb thriller', and read it through the conventions of the empire as 'the best film of its sort since *The Lives of a Bengal Lancer*'.[65] The reviewer in the *Evening News* read the film as an American tribute to British Second World War heroism, much like Harsch's later tribute to Churchill. Calling it 'as thrilling an adventure film as was ever made', the reviewer emphasized that 'it was an American producer, Sam Spiegel, who promoted this remarkable tribute to the British spirit in war'.[66]

This range of readings no doubt reflected the ambivalence of the film—its anti-romance themes undercut by the need to read it through the conventions of the war and empire genres. Like these genres, it is obsessed with questions of martial masculinity and heroism. The criticism of British martial masculinity develops alongside increasing suspense in sequences that merge these genres, and the dramatic explosion of the bridge marks the climax of an exciting adventure narrative, undermining the final

[63] *Evening Standard*, 3 Oct. 1957: *Reynolds News*, 6 Oct. 1957.
[64] *Daily Mirror*, 3 Oct. 1957.
[65] *Financial Times*, 7 Oct. 1957.
[66] *Evening News*, 3 Oct. 1957.

message of the film—'Madness! Madness!' But readings which praised the film as a tribute to British heroism also suggest the extent to which Second World War narratives of the 1950s raised expectations of a romance of manliness, and the continuing investment in such a romance.

Shears's American verdict on the British officers in *The Bridge On the River Kwai* contrasted strongly with American tributes to Churchill in the week of his funeral. Churchill had been made an honorary citizen of the United States in 1963, and the ceremony, which Churchill was not well enough to attend, was broadcast live from America to Britain over satellite. In funeral week, *Time* magazine carried Churchill's picture on a cover that named him 'Giant of the Century'. Heroes who represented traditional British martial masculinity and high-minded stoicism, like Nicholson in *The Bridge On the River Kwai*, were not popular in America. Hollywood celebration of the British imperial hero before 1945 showed him as buccaneering and romantic. British Second World War films of the 1950s never gained strong markets or popularity in America, while *Scott of the Antarctic* (1948)—perhaps the most quintessential representation of a stiff-upper-lip hero—had only one showing there: a charity premiere at the White House.[67] Churchill's story celebrated a man of action. His funeral, broadcast live on American television, attracted a larger audience than that of John F. Kennedy in 1963.[68]

In Britain, the cult of Churchill demonstrated the continuing investment in a romance of manliness, and the enduring appeal of an epic story of national destiny. The media image of a nation united in a common focus on a naval gun carriage obscured divisions, indifference, and hostility. But in a week when the cult of Churchill reached its height, there could be no possible criticism of what Churchill represented as outmoded. The idea that he *was* Britain meant that criticism of his life or funeral in the British media was at best highly unpatriotic. At worst, Goronwy Rees noted, asking what the funeral meant 'seemed almost blasphemous'.[69]

Effete Metropolis

In a piece of journalism written in 1956—the same year that *Look Back in Anger* was first staged—John Osborne posed the question: 'what's gone wrong with women?' Diagnosing a post-war malaise of caution and fatigue, Osborne argued that this attitude 'on every level stems from woman... Never before have women had so much freedom, so much power, or so

[67] Michael Balcon, *Michael Balcon Presents a Lifetime of Films* (London: Hutchinson, 1969), 174.
[68] Ramsden, *Man of the Century*, 22.
[69] Goronwy Rees, 'After the Ball was Over', *Encounter*, Nov. 1965, 3.

much influence. Men have lost their dynamic... We are becoming dominated by female values.' The article concluded: 'Something is going wrong, something is rotten, something is unsatisfactory. Just think about it for five minutes—you might even get a little angry.'[70]

John Osborne, as well as his creation Jimmy Porter in *Look Back in Anger*, was the archetype of the 'Angry Young Man'. First performed on stage at the Royal Court Theatre in London in May 1956, *Look Back in Anger* reached a wide audience when it was televised live from the Royal Court on the recently opened commercial television channel, and subsequently made into a film directed by Tony Richardson in 1959.[71] *Look Back in Anger* was representative of a range of theatrical, literary, and filmic work produced by men who were more or less youthful, which featured young male characters who express a range of dissatisfactions with the age in which they live, and articulate a sense—often left quite vague—that something is wrong.

In 1959, Tony Richardson enthusiastically hailed the 'Angry Young Man' as a figure capable of rejuvenating British culture. 'It is absolutely vital', he said, 'to get into British films the same sort of impact and sense of life that what you can loosely call the Angry Young Man cult has had in the theatre and literary worlds.'[72] In the late 1950s and early 1960s, the production of 'New Wave' films of working-class realism—a number directed by Tony Richardson—was widely seen as fulfilling his hopes. Made at a moment just after the introduction of commercial television in Britain, when the decline of cinema audiences accelerated, 'New Wave' films were seen as offering a new 'frankness' and 'openness' about sex—a strong selling-point in a period when film censorship was becoming increasingly relaxed. Made at a moment when there was much criticism of British theatre and cinema—including the Second World War genre—as stiflingly conventional, they were seen by many critics as marking an exhilarating break with the past.

Jimmy's noise is a constant feature of *Look Back in Anger* in his lengthy verbal, psychological, and sometimes physical assaults on others when he is on stage, enacting his dissatisfaction and sense of malaise. But his noise also demonstrates his vitality, and his jazz trumpet acts as a reminder of his presence for much of the time that he is offstage. The film elaborates this, opening with jazz, young people dancing, and the exuberance of Jimmy's trumpet playing. As he leaves the performance and goes out into rainy streets, Jimmy (Richard Burton) disrupts the quiet respectability of a residential area, playing his trumpet into a pillar-box, which answers with

[70] John Osborne, 'What's Gone Wrong with Women', *Daily Mail*, 14 Nov. 1956.

[71] John Osborne, *Look Back in Anger* (London: Faber and Faber, 1962); *Look Back in Anger* (Tony Richardson, 1959).

[72] Quoted in Spicer, *Typical Men*, 151.

an echo. Like his creator, John Osborne, Jimmy was acclaimed as new and radical, and credited with a distinctively modern voice, speaking on behalf of a post-war generation.

If Jimmy Porter speaks on behalf of a post-war generation, however, his is a voice that is strongly preoccupied with looking back. *Look Back in Anger* makes reference to the passing of a number of worlds, and demonstrates considerable nostalgia for them. One is the world of working-class community with which Jimmy strongly identifies. Although his own origins are left quite vague, and he has been to university—one that is 'not even red brick but white tile'—Jimmy runs a sweet stall in a working-class market. He has been set up there by Mrs Tanner—his wife informing her father that Mrs Tanner is 'what Jimmy insists on calling working-class. A charwoman who married an actor.' Jimmy's attachment to the vitality of traditional working-class culture is enacted as he fools with his old friend Cliff, performing versions of music-hall sketches. In the film version, this is extended to a contrast with the moribund English theatre, as Jimmy and Cliff disrupt a rehearsal for a cliched and conventional middle-class play with their double-act. It is, however, through his bond with Mrs Tanner that Jimmy's identification with working-class community is most apparent, and Mrs Tanner's death signifies nostalgia for the passing of this world.

While Mrs Tanner is exempted from Jimmy's characteristic contempt for women, Colonel Redfern, his father-in-law, is exempted from his characteristic ranting against the upper classes. Redfern, who has spent most of his adult life in India, articulates a nostalgia for Britain's imperial past: 'I had the Maharaja's army to command—that was my world and I loved it, all of it. At the time it looked like going on for ever . . . Those long, cool evenings up in the hills, everything purple and golden.' Unexpectedly, Jimmy is quite open about a nostalgia of his own that parallels Redfern's:

I hate to admit it, but I think I can understand how her Daddy must have felt when he came back from India, after all those years away. The old Edwardian brigade do make their brief little world look pretty tempting . . . Always the same picture: high summer, the long days in the sun, slim volumes of verse, crisp linen, the smell of starch. What a romantic picture. Phoney too, of course. It must have rained sometimes. Still, even I regret it somehow, phoney or not. If you've no world of your own, it's rather pleasant to regret the passing of someone else's. I must be getting sentimental.[73]

The apologetic tone with which Jimmy starts this speech, his acknowledgement of interest in Redfern's past, and his attempt to understand the feelings of another person are all reversals of Jimmy's normal obsessive preoccupation with his own feelings and his own past. His view of Redfern

---

[73] Osborne, *Look Back*, 17.

is also a reversal of his intense anger and hatred towards the upper classes as represented by his wife, Alison, who tells Redfern that 'he [Jimmy] hates all of us', but later modifies this: 'I think he rather likes you.'[74] Jimmy's identification with Redfern suggests that when he laments that 'there aren't any good, brave causes left', he is lamenting the passing of a romance of manliness that encompasses not only his father's struggles in the Spanish Civil War, but also Redfern's imperialism.

Redfern is the only character in *Look Back in Anger* who is given a history that is not centred on relationship with Jimmy. His own feelings about the loss of his world are expressed within the play and the film, and dated very precisely to 1947 and Indian independence:

I think the last day the sun shone was when that dirty little train steamed out of that crowded suffocating Indian station, and the battalion band playing for all it was worth. I knew in my heart it was all over then. Everything.[75]

Alison's comment to her father on this speech suggests another parallel between Jimmy and Redfern—a common masculine malaise about the post-war world: 'You're hurt because everything is changed. Jimmy is hurt because everything is the same. And neither of you can face it. Something's gone wrong somewhere, hasn't it?'[76] The dialogue between Alison and her father takes place in the flat where she is packing to leave Jimmy, but the film version gives them further dialogue in Redfern's garden after she has left. The imagery of Redfern (Glen Byam Shaw) at home extends the idea of a parallel between the ways in which male lives are marked by the end of empire. Redfern is an ex-imperial soldier, repatriated, retired. This is the point at which he gains Jimmy's understanding of how he must have felt returning home from India to a diminished world. Like Jimmy, Redfern spends a good deal of his time at home with women.

Jimmy's considerable nostalgia for a romance of manliness in empire, embodied in the figure of a father-in-law who commanded the Maharaja's army, is an incongruous feature of a play in which Jimmy's voice was widely seen as new and radical. The film adaptation retains the nostalgia for Redfern's imperial past, but adds some sequences which elaborate Jimmy's claims to represent a modern voice against an old imperial figure. It shows Jimmy watching an old empire film in a local cinema with contempt. It is at pains to establish Jimmy's liberal credentials on questions of race, introducing an Indian character—Kapoor (S. P. Kapoor)—who does not feature in the play. Like Jimmy, Kapoor is a market stall-holder, and his brief appearance serves to mark Jimmy out as anti-racist through his support for Kapoor

---

[74] Osborne, *Look Back*, 65–6.　　　[75] Ibid. 68.　　　[76] Ibid.

against other white stall-holders who object to Kapoor underselling them, and the market supervisor who withdraws his licence. Thus, Jimmy's sense of male solidarity encompasses not only Redfern as a representative of the Raj, but also Kapoor as a representative of the Indians the Raj had ruled. Even the white stall-holders are exempt from the main burden of his anger against racism, which is directed against his wife, Alison, in his accusation that she sees herself as a member of the 'master race'. But male solidarity does not extend to 'Brother Nigel'—Alison's politician brother—who is accused by Jimmy of 'selling out his countryman all these years'. *Look Back in Anger* blames what Osborne later called 'the sightless, feeble, betrayed body of my country' not only on women, but also politicians.[77]

Many films of the British 'New Wave' focused on Northern masculinity to represent vitality and toughness. The associations of the North with heavy industry, manual labour, and harsh landscapes gave it greater masculine credentials than a more comfortable and cosy South—an opposition that was reinforced in documentary cinema between the wars. The interwar documentary movement paid considerable attention to the male working classes in a Northern urban and industrial landscape, endowing manual labour with nobility and heroism. Their imagery of working-class masculinity has been described by Kathryn Dodd and Philip Dodd as providing a 'new, alternative version of manly Englishness' where the Northern man became 'the new icon of a manly nation'. A new icon was needed, they argue, not only to compensate for the decline of imperial masculinity, but also to set against the feminization of national identity between the wars, when national life was increasingly imagined in terms of the domestic and the private.[78]

In their realist intention, focus on Northern masculinity, and relocation of the nation in the North of England, 'New Wave' films shared ground with interwar documentaries, but their image of working-class masculinity shifted considerably. Pre-1939 documentaries had focused on the world of work, and the endeavours of men who inhabit a homosocial word, offering models of solidarity and community. The qualities that they assign these men resemble those of the high-minded imperial hero—self-control, dignity, and stoicism—but there is also considerable attention to their physicality. In documentaries that focus on the fishing industry, like *Drifters* (1929), *Granton Trawler* (1934), and *North Sea* (1938), working-class men demonstrate their manhood in a struggle against an inhospitable and

---

[77] Quoted in Richard Weight, *Patriots: National Identity in Britain 1940–2000* (Basingstoke: Macmillan, 2002), 290.

[78] Kathryn Dodd and Philip Dodd, 'Engendering the Nation: British Documentary Film, 1930–1939', in Andrew Higson (ed.), *Dissolving Views: Key Writings on British Cinema* (London: Cassell, 1996), 48–50.

dangerous natural world, fighting against the elements.[79] In documentaries that focus on heavy industry, like *Industrial Britain* (1933) and *Coal Face* (1935), they demonstrate physical strength, toughness, and endurance— the camera focusing on their bodies and muscularity.[80]

'New Wave' films produce a very different version of masculine identity. The world of work has largely disappeared, and with it the emphasis on a homosocial world. Although often understood by contemporaries as films about class, the youthful male protagonists of 'New Wave' films are marked by an aggressive heterosexuality and individuality that offers a modernized version of Northern masculinity, and they are in quest of heterosexual adventures. Like Jimmy Porter, they spend a good deal of their time with women.

In *Look Back in Anger*, Jimmy's regret at the passing of Redfern's romantic world in India is set against the Americanized world of the present: 'I must say it's pretty dreary living in the American Age—unless you're American of course. Perhaps all our children will be Americans.'[81] Hostility to Americanization was common to many 'New Wave' films, which construct Northern masculinity against a generalized Americanized commercialism and consumerism associated with women. Television, in particular, is identified as a feminizing influence, threatening traditional masculine working-class culture. At the beginning of *Saturday Night and Sunday Morning* (1960) Arthur Seaton's father is prone in front of the television—an entirely passive figure.[82] In *A Kind of Loving* (1962) the early vitality of Vic (Alan Bates) is stemmed by his move to the suburban new estate, where he is forced to sit in front of a television with women, in a domestic setting, watching a quiz show.[83] In *The Loneliness of the Long Distance Runner* (1962) the mother of the male protagonist, indulging in a spending spree with the compensation money from her husband's death, purchases a television and avidly watches advertisements.[84] A modernized masculinity is thus constructed against many aspects of modernity, and especially the television.

The highly popular James Bond films, beginning with the production of *Doctor No* (1962), dealt with American power differently.[85] They dispatched it through a fantasy world in which Bond takes complete command of all situations, the CIA agent Felix Leiter is a subordinate partner, and

[79] *Drifters* (John Grierson, 1929); *Granton Trawler* (John Grierson, 1934); *North Sea* (Harry Watt, 1938).
[80] *Industrial Britain* (Robert Flaherty, 1931); *Coal Face* (Alberto Cavalcanti, 1935).
[81] Osborne, *Look Back*, 17.
[82] *Saturday Night and Sunday Morning* (Karel Reisz, 1960).
[83] *A Kind of Loving* (John Schlesinger, 1962).
[84] *The Loneliness of the Long Distance Runner* (Tony Richardson, 1962).
[85] *Doctor No* (Terence Young, 1962).

Britain has not been superseded as a world power by America. Raymond Durgnat's comments on Bond as 'the last man in the British Empire's Superman XI' and 'an Edwardian in modern drag' suggest the extent to which Bond films offered a version of a romance of manliness where Bond triumphed over all external obstacles and adversaries.[86] But if these films looked back, like Jimmy Porter, they also modernized heroics. Many evoked the contemporary Cold War rather than the colonial past. All displayed a range of modern technological gadgetry, emphasizing the pleasures of consumption, and celebrating a playful, hedonistic, and highly sexualized hero. Like the anti-heroes of 'New Wave' films, James Bond is in quest of sexual adventure.[87]

The quest for sexual adventure did not feature in the traditional romance of manliness. But if Bond films offer a fantasy solution to post-war malaise, showing a Britain that retains its great power status, 'New Wave' films associate men with vitality and potency chiefly through sexual politics. Their diagnosis of malaise is framed around the question that Osborne asks: 'What's gone wrong with women?'[88] Women are shown as threatening in various ways—emasculating or domesticating men, draining them of vitality, feminizing traditional working-class culture—and they attract a range of punishments particularly for their sexuality. The 'Angry Young Man' thus expresses a sense of malaise primarily through gender, and works it out against women. Against the loss of different worlds that had embodied a manly England—empire, war, and working-class community—he promises to reinstate a version of vital and virile masculinity, represented through a culture of youthful male rebellion. In a context where ideas of masculinity were increasingly polarized between the old homosocial world of male heroism, and the modern feminized world of the 'new man', he embodies and claims a new type of male heroics. He asserts his manhood not in a homosocial world of male endeavour and struggle, but through an aggressive heterosexuality that claims the power to humiliate and degrade women as a male entitlement.

If the 'Angry Young Man' movement characteristically framed its explorations of national malaise around John Osborne's question, 'What's gone wrong with women?', others highlighted a different question: 'What's

---

[86] Raymond Durgnat, *A Mirror for England* (London: Faber, 1970), 151.

[87] See Tony Bennett and Janet Woollacott, *Bond and Beyond: The Political Career of a Popular Hero* (Basingstoke: Macmillan, 1987); James Chapman, *License to Thrill: A Cultural History of the James Bond Films* (London: I. B. Tauris, 1999); David Cannadine, *In Churchill's Shadow: Confronting the Past in Modern Britain* (London: Allen Lane, 2002).

[88] John Hill, 'Working-Class Realism and Sexual Reaction: Some Theses on the British "New Wave"', in James Curran and Vincent Porter (eds.), *British Cinema History* (London: Weidenfeld and Nicolson, 1983), 303–11; John Hill, *Sex, Class and Realism: British Cinema 1956–1963* (London: British Film Institute, 1986); Terry Lovell, 'Landscapes and Stories in 1960s British Realism', *Screen*, 31 (1990), 357–76.

gone wrong with politicians?' The 1960s satire boom made etiolated politicians, especially Harold Macmillan, the symbol of an effete metropolis. This was also a characteristic theme of colonial wars in Malaya and Kenya, where white settler communities, voicing demands for stern action, identified a metropolis that was weak and vacillating. Ian Smith drew on this diagnosis in 1965 when he signed the Proclamation of Independence. Against a metropolis that was committed to black majority rule in Rhodesia, Smith championed the cause of white settlers. Smith himself had been born in Rhodesia, but many white settlers were first-generation immigrants, including many Britons who immigrated after 1945.

Smith's rebellion was unprecedented in its claim to act on behalf of a racial community of Britons. Media representations of colonial wars in Malaya and Kenya had shown such a racial community under siege by uprisings of the colonized. In the context of a rebellion by white settlers themselves, British politicians potentially looked doubly impotent. The Labour government disavowed a racial community of Britons and insisted on 'unimpeded progress' towards black majority rule, prompting the Marquess of Salisbury, speaking in the House of Lords, to attack Britain's 'supine repudiation' of her own kith and kin.[89] At the same time, the government limited itself to the imposition of economic sanctions against the rebels. Military intervention, used in Malaya and Kenya, was legitimized as protection for white settlers, but could not be so readily used when it involved the use of force against 'our own people'.[90]

By contrast, Ian Smith's claim that if Churchill had been alive, he would have emigrated to Rhodesia, associated Rhodesia—and by extension himself as its leader—with Churchill's manly virtues. It was an association strengthened by Smith's own record in the Second World War, when he had served as an RAF pilot, and received a wound that immobilized half his face, making it difficult for him to smile. Against the view that Rhodesia now represented the best of Churchill's Britain, the charge that British politicians had lost manliness had resonance for some Britons. The Labour Prime Minister in 1965 was the pipe-smoking Harold Wilson, who courted popularity through awarding the Order of the British Empire to the Beatles. A letter-writer in the *Daily Express* suggested that 'In Ian Smith the Rhodesians have a Prime Minister who thinks about his own people first. He is a man, not a spineless politician, who puts the welfare of his own nation before others.'[91]

---

[89] The *Times*, 16 Nov. 1965.

[90] This was Lady Hoare's phrase in a letter to the *Daily Express*, 19 Nov. 1965. A characteristic phrase used to denote the ties between a racial community of Britons in the context of Rhodesian UDI was 'kith and kin'.

[91] *Daily Express*, 13 Nov. 1965.

In *Guns at Batasi* (1964) a diagnosis of national malaise that simultaneously blamed women and politicians for reducing men to impotence is supplied through the figure of a female Member of Parliament—Miss Barker-Wise (Flora Robson).[92] *Guns at Batasi* offered a different image of British martial masculinity from the Second World War narratives that developed once the war was over, with their focus on a male elite. Set somewhere unspecified in post-colonial Africa, the film focuses on the Warrant Officers and Non-Commissioned Officers of the British army to whom it is dedicated. It shows them as increasingly impotent, immobilized by the process of decolonization, pinned down in barracks. When they do take action it is to move only a few yards, still within sight of the mess. *Guns at Batasi* explores the impact of loss of empire on British masculinity, provides an elegy for the soldier hero, particularly the imperial soldier, and is infused by imperial nostalgia. It continuously asserts the racial superiority of the British and at the same time shows that such superiority no longer provides any guarantee of authority or power.

Guns at Batasi invokes British racial superiority particularly through a contrast between African mayhem and British order. In early sequences of the film, all the action is African as Africans stage a *coup*, demonstrating on the streets and setting fire to cars. As the British hand over command to the African Captain Abraham (Earl Cameron), in line with their policy of non-involvement, supporters of the *coup*, led by Lieutenant Boniface (Errol John), take Abraham prisoner and raid an ammunition store to arm themselves. Shot from a white British perspective, Africans are shown as a threatening mob in the opening sequence of the film, as British soldiers driving an army truck encounter African demonstrators, and in a later sequence which shows African demonstrators attacking a car from the point of view of whites inside it. Following both these sequences there are cuts to the barracks and the mess as places where the British maintain order. Such order is symbolized by Sergeant Major Lauderdale (Richard Attenborough), who rules the mess with a rod of iron. In the first mess sequence a soldier takes down a portrait of the Queen, betting that Lauderdale will notice its absence within two minutes of arrival, and wins the bet. In the second mess sequence this order is connected with pre-1939 British colonial rule as the men swap stories about 'best stations', recalling 'church parade in Singapore before the war', and India—'Jewel of the East they used to call it—what a pity they had to give it away'.

As in colonial war films, the emphasis on the domestic world inhabited by the British provides an ambivalent image, for the mess is not only a place of British order but also the place where, throughout the first half of the

---

[92] *Guns at Batasi* (John Guillermin, 1964).

film, British soldiers are confined—under orders from their Colonel Deal (Jack Hawkins) to stay there until what he calls 'this little spot of bother' blows over. Against scenes of African action, they are shown indoors, drinking, chatting, and playing billiards. Their passivity is emphasized by the comments of one soldier: 'Bloody marvellous! Two hot chocolate mechanics chuck bricks at each other and the whole British army is immobilised.' He is rebuked by Lauderdale: 'They're not hot chocolate mechanics, they're Africans.'

As the men dine in the mess on the Queen's birthday and a loyal toast is proposed, African mayhem disrupts the orderly scene as Abraham, who has been wounded while escaping from arrest by Boniface, bursts in, collapsing on the billiard table. This is the watershed of the film. Thereafter the British move away from confinement, immobilization, and impotence. Defending his men, his mess, and Captain Abraham, against what he sees as Boniface's 'mutiny', Lauderdale takes action which culminates in his movement out of the mess to blow up guns trained on it by Boniface. The image of a British soldier resisting a mutineer is linked to images of other British soldier heroes by Lauderdale, who, in a set-piece confrontation with Boniface, tells him about serving on the North-West frontier: 'Sometimes, Mr Boniface, I'd lie awake in my tent with a hurricane lamp, sometimes in the middle of a blizzard, reading about the exploits of other British soldiers. Sometimes I'd be lying there in my freezing cold tent actually sweating. Beads of sweat pouring down my face from a battle two hundred years old.'

If Lauderdale symbolizes the values of old imperial Britain, it is Miss Barker-Wise who symbolizes the new era of loss of imperial power. The contrast between them is thus represented through sexual difference. Like Lauderdale, Miss Barker-Wise is unmarried and middle-aged, drinks whisky, smokes cigarettes, and speaks forcefully and with authority. The film makes clear that these are undesirable qualities in a woman, showing the acceptable unmarried female in a sergeant's mess through the figure of Karen Ericksson (Mia Farrow) who is youthful, pretty, and sexy. Miss Barker-Wise is greeted with considerable derision by the men in the mess for her failings as a woman, and Lauderdale's verdict—that she is an 'old bag'—is endorsed by the film. And Miss Barker-Wise has other failings— what Lauderdale calls 'smarmy, silly, bloody half-baked ideas'. This is a verdict that the film also endorses. Miss Barker-Wise champions Africans in general, and Boniface in particular: a student that she taught in England. She claims him on various occasions as 'a very humane man' whose 'principles are very sound' and 'a civilized and cultured man'. The film heavily underlines her error, showing Boniface as cruel, untrustworthy, and unprincipled. When Miss Barker-Wise leaves the mess against Lauderdale's commands, to seek medical aid for Abraham from Boniface, she discovers this for herself. Boniface's idea of medical aid for Abraham is sending African soldiers to arrest him on a charge of treason.

In the closing sequences of the film Miss Barker-Wise admits to Lauderdale: 'I disapprove of his [Boniface's] methods as much as I do of yours.' She also informs him that Boniface is now a Colonel. It is not Lauderdale but Boniface who has the last word, for the *coup* is successful, and Boniface demands that Lauderdale leave the country. The British Colonel confesses his own impotence as he orders Lauderdale to return to England by the next available plane, at the same time admitting that in Lauderdale's place he would have done exactly the same, 'step for step'. The action of the soldier hero in the aftermath of loss of empire is thus shown as more likely to earn punishment than medals. In a brief moment of frustration and anger, Lauderdale disrupts British order, hurling a glass at the main symbol of authority in the mess—the portrait of the Queen. He then quickly reverts to his own meticulous standards, sweeping up the shattered glass, straightening the portrait, and marching briskly—even jauntily—away from the mess. Despite its closing image of an undaunted Lauderdale, *Guns at Batasi* is imbued with sadness for a lost world, and shows the British army profoundly affected by decolonization—its capacity for action eroded to the point of immobility, its authority diminished, and its soldier heroes unhonoured.

In endorsing Lauderdale's verdict on Miss Barker-Wise's liberal views on Africans as 'bloody half-baked', *Guns at Batasi* draws on a familiar analysis made by white settler communities in Africa, including the white settler community in Rhodesia under the leadership of Ian Smith. When Lauderdale tells Barker-Wise: 'You're not in Parliament now. This isn't England. And I know more about these people than you do', he echoes a view frequently pronounced in white settler communities: metropolitan administrators and politicians are ignorant of Africa and Africans, knowing nothing at first hand.[93] In its portrayal of Miss Barker-Wise, the film suggests Smith's verdict on contemporary Britain and its politicians: they betray the values of empire and, far from supporting a racial community of Britons, are enthusiasts for granting independence to Africans, putting at risk the livelihoods—even the lives—of whites. In its contrast between African mayhem and British order, the film shows the consequences of such policies. When Boniface taunts Lauderdale with his power to train guns on the mess, the film echoes another view familiar in white settler communities—black Africans are getting the upper hand, and British politicians do nothing to stop them. While Lauderdale is successful in

[93] See Wendy Webster, 'Elspeth Huxley: Gender, Empire and Narratives of Nation, 1935–64', *Women's History Review*, 8 (1999), 528.

blowing up these guns, it is Boniface who becomes a Colonel and orders Lauderdale out of the country.

While *Guns at Batasi* portrays Africa in terms that correspond closely to the views of white settler communities in Africa, it also invites comparison to *Look Back in Anger*. In many ways, these works could not be more different. *Look Back in Anger* was a highly acclaimed play that gained a wide audience through its commercial television broadcast and film adaptation, while *Guns at Batasi* was a low-budget film which, unusually for the empire genre, was made in black and white. The middle-aged professional soldier Lauderdale, dedicated to the virtues of discipline, and lying awake to read stories of British heroism, is very far removed from the Angry Young Man. Despite these differences, *Look Back in Anger* and *Guns at Batasi* both register the loss of a romance of manliness, offering similar analyses of national malaise. Why are there 'no good, brave causes left'?—Jimmy Porter's lament. Why are British soldiers reduced to impotence?—the lament of *Guns at Batasi*. They are betrayed by politicians and by women.

Flawed and Flawless Heroes

Lawrence of Arabia (1962) looked nothing like *Guns at Batasi*.[94] It was made in Technicolor with a huge budget of 13 million dollars, and by the same British–American team that made *The Bridge on the River Kwai*—Sam Spiegel producing and David Lean directing. Its heroic actions involve epic journeys and military campaigns mounted on camels, feature vast and expansive desert sandscapes, and are planned from Arab tents. In *Guns at Batasi*, action is planned from the European sergeants' mess to which soldiers are confined for most of the film, and involves a walk of only a few yards. Yet Graham Dawson's comment on the ending of *Lawrence of Arabia*—'it laments the loss of Empire as a possible location where adventure romance could continue to be imagined'—makes it possible to look at connections between the two films.[95] *Guns at Batasi* laments the loss of such romance and demonstrates just how far it has become impossible to imagine romance in a post-colonial context. *Lawrence of Arabia*, set during the First World War, appears to offer a romance and, like the cult of Churchill, looks back to an imperial past to tell an epic story. But it is also imbued with sadness for a lost world: a romance of manliness that registers the loss of such romance.

---

[94] *Lawrence of Arabia* (David Lean, 1962).
[95] Dawson, *Soldier Heroes*, 227.

Lawrence of Arabia became a media event. Queen Elizabeth II attended its opening performance in London in December 1962, and it opened in New York a week later, winning seven Oscars, including Oscar for best picture and best director.[96] In reworking the story of Lawrence for a contemporary film, it began to claim empire as part of British heritage produced for an international, and particularly for an American, audience. It produced wide publicity not only for those who worked on location as actors, producers, and writers, but for its historical character, T. E. Lawrence, whose story was retold and reworked across a range of radio and television programmes, newspapers, and magazines. The *Daily Express* serialized the story alongside exhortations to its readers to 'Make Britain great again' in the week that produced furore over the American ex-Secretary of State Dean Acheson's pronouncement that 'Great Britain has lost an empire and has not yet found a role'.[97]

It is a measure of its very considerable departure from the racial imagery of the traditional empire genre that the first half of the film shows its hero finding love and camaraderie in a homosocial world, but among Arabs, not British. Lawrence (Peter O'Toole) shares his manly qualities with the Arab men he leads on a series of epic journeys and military campaigns in the desert, and through these he discovers and demonstrates his own manhood. For much of the first half of the film, Arabs are shown as exemplars of martial masculinity—natural warriors of great physical prowess and courage like Auda abu Tayi (Anthony Quinn), who claims: 'I carry twenty-three great wounds, all got in battle. Seventy-five men have I killed with my own hands—in battle.'

With the notable exception of Lawrence, the British are shown as completely ignorant of these warriors' prowess—routinely racist to Arabs they call 'wogs', and regard as dirty, useless, and primitive. After Lawrence has led an Arab army to take Akaba—shown as an act of enormous courage and endurance involving an epic journey through the desert—his return to the British headquarters at Cairo involves him in a further epic journey across Sinai. As he enters the officers' mess in Arab robes, the contrast is between the epic scenes the audience has witnessed, and the domestic imagery of British officers in a mess, drinking and playing snooker, who respond to Lawrence's arrival with his Arab servant: 'Clear off Lawrence!' 'Get that wog out of here! Take that little wog out!' Their racism is pointed up by Lawrence in his announcement that Akaba has been taken. When asked who has taken it his reply is replete with a claim to heroism and

[96] For an account of the American publicity for *Lawrence of Arabia* and American responses, see Steven Caton, *Lawrence of Arabia: A Film's Anthropology* (Berkeley: University of California Press, 1999).

[97] *Daily Express*, 12 Dec. 1962.

manliness that crosses racial boundaries: 'We have ... Our side in the war has. The wogs have. We have.'

This romance of manliness does not have a conventional hero at its centre. In the opening sequences, before he journeys into the desert, Lawrence is confined and constrained within his British soldier's uniform and role, clumsy and awkward, refusing the upright bearing of a soldier. It is among Arab men that he discovers an expansive masculinity, discarding his British soldier's uniform to take on the identity of el Aurens, dressed in Arab robes. These exchanges mark an exemplary act of courage by Lawrence in rescuing a member of the army, Gasim (I. S. Johar), as well as his developing friendship with Sharif Ali (Omar Sharif), who awards him both the robes and the name. They are accompanied by increasing acclaim of Aurens as heroic leader by the Arab army. Such acclamation is reinforced when Akaba is taken, and Ali tells him: 'the miracle is accomplished—garlands for the conqueror'.

The epic adventure, celebrating Lawrence and the victory at Akaba, is disturbed even in the first half of the film. The martial masculinity of Arabs is shown as deficient in discipline when they loot Akaba, and warring between Arab tribes is emphasized throughout. It is to avoid a blood feud between rival Arab tribes that Lawrence has to execute Gasim—the man he rescued. Moreover, there are hints that Lawrence's heroism is flawed when, on return to Cairo Headquarters, in a confessional moment with the British General Allenby (Jack Hawkins), he speaks of his enjoyment of this execution. The idea that Lawrence, who sees himself leading the Arab people to freedom, may simply be a pawn of British interests, is sketched in the portrait of Allenby, who is duplicitous, promising artillery to Lawrence which he has no intention of providing. This suggests that other assurances he has given—that 'we [the British] have no ambitions in Arabia'—will not be honoured. The final words before the intermission are Allenby's, and attribute his decisions to politicians: 'I've got orders to obey thank God. Not like that poor devil (Lawrence). He's reaping the whirlwind.'

In the second half of the film, these disruptions of a conventional romance of manliness are very considerably extended. In the year after Hollywood removed its ban on overt representations of homosexuality, and the first British film featuring a campaign against the law on homosexuality had been made, representation of male rape on screen was unthinkable.[98] Even so, *Lawrence of Arabia* sketches in the rape of Lawrence by a Turkish officer. The introduction of a new character—Jackson Bentley

---

[98] *Victim* (Basil Dearden, 1961) starred Dirk Bogarde as a lawyer campaigning against the law that criminalized homosexuality.

(Arthur Kennedy), an American journalist—further undermines romance, for his mission is to create Lawrence as hero for an American audience, and he is quite open about the American appetite for pictures and stories of an adventure hero. Bentley thus provides a film-within-a-film, snapping furiously. His shots of Lawrence replicate much of what the audience has been offered in the first half of the film: Lawrence as the hero of an exciting and romantic adventure created by the camera for the benefit of an American audience.

Bentley's shots of Lawrence do not always portray him as heroic. The theme of flawed heroism is dramatically extended in the second half of the film. Lawrence, campaigning to take Damascus, is shown descending on the village of Tafas, where Turks have massacred Arabs, with a cry of 'No Prisoners! No Prisoners!' and engaging in a bout of frenzied killing, stupefied with excitement. Lawrence shoots a surrendering Turkish soldier at point blank range. As he gives way to murderous bloodlust, his behaviour is registered through the reaction of his Arab friend Ali, who is deeply shocked, and returns to him, with heavy irony, the verdict that Lawrence had earlier pronounced: 'Arabs are barbarous and cruel.'

Despite Ali's verdict, and like the courageous martial masculinity of the first half of the film, this is a masculinity that crosses racial boundaries. The 'we' uniting 'wogs' with the British Lawrence excludes Ali, but is otherwise a common male brutality. It is from an Arab man that Lawrence has picked up the cry 'No Prisoners! No Prisoners!' and the Arab men he leads who demonstrate, like him, the capacity for monstrous violence. After Tafas, the disillusionment of the second half is almost complete. The Arab army take Damascus and set up a National Arab Council to administer the city, but rivalry between Arab tribes prevents the establishment of order. Allenby is shown negotiating with King Feisal, effectively ensuring, against his earlier assurance to Lawrence, that the British not only have ambitions in Arabia but are about to realize these.

In attempting to establish liberal credentials on race, *Lawrence of Arabia* is in striking contrast to *Guns at Batasi*'s endorsement of the idea that liberal views are 'bloody half-baked'. But liberal credentials on race were a characteristic preoccupation of films of the empire genre in the 1960s. Both *Zulu* (1964) and *Khartoum* (1966)—a film about General Gordon that attempted to trade on the success of *Lawrence of Arabia*—expose and repudiate a British racism in empire that they represent as organized around ideas of masculinity. Both begin with images of the massacres of modern armies, which they attribute to British failure to recognize that native peoples are worthy opponents—manly warriors like them.[99] Like *Lawrence*

---

[99] *Khartoum* (Basil Dearden, 1966).

of Arabia, *Zulu* (1964) shows manly qualities that cross racial boundaries, and quickly disabuses its audience of the idea that Zulu are 'cowardly blacks', as one soldier suggests at the outset. Like their British opponents, and like the Arab army in *Lawrence of Arabia*, Zulu are attributed martial masculinity, and shown as natural warriors of great physical prowess, courage, and discipline.[100]

The establishment of liberal credentials on race serves to modernize 1960s films and distance them from some of the traditions of the empire genre. But they are modernized particularly through drawing on psychology to depict flawed heroes. As individualists, acting independently against the values of generals and politicians, the heroes of *Lawrence of Arabia* and *Khartoum* bear some resemblance to the 'Angry Young Man'. But their flaws are wide-ranging, and include the possibility that heroic masculinity draws variously on masochism, exhibitionism, and desire for self-glorification. These films' modernity lies in part in their self-consciousness about their themes. In representing men of destiny, they play with psychological awareness of the claim to supernatural powers as fantasy and egotism. They also play with the love of the desert as romantic fantasy. Indeed, in *Lawrence of Arabia* King Feisal charges Lawrence with being like Gordon of Khartoum—another of those English who 'have a great hunger for desolate places', another of 'these desert-loving Englishmen'. But if Lawrence is in love with desert, so are the cameras that shoot the film of his adventures there. Although the character of Bentley adds a further element of self-awareness of what cameras can do to create romantic fantasy, *Lawrence of Arabia* offers epic sandscapes as a major source of visual pleasure to its audience.

The power of this imagery is strongly evoked at the end of *Lawrence of Arabia* in a moment of intense nostalgia. The final word of the film is given to the British soldier who chauffeurs Lawrence in a staff car which is taking him to a ship sailing for England—'home'. From the confines of a British soldier's uniform in the staff car, Lawrence stands up to look at Arab men on camels from whom he is now utterly separated, and who offer him no sign of recognition. A motorbike speeds past, foreshadowing Lawrence's death in England in the motorbike accident with which the film begins. Lawrence is shown as terribly diminished by this final word. 'Home' signifies his loss of the expansive homosocial world of manly adventure that he has inhabited throughout much of the film, and the route he is taking to containment and immurement in a smaller world. 'Home' signifies a diminished identity,

---

[100] *Zulu* (Cyril Endfield, 1964). British racism was also depicted in *The Long Duel* (Ken Annakin, 1967), set in India. But the main focus on the film was on manly qualities that cross racial boundaries—the growing respect between the British officer (Trevor Howard) and the tribal chieftain (Yul Brynner).

even death. It is all that remains for Lawrence, and for Lauderdale at the end of *Guns at Batasi* where the order to return to England embodies all that has been lost in a post-colonial world—British authority and capacity for action in Africa, the soldier hero, a romance of manliness. Like Lawrence, Lauderdale has been betrayed by politicians and generals from home.

The sense of a diminished identity that haunts the endings of *Guns at Batasi* and *Lawrence of Arabia* also haunted Enoch Powell's thinking about empire in the 1960s. Powell, who had declared in 1952 that Britain was dependent on empire for the very structure of its existence, now, in a startling formulation, denied that Britain had an imperial past. Powell conjured a version of nation that was shorn of imperial identity, not through the process of decolonization, but through dismissal of its imperial past as a 'myth'.[101] He characterized the nation by 'the continuity of her existence . . . unbroken when the looser connections which had linked her with distant continents and strange races fell away'. The empire, if it ever existed—and Powell had considerable problems in altogether denying this—had been a distraction, but fortunately 'the nationhood of the mother country remained unaltered through it all'.[102] Reversing the meaning of 'home' in *Lawrence of Arabia*, Powell saw his generation as 'like one which comes home again from years of distant wandering'.[103] Without the distractions of empire, the nation can return to an unsullied core identity—Englishness, not Britishness. Powell makes return to England—a moment of diminishment and loss in *Lawrence of Arabia* and *Guns at Batasi*—into a homecoming to a domestic sanctuary.

Powell's denial of an imperial past in 1964 brought his view about empire in line with his view of the Commonwealth: both were dangerous illusions. A more common response in the 1960s, as at Churchill's funeral, consigned empire to the past, but unyoked it from the Commonwealth. At the BBC in 1968, Max Morgan-Witts suggested that the BBC's most popular television channel should celebrate the imperial past in colour, and that the final end of empire should therefore be postponed until 1970. He wrote:

By 1970, the fall of Britain's influence as a world power will be pretty well complete. By then, we will have to face the fact, but we will still have our memories . . . With the advent of colour on Channel 1 in 1970, might it not be a good year to remind our audience of our past glories (?) and to prepare ourselves for our new role—without feeling sorry for ourselves.[104]

---

[101] J. Enoch Powell, Speech at Trinity College Dublin, 13 November 1964, in John Wood (ed.), *Freedom and Reality* (London: Batsford, 1969), 245–53.

[102] J. Enoch Powell, Speech to Royal Society of St George, 22 Apr. 1964, ibid. 254–7.

[103] Ibid. 255.

[104] Memorandum from Max Morgan-Witts, 5 Feb. 1968, BBC WAC T64/51/1.

The television series made as a result of Morgan-Witts's suggestion—*The British Empire*—was broadcast in 1972.[105] While Morgan-Witts had put a question mark against the idea of empire as 'past glories', the series generally did not. It was accompanied by a series of magazines, from BBC television in conjunction with Time-Life Books, which told their readers:

In the months to come, we shall be journeying together through the centuries when British men and women laboured and fought and died to build their great empire. It will be a journey packed with discovery and emotion: of joy in moments of triumph, of sorrow in moments of tragedy, and even—in moments of horror—of disgust; but overwhelmingly of pride in the lasting accomplishments of generations of soldiers, sailors and civil servants, of missionaries, merchants and planters. Their achievements have indeed lasted: they have moulded much of the modern world.[106]

Once empire was consigned to the past, it could be celebrated as part of British history and heritage.

Churchill's funeral made him an icon of national history, honouring a great leader who, far from betraying the nation, provided a model of 'exceptional manliness' against those who did. Unlike Lawrence, he was not the subject of psychobiography. In the same year that the BBC broadcast *The British Empire* on television, *The Young Winston* was released. Like the television series, it moved to claim empire as national heritage.[107] The focus of the film was not the Second World War, but Churchill's imperial exploits and adventures as a young man in India, the Sudan, and South Africa. The film draws on psychology—offering the story of Churchill's difficult relationship with his father to suggest that he needed military adventure to demonstrate his manhood against his father's disappointment in him. But any element of psychobiography is very limited and the dominant image is of imperial heritage as manly, heroic adventure, including Churchill's participation in the last full charge of the British cavalry. Churchill is shown as a young man in quest of military glory who wants to 'win a reputation for courage and daring', to 'be mentioned in dispatches', to win 'lots and lots of medals'. When he kills in battle, this is not murderous bloodlust or pointless butchery, but a display of the courage and daring he desires. *The Young Winston* demonstrates the key themes around which ideas of national greatness continued to be organized. Imperial masculinity was consigned to the past but by no means discredited.

Churchill's funeral, while a moment of intense nostalgia, provided reaffirmation of an undiminished identity. The idea that Churchill spoke for Britain through his great wartime oratory, in the speeches read by Paul

[105] *The British Empire*, BBC television, 1972.
[106] *The British Empire*, Time-Life/BBC1 (1971), 1.
[107] *The Young Winston* (Richard Attenborough, 1972).

Scofield on the commercial television broadcast of his funeral, was commonplace. J. B. Priestley, the personification of the quiet pipe-smoking Englishman and the temperate masculine hero of the people's war, had faded. But Churchill was also credited with speaking for the nation on a deeper level—as an imperialist who had loved the British Empire, as a historian who had celebrated the great deeds of nation and empire, above all as a great exemplar of martial masculinity who had defended the nation against aggression, and won a great victory. An editorial in the *Daily Telegraph* on the day following Churchill's death imagined what message he would send to the British people from the shades. It concluded: 'we may be very sure that it would be a call to quit ourselves like men'.[108]

The funeral, as a moment of intense nostalgia, reaffirming a history of national greatness, produced some anxiety about Britain's diminished identity since the Second World War. There was much unfavourable comparison of the present with the past. This used gendered imagery, where national 'feebleness' and the 'simperings and pettiness of our recent politics' was set against the idea of past national greatness that Churchill personified.[109] Patrick O'Donavan, affirming that the funeral had been a celebration of 'the fact of Britain', addressed those who thought that it 'marked the final act of Britain's greatness'.[110] Quintin Hogg, asking, 'Can Britain ever be great again?', addressed 'those who preach that Britain is finished'.[111] Both saw the occasion as one for renewal and rededication and this was a message that many preached.

Goronwy Rees, writing about Churchill's funeral in 1965, saw it as an elegy for empire. 'One could not', he wrote, 'help feeling that so public an extravagance of grief and mourning could not really have been inspired by one man, that it was not Churchill the nation was burying, but a part of their own history, not a statesman but an Empire, not a hero but themselves, as they once were and never would be again.'[112] But while imperial identity was woven into Churchill's story and into tributes that claimed that Churchill *was* Britain, his funeral was also a culminating moment in the process through which an old imperial romance of manliness was transposed onto the Second World War. Funeral week demonstrated the very considerable resonance that such a romance retained in British culture. It remained a compelling story, enlarging and dignifying Britishness, and offering a potent myth of national greatness, the assurance of a manly heritage, and a flawless hero.

[108] *Daily Telegraph*, 25 January 1965.
[109] *Sunday Times*, 31 January 1965.
[110] O'Donavan, 'Requiem'.
[111] Quintin Hogg, 'Can Britain Ever Be Great Again?', *Sunday Express*, 31 Jan. 1965.
[112] Goronwy Rees, 'After the Ball Was Over', *Encounter*, Nov. 1965, 3–9.

Epilogue

As a teenager, Margaret Thatcher went to the cinema. She records that 'for nine pence you had a comfortable seat in the darkness while the screen showed first the trailer for forthcoming attractions, then the *British Movietone News* with its chirpy optimistic commentary'. Among the films that she remembers viewing were *The Drum* (1938) and *The Four Feathers* (1939)— both in the Korda trilogy on the British empire.[1] Thatcher was in her early teens when these films were released, and perhaps too young, aged 10, to see the first of the trilogy, *Sanders of the River* (1935). She does not record her response, nor how far it corresponded to that of another British female viewer of empire films in the 1930s—'exultant pride in my own country, and her achievements'.[2]

There can be more confidence about Thatcher's response to the popular narratives from the post-war period that registered loss of imperial power or reworked imperial narratives. She reproduced and developed these, extending their currency into the late twentieth century. In particular, in the context of the Falklands/Malvinas conflict of 1982, she drew on Britain's imperial past and the Second World War in an attempt to write a new epic story of national greatness and national destiny. At the same time, her own identity as a female politician—the first woman Prime Minister—gave this narrative new meaning.

As leader of the Conservative party, before her first election victory, Thatcher produced a classic statement of black immigration as a threat to Britishness. In taking up a familiar narrative from the 1950s, she gave it considerable legitimacy through her position as leader of a major political party. Labour and Conservative committees had met in secret in the 1950s to discuss ways of controlling immigration. Thatcher's announcement of her view was very public—made in 1978 in a television interview:

People are really rather afraid that this country might be rather swamped by people with a different culture and you know, the British character has done so much for democracy, for law and done so much throughout the world that if there is any fear

---

[1] Margaret Thatcher, *The Path to Power* (London, HarperCollins, 1995), 14.

[2] Quoted in J. P. Mayer, *British Cinemas and their Audiences* (London, Dennis Dobson, 1948), 84.

that it might be swamped people are going to react and be rather hostile to them coming in. So, if you want good race relations, you have got to allay people's fears on numbers.[3]

Thatcher's statement was notable for the way it mobilized ideas about British attachment to democratic values and its role in spreading these throughout the world—a strong element in the idea of a decent and tolerant Britain and empire—to legitimate opposition to immigration.

Thatcher's development of the epic story of national greatness told in the week of Churchill's funeral awaited the Falklands/Malvinas war of 1982. In response to Argentinian invasion and occupation of the Falkland Islands— British dependent territories in the South Atlantic with a population of nearly 2,000 people—Britain sent a task force of 20 warships with support aircraft and 6,000 troops to recover the islands. In the media, the conflict evoked strong popular memories of the Second World War and Thatcher— by then Prime Minister—was insistently compared to Churchill. Thatcher herself made many references to the Second World War which invoked the figure of Churchill—and she increasingly referred to him as 'Winston'. In a television programme in 1983 she showed Sir Laurens Van der Post the chair 'where Winston used to sit', and confided in him that she had thought of Churchill very much during the Falklands conflict.[4] Churchill, she told an audience in Washington the following September, 'was a giant'.[5]

As in Churchill's funeral week, the celebration of the Second World War as a main symbol of national greatness was linked to Britain's imperial past. When Thatcher went to the House of Commons to make her announcement of Argentinian surrender in the Falklands, she spoke to the crowds in Downing Street telling them that 'today has put the Great back into Britain'. When she spoke to a Conservative rally at Cheltenham racecourse in July 1982, she elaborated on what putting the 'Great' back into Britain meant:

There were those who thought we could no longer do the great things which we once did. Those who believed that our decline was irreversible . . . those [who feared] that Britain was no longer the nation that had built an Empire and ruled a quarter of the world. Well, they were wrong. The lesson of the Falklands is that Britain has not changed and that this nation still has those sterling qualities that shine through our history. This generation can match their fathers and grandfathers in ability, in courage, and in resolution . . . We rejoice that Britain has rekindled that spirit which has fired her for generations past and which today has begun to burn as brightly as before.[6]

---

[3] Margaret Thatcher interview, Granada television, 30 Jan. 1978.

[4] Michael Cockerell, *Live from Number Ten* (London: Faber and Faber, 1988), 269.

[5] Margaret Thatcher, *Speeches on Britain's Relations with the World 1976–1986* (London: Aurum, 1986), 90.

[6] Margaret Thatcher's speech at Cheltenham race course is reproduced in Anthony Barnett, *Iron Britannia* (London: Allison and Busby, 1983), 149–53.

In portraying the Falklands conflict as a further instalment in a great imperial history in 1982, Thatcher expressed sentiments that closely corresponded to those of the female viewer of empire films in the 1930s: 'exultant pride in my own country, and her achievements'. Thatcher used victory to attempt to write a new energizing myth of nation.

In the 1960s, those who had reclaimed Britain's imperial past as British national heritage unyoked this from a Commonwealth that was increasingly repudiated and criticized. This was another story that Thatcher extended. The fading importance of any need to take note of Commonwealth opinion was embodied in her opposition as Prime Minister to the imposition of sanctions against South Africa at Heads of Governments Commonwealth conferences in Melbourne in 1981, New Delhi in 1983, and Nassau in 1985. Her opposition to measures that were supported by the vast majority of other Commonwealth countries, whose anger at British policy prompted 32 countries to boycott the Edinburgh Commonwealth Games in 1986, threatened a break-up of the Commonwealth. Thatcher was undismayed, telling an interviewer that 'It's not the British Commonwealth any longer. It's their club, their Commonwealth. If they wish to break it up, I think that's absurd.'[7] Thatcher's objection to the name of the Commonwealth echoed Churchill's objections to the dropping of the adjective 'British' in 1948. As in the 1960s, and even more so by 1985, this summary dismissal of the Commonwealth articulated a perception that, unlike the imperial past, it did little to enlarge or dignify Britishness.

Thatcher's dismissal of the Commonwealth contrasted strongly with her enthusiasm for a 'special relationship' with America—especially after the inauguration of Ronald Reagan as President in 1981. In his turn, Ronald Reagan called Thatcher 'the best man in England'. But the American invasion and occupation of Grenada in 1983—with a task force of 6,000 troops and 15 warships—meant that Thatcher also experienced loss of imperial power particularly acutely through America. The Caribbean island of Grenada had been part of the British Windward Islands Crown Colony and, on gaining independence in 1974, became a member of the Commonwealth. Queen Elizabeth II was its Head of State. America invaded Grenada without informing or consulting the British government, and the Queen's Governor-General on the island was forced to accept the invasion. Thatcher was enraged by such lack of consultation, but there was little she could do.[8] In the aftermath of the Falklands victory, she had declared that 'Britain found herself again in the South Atlantic' and that 'now once again

---

[7] Quoted in Hugo Young, *One of Us: A Biography of Margaret Thatcher* (Basingstoke: Macmillan, 1989), 486.

[8] See ibid. 345–50.

Britain is not prepared to be pushed around'.[9] But Britain was powerless in the face of the American invasion of a member of the Commonwealth.

In 1975, in her first leadership speech to the Conservative party conference Thatcher criticized those who wrote about the past for their failure to focus on themes of national greatness:

We are witnessing a deliberate attack on our values, a deliberate attack on our heritage and our great past, and there are those who gnaw away at our national self-respect, rewriting British history as centuries of unrelieved gloom, oppression and failure—as days of hopelessness, not days of hope.[10]

In the context of the Falklands victory, Thatcher attempted to refocus attention on national greatness as a more or less seamless story, briefly interrupted by post-1945 decline and especially by the 1960s—which she identified as a decade of 'fashionable theories and permissive claptrap' that 'set the scene for a society in which the old virtues of discipline and self-restraint were denigrated'.[11] Her story, linking Britain's imperial past to Britain in the 1980s, was embellished with many heroes. While Churchill was the most notable of these, Thatcher, taking Laurens Van der Post around Number Ten on television, not only showed him the chair 'where Winston used to sit' but also the portraits of great English heroes which she had installed to replace Italian paintings: Clive of India, Nelson, and Wellington.

Thatcher was not an easy figure to incorporate into a romance of manliness. But the narrative of the Falklands showed her inhabiting a homosocial world and developed a quest plot where she was victorious against all external obstacles and enemies. In the aftermath of the Falklands victory, many media representations acclaimed her as 'the best man in the Cabinet' and 'the best man in England'. According to the Conservative party campaign song in the 1983 General Election, there was 'not a man around to match her'. In the context of the Falklands, Thatcher could also be understood as the type of doughty and intrepid female imperial pioneer depicted in colonial war films of the 1950s, and increasingly celebrated in the aftermath of the Falklands conflict. Like the title of a book by Joanna Trollope, published in 1983, Thatcher could be seen as one of Britannia's daughters imbued with the pioneering spirit of the empire and what Trollope, writing of the women of the British empire, celebrated as their 'endurance, resourcefulness and achievement'.[12]

---

[9] Barnett, *Iron Britannia*, 151.

[10] Quoted in John Osmond, *The Divided Kingdom* (London: Constable, 1988), 198.

[11] Margaret Thatcher, speaking to Conservatives in Harrogate in March 1982, quoted in Andrew Thomson, *Margaret Thatcher: The Woman Within* (London: W. H. Allen, 1989), 120.

[12] Joanna Trollope, *Britannia's Daughters: Women of the British Empire* (London: BCA, 1995; first published 1983), 37.

Thatcher herself peppered the story of the Falklands victory with sexual politics. As early as 1980, two years before the conflict, she began to call many of her male colleagues who did not find favour with her 'wets'. She used the term particularly for the traditional Tory gentleman, but it encompassed all those she considered feeble, weak, vacillating, and spineless. In 1982, when she spoke of those who thought that Britain was no longer the nation that had built an empire and ruled a quarter of the world, she often called them 'the waverers and the fainthearts'. This phrase encompassed a wide constituency who did not share her energizing vision of imperial history, including some of her male colleagues.

In blaming politicians for a national malaise that had sapped the spirit of the nation since 1945, Thatcher produced a verdict that had been widely articulated in the 1960s. She reserved particular scorn for men she judged to represent etiolated masculinity. In her turn, she was often portrayed in the media, like Churchill, as a politician who did not betray the nation. She could be trusted to deliver on a promise to turn back the tide of post-1945 decline and loss of imperial power. But Thatcher's identity as a woman and a politician added a new resonance to stories of post-war national malaise, reversing the gendering of the story in *Guns at Batasi*, where betrayal of imperial values is embodied in the figure of Miss Barker-Wise—a female politician. When Thatcher—a female politician—castigated a range of British men as 'wets' and 'waverers and fainthearts', there were a variety of ways in which her message could be understood. In the context of the Falklands it had an imperial resonance. British men had proved weak and vacillating, giving up on empire. A British woman—defiant, resolute, courageous, and indomitable—was made of sterner stuff.

Bibliography

Primary Sources

ARCHIVAL COLLECTIONS

BBC Written Archives Centre, Caversham Park, Reading:
  BBC Radio Scripts
  BBC Television Scripts
  BBC Programme Files
  BBC Scriptwriter Files
  BBC Policy Files
  BBC Audience Research Files
Public Records Office, Kew:
  Colonial Office Files (CO)
  Ministry of Information Files (INF)

PRINTED MEDIA: NEWSPAPERS AND MAGAZINES

Auckland Star
Bolton Evening News
Daily Express
Daily Herald
Daily Mail
Daily Mirror
Daily Sketch
Daily Telegraph
Encounter
Evening News
Evening News and Star
Evening Standard
Financial Times
Illustrated London News
Lancashire Daily Post
Listener
Liverpool Evening Express
Manchester Guardian
National Geographic
News Chronicle
News of the World
New York Herald Tribune

Northern Echo
Observer
Picture Post
Punch
Radio Times
Reynolds News
Sight and Sound
Star
Sunday Chronicle
Sunday Express
Sunday Telegraph
Sunday Times
The Times
Wembley News
Yorkshire Post

VISUAL MEDIA: NEWSREELS

British Movietone News
British Paramount News
Gaumont British News
Pathé Gazette
Pathé News
Universal News
War Pictorial News

VISUAL MEDIA: FILMS AND TELEVISION PROGRAMMES

Drifters (John Grierson, 1929).
Industrial Britain (Robert Flaherty, 1931).
Granton Trawler (John Grierson, 1934).
Lives of a Bengal Lancer (Henry Hathaway, US 1934).
Coal Face (Alberto Cavalcanti, 1935).
The Ghost Goes West (Rene Clair, 1935).
Housing Problems (Arthur Elton and Edgar Anstey, 1935).
Ruggles of Red Gap (Leo McCarey, US 1935).
Sanders of the River (Alexander Korda, 1935).
Charge of the Light Brigade (Michael Curtiz, US 1936).
The Great Barrier (Milton Rosmer and Geoffrey Barkas, 1936).
Night Mail (Harry Watt and Basil Wright, 1936).
Rhodes of Africa (Berthold Vietel, 1936).
King Solomon's Mines (Robert Stevenson, 1937).
Wee Willie Winkie (John Ford, US 1937).
The Drum (Zoltan Korda, 1938).
Four Men and a Prayer (Kenneth MacGowan, US 1938)
North Sea (Harry Watt, 1938).
A Yank at Oxford (Jack Conway, US 1938).

The First Days (Humphrey Jennings and Harry Watt, 1939).
The Four Feathers (Zoltan Korda, 1939).
Gunga Din (George Stevens, US 1939).
A Midsummer Day's Work (GPO Film Unit, 1939).
Nine for Six (GPO Film Unit, 1939).
The Proud Valley (Pen Tennyson, 1939).
The Rains Came (Clarence Brown, US 1939).
Stagecoach (John Ford, US 1939)
The Sun Never Sets (Rowland Lee, US 1939).
Wings Over Empire (Stuart Legg, 1939).
Britain at Bay (Ministry of Information, 1940).
Britain Can Take It! (Harry Watt and Humphrey Jennings, 1940).
The Front Line (Harry Watt, 1940).
Men of the Lightship (David Macdonald, 1940).
Planes of Hindustan (G. Radcliffe Genge, 1940).
Arms from India (Indian Film Unit, 1941).
Christmas Under Fire (Harry Watt, 1941).
Defenders of India (Indian Film Unit, 1941).
The Empire Marches (Universal, 1941).
The Foreman Went to France (Charles Frend, 1941).
The 49th Parallel (Michael Powell, 1941).
From the Four Corners (Denham and Pinewood Studios, 1941).
India Marches (Bombay Talkies, 1941).
Ohm Kruger (Hans Steinhoff, Germany 1941).
Sundown (Henry Hathaway, US 1941).
They Flew Alone (Herbert Wilcox, 1941).
A Yank in the RAF (Henry King, US 1941).
In Which We Serve (Noel Coward and David Lean, 1942).
Listen to Britain (Humphrey Jennings, 1942).
Mrs Miniver (William Wyler, US 1942).
War Came to Kenya (Information Office of Kenya, 1942).
A Yank at Eton (Norman Taurog, US 1942).
The Bells Go Down (Basil Dearden, 1943).
The Gentle Sex (Leslie Howard and Maurice Elvey, 1943).
Letter from Ulster (Brian Desmond Hurst, 1943).
The Life and Death of Colonel Blimp (Michael Powell and Emeric Pressburger, 1943).
Millions Like Us (Frank Launder and Sidney Gilliat, 1943).
San Demetrio London (Charles Frend, 1943).
We Dive at Dawn (Anthony Asquith, 1943).
Welcome to Britain (Anthony Asquith, 1943).
West Indies Calling (John Page, 1943).
A Canterbury Tale (Michael Powell and Emeric Pressburger, 1944).
The Canterville Ghost (Jules Dassin, US 1944).
Know Your Ally: Britain (Frank Capra, US 1944).
Maximum Effort (Michael Hankinson, 1944).

Two Thousand Women (Frank Launder, 1944).

A Diary for Timothy (Humphrey Jennings, 1945).

I Live in Grosvenor Square (Herbert Wilcox, 1945).

The Way to the Stars (Anthony Asquith, 1945).

The Captive Heart (Basil Dearden, 1946).

Learie Constantine (Colonial Film Unit, 1946).

A Matter of Life and Death (Michael Powell and Emeric Pressburger, 1946).

Men of Two Worlds (Thorold Dickinson, 1946).

The Overlanders (Harry Watt, 1946).

Piccadilly Incident (Herbert Wilcox, 1946).

The Victory Parade (Colonial Film Unit, 1946).

The Victory Parade (Castleton-Knight Productions, 1946).

Victory Parade (H. R. Dance, Chelsea Colour films, 1946).

Black Narcissus (Michael Powell and Emeric Pressburger, 1947).

Women Must Work (Central Office of Information, 1947).

Fury at Furnace Creek (H. Bruce Humberstone, US 1948).

Scott of the Antarctic (Charles Frend, 1948).

Diamond City (David MacDonald, 1949).

Eureka Stockade (Harry Watt, 1949).

Passport to Pimlico (Henry Cornelius, 1949).

The Adventurers (David MacDonald, 1950).

Bitter Springs (Ralph Smart, 1950).

Odette (Herbert Wilcox, 1950).

Pool of London (Basil Dearden, 1950).

The Wooden Horse (Jack Lee, 1950).

Kim (Victor Saville, 1951).

Outcast of the Islands (Carol Reed, 1951).

Soldiers Three (Tay Garnett, 1951).

Where No Vultures Fly (Harry Watt, 1951).

Appointment in London (Philip Leacock, 1952).

The Planter's Wife (Ken Annakin, 1952).

The Titfield Thunderbolt (Charles Crichton, 1952).

The Conquest of Everest (BBC television, 14 July 1953).

The Conquest of Everest (Countryman Films, 1953).

The Coronation of Queen Elizabeth II (BBC television, 2 June 1953).

The Cruel Sea (Charles Frend, 1953).

Her People Rejoiced (BBC television, 16 May 1953).

The Maggie (Alexander Mackendrick, 1953).

Malta Story (Brian Desmond Hurst, 1953).

Mogambo (John Ford, US 1953).

A Queen is Crowned (Castelton Knight, J. Arthur Rank Organisation, 1953).

The Second Elizabeth (BBC television, 1953).

The Colditz Story (Guy Hamilton, 1954).

King of the Khyber Rifles (Henry King, US 1954).

The Purple Plain (Robert Parrish, 1954).

The Seekers (Ken Annakin, 1954).

West of Zanzibar (Harry Watt, 1954).

The Dam Busters (Michael Anderson, 1955).

Has Britain a Colour Bar? (BBC television, 1955).

Bhowani Junction (George Cukor, 1956).

The Ship That Died of Shame (Basil Dearden, 1955).

Simba (Brian Desmond Hurst, 1955).

The Black Tent (Brian Desmond Hurst, 1956).

Private's Progress (John Boulting, 1956).

Reach for the Sky (Lewis Gilbert, 1956).

Rock Around the Clock (Fred Sears, US 1956).

Safari (Terence Young, 1956).

A Town Like Alice (Jack Lee, 1956).

We The British Are We In Decline? (BBC television, 1956).

Zarak (Terence Young, 1956).

The Bridge on the River Kwai (David Lean, 1957).

Something of Value (Richard Brooks, US 1957).

Windom's Way (Ronald Neame, 1957).

The Yangtse Incident (Michael Anderson, 1957).

The Bandit of Zhobe (John Gilling, 1958).

Carve Her Name with Pride (Lewis Gilbert, 1958).

Harry Black (Hugo Fregonese, 1958).

Mixed Marriages (Associated Rediffusion, 1958).

Room at the Top (Jack Clayton, 1958).

The Wind Cannot Read (Ralph Thomas, 1958).

Carlton-Browne of the FO (Jeffrey Dell and Roy Boulting, 1959).

Look Back in Anger (Tony Richardson, 1959).

North West Frontier (J. Lee Thompson, 1959).

Sapphire (Basil Dearden, 1959).

The Battle of the Sexes (Charles Crichton, 1960).

Hot Summer Night (BBC television, 1960).

Saturday Night and Sunday Morning (Karel Reisz, 1960).

Sink the Bismarck! (Lewis Gilbert, 1960).

Tunes of Glory (Ronald Neame, 1960).

Flame in the Streets (Roy Baker, 1961).

A Taste of Honey (Tony Richardson, 1961).

The Valiant Years (Jack Le Vien, BBC television, 1961).

Victim (Basil Dearden, 1961).

Commonwealth Crisis: Britain and the Old Dominions (BBC television, 4 September 1962).

The Commonwealth in London (BBC television, 17 November 1962).

Doctor No (Terence Young, 1962).

A Kind of Loving (John Schlesinger, 1962).

Lawrence of Arabia (David Lean, 1962).

The Loneliness of the Long Distance Runner (Tony Richardson, 1962).

Death Drums Along the River (Lawrence Huntington, 1963).
Black Marries White: The Last Barrier (Association Rediffusion, 1964).
The Colony, (Philip Donnellan, BBC television, 1964).
Guns at Batasi (John Guillermin, 1964).
Zulu (Cyril Endfield, 1964).
The High Bright Sun (Ralph Thomas, 1965).
'Memories of Sir Winston', *Panorama* (BBC television, 25 January 1965).
The Negro Next Door (Associated Rediffusion, 1965).
The State Funeral of Sir Winston Churchill (Anthony Gaxton, BBC television, 1965).
The State Funeral of Sir Winston Churchill (Peter Morley, ITV, 1965).
Born Free (James Hill, 1966).
Khartoum (Basil Dearden, 1966).
The Long Duel (Ken Annakin, 1967).
Carry On Up the Khyber (Gerald Thomas, 1968).
The Virgin Soldiers (John Dexter, 1969).
The British Empire (BBC television, 1972).
The Young Winston (Richard Attenborough, 1972).
Margaret Thatcher interview (Granada television, 30 January 1978).
Flame Trees of Thika (Thames television, 1981).
Heat and Dust (James Ivory, 1982).
The Far Pavilions (ITV, 1984).
Jewel in the Crown (ITV: a fourteen-episode television serial which was adapted from
    Paul Scott's *The Raj Quartet*, 1984).
A Passage to India (David Lean, 1984).
Out of Africa (Sydney Pollack, 1985).

Secondary Sources

ALDGATE, ANTHONY, and RICHARDS, JEFFREY, *Britain Can Take It: The British
    Cinema in the Second World War* (Edinburgh: Edinburgh University Press, 1994).
ANDERSON, BENEDICT, *Imagined Communities: Reflections on the Origin and
    Spread of Nationalism* (London: Verso, 1983).
BALCON, MICHAEL, 'Let British Films Be Ambassadors to the World', *Kinemato-
    graph Weekly*, 11 January 1945.
—— *Michael Balcon Presents a Lifetime of Films* (London: Hutchinson, 1969).
BARNETT, ANTHONY, *Iron Britannia* (London: Allison and Busby, 1983).
BARR, CHARLES, 'Introduction: Amnesia and Schizophrenia', in Charles Barr
    (ed.), *All Our Yesterdays* (London: British Film Institute, 1986).
BAUCOM, IAN, *Out of Place: Englishness, Empire and the Locations of Identity*
    (Princeton: Princeton University Press, 1999).
BAXENDALE, JOHN, '"I Had Seen a Lot of Englands": J. B. Priestley, Englishness
    and the People', *History Workshop Journal*, 51 (2001), 87–111.
BELICH, JAMES, *Paradise Reforged: A History of the New Zealanders from the 1880s
    to the Year 2000* (London: Allen Lane, 2001).

BENNETT, TONY, and WOOLLACOTT, JANET, *Bond and Beyond: The Political Career of a Popular Hero* (Basingstoke: Macmillan, 1987).

BERGONZI, BERNARD, *Heroes' Twilight: A Study of the Literature of the Great War* (London: Constable, 1965).

BERKELEY, HUMPHREY, *The Odyssey of Enoch: A Political Memoir* (London: Hamilton, 1977).

BLUNT, ALISON, 'Embodying War: British Women and Domestic Defilement in the Indian "Mutiny", 1857–8', *Journal of Historical Geography*, 26 (2000), 403–28.

BOUSQUET, BEN, and DOUGLAS, COLIN, *West Indian Women at War: British Racism in World War II* (London: Lawrence and Wishart, 1991).

BOYD, KELLY, *Manliness and the Boys' Story Paper in Britain: A Cultural History, 1855–1940* (Basingstoke: Palgrave, 2003).

BRANTLINGER, PATRICK, *Rule of Darkness: British Literature and Imperialism, 1830–1914* (Ithaca: Cornell University Press, 1988).

BROWN, JUDITH, and LOUIS, WM ROGER (eds.), *The Oxford History of the British Empire*, Vol. IV: *The Twentieth Century* (Oxford: Oxford University Press, 1999).

BRUNSDON, CHARLOTTE, and MOSELEY, RACHEL, ' "She's a Foreigner Who's Become a British Subject": *Frieda*', in Alan Burton, Tim O'Sullivan, and Paul Wells (eds.), *Liberal Directions: Basil Dearden and Postwar British Film Culture* (Trowbridge: Flicks Books, 1997), 129–36.

BRUNT, ROSALIND, 'The Family Firm Restored: Newsreel Coverage of the British Monarchy 1936–45', in Christine Gledhill and Gillian Swanson (eds.), *Nationalising Femininity: Culture, Sexuality and British Cinema in the Second World War* (Manchester: Manchester University Press, 1996), 140–51.

BURNS, JAMES, 'Watching Africans Watch Films: Theories of Spectatorship in British Colonial Africa', *Historical Journal of Film, Radio and Television*, 20 (2000), 197–211.

BURTON, ANTOINETTE, *Burdens of History: British Feminists, Indian Women, and Imperial Culture, 1865–1915* (London: Chapel Hill, 1994).

——*At the Heart of Empire: Indians and the Colonial Encounter in Late Victorian Britain* (Berkeley: University of California Press, 1998).

BUSH, BARBARA, *Imperialism, Race and Resistance: Africa and Britain 1919–1945* (London: Routledge, 1999).

CAIN, P. J., and HOPKINS, A. G., *Crisis and Deconstruction, 1914–1990* (London: Longman, 1993).

CALDER, ANGUS, *The People's War: Britain 1939–1945* (London: Panther, 1971).

CAMERON, KENNETH, *Into Africa: The Story of the East African Safari* (London: Constable, 1990).

CANNADINE, DAVID, *Ornamentalism: How the British Saw Their Empire* (London: Allen Lane, 2001).

——*In Churchill's Shadow: Confronting the Past in Modern Britain* (London: Allen Lane, 2002).

CARPENTER, HUMPHREY, *That Was Satire That Was: The Satire Boom of the 1960s* (London: Victor Gollancz, 2000).

CARRUTHERS, SUSAN, *Winning Hearts and Minds: British Governments, the Media and Colonial Counter-Insurgency 1944–1960* (London: Leicester University Press, 1995).

CASTLE, KATHRYN, *Britannia's Children: Reading Colonialism Through Children's Books and Magazines* (Manchester: Manchester University Press, 1996).

CATON, STEVEN, *Lawrence of Arabia: A Film's Anthropology* (Berkeley: University of California Press, 1999).

CAVENDISH, RICHARD, 'Britain Abandons the Groundnuts Scheme, January 9th 1951', *History Today*, January 2001.

CHAMBERLAIN, MARY, 'Gender and the Narratives of Migration', *History Workshop Journal*, 43 (1997), 86–108.

—— *Narratives of Exile and Return* (London: Macmillan, 1997).

CHAPMAN, JAMES, '"The Yanks Are Shown To Such Advantage": Anglo-American Rivalry in the Production of *The True Glory*', *Historical Journal of Film, Radio and Television*, 16 (1996), 533–54.

—— *The British At War: Cinema, State and Propaganda 1939–1945* (London: I. B. Tauris, 1998).

—— 'Our Finest Hour Revisited: The Second World War in British Feature Films Since 1945', *Journal of Popular British Cinema*, 1 (1998), 63–75.

—— *License to Thrill: A Cultural History of the James Bond Films* (London: I. B. Tauris, 1999).

CHAUDHURI, NUPUR, and STROBEL, MARGARET (eds.), *Western Women and Imperialism: Complicity and Resistance* (Bloomington: Indiana University Press, 1992).

CHEW, SHIRLEY, and RUTHERFORD, ANNA (eds.), *Unbecoming Daughters of the Empire* (Sydney: Dangaroo Press, 1993).

CHIBNALL, STEVE, *J. Lee Thompson* (Manchester: Manchester University Press, 2000).

CHOWDHRY, PREM, *Colonial India and the Making of Empire Cinema: Image, Ideology and Identity* (Manchester: Manchester University Press, 2000).

COCKERELL, MICHAEL, *Live from Number Ten* (London: Faber and Faber, 1988).

COHEN, STEVE, 'Anti-Semitism, Immigration Controls and the Welfare State', *Critical Social Policy*, 13 (Summer 1985), 73–92.

COLLEY, LINDA, 'Britishness and Otherness: An Argument', *Journal of British Studies*, 31 (1992), 309–29.

—— *Britons: Forging the Nation 1707–1837* (New Haven: Yale University Press, 1992).

—— *Captives: Britain, Empire and the World, 1600–1850* (London: Jonathan Cape, 2002).

COLLINGHAM, E. M., *Imperial Bodies: The Physical Experience of the Raj c.1800–1947* (Cambridge: Polity, 2001).

COLPI, TERRI, *The Italian Factor: The Italian Community in Britain* (Edinburgh: Mainstream, 1991).

CONEKIN, BECKY, *The Autobiography of a Nation: The 1951 Festival of Britain* (Manchester: Manchester University Press, 2003).

—— MORT, FRANK, and WATERS, CHRIS (eds.), *Moments of Modernity: Reconstructing Britain 1945–1964* (London: Rivers Oram, 1999).

CONSTANTINE, STEPHEN, 'Migrants and Settlers', in JUDITH BROWN and WM ROGER LOUIS (eds.), *The Oxford History of the British Empire*, Vol. IV: *The Twentieth Century* (Oxford: Oxford University Press, 1999), 163–87.

COOMBES, ANNIE, *Reinventing Africa: Museums, Material Culture and Popular Imagination in Late Victorian and Edwardian England* (New Haven: Yale University Press, 1994).

COOPER, FREDERICK, *Decolonisation and African Society: The Labour Question in French and British Africa* (Cambridge: Cambridge University Press, 1996).

CROFTS, WILLIAM, *Coercion or Persuasion? Propaganda in Britain After 1945* (London: Routledge, 1989).

CULL, NICHOLAS, *Selling War: The British Propaganda Campaign Against American 'Neutrality' in World War II* (Oxford: Oxford University Press, 1995).

DARWIN, JOHN, *Britain and Decolonization: The Retreat from Empire in the Post-War World* (Basingstoke: Macmillan, 1988).

—— *The End of the British Empire: The Historical Debate* (Basingstoke: Macmillan, 1991).

—— 'Decolonization and the End of Empire', in Robin Winks (ed.), *The Oxford History of the British Empire*, Vol. V: *Historiography* (Oxford: Oxford University Press, 1999), 541–57.

DAVIES, ALISTAIR, and SINFIELD, ALAN (eds.), *British Culture of the Postwar: An Introduction to Literature and Society* (London: Routledge, 2000).

DAVIS, FRED, *Yearning for Yesterday: A Sociology of Nostalgia* (New York: Free Press, 1979).

DAWSON, GRAHAM, 'The Blond Bedouin: Lawrence of Arabia. Imperial Adventure and the Imaginings of English-British Masculinity', in Michael Roper and John Tosh (eds.), *Manful Assertions: Masculinities in Britain since 1800* (London: Routledge, 1991), 113–44.

—— *Soldier Heroes: British Adventure, Empire and the Imagining of Masculinities* (London: Routledge, 1994).

DENNISTON, ROBIN, *Trevor Huddleston: A Life* (London: Macmillan, 1999).

DICKINSON, MARGARET, and STREET, SARAH, *Cinema and State: The Film Industry and the Government, 1927–1984* (London: British Film Institute, 1985).

DILKE, SIR CHARLES WENTWORTH, *Greater Britain: A Record of Travel in English Speaking Countries During 1866 and 1867* (1st edn. 1867; 5th edn. London: Macmillan, 1870).

DIMBLEBY, JONATHAN, *Richard Dimbleby: A Biography* (London: Hodder and Stoughton, 1975).

DIMBLEBY, RICHARD, 'My Coronation Commentary', in Leonard Miall (ed.), *Richard Dimbleby by his Colleagues* (London: BBC, 1966).

DIXON, WHEELER WINSTON (ed.), *Re-viewing British Cinema 1900–1992* (Achany, NY: State University of New York Press, 1994).

DODD, KATHRYN, and DODD, PHILIP, 'Engendering the Nation: British Documentary Film, 1930–1939', in Andrew Higson (ed.), *Dissolving Views: Key Writings on British Cinema* (London: Cassell, 1996), 38–50.

DONNELLY, MARK, *Britain in the Second World War* (London: Routledge, 1999).

DURGNAT, RAYMOND, *A Mirror for England* (London: Faber, 1970).

DYER, RICHARD, 'White', *Screen*, 29 (1988), 44–64.

—— *White* (London: Routledge, 1997).

ELEY, GEOFF, 'Finding the People's War: Film, British Collective Memory, and World War II', *American Historical Review*, 106 (June 2001), 818–38.

ELTON, LORD, *Imperial Commonwealth* (London: Collins, 1945).

EVANS, G. K., *Public Opinion on Colonial Affairs, June 1948* (London: HMSO, 1948).

FIELDHOUSE, DAVID, 'Can Humpty Dumpty Be Put Together Again? Imperial History in the 1980s', *Journal of Imperial and Commonwealth History*, 12 (1984), 9–23.

FINCH, JANET, and SUMMERFIELD, PENNY, 'Social Reconstruction and the Emergence of Companionate Marriage', in David Clark (ed.), *Marriage, Domestic Life and Social Change* (London: Routledge, 1991).

FLEMING, TOM (ed.), *Voices Out of the Air: The Royal Christmas Broadcasts 1932–1981* (London: Heinemann, 1981).

FRANCIS, MARTIN, 'The Labour Party: Modernisation and the Politics of Restraint', in Becky Conekin, Frank Mort, and Chris Waters (eds.), *Moments of Modernity: Reconstructing Britain 1945–1964* (London: Rivers Oram, 1999), 152–70.

—— 'Tears, Tantrums, and Bared Teeth: The Emotional Economy of Three Conservative Prime Ministers, 1951–1963', *Journal of British Studies*, 41 (July 2002), 354–87.

—— 'The Domestication of the Male? Recent Research on Nineteenth- and Twentieth-Century British Masculinity', *The Historical Journal*, 45 (2003), 637–52.

FUSSELL, PAUL, *The Great War and Modern Memory* (Oxford: Oxford University Press, 1975).

GABRIEL, JOHN, *Whitewash: Racialised Politics and the Media* (London: Routledge, 1998).

GAMBLE, ANDREW, *Britain in Decline: Economic Policy, Political Strategy and the British State* (3rd edn. Basingstoke: Macmillan, 1990).

GEDDES, ANDREW, 'Immigrant and Ethnic Minorities and the EU's "Democratic Deficit"', *Journal of Common Market Studies*, 33 (1995), 197–217.

GERAGHTY, CHRISTINE, *British Cinema in the Fifties: Gender, Genre and the 'New Look'* (London: Routledge, 2000).

GIKANDI, SIMON, *Maps of Englishness: Writing Identity in the Culture of Colonialism* (New York: Columbia University Press, 1996).

GILLESPIE, STIRLING, *Celluloid Safari: Filming Big Game from Cape to Cairo* (London: Blackie, 1939).

GILROY, BERYL, *Black Teacher* (London: Bogle L'Ouverture Press, 1976).

GILROY, PAUL, '*There Ain't No Black in the Union Jack': The Cultural Politics of Race and Nation* (London: Hutchinson, 1987).

—— *The Black Atlantic: Modernity and Double Consciousness* (London: Verso, 1993).

GIZZO, SUZANNE DEL, '"Peephole to the Jungle": A Study of Safari from Imperial Preservation to Global Conservation', *Proteus*, 15 (1998), 37–42.

GLANCY, H. MARK, *When Hollywood Loved Britain: The Hollywood 'British' Film 1939–45* (Manchester: Manchester University Press, 1999).

GLEDHILL, CHRISTINE, and SWANSON, GILLIAN (eds.), *Nationalising Femininity: Culture, Sexuality and British Cinema in the Second World War* (Manchester: Manchester University Press, 1996).

GOLDSWORTHY, DAVID, *Colonial Issues in British Politics, 1945–1961* (Oxford: Clarendon Press, 1971).

GREEN, MARTIN, *Dreams of Adventure, Deeds of Empire* (London: Routledge and Kegan Paul, 1980).

GREWAL, INDERPAL, *Home and Harem: Nation, Gender, Empire and the Cultures of Travel* (London: Leicester University Press, 1996).

GRUNDY, KENNETH, *Soldiers Without Politics: Blacks in the South African Armed Forces* (Berkeley: University of California Press, 1983).

HAGGIS, JANE, 'Gendering Colonialism or Colonising Gender? Recent Women's Studies Approaches to White Women and the History of British Colonialism', *Women's Studies International Forum*, 13 (1990), 105–15.

HAGGITH, TOBY, 'Citizenship, Nationhood and Empire in British Official Film Propaganda', in Richard Weight and Abigail Beach (eds.), *The Right to Belong: Citizenship and National Identity in Britain, 1930–1960* (London: I. B. Tauris, 1998), 59–88.

HAJKOWSKI, THOMAS, 'The BBC, the Empire, and the Second World War, 1939–1945', *Historical Journal of Film, Radio and Television*, 22 (2002), 135–55.

HALL, CATHERINE, *White Male and Middle Class: Explorations in Feminism and History* (Cambridge: Polity, 1992).

—— *Civilising Subjects: Metropole and Colony in the English Imagination, 1830–1867* (Cambridge: Polity, 2002).

HANSEN, PETER, 'Albert Smith, the Alpine Club, and the Invention of Mountaineering in Mid-Victorian Britain', *Journal of British Studies*, 34 (1995), 300–24.

—— 'Vertical Boundaries, National Identities: British Mountaineering on the Frontiers of Europe and the Empire', *Journal of Imperial and Commonwealth History*, 24 (1996), 48–71.

—— 'The Dancing Lamas of Everest: Cinema, Orientalism, and Anglo-Tibetan Relations in the 1920s', *American Historical Review*, 101 (June 1996), 712–47.

—— 'Debate: Tenzing's Two Wrist-Watches: The Conquest of Everest and Late Imperial Culture, 1921–1953: Comment', *Past and Present*, 157 (1997), 159–77.

—— 'Confetti of Empire: The Conquest of Everest in Nepal, India, Britain, and New Zealand', *Comparative Studies in Society and History*, 42 (2000), 307–32.

—— 'Coronation Everest: The Empire and Commonwealth in the "Second Elizabethan Age"', in Stuart Ward (ed.), *British Culture and the End of Empire* (Manchester: Manchester University Press, 2001), 57–72.

HARAWAY, DONNA, *Simians, Cyborgs and Women: The Reinvention of Nature* (London: Free Association, 1991).

HARPER, SUE, and PORTER, VINCENT, 'Cinema Audience Tastes in 1950s Britain', *Journal of Popular Cinema*, 2 (1999), 66–82.

HARRISSON, TOM, *Living Through the Blitz* (London: Collins, 1976).

HARVEY, A. D., *Collision of Empires: Britain in Three World Wars, 1793–1945* (London: Phoenix, 1992).

HEBIDGE, DICK, *Hiding in the Light* (London: Routledge, 1988).

HEFFER, SIMON, *Like the Roman: The Life of Enoch Powell* (London: Weidenfeld and Nicolson, 1998).

HEILBRUN, CAROLYN, *Writing a Woman's Life* (London: Women's Press, 1989).

HIGSON, ANDREW, *Waving the Flag: Constructing a National Cinema in Britain* (Oxford: Clarendon Press, 1995).

—— (ed.), *Dissolving Views: Key Writings on British Cinema* (London: Cassell, 1996).

—— and MALTBY, RICHARD (eds.), *'Film Europe' and 'Film America': Cinema, Commerce and Cultural Exchange 1920–1939* (Exeter: University of Exeter Press, 1999).

HILL, JOHN, 'Working-Class Realism and Sexual Reaction: Some Theses on the British "New Wave"', in James Curran and Vincent Porter (eds.), *British Cinema History* (London: Weidenfeld and Nicolson, 1983), 303–11.

—— *Sex, Class and Realism: British Cinema 1956–1963* (London: British Film Institute, 1986).

—— *British Cinema in the 1980s* (Oxford: Clarendon Press, 1999).

HILLARY, EDMUND, *High Adventure* (London: Companion Book Club, 1956).

HOLLAND, R. F., *European Decolonization 1918–1981: An Introductory Survey* (Basingstoke: Macmillan, 1985).

HOLMES, COLIN, *John Bull's Island: Immigration and British Society, 1871–1971* (Basingstoke: Macmillan, 1988).

—— *A Tolerant Country? Immigrants, Refugees and Minorities in Britain* (London: Faber, 1991).

HOUSE, ADRIAN, *The Great Safari: The Lives of George and Joy Adamson* (London: Harvill, 1993).

HOWE, STEPHEN, *Anti-Colonialism in British Politics: The Left and the End of Empire 1939–1964* (Oxford: Oxford University Press, 1993).

—— 'Internal Decolonization? British Politics since Thatcher as Post-Colonial Trauma', *Twentieth Century British History*, 14 (2003), 286–304.

HUNT, JOHN, *The Ascent of Everest* (London: Hodder and Stoughton, 1953).

HUXLEY, ELSPETH, *The Flame Trees of Thika: Memories of an African Childhood* (London: Chatto and Windus, 1959).

—— *Back Street New Worlds: A Look at Immigrants in Britain* (London: Chatto and Windus, 1964).

JAMES, C. L. R., *Beyond a Boundary* (London: Hutchinson, 1963).

JAMES, WINSTON, and HARRIS, CLIVE (eds.), *Inside Babylon: The Caribbean Diaspora in Britain* (London: Verso, 1993).

JARRETT-MACAULEY, DELIA, *The Life of Una Marson, 1905–65* (Manchester: Manchester University Press, 1998).

JOHNSON, PAUL (ed.), *Twentieth Century Britain: Economic, Social and Cultural Change* (Harlow: Addison Wesley Longman, 1994).

KAPLAN, E. ANN, *Looking for the Other: Feminism, Film, and the Imperial Gaze* (London: Routledge, 1997).

KAY, DIANA, and MILES, ROBERT, *Refugees or Migrant Workers? European Volunteer Workers in Britain 1946–1951* (London: Routledge, 1992).

KEARTON, CHERRY, *In the Land of the Lion* (London: Arrowsmith, 1929).

KEATING, PETER (ed.), *Into Unknown England 1866–1913: Selections from the Social Explorers* (London: Fontana, 1976).

KENNEDY, DANE, 'Imperial History and Post-Colonial Theory', *Journal of Imperial and Commonwealth History*, 24 (1996), 345–63.

KENT, SUSAN KINGSLEY, *Making Peace: The Reconstruction of Gender in Interwar Britain* (Princeton: Princeton University Press, 1993).

—— *Gender and Power in Britain, 1640–1990* (London: Routledge, 1999).

KIPNIS, LAURA, 'The Phantom Twitchings of an Amputated Limb: Sexual Spectacle in the Post-Colonial Epic', *Wide Angle*, 11 (1989), 42–51.

KIRK-GREENE, ANTHONY, '"Damnosa Hereditas": Ethnic Ranking and the Martial Races Imperative in Africa', *Ethnic and Racial Studies*, 3 (1983), 393–414.

KUSHNER, TONY, 'Remembering to Forget: Racism and Anti-Racism in Postwar Britain', in Bryan Cheyette and Laura Marcus (eds.), *Modernity, Culture and 'The Jew'* (Cambridge: Polity, 1998).

—— and KNOX, KATHARINE, *Refugees in an Age of Genocide: Global, National and Local Perspectives During the Twentieth Century* (London: Frank Cass, 1999).

LANDY, MARCIA, *British Genres: Cinema and Society, 1930–1960* (Princeton: Princeton University Press, 1991).

LANT, ANTONIA, 'The Female Spy: Gender, Nationality, and War in *I See a Dark Stranger*', in Robert Sklar and Charles Musser (eds.), *Resisting Images: Essays on Cinema and History* (Philadelphia: Temple University Press, 1990), 173–99.

—— *Blackout: Reinventing Women for Wartime British Cinema* (Princeton: Princeton University Press, 1991).

LAPPING, BRIAN, *End of Empire* (London: Granada, 1985).

LIGHT, ALISON, *Forever England: Femininity, Literature and Conservatism Between the Wars* (London: Routledge, 1991).

LOOMBA, ANIA, *Colonialism/Postcolonialism* (London: Routledge, 1998).

LOUIS, WM ROGER, and BULL, HEDLEY (eds.), *The Special Relationship: Anglo-American Relations Since 1945* (Oxford: Oxford University Press, 1986).

LOVELL, TERRY, 'Landscapes and Stories in 1960s British Realism', *Screen*, 31 (1990), 357–76.

LUNN, KENNETH, 'Reconsidering "Britishness": The Construction and Significance of National Identity in Twentieth Century Britain', in Brian Jenkins and Spyros Sofos (eds.), *Nation and Identity in Contemporary Europe* (London: Routledge, 1996), 83–100.

McClintock, Anne, *Imperial Leather: Race, Gender and Sexuality in the Colonial Contest* (London: Routledge, 1995).

McClure, John, *Late Imperial Romance* (London: Verso, 1994).

Macdonald, Kevin, *Emeric Pressburger: The Life and Death of a Screenwriter* (London: Faber, 1994).

MacInnes, Colin, 'A Short Guide for Jumbles to the Life of their Coloured Brethren in England', in Colin MacInnes, *England: Half English* (London: MacGibbon and Kee, 1961, first published 1956).

McIntyre, W. David, *British Decolonization 1946–1997* (Basingstoke: Macmillan, 1998).

—— 'The Strange Death of Dominion Status', *Journal of Imperial and Commonwealth History*, 27 (May 1999), 193–212.

MacKenzie, John, *Propaganda and Empire: The Manipulation of British Public Opinion 1880–1960* (Manchester: Manchester University Press, 1984).

—— (ed.), *Imperialism and Popular Culture* (Manchester: Manchester University Press, 1986).

—— 'The Imperial Pioneer and Hunter and the British Masculine Stereotype in Late Victorian and Edwardian Times', in J. A. Mangan and James Walvin (eds.), *Manliness and Morality: Middle-Class Masculinity in Britain and America 1800–1940* (Manchester: Manchester University Press, 1987), 176–98.

—— *The Empire of Nature: Hunting, Conservation and British Imperialism* (Manchester: Manchester University Press, 1988).

—— 'Heroic Myths of Empire' in John MacKenzie (ed.), *Popular Imperialism and the Military* (Manchester: Manchester University Press, 1992), 109–37.

—— *Orientalism: History, Theory and the Arts* (Manchester: Manchester University Press, 1995).

—— 'The Popular Culture of Empire in Britain', in Judith Brown and Wm Roger Louis (eds.), *The Oxford History of the British Empire*, Vol. IV: *The Twentieth Century* (Oxford: Oxford University Press, 1999), 212–31.

Malik, Kenan, *The Meaning of Race: Race, History and Culture in Western Society* London: Macmillan, 1996).

Malik, Sarita, *Representing Black Britain: A History of Black and Asian Images on British Television* (London: Sage, 2002).

Mander, John, *Great Britain or Little England?* (Harmondsworth: Penguin, 1963).

Mansell, Gerard, *Let Truth Be Told: Fifty Years of BBC External Broadcasting* (London: Weidenfeld and Nicolson, 1982).

Marr, Andrew, *The Day Britain Died* (London: Profile Books, 2000).

Marshall, P. J., 'Imperial Britain', *Journal of Imperial and Commonwealth History*, 23 (1995), 379–94.

May, Alex, ' "Commonwealth or Europe?" Macmillan's Dilemma, 1961–1963', in Alex May (ed.), *Britain, the Commonwealth and Europe: The Commonwealth and Britain's Application to Join the European Communities* (Basingstoke: Palgrave, 2001), 82–110.

MAYER, J. P., *British Cinemas and their Audiences: Sociological Studies* (London: Dennis Dobson, 1948).

MEDHURST, ANDY, '1950s War Films', in Geoff Hurd (ed.), *National Fictions: World War Two in British Films and Television* (London: BFI Publishing, 1984), 35–9.

MEHROTRA, S. R., 'On the Use of the Term "Commonwealth"', *Journal of Commonwealth Political Studies*, 2 (1963), 1–16.

MERCER, KOBENA, *Welcome to the Jungle: New Positions in Black Cultural Studies* (London: Routledge, 1994).

MIALL, LEONARD (ed.), *Richard Dimbleby by his Colleagues* (London: BBC, 1966).

MIDGLEY, CLARE, *Women Against Slavery: The British Campaigns, 1780–1870* (London: Routledge, 1992).

—— (ed.), *Gender and Imperialism* (Manchester: Manchester University Press, 1998).

MILES, ROBERT, *Racism After 'Race Relations'* (London: Routledge, 1993).

MILLIGAN, SPIKE, *The Goon Show Scripts* (London: Woburn Press, 1972).

MOON, JEREMY, *European Integration in British Politics 1950–1963: A Study of Issue Change* (Aldershot: Gower, 1985).

MORGAN, DAVID, and EVANS, MARY, *The Battle for Britain: Citizenship and Ideology in the Second World War* (Routledge: London, 1993).

MORRIS, JAMES, *Farewell the Trumpets: An Imperial Retreat* (London: Faber and Faber, 1978).

MORRIS, KATE, *British Techniques of Public Relations and Propaganda for Mobilizing East and Central Africa During World War II* (Lewiston, NY: Edwin Mellen, 2000).

MUNRO, KENNETH, 'Canada as Reflected in her Participation in the Coronation of her Monarchs in the Twentieth Century', *Journal of Historical Sociology*, 14 (Mar. 2001), 21–46.

MURPHY, PHILIP, *Party Politics and Decolonization: The Conservative Party and British Colonial Policy in Tropical Africa, 1951–1964* (Oxford: Clarendon Press, 1995).

MURPHY, ROBERT (ed.), *The British Cinema Book* (London: British Film Institute, 1997).

NAIRN, TOM, *The Break-Up of Britain: Crisis and Neo-Nationalism* (London: New Left Books, 1981).

NEHRING, NEIL, *Flowers in the Dustbin: Culture, Anarchy, and Postwar England* (Michigan: University of Michigan Press, 1993).

NEWSINGER, JOHN, 'A Counter-Insurgency Tale: Kitson in Kenya', *Race and Class*, 31 (1990), 61–72.

—— 'The Military Memoir in British Imperial Culture: The Case of Malaya', *Race and Class*, 35 (1994), 47–62.

NICHOLAS, SIAN, *The Echo of War: Home Front Propaganda and the Wartime BBC, 1939–45* (Manchester: Manchester University Press, 1996).

—— 'From John Bull to John Citizen: Images of National Identity and Citizenship on the Wartime BBC', in Richard Weight and Abigail Beach (eds.), *The Right to*

Belong: Citizenship and National Identity in Britain, 1930–60 (London: I. B. Tauris, 1998), 36–75.

—— '"Brushing Up Your Empire": Dominion and Colonial Propaganda on the BBC's Home Services, 1939–45', *Journal of Imperial and Commonwealth History*, 31 (May 2003), 207–30.

NOCON, ANDREW, 'A Reluctant Welcome? Poles in Britain in the 1940s', *Oral History* (Spring 1996), 79–87.

NORGAY, TENZING, in collaboration with RAMSEY ULLMAN, JAMES, *Tiger of the Snows* (New York: G. P. Putnam, 1955). This book was published in Britain as *Man of Everest: The Autobiography of Tenzing* (London: Reprint Society, 1955).

—— *After Everest: An Autobiography by Tenzing Norgay Sherpa as told to Malcolm Barnes* (London: Allen and Unwin, 1977).

ORTNER, SHERRY, *Life and Death on Mount Everest: Sherpas and Himalayan Mountaineering* (Princeton: Princeton University Press, 1999).

OSBORNE, JOHN, *Look Back in Anger* (London: Faber and Faber, 1957).

—— *Damn You, England: Collected Prose* (London: Faber and Faber, 1994).

OSMOND, JOHN, *The Divided Kingdom* (London: Constable, 1988).

O'SULLIVAN, TIM, 'Listening Through: The Wireless and World War Two', in Pat Kirkham and David Thoms (eds.), *War Culture: Social Change and Changing Experience in World War Two* (London: Lawrence and Wishart, 1995), 173–85.

OWEN, NICHOLAS, '"More Than a Transfer of Power": Independence Day Ceremonies in India, 15 August 1947', *Contemporary Record*, 6 (1992), 415–51.

—— 'Decolonisation and Postwar Consensus', in Harriet Jones and Michael Kandiah (eds.), *The Myth of Consensus: New Views on British History* (Basingstoke: Macmillan, 1996), 157–81.

OWUSU, KWESI (ed.), *Black British Culture and Society: A Text Reader* (London: Routledge, 2000).

PALMER, ALAN, *Dictionary of the British Empire and Commonwealth* (London: John Murray, 1996).

PAREKH, BHIKHU, *The Future of Multi-Ethnic Britain* (London: Profile Books, 2000).

PARIS, MICHAEL, *Warrior Nation: Images of War in British Popular Culture 1850–2000* (London: Reaktion, 2000).

PARSONS, TIMOTHY, *The African Rank-and-File: Social Implications of Colonial Military Service in the King's African Rifles 1902–1964* (Portsmouth: Heinemann, 1999).

PATTERSON, SHEILA, *Dark Strangers: A Sociological Study of the Absorption of a Recent West Indian Migrant Group in Brixton, South London* (London: Tavistock, 1963).

—— 'The Poles: An Exile Community in Britain', in James Watson (ed.), *Between Two Cultures: Migrants and Minorities in Britain* (Oxford: Blackwell, 1977).

PAUL, KATHLEEN, '"British Subjects" and "British Stock": Labour's Post-War Imperialism', *Journal of British Studies*, 34 (Apr. 1995), 233–76.

—— *Whitewashing Britain: Race and Citizenship in the Postwar Era* (Ithaca: Cornell University Press, 1997).

PEARSON, GEORGE, *Flashback: The Autobiography of a British Film Maker* (London: George Allen and Unwin, 1957).

PELLS, RICHARD, *Not Like Us: How Europeans Have Loved, Hated, and Transformed American Culture Since World War II* (New York: Basic Books, 1997).

PHILLIPS, RICHARD, *Mapping Men and Empire: A Geography of Adventure* (London: Routledge, 1997).

PIMLOTT, BEN, *The Queen: A Biography of Elizabeth II* (London: Harper Collins, 1996).

PORTER, ANDREW (ed.), *The Oxford History of the British Empire*, Vol. III: *The Nineteenth Century* (Oxford: Oxford University Press, 1999).

PORTER, VINCENT, 'Methodism Versus the Market Place: The Rank Organisation and British Cinema', in Robert Murphy (ed.), *The British Cinema Book* (London: British Film Institute, 1997), 122–32.

POWELL, J. ENOCH, Speech at Trinity College Dublin, 13 November 1964, in John Wood (ed.), *Freedom and Reality* (London: Batsford, 1969), 245–53.

—— Speech at Birmingham, 20 April 1968, in John Wood (ed.), *Freedom and Reality* (London: Batsford, 1969), 213–19.

POWELL, MICHAEL, *A Life in the Movies: An Autobiography* (London: Heinemann, 1986).

PRAKASH, GYAN (ed.), *After Colonialism: Imperial Histories and Postcolonial Displacements* (Princeton: Princeton University Press, 1994).

PRATT, MARY LOUISE, *Imperial Eyes: Travel Writing and Transculturation* (London: Routledge, 1992).

PRIESTLEY, J. B., *English Journey* (London: William Heinemann, 1934).

—— *Postscripts* (London: William Heinemann, 1940).

PRONAY, NICHOLAS, 'The British Post-Bellum Cinema: A Survey of the Films Relating to World War II Made in Britain between 1945 and 1960', *Historical Journal of Film, Radio and Television*, 8 (1988), 39–54.

—— and CROFT, JEREMY, 'British Film Censorship and Propaganda Policy During the Second World War', in James Curran and Vincent Porter (eds.), *British Cinema History* (London: Weidenfeld and Nicolson, 1983), 144–63.

RAMSDEN, JOHN, 'How Winston Churchill Became the Greatest Living Englishman', *Contemporary British History*, 12 (Autumn 1998), 1–40.

—— 'Refocusing "The People's War": British War Films of the 1950s', *Journal of Contemporary History*, 33 (1998), 35–63.

—— *Man of the Century: Winston Churchill and his Legend Since 1945* (London: HarperCollins, 2003).

RATTIGAN, NEIL, 'The Last Gasp of the Middle Class: British War Films of the 1950s', in Wheeler Dixon (ed.), *Re-viewing British Cinema, 1900–1992* (Albany, NY: State University of New York Press, 1994), 143–52.

REYNOLDS, DAVID, *Rich Relations: The American Occupation of Britain 1942–1945* (London: HarperCollins, 1996).

RICH, PAUL, *Race and Empire in British Politics* (Cambridge: Cambridge University Press, 1990).

RICHARDS, JEFFREY, *Visions of Yesterday* (London: Routledge and Kegan Paul, 1973).

—— '"Patriotism with Profit": British Imperial Cinema in the 1930s', in James Curran and Vincent Porter (eds.), *British Cinema History* (London: Weidenfeld and Nicolson, 1983), 245–56.

—— 'Boy's Own Empire: Feature Films and Imperialism in the 1930s', in John MacKenzie (ed.), *Imperialism and Popular Culture* (Manchester: Manchester University Press, 1986), 140–64.

—— *Films and British National Identity: From Dickens to Dad's Army* (Manchester: Manchester University Press, 1997).

—— and SHERIDAN, DOROTHY (eds.), *Mass-Observation at the Movies* (London: Routledge and Kegan Paul, 1987).

ROBBINS, KEITH, '"This Grubby Wreck of Old Glories": The United Kingdom and the End of the British Empire', *Journal of Contemporary History*, 15 (1980), 81–95.

ROBINSON, RONALD, and GALLAGHER, JOHN, with DENNY, ALICE, *Africa and the Victorians: The Official Mind of Imperialism* (London: Macmillan, 1961).

ROSE, SONYA, 'Sex, Citizenship, and the Nation in World War II Britain', *American Historical Review*, 103 (Oct. 1998), 1147–76.

—— 'Race, Empire and British Wartime National Identity, 1939–45', *Historical Research*, 74 (2001), 220–37.

—— *Which People's War? National Identity and Citizenship in Wartime Britain 1939–1945* (Oxford: Oxford University Press, 2003).

Royal Commission on Population, *Report* (London: HMSO, 1949).

RYALL, TOM, *Britain and the American Cinema* (London: Sage, 2001).

RYAN, JAMES, *Picturing Empire: Photography and the Visualisation of the British Empire* (London: Reaktion, 1997).

SCHWARZ, BILL, 'Black Metropolis, White England', in Mica Nava and Alan O'Shea (eds.), *Modern Times: Reflections on a Century of English Modernity* (London: Routledge, 1996), 182–207.

—— (ed.), *The Expansion of England: Race, Ethnicity and Cultural History* (London: Routledge, 1996).

—— '"The Only White Man In There": The Re-Racialisation of England, 1956–1968', *Race and Class*, 38 (1996), 65–78.

—— 'Politics and Rhetoric in the Age of Mass Culture', *History Workshop Journal*, 46 (1998),

—— 'Reveries of Race: The Closing of the Imperial Moment', in Becky Conekin, Frank Mort, and Chris Waters (eds.), *Moments of Modernity: Reconstructing Britain 1945–1964* (London: Rivers Oram, 1999), 189–207.

—— 'Claudia Jones and the *West Indian Gazette*: Reflections on the Emergence of Post-Colonial Britain', *Twentieth Century British History*, 14 (2003), 264–85.

SEGAL, LYNNE, 'Look Back in Anger: Men in the Fifties', in Rowena Chapman and Jonathan Rutherford (eds.), *Male Order: Unwrapping Masculinity* (London: Lawrence and Wishart, 1988), 68–96.

SHARPE, JENNY, *Allegories of Empire: The Figure of the Woman in the Colonial Text* (Minneapolis: University of Minnesota Press, 1993).

SHERWOOD, MARIKA, *Many Struggles: West Indian Workers and Service Personnel in Britain, 1939–45* (London: Karia Press, 1985).

SHOHAT, ELLA, and STAM, ROBERT, *Unthinking Eurocentrism: Multiculturalism and the Media* (London: Routledge, 1994).

SHOWALTER, ELAINE, 'Rivers and Sassoon: The Inscription of Male Gender Anxieties', in Margaret Higonet (ed.), *Behind the Lines: Gender and the Two World Wars* (New Haven: Yale University Press, 1987), 61–9.

SINFIELD, ALAN, *Literature, Politics and Culture in Postwar Britain* (Oxford: Blackwell, 1989).

SINHA, MRINALINI, *Colonial Masculinity: The 'Manly Englishman' and the 'Effeminate Bengali' in the Late Nineteenth Century* (Manchester: Manchester University Press, 1995).

SMITH, GRAHAM, *When Jim Crow Met John Bull: Black American Soldiers in World War II Britain* (London: I. B. Tauris, 1987).

SMITH, HOWARD, 'The BBC Television Newsreel and the Korean War', *Historical Journal of Film, Radio and Television*, 8 (1988), 227–52.

—— 'Apartheid, Sharpeville and Impartiality: The Reporting of South Africa on BBC Television 1948–1961', *Historical Journal of Film, Radio and Television*, 13 (1993), 251–98.

SMITH, MALCOLM, *Britain and 1940: History, Myth and Popular Memory* (London: Routledge, 2000).

SMYTH, ROSALEEN, 'Britain's African Colonies and British Propaganda During the Second World War', *Journal of Imperial and Commonwealth History*, 41 (1985), 65–82.

—— 'The British Colonial Film Unit and Sub-Saharan Africa, 1939–1945', *Historical Journal of Film, Radio and Television*, 8 (1988), 285–98.

—— 'The Post-War Career of the Colonial Film Unit in Africa: 1946–1955', *Historical Journal of Film, Radio and Television*, 12 (1992), 163–77.

SPICER, ANDREW, 'Male Stars, Masculinity and British Cinema 1945–1960', in Robert Murphy (ed.), *The British Cinema Book* (London: British Film Institute, 1997), 144–53.

—— *Typical Men: The Representation of Masculinity in Popular British Cinema* (London: I. B. Tauris, 2001).

SPIVAK, GAYATRI, *Outside in the Teaching Machine* (London: Routledge, 1993).

STEWART, GORDON, 'Tenzing's Two Wrist-Watches: The Conquest of Everest and Late Imperial Culture in Britain 1921–1953', *Past and Present*, 149 (1995), 170–97.

STOLER, ANN, *Race and the Education of Desire: Foucault's History of Sexuality and the Colonial Order of Things* (Durham, NC: Duke University Press, 1995).

STREET, SARAH, *British National Cinema* (London: Routledge, 1997).

STROBEL, MARGARET, *European Women and the Second British Empire* (Bloomington: Indiana University Press, 1991).

SWANN, PAUL, *The Hollywood Feature Film in Postwar Britain* (London: Croom Helm, 1987).

SYMONDS, RICHARD, *Oxford and Empire: The Last Lost Cause?* (London: Macmillan, 1986).

TABILI, LAURA, *'We Ask for British Justice': Workers and Racial Difference in Late Imperial Britain* (Ithaca: Cornell University Press, 1994).

THANE, PAT, 'Population Politics in Post-War British Culture', in Becky Conekin, Frank Mort, and Chris Waters (eds.), *Moments of Modernity: Reconstructing Britain 1945–1964* (London: Rivers Oram Press, 1999), 114–33.

THATCHER, MARGARET, *The Path to Power* (London, HarperCollins, 1995).

—— *Speeches on Britain's Relations with the World 1976–1986* (London: Aurum, 1986).

THOMSON, ANDREW, *Margaret Thatcher: The Woman Within* (London: W. H. Allen, 1989).

THORNE, SUSAN, '"The Conversion of Englishmen and the Conversion of the World Inseparable": Missionary Imperialism and the Language of Class in Early Industrial Britain', in Frederick Cooper and Ann Stoler (eds.), *Tensions of Empire: Colonial Cultures in a Bourgeois World* (Berkeley: University of California Press, 1997), 238–62.

TIDRICK, KATHRYN, *Empire and the English Character* (London: I. B. Tauris, 1990).

TROLLOPE, JOANNA, *Britannia's Daughters: Women of the British Empire* (London: BCA, 1995; first published 1983).

TURNER, BARRY, and RENNELL, TONY, *When Daddy Came Home: How Family Life Changed Forever in 1945* (London: Hutchinson, 1995).

TURNER, JOHN, *Filming History: The Memoirs of John Turner, Newsreel Cameraman* (London: BUFVC, 2001).

WALKER, ALEXANDER, *Hollywood, England: The British Film Industry in the Sixties* (London: Michael Joseph, 1974).

WANDOR, MICHELENE, *Look Back in Gender: Sexuality and the Family in Post-War British Drama* (London: Methuen, 1987).

WARD, STUART, (ed.), *British Culture and the End of Empire* (Manchester: Manchester University Press, 2001).

—— 'The End of Empire and the Fate of Britishness', paper delivered to British World Conference II, University of Calgary, July 2003.

WARE, VRON, *Beyond the Pale: White Women, Racism and History* (London: Verso, 1992).

WATERS, CHRIS, '"Dark Strangers" in our Midst: Discourses of Race and Nation in Britain, 1947–1963', *Journal of British Studies*, 36 (1997), 207–38.

—— 'Disorders of the Mind, Disorders of the Body Social: Peter Wildeblood and the Making of the Modern Homosexual', in Becky Conekin, Frank Mort, and Chris Waters (eds.), *Moments of Modernity: Reconstructing Britain 1945–1964* (London: Rivers Oram, 1999), 134–51.

WEBSTER, WENDY, *Imagining Home: Gender, 'Race' and National Identity 1945–64* (London: UCL Press, 1998).

—— 'Elspeth Huxley: Gender, Empire and Narratives of Nation, 1935–64', *Women's History Review*, 8 (1999), 527–45.

—— 'Defining Boundaries: European Volunteer Worker Women in Britain and Narratives of Community', *Women's History Review*, 9 (2000), 257–76.

—— 'Reconstructing Boundaries: Gender, War and Empire in British Cinema 1945–50', *Historical Journal of Film, Radio and Television*, 23 (2003), 43–57.

WEIGHT, RICHARD, *Patriots: National Identity in Britain 1940–2000* (Basingstoke: Macmillan, 2002).

WIENER, MARTIN, *English Culture and the Decline of the Industrial Spirit 1850–1980* (Cambridge: Cambridge University Press, 1981).

WILCOCK, H. D., 'Public Opinion: Attitudes towards America and Russia', *Political Quarterly*, 19 (1948), 61–72.

WILMUT, ROGER, *From Fringe to Flying Circus: Celebrating a Unique Generation of Comedy 1960–1980* (London: Book Club Associates, 1981).

WINKS, ROBIN (ed.), *The Oxford History of the British Empire*, Vol. V: *Historiography* (Oxford: Oxford University Press, 1999).

WOHL, ROBERT, *The Generation of 1914* (London: Weidenfeld and Nicolson, 1980).

WOLTON, SUKE, *Lord Hailey, the Colonial Office and the Politics of Race and Empire* (Houndsmill: Macmillan Press, 2000).

WOODS, PHILIP, 'From Shaw to Shantaram: The Film Advisory Board and the Making of British Propaganda Films in India, 1940–1943', *Historical Journal of Film, Radio and Television*, 21 (2001), 293–308.

WOOLLACOTT, ANGELA, *To Try Her Fortune in London: Australian Women, Colonialism and Modernity* (Oxford: Oxford University Press, 2001).

WORTHY, SCOTT, 'A Martial Race? Maori and Pakeha New Zealand Soldiers of the Great War in Imperial Context', paper delivered to British World Conference II, University of Calgary, July 2003.

YOUNG, HUGO, *One of Us: A Biography of Margaret Thatcher* (Basingstoke: Macmillan, 1989).

YOUNG, LOLA, *Fear of the Dark: 'Race', Gender and Sexuality in the Cinema* (London: Routledge, 1996).

Index